LIBRARY OF HEBREW BIBLE/ OLD TESTAMENT STUDIES

732

Formerly Journal for the Study of the Old Testament Supplement Series

Editors
Laura Quick, Oxford University, UK
Jacqueline Vayntrub, Yale University, USA

Founding Editors
David J. A. Clines, Philip R. Davies and David M. Gunn

Editorial Board
Sonja Ammann, Alan Cooper, Steed Davidson, Susan Gillingham,
Rachelle Gilmour, John Goldingay, Rhiannon Graybill, Anne Katrine Gudme,
Norman K. Gottwald, James E. Harding, John Jarick, Tracy Lemos,
Carol Meyers, Eva Mroczek, Daniel L. Smith-Christopher,
Francesca Stavrakopoulou, James W. Watts

UNITY IN THE BOOK OF ISAIAH

Edited by
Benedetta Rossi, Dominic S. Irudayaraj
and Gina Hens-Piazza

LONDON • NEW YORK • OXFORD • NEW DELHI • SYDNEY

T&T CLARK

Bloomsbury Publishing Plc, 50 Bedford Square, London, WC1B 3DP, UK
Bloomsbury Publishing Inc, 1359 Broadway, New York, NY 10018, USA
Bloomsbury Publishing Ireland, 29 Earlsfort Terrace, Dublin 2, D02 AY28, Ireland

BLOOMSBURY, T&T CLARK and the T&T Clark logo
are trademarks of Bloomsbury Publishing Plc

First published in Great Britain 2024
Paperback edition published 2025

Copyright © Benedetta Rossi, Dominic S. Irudayaraj, Gina Hens-Piazza and contributors, 2024

Benedetta Rossi, Dominic S. Irudayaraj, Gina Hens-Piazza have asserted their right under the
Copyright, Designs and Patents Act, 1988, to be identified as Editors of this work.

The acknowledgments on p. ix constitute an extension of this copyright page.

All rights reserved. No part of this publication may be: i) reproduced or transmitted
in any form, electronic or mechanical, including photocopying, recording or by means
of any information storage or retrieval system without prior permission in writing from
the publishers; or ii) used or reproduced in any way for the training, development or
operation of artificial intelligence (AI) technologies, including generative AI technologies.
The rights holders expressly reserve this publication from the text and data mining
exception as per Article 4(3) of the Digital Single Market Directive (EU) 2019/790.

Bloomsbury Publishing Plc does not have any control over, or responsibility for, any third-party
websites referred to or in this book. All internet addresses given in this book were correct at the
time of going to press. The author and publisher regret any inconvenience caused if addresses have
changed or sites have ceased to exist, but can accept no responsibility for any such changes.

A catalogue record for this book is available from the British Library.
A catalogue record for this book is available from the Library of Congress.

ISBN: HB: 978-0-5677-0593-8
PB: 978-0-5677-0596-9
ePDF: 978-0-5677-0594-5

Series: Library of Hebrew Bible/Old Testament Studies, volume 732
ISSN 2513-8758

Typeset by Trans.form.ed SAS

For product safety related questions contact productsafety@bloomsbury.com.

To find out more about our authors and books visit www.bloomsbury.com
and sign up for our newsletters.

CONTENTS

Acknowledgments ix
Abbreviations xi
Contributors xv

Chapter 1
INTRODUCTION
    Gina Hens-Piazza, Dominic S. Irudayaraj and Benedetta Rossi   1

SECTION ONE
WORLD BEHIND THE TEXT

Chapter 2
THE "UNITY" OF THE BOOK OF ISAIAH:
A PERSONAL REVIEW AND OUTLOOK
    Ulrich Berges   13

Chapter 3
TWO STEPS FORWARD, ONE STEP BACK:
METHODOLOGICAL REFLECTIONS ON READING ISAIAH AS A UNITY
    H. G. M. Williamson   28

Chapter 4
E PLURIBUS UNUM:
FINDING INTERTEXTUAL THREADS THAT UNITE THE BOOK OF ISAIAH
    Hyun Chul Paul Kim   38

Chapter 5
TRACKING THE SCRIBAL TRAILS IN THE BOOK OF ISAIAH:
THE SABBATH AFFAIR
    Benedetta Rossi   56

Chapter 6
CONCEPT OF HISTORY IN THE BOOK OF ISAIAH
    Peter Dubovský   76

Chapter 7
THE REMNANTS OF A FIGURAL PAST:
SYMMETRY, ANALOGY, AND THE SEARCH FOR A HOLY SEED
IN THE BOOK OF ISAIAH
 Jacob Stromberg   94

SECTION TWO
WORLD OF THE TEXT

Chapter 8
THE UNITY OF THE BOOK OF ISAIAH: MORE THAN A MEMORY GAME
OR A FATA MORGANA?
 Willem A. M. Beuken   129

Chapter 9
JACOB AS A UNIFYING MOTIF
IN THE BOOK OF ISAIAH
 Marvin A. Sweeney   144

Chapter 10
CAN JEREMIAH QUOTE DEUTERO- OR TRITO-ISAIAH?
ITS IMPACT ON THE "UNITY" MOVEMENT IN ISAIAH STUDIES
 Georg Fischer   157

Chapter 11
BLINDNESS IN DISCOURSE:
COGNITIVE LINKS IN ISAIAH THROUGH THE METAPHORS
IN ISAIAH 42–43 AS TEST CASES
 Boris Lazzaro   167

SECTION THREE
WORLD IN FRONT OF THE TEXT

Chapter 12
"DESOLATE" DEPICTIONS IN ISAIAH:
APPROACHING THE UNITY QUESTION, ANEW!
 Dominic S. Irudayaraj   185

Chapter 13
ZION'S DESTINY AS THEOLOGICAL DISCLOSURE:
MAPPING OF A METAPHOR ACROSS ISAIAH
 Gina Hens-Piazza   199

Chapter 14
Between Absurdity and Hope:
Suffering in the Book of Isaiah
    Blaženka Scheuer   212

Chapter 15
The Isaianic "Unity Movement"
from a Perspective of Trauma Studies:
With a Special Focus on Isaiah 1–12
    Elizabeth Esterhuizen and Alphonso Groenewald   225

Chapter 16
Unity and Translation Criticism:
The Case of the Peshitta Translation
    Attila Bodor   238

Bibliography   248
Index of References   271
Index of Authors   286

ACKNOWLEDGMENTS

A change of venue and a chat over a cup of coffee marked the modest beginning of this edited volume. When SBL chose Rome as the venue for its 2019 International Meeting, the hosting institutions—Pontifical Biblical Institute and the Pontifical Gregorian University—were invited to propose and plan a few sessions. To brainstorm on some themes within the sphere of Prophetic Literature, we met and discussed—of course, with an aromatic and inviting cappuccino to go with! The book of Isaiah and the theme of unity soon emerged as our preferred theme. An initial description of the session was composed, debated, and refined. The approved description was sent out with the title *Promises and Challenges of "Unity" Movement for Isaiah Studies*. The intended scare quotes, on their part, echoed the challenging nature of the unity pursuit within the ambit of the book of Isaiah.

With three sessions scheduled on 3 July 2019, a total of ten scholars braved the Roman summer and presented their research findings on the chosen theme. The well-attended sessions and the lively exchanges that ensued were early attestations to the promise of the unity theme as well as its attendant challenges. Among the audience was Claudia Camp, then commissioning editor of LHBOTS series from Bloomsbury T&T Clark, who showed both interest in and encouragement to taking the session discussion further. Thus, the plan to run a sequel session on the same theme at the following International SBL Meeting in Adeleide (2020) was set in motion. Despite the official approval of our proposal, thanks to the session chair Alphonso Groenewald, the planned session did not see the light as the pandemic came in our way.

After some time, an alternative idea to proceed further was broached. Even as our contributors were graciously working on their conference papers and providing us with the revised editions of their papers, a few invited scholars who, though never having had the occasion to be part of the conference discussions, generously contributed their share to enrich the unity discussions. We are grateful to each one of them. The project therefore demanded more time and effort than we had initially anticipated. So, we gratefully acknowledge our institutions—Jesuit School of Theology of Santa Clara University, Berkeley, CA and Pontifical Biblical Institute, Rome—for graciously granting us the time and continued support in bringing this work to completion.

We thank Laura Quick and Jacqueline Vayntrub (LHBOTS Series Editors), Dominic Mattos and Katherine Jenkins for overseeing the project, their suggestions, and encouragement. And finally, for the elegant typesetting, our grateful regards go out to Duncan Burns.

ABBREVIATIONS

1QIsa^a	Qumran Scroll Isaiah^a
AB	Anchor Bible
ABC	Albert K. Grayson, *Assyrian and Babylonian Chronicles* (Locust Valley, NY: J.J. Augustin, 1975)
AcBib	Academia Biblica
ACEBTSup	Amsterdamse cahiers voor exegese van de Bijbel en zijn traditites. Supplement Series
AnBib	Analecta Biblica
ANE	Ancient Near East
AOAT	Alter Orient und Altes Testament
ATD	Das Alte Testament Deutsch
AUSCLL	American University Studies, Series 17: Classical Languages and Literature
BBB	Bonner Biblischen Beiträge
BCAT	Biblischer Commentar über das Alte Testament
BETL	Bibliotheca Ephemeridum Theologicarum Lovaniensium
Bib	*Biblica*
BibInt	*Biblical Interpretation: A Journal of Contemporary Approaches*
BibOri	Biblica et Orientalia
BIS	Biblical Interpretation Series
BiTr	*The Bible Translator*
BN	*Biblische Notizen*
BThSt	Biblisch-theologische Studien
BWANT	Beiträge zur Wissenschaft vom Alten und Neuen Testament
BZ	*Biblische Zeitschrift*
BZAW	Beihefte zur Zeitschrift für die alttestamentliche Wissenschaft
CBQ	*Catholic Biblical Quarterly*
CEB	Common English Bible
CG	Hélène Lozachmeur, ed., *La Collection Clermont-Ganneau. Ostraca, épigraphes sur Jarre étiquettes de bois.* Vol. 1 (Mémoires de L'Académie des Inscriptions et Belles-Lettres 35) (Paris: De Boccard, 2006)
CHANE	Culture and History of the Ancient Near East
ConBOT	Coniectanea Biblica: Old Testament Series
COS	William W. Hallo and K. Lawson Younger, eds., *The Context of Scripture*, 3 vols. (Leiden: Brill, 1997–2002)
DCH	David J.A. Clines, *The Dictionary of Classical Hebrew*, 8 vols. (Sheffield: Academic Press/Phoenix Press, 1993–2011)

DCLS	Deuterocanonical and Cognate Literature Studies
DJD	Discoveries in the Judean Desert
ECC	The Eerdmans Critical Commentary
EstBib	*Estudios biblicos*
ET	English Translation
ETL	*Ephemerides theologicae Lovanienses*
FAT	Forschungen zum Alten Testament
FAT/II	Forschungen zum Alten Testament. 2. Reihe
FOTL	Forms of the Old Testament Literature
FRLANT	Forschungen zur Religion und Literatur des Alten und Neuen Testaments
FzB	Forschung zur Bibel
GKC	Heinrich F.W. Gesenius, *Gesenius' Hebrew Grammar*. As edited and enlarged by the late E. Kautzsch. 2nd English edition revised in accordance with the twenty-eight German edition (1909) by A.E. Cowley (Oxford: Clarendon Press, 1910)
HALOT	*The Hebrew and Aramaic Lexicon of the Old Testament*. Ludwig Koehler, Walter Baumgartner and Johann J. Stamm. Translated and edited under the supervision of Mervyn E. J. Richardson. 5 vols. (Leiden: Brill, 1994–2000)
HBAI	*Hebrew Bible and Ancient Israel*
HBM	Hebrew Bible Monographs
HBS	Herders biblische Studien. Herder's Biblical Studies
HCOT	Historical Commentary on the Old Testament
HS	*Hebrew Studies*
HThKAT	Herders theologischer Kommentar zum Alten Testament
HTR	*Harvard Theological Review*
IB	*The Interpreter's Bible: The Holy Scriptures in the King James and Revised Standard Versions with General Articles and Introduction, Exegesis, Exposition for Each Book of the Bible in Twelve Volumes*. Edited by George Arthur Buttrick et al. (New York: Abingdon-Cokesbury Press, 1952–57)
IBHS	Bruce K. Waltke and Michael O'Connor, *An Introduction to Biblical Hebrew Syntax* (Winona Lake, IN: Eisenbrauns, 1990)
ICC	International Critical Commentary
Int	*Interpretation*
IOSOT	International Organization for the Study of the Old Testament
JAAS	*Journal of Assyrian Academic Studies*
JAOS	*Journal of the American Oriental Society*
JBL	*Journal of Biblical Literature*
JBQ	*The Jewish Bible Quarterly*
JBTh	Jahrbuch für biblische Theologie
JCS	*Journal of Cuneiform Studies*
JESOT	*Journal for the Evangelical Study of the Old Testament*
JNES	*Journal of Near Eastern Studies*
Joüon	Joüon, Paul, *A Grammar of Biblical Hebrew*. Translated and revised by T. Muraoka, 2 vols. (Rome: Pontifical Biblical Institute, 1991)

JPS	Jewish Publication Society
JQR	*Jewish Quarterly Review*
JSem	*Journal for Semitics*
JSJSup	Supplements to the Journal for the Study of Judaism
JSOT	*Journal for the Study of the Old Testament*
JSOTSup	Journal for the Study of the Old Testament. Supplement Series
KAT	Kommentar zum Alten Testament
LCBI	Literary Currents in Biblical Interpretation
LHBOTS	The Library of Hebrew Bible/Old Testament Studies
LSTS	Library of Second Temple Studies
LXX	Septuagint
Lys	Plutarchus, *Life of Lysander*
MPIL	Monographs of the Peshitta Institute
NCBC	The New Century Bible Commentary
NIB	The New Interpreter's Bible. General Articles & Introduction, Commentary, & Reflections for each Book of the Bible including the Apocryphal / Deuterocanonical Books in Twelve Volumes (Nashville, TN: Abingdon, 1994–2004)
NKJV	New King James Version
NRSV	New Revised Standard Version
NSBT	New Studies in Biblical Theology
NSK.AT	Neuer Stuttgarter Kommentar. Altes Testament
OBO	Orbis Biblicus et Orientalis
ÖBS	Österreichische biblische Studien
OBT	Overtures in Biblical Theology
OED	*Oxford English Dictionary*
OG	Old Greek
OL	Old Latin
OTE	*Old Testament Essays*
OTL	Old Testament Library
OTM	Oxford Theological Monographs
OTS	Oudtestamentische Studien. Old Testament Studies
PNAE	*The Prosopography of the Neo-Assyrian Empire*
POuT	De Prediking van het Oude Testament
RB	*Revue Biblique*
RC	*Religion Compass*
RIMB	Royal Inscriptions of Mesopotamia. Babylonian Periods
RINAP	The Royal Inscriptions of the Neo-Assyrian Period
RSB	Ricerche Storico Bibliche
RSR	*Recherches de science religieuse*
s.v.	*sub verbo* (under the word)
SAAS	State Archives of Assyria Studies
SBB	Stuttgarter Biblische Beiträge
SBL	Society of Biblical Literature
SBLAcBib	Society of Biblical Literature Academia Biblica
SBLAIL	Society of Biblical Literature Ancient Israel and Its Literature
SBLANEM	Society of Biblical Literature Ancient Near East Monographs

SBLDS	Society of Biblical Literature Dissertation Series
SBLMS	Society of Biblical Literature Monograph Series
SBLStBibLit	Society of Biblical Literature Studies in Biblical Literature
SBS	Stuttgarter Bibelstudien
SJOT	*Scandinavian Journal of the Old Testament*
SSN	Studia Semitica Neerlandica
STDJ	Studies on the Texts of the Desert of Judah
sVtg	Septuaginta Vetus Testamentum Graecum
TAD	Bezalel Porten and Ada Yardeni, eds., *Textbook of Aramaic Documents from Ancient Egypt. Volume IV. Ostraca & Assorted Inscriptions* (Winona Lake, IN: Eisenbrauns, 1999)
TDOT	*Theological Dictionary of the Old Testament*. Edited by G. Johannes Botterweck and Helmer Ringgren. Translated by John T. Willis et al. 8 vols. (Grand Rapids, MI: Eerdmans, 1974–2006)
THBS	Supplements to the Textual History of the Hebrew Bible
ThWAT	*Theologisches Wörterbuch zum Alten Testament*. Edited by G. Johannes Botterweck and Helmer Ringgren. 10 vols. (Stuttgart: Kohlhammer, 1973–2000)
TRu	*Theologische Rundschau*
TSAJ	Texts and Studies in Ancient Judaism. Texte und Studien zum antiken Judentum
TZ	*Theologische Zeitschrift*
UCOP	University of Cambridge Oriental Publications
UTB	Uni-Taschenbücher
VT	*Vetus Testamentum*
VTSup	Supplements to Vetus Testamentum
WBC	Word Biblical Commentary
WMANT	Wissenschaftliche Monographien zum Alten und Neuen Testament
WUNT	Wissenschaftliche Untersuchungen zum Neuen Testament
WUNT/II	Wissenschaftliche Untersuchungen zum Neuen Testament. 2. Reihe
ZAR	*Zeitschrift für Altorientalische und Biblische Rechtsgeschichte*
ZAW	*Zeitschrift für die Alttestamentliche Wissenschaft*
ZBK	Zürcher Bibelkommentare

CONTRIBUTORS

Ulrich Berges is Professor for Old Testament Studies at University of Bonn, and Extraordinary Professor in the Faculty of Theology of the University of Pretoria. He has published the volumes on Isa 40–48 and Isa 49–54 in the Herders Theologischer Kommentar zum Alten Testament series.

Willem A. M. Beuken is Professor Emeritus of Old Testament at KU Leuven. He is author of the volumes on Isa 1–39 in Herders Theologischer Kommentar zum Alten Testament series.

Attila Bodor is a Humboldt Postdoctoral Research Fellow at the University of Göttingen, Germany. He has recently published *The Theological Profile of the Book of Isaiah* (Brill, 2021).

Peter Dubovský is the Rector at the Pontifical Biblical Institute, Rome and professor of the Old Testament and history. He is the author of *The Building of the First Temple: A Study in Redactional, Text-critical and Historical Perspective* (Mohr Siebeck, 2015).

Elizabeth (Liza) Esterhuizen is a Research Associate at the University of Pretoria. She is an Old Testament and psychology scholar with a special interest in the prophetic books of Isaiah and Nahum. Her main research focus is the reading of the book of Isaiah through a trauma lens as pertaining to her psychology background.

Georg Fischer is Professor Emeritus (Old Testament) at Theological Faculty of the Leopold-Franzens-University, Innsbruck, Austria. His recent publications include the volume *Jeremiah Studies* (Mohr Siebeck, 2020).

Alphonso Groenewald is a Professor in the Department of Old Testament and Hebrew Scriptures at the Faculty of Theology and Religion, University of Pretoria. His research focus is on the book of Isaiah, and he combines his exegetical analysis of Isaiah with a trauma theory lens.

Gina Hens-Piazza is the Joseph S. Alemany Professor of Biblical Studies at the Jesuit School of Theology of Santa Clara University in Berkeley CA.

Dominic S. Irudayaraj is Associate Professor at the Pontifical Biblical Institute, Rome; Visiting Professor at Hekima College, Nairobi; Research Associate at University of Pretoria, South Africa. His publications include *Violence, Otherness, and Identity in Isaiah 63:1–6* (Bloomsbury T&T Clark, 2017).

Hyun Chul Paul Kim is Harold B. Williams Professor of Hebrew Bible at the Methodist Theological School in Ohio (MTSO), Delaware, Ohio, USA, and his recent publications include *Reading Isaiah: A Literary and Theological Commentary* (Smyth & Helwys, 2016).

Boris Lazzaro is Professor of Old Testament at the Pontifical Urbaniana University, Rome. Among his publications is the monograph about the poetics of obscurity in First Isaiah: *Isaia l'oscuro. Forme dell'oscurità linguistica isaiana e storia della loro recezione nell'attestazione di Is 29* (G&B Press, 2020).

Benedetta Rossi is Associate Professor of Old Testament Exegesis at the Pontifical Biblical Institute in Rome. She recently coedited (with Danilo Verde) *Cultural Hegemony, Ideological Conflicts, and Power in Second Temple Judaism* (Leuven: Peeters, forthcoming).

Blaženka Scheuer is a Senior Lecturer at the Centre for Theology and Religious Studies, Lund University. She is the author of *Bees, Wasps, and Weasels: Zoomorphic Slurs and the Delegitimation of Deborah and Huldah in the Babylonian Talmud* (Lexington Books, forthcoming).

Jacob Stromberg is Lecturer in Old Testament at Duke Divinity School and co-editor (with Todd Hibbard) of *The History of Isaiah* (Mohr Siebeck, 2021) and (with Michael Lyons) of *Isaiah's Servants in Early Judaism and Christianity* (Mohr Siebeck, 2021).

Marvin A. Sweeney is Professor of Hebrew Bible at the Claremont School of Theology. He is the author of the volumes on Isa 1–39 and Isa 40–66 in the Forms of the Old Testament Literature Commentary Series (Eerdmans, 1996, 2016) and many other studies.

H. G. M. Williamson is the Emeritus Regius Professor of Hebrew at Oxford University. He has published two volumes so far in the ICC commentary series on Isa 1–5 and Isa 6–10.

Chapter 1

INTRODUCTION

Gina Hens-Piazza, Dominic S. Irudayaraj and Benedetta Rossi

"The essence of the beautiful is unity in variety."
                                                    Felix Mendelssohn

The book of Isaiah qualifies as one of the longest and most complex books of the Bible. Its composition possibly spans as many as four tumultuous periods of Israelite history—the era of Assyrian sovereignty, followed by the rise of Babylonian dominance, the period of Persian occupation and finally the era of Hellenistic imperialism. A *montage* featuring disparate traditions crafts its content and a host of unidentified voices echoes across at least two-thirds of its sixty-six chapters. With such a conglomerate history of origin, one might question if the words "unity" and "Isaiah" appropriately belong together in a book title or whether such a juxtaposition might be construed as merely oxymoronic.

It is small wonder that such a lengthy and complicated book as Isaiah has been the focus of numerous scholarly overtures. For centuries, the premodern era considered it the work of one author who, through divine inspiration, could anticipate and speak to generations far beyond his eighth-century setting.[1] Even as late as the eighteenth century, Georg Seiler imagined the prophet Isaiah as the book's sole author, speaking in the eighth century through the Babylonian exile and far into the early Christian era.[2] Around the same period, Robert Lowth,

---

1. Even today, some groups share a similar view supported by their religious affiliation or understanding of inspiration or both.
2. Georg Friedrich Seiler, *Das größre biblische Erbauungsbuch: Des alten Testamentes siebenter Theil: Die Propheten Jesaias und Jeremias*, 8 vols. (Erlangen: zu finden in der Bibelanstalt, 1792), 12, as cited in Andrew Abernethy, *Discovering Isaiah: Content, Interpretation, Reception* (Grand Rapids, MI: Eerdmans, 2021), 25.

who offered a translation of the whole of Isaiah and a commentary celebrating its exquisite poetry, also wrote with the presumption of one author.[3]

The rise of historical-critical scholarship in the late eighteenth century raised questions about such assumptions and instigated a major shift in the consideration of this book. Based upon various textual references to historical events, such as the crisis of Jerusalem, the Syro-Ephraimite conflict, prophecies from the time of Sargon, the Babylonian exile, Cyrus of Persia, and the post-exilic circumstances, an extensive dissecting process began that sought to identify various passages of Isaiah with different historical periods. Prompted by studies of Johann Gottfried Eichhorn[4] and Johann Christoph Döderlein,[5] Heinrich Ewald's work[6] was particularly influential, arguing that Isaiah consisted of two books, one made up of traditions identified with the eighth-century prophet, Isaiah ben Amoz, and another collection of passages stemming from the exilic and post-exilic setting.[7] On this impetus, scholars worked for the next forty years to parcel out the traditions of this book, slotting passages into one or other of these two detailed time frames. Such close historical scrutiny eventually gave rise to Bernhard Duhm's most influential work, *Das Buch Jesaia*, in which he makes a compelling case for the Isaiah corpus comprising three books.[8] While recognizing other materials added to the book as late as the first century BCE, Duhm's identification of an Isaiah (chs. 1–39) tied to the eighth-century prophet, a Second Isaiah (chs. 40–55) written during exile (540s BCE) and a Third Isaiah (chs. 56–66) composed in the post-exilic period from Jerusalem, established a template for scholarly study that still continues today.

With the tentative and often hypothetical character of historical critical proposals, a turn from this methodological hegemony in biblical studies was well under way by mid-twentieth century. Regarding Isaiah, a decreasing consensus characterized research on topics such as the actual redactional layers of Isa 1–39,

---

3. Robert Lowth, *Isaiah: A New Translation, With a Preliminary Dissertation, and Notes, Critical, Philological, and Explanatory* (London: J. Nichols, for J. Dodsley, and T. Cadell, 1778), i–ii.

4. Johann Gottfried Eichhorn, *Einleitung in das Alte Testament*, 5 vols. (Leipzig: Weidmann, 1780–83).

5. Johann Christoph Döderlein, *Esaias ex recensione textus hebraei ad fidem codd. quorundam mss et versionum antiquarum latine vertit notasque varii argumenti*, 3rd ed. (Norimbergae et Altdorfi: George Peter Monath, 1789).

6. Georg Heinrich August Ewald, *Commentary on the Prophets of the Old Testament*, 5 vols, trans. J. Frederick Smith (London: Williams & Norgate, 1875–81), as cited in Abernethy, *Discovering Isaiah*, 26.

7. Actually, perhaps the earliest allusion to a bipartite division finds a place in the commentary of Abraham Ibn Ezra (who himself builds on the views of the eleventh-century thinker Moshe ben Shemuel HaKohen ben Jaqtila). Cf. Shalom M. Paul, *Isaiah 40–66: A Commentary*, ECC (Grand Rapids, MI: Eerdmans, 2012), 3.

8. Bernhard Duhm, *Das Buch Jesaia*, 4th ed., Göttinger Handcommentar zum Alten Testament (Göttingen: Vandenhoeck & Ruprecht, 1922).

the location from which Second Isaiah wrote, the assignment of dates to the oracles against the nations, the macro-structure of chs. 1–39, as well as many other topics. Moreover, the on-going dissection of these sixty-six chapters in the interest of merely a conjectural history was sacrificing or even obfuscating the literary genius, theological message, and the instructional materials of the faith communities comprising this book.

In the 1950s Leon Liebreich, who still appealed to the author/editor's intention, noted terms in parallels between the first and final chapters of Isaiah, suggesting the "intention and fixed determination to make the book end in the same way in which it begins."[9] In subsequent essays, he cited even more correspondences between Isa 1 and 65–66.[10] Around the same time, James Muilenburg's commentary on Isa 40–66 (1956) read past the historical and redactional segmentation that had preoccupied scholars' work on these chapters and interpreted large blocks of this material as a literary whole.[11] His work not only disclosed that when taken together, these chapters displayed monumental poetic integrity but also demonstrated the potential theological meaning made evident by this holistic approach. It is no surprise that this impetus to read the text of Isaiah as a whole coincided with Muilenberg's 1969 Society of Biblical Literature presidential address, which became a clarion call to move beyond solely historical studies and consider the yield of literary approaches to the biblical text.[12] At about the same time, both Claus Westermann's (1964) and Roy Melugin's work on Isa 40–55 (1976) set the stage, urging a synchronic reading of these chapters. Thus, the seeds of the unity movement in the study of Isaiah were sown.[13] Melugin, in his comprehensive study, credits the work of Peter Ackroyd (1978), Roland Clements (1982), and Rolf Rendtorff (1984) as founders of the movement.[14] But in the years to come, Melugin himself, along with Marvin Sweeney, played key roles in initiating and expanding this holistic approach to Isaiah.[15]

---

9. Leon J. Liebreich, "The Compilation of the Book of Isaiah," *JQR* 46 (1956): 259–77 (276).

10. See also his follow-up essay that same year: Leon J. Liebreich, "The Compilation of the Book of Isaiah," *JQR* 47 (1956): 114–38.

11. James Muilenburg, "The Book of Isaiah: Chapters 40–66," in *IB* 5 (Nashville, TN: Abingdon, 1956), 381–733.

12. James Muilenburg, "Form Criticism and Beyond," *JBL* 88 (1969): 1–18.

13. Claus Westermann, "Sprache und Struktur der Prophetic Deuterojesajas," in *Forschung am Alten Testament: Gesammelte Studien*, Theologische Bücherei. Altes Testament 24 (Munich: Chr Kaiser, 1964), 92–170; and Roy F. Melugin, *The Formation of Isaiah 40–55*, BZAW 141 (Berlin: de Gruyter, 1976).

14. See Roy F. Melugin, "Isaiah 40–66 in Recent Research: The Unity Movement," in *Recent Research on the Major Prophets*, ed. Alan J. Hauser, Recent Research in Biblical Studies 1 (Sheffield: Sheffield Phoenix Press, 2008), 148.

15. See the collection of essays edited by Roy F. Melugin and Marvin A. Sweeney, *New Visions of Isaiah*, JSOTSup 214 (Sheffield: Sheffield Academic Press, 1996).

The question of how the parts compose the whole and relate to each other also influenced the redaction work of historical critics. Rendtorff had argued that Isa 40–55 constituted the centerpiece of the whole book and that Third Isaiah, whom he identified as the final editor, added sections to First Isaiah to more fully integrate and connect it to the message of Second Isaiah.[16] Thus Rendtorff's redaction-critical study led him to observe that Third Isaiah in "56:1 uses 'righteousness' both morally as it is in First Isaiah and salvifically as it is used in Second Isaiah."[17] Later, H. G. M. Williamson also proposed how particular passages and expressions of First Isaiah such as "the Holy One of Israel," which is repeatedly used in Isa 40–55, clearly influenced the composition of Second Isaiah.[18] Williamson notes in particular the impact of Isa 6 on the oracles in Second Isaiah, as well as the title "Holy One of Israel" in 41:20, which is likely drawn from seven occurrences in First Isaiah. Later his student Jacob Stromberg (2011) would advance this view, showing how allusions from Third Isaiah can be traced back to passages in Isa 1–55.[19]

From the 1970s onward, the surge in literary criticism did not deny the composite nature of Isaiah or other compelling research regarding the world behind this text; instead, its gaze fixed more exclusively upon the whole text and its artistry. Recurring vocabulary, themes such as Zion, repetitions of key terms such as "righteousness," chiastic structures that cut across previous divisions of the three-book hypothesis, and intra- and intertextual connections all revealed an accord and integrity that disclosed unifying dimensions across these sixty-six chapters. Like Liebreich's earlier observation, many interpreters recognized and elaborated further the connection between the opening of the book and the final two chapters. Others recognized parallels and contrasts that draw together parts of chapters. For example, Christopher Seitz, Rolf Rendtorff, and Rainer Albertz noted the connections between Isa 40:1–8, the commission report, and Isaiah's call in 6:1–13.[20]

---

16. Rolf Rendtorff, "Zur Komposition des Buches Jesaja," *VT* 34 (1985): 295–320.

17. As quoted by Abernethy, *Discovering Isaiah*, 30.

18. H. G. M. Williamson, *The Book Called Isaiah: Deutero-Isaiah's Role in Composition and Redaction* (Oxford: Clarendon, 1994), 37–8.

19. Jacob Stromberg, *Isaiah after Exile: The Author of Third Isaiah as Reader and Redactor of the Book*, OTM (Oxford: Oxford University Press, 2011).

20. Christopher Seitz, "The Divine Council: Temporal Transition and New Prophecy in the Book of Isaiah," *JBL* 109 (1990): 238–43; Rolf Rendtorff, "Jesaja 6 im Rahmen der Komposition des Jesajabuches," in *The Book of Isaiah: Le Livre d'Isaïe. Les oracles et leurs relectures. Utilité et complexité de l'ouvrage*, ed. Jacques Vermeylen, BETL 81 (Leuven: Leuven University Press, 1989), 73–82 (79–81); Rainer Albertz, "Das Deuterojesaja-Buch als Fortschreibung der Jesaja-Prophetie," in *Die hebräische Bibel und ihre zweifache Nachgeschichte: Festschrift für Rolf Rendtorff zum 65. Geburtstag*, ed. Erhard Blum, G. Christian Macholz, and Ekkehard Stegemann (Neukirchen-Vluyn: Neukirchener Verlag, 1990), 241–56 (244–8).

In 1990, the SBL seminar on The Formation of the Book of Isaiah was established and co-chaired by Melugin and Sweeney. During its four-year run, the seminar featured an increasing number of papers related to the topic of unity across the book.[21] In addition, a few of these studies not only attended to the dimensions of literary artistry but also began to assess indicators for the implied readers of these texts. For example, Edgar Conrad's interpretive reading of the final form of Isaiah not only mapped parallels, narrative connections, and repetitions across the whole of the book but also investigated clues for the implied reader or audience receiving and hearing this text.[22] Around the same time, Katheryn Pfisterer Darr also considered how the implied reader in the post-exilic period would receive and hear Isaiah.[23] In particular, she tracked the images of child and family from the opening to the conclusion of the book. This attention to the implied reader would instigate another turn in the study of Isaiah where readers in a variety of contexts would receive and interpret the book from the particularities and concerns of their settings.

Studies of themes that cut across separate chapters or even the whole book have also occupied literary studies. Most recently, *The Oxford Handbook of Isaiah* devotes a whole subsection to ten essays that trace themes and literary motifs that span the entire corpus.[24] Topics such as the character of God, sin and punishment, the portrait of Zion/Jerusalem, exile, elements of wisdom, the notion of a remnant, and even eschatology are shown to occupy prominence and they occasion discussions relating to thematic development throughout the entire book.

This more integrated and what became known as a unifying approach to Isaiah would not be confined to redaction-critical studies or the variety of literary approaches but would soon be influenced by the increased attention to the role of the real reader and the reading community. This trajectory of biblical interpretation featured readers and how their experiences and ideological orientations influenced the interpretation of texts such as Isaiah. As this world in front of the text became a formalized interpretive lens, a further array of interpretive studies (i.e., postcolonial, feminist/womanist, ecological, subaltern, etc.) that read the final form of Isaiah emerged. In 2006, Mark Gray's volume *Rhetoric and Social Justice in Isaiah* enlists his pastoral experience in social justice in Africa, his reading of Jacques Derrida and other postmodern thinkers, along with postcolonial African commentators to wrestle the justice issues across the biblical book.[25]

---

21. See Melugin's extensive overview of these studies in "Isaiah 40–66 in Recent Research: The Unity Movement."

22. Edgar W. Conrad, *Reading Isaiah*, OBT (Minneapolis, MN: Fortress, 1991), 1, 30–1.

23. Katheryn Pfisterer Darr, *Isaiah's Vision and the Family of God*, LCBI (Louisville, KY: Westminster/John Knox Press, 1994).

24. Lena-Sofia Tiemeyer, ed., *The Oxford Handbook of Isaiah* (New York: Oxford University Press, 2020), 201–376.

25. Mark Gray, *Rhetoric and Social Justice in Isaiah*, LHBOTS 432 (London: T&T Clark, 2006).

Patricia K. Tull's essay, "Persistent Vegetative States: People as Plants and Plants as People in Isaiah," exercises an ecological lens focusing on numerous images drawn from the world of agriculture: vineyards and cucumber fields, plowshares, pruning hooks, and threshing sledges.[26] Tull summons readers to hear across this prophetic text that we "belong to the ground beneath us, and we cannot afford to let ourselves be cut off from its sustaining power."[27]

In his recent essay, "Postcolonial Readings of Isaiah," Mark Brett observes that the imperial contexts of Neo-Assyrian, Neo-Babylonian, Persian, and Hellenistic Empires, during which time the book of Isaiah was composed, invites a postcolonial scrutiny of several key motifs across the book.[28] His interpretation takes up matters such as the multiple layers of power in a colonial situation, cultural hybridity, and the role of empire resident there. Given the imperial politics during the Persian period, Brett considers the potential of religious texts such as Isaiah to function propagandistically, directly informing readers' thinking concerning these issues today.

With its numerous female images, the book of Isaiah also has invited interpretations from feminist and womanist approaches. In her essay, "Isaiah: The Book of Female Metaphors," Irmtraud Fischer offers a feminist assessment of the female portraits across the whole of Isaiah and the importance of understanding their ancient sociocultural signification as it reaps consequences for women readers today.[29] And most recently, Sharon Moughtin-Mumby's "Feminist/Womanist Readings in Isaiah" offers an overview of six trajectories she traces throughout Isaiah that have consequences and pose challenges for women readers of this book.[30]

As Melugin's overview demonstrated, the search for unity in Isaiah erects a tent within which an extensive variety of studies reside. Our study stands on the shoulders of those who have come before us and humbly continues to build upon this expanding foundation with particular attention to perspective and how that becomes an organizing principle in this pursuit. A session on unity in Isaiah at the

---

26. Patricia K. Tull, "Persistent Vegetative States: People as Plants and Plants as People in Isaiah," in *The Desert Will Bloom: Poetic Visions in Isaiah*, ed. A. Joseph Everson and Hyun Chul Paul Kim, SBLAIL 4 (Atlanta, GA: SBL Press, 2009), 17–34.

27. Tull, "Persistent Vegetative States," 34. More recently, see Hilary Marlow, "Reading from the Ground Up: Nature in the Book of Isaiah," in *The Oxford Handbook of the Bible and Ecology*, ed. Hilary Marlow and Mark Harris (New York: Oxford University Press, 2022), 123–35.

28. Mark G. Brett, "Postcolonial Readings of Isaiah," in Tiemeyer, ed., *The Oxford Handbook of Isaiah*, 621–36.

29. Irmtraud Fischer, "Isaiah: The Book of Female Metaphors," in *Feminist Biblical Interpretation: A Compendium of Critical Commentary on the Books of the Bible and Related Literature*, ed. Luise Schottroff and Marie-Theres Wacker (Grand Rapids, MI: Eerdmans, 2012), 303–18.

30. Sharon Moughtin-Mumby, "Feminist/Womanist Readings in Isaiah," in Tiemeyer, ed., *The Oxford Handbook of Isaiah*, 601–20.

International SBL in Rome in 2019 provided impetus for this project. For while each paper made a case for unity in Isaiah, the rich discussion among participants often fixed attention upon the diversity of the methodological perspectives arguing for unity. Further, the question of what was meant by the word "unity" surfaced frequently, as well as the matter of whether we should be speaking of "unities" rather than "unity." As we continue to ponder these important inquires, the great nineteenth-century German composer Felix Mendelssohn's observation may be helpful in the midst of these musings: "The essence of the beautiful is unity in variety."

Unity, whether within a text or elsewhere, is not about sameness, uniformity, or even equivalence. In the case of Isaiah, such an understanding would risk obscuring the rich plurality resident there.[31] Rather the case for unity is based first upon the recognition of features across the text as a whole, as well as that this recognition depends upon the perspective of the viewer. Linguistic correlations, macro textual structures, enduring themes, iterative concepts, repeated literary patterns, allusions perceived between words, or even whole portions of texts that in relation to each other collectively yield meaning all number among these features. It is a well-known adage that beauty is in the eye of the beholder. Thus, perspective also will qualify what unity is discerned here. Whether one is interpreting from the perspective of the world behind the text, the world of the text, or the world in front of the text (the three broad categories around which the three sections of this volume are arranged) has a determining impact on the outcome. Thus, as in the past, the ongoing scholarship in these essays, which continues to uncover other unifying interpretations of Isaiah, may well contribute to the variety that Mendelssohn describes. Thus, "the beautiful," and in this case, the beautiful in Isaiah, continues to disclose "unity" in all this variety.

Participating in the unity in Isaiah movement, this study will arrange its essays according to the interpreter's perspective in relation to the text. None of these points of view (world behind the text, world of the text, and world in front of the text) is exclusive and, within most interpretations, some crossover among the perspectives exists. That this is the case bespeaks the importance for the enlistment of cross-disciplinary and multi-methodological routes to pursue the interpretive richness of Isaiah as a whole. Thus, we intend the three-world perspectives to serve merely as helpful organizational groupings for this eclectic collection of scholarly essays.

The first group of essays tends toward a diachronic approach but with varying qualifications. In the opening essay, Ulrich Berges redefines the issue in reading Isaiah as not a matter of unity or complexity but rather as unity *in* complexity. Therefore, as an appropriate paradigm, he focuses upon sectional compositions (*Teilkompositionen*) which build upon one another. To this end, Berges proposes a "diachronically reflected synchrony" approach and demonstrates the same by tracing three key themes in Trito-Isaiah (Zion, accusation and demand for justice, and the extent of YHWH's congregation and servants). Thus he concludes that

---

31. David Carr, "Reaching for Unity in Isaiah," *JSOT* 57 (1993): 61–80 (80).

each major section of Isaiah represents the book in a nutshell under different aspects but always from the perspective of Israel in the Persian period.

Following, H. G. M. Williamson assesses varying methods and outcomes of select monographs that consider significant themes in Isaiah as a whole. He then interrogates relationships between synchronic and diachronic approaches as well as between sequential or episodic reading strategies. Grounded in these assessments, the author makes a case for a more integrated process of composition in which literary dependence ran in two directions, from earlier chapters in the book to later and *vice versa*. Williamson then concludes with an affirmation that the best way to a synchronic reading is through the diachronic.

For his part, Hyun Chul Paul Kim also surveys scholarly studies that investigate key thematic threads across Isaiah. The author then undertakes a synchronic analysis of Isa 34 and lists some pervasive and persuasive allusions and connections to other parts of the book, which paves the way for his diachronic assessment. Thus, Kim concludes that Isa 34 was a late redaction by a final editor who intentionally summons readers to recognize these thematic and theological connections across the book.

Addressing the unity question, the next two essays narrow their focus to more explicit historical considerations at play in the world behind the text. Benedetta Rossi examines the scribal processes at work in the book of Isaiah. With Isa 56:1–8 as a test case, she situates the pericope against the background of the tension between Sabbath and justice, both in framing texts (1:13 in 1:2–20) and in secondary additions (Isa 58:13–14). Here Rossi notes how several cross-references connect the new texts to the more extensive collection and thus attest to the scribal authority in expressing new ideas (an unprecedented Sabbath development) by employing textual material already available.

The focus on the scribes continues in Peter Dubovský's chapter which takes into account direct references to historical events and persons in the book of Isaiah. In addition, he highlights the division of history into three periods as reflecting Exodus' paradigm of oppression and liberation. Further, Dubovský notes how these direct references betray a vision of history organizing the otherwise disconnected prophecies into a unity that at the same time offers a new interpretation of the history of humanity.

Closing this section, Jacob Stromberg approaches the book of Isaiah as an historian of ancient Israelite literature with a view to highlight the literary competence in antiquity. The said competence is attested in the comparison between the two halves of the book by the ancient reader. To demonstrate, the author observes that the book of Isaiah employs symmetry and analogy to portray a history wherein the past portends the future. In this figural history, the remnants of the past—the survivors of the Assyrian and Babylonian eras—were to carry a lesson for the holy seed of the future.

The second set of essays proposes unity from primarily a text centered perspective. Willem Beuken's chapter demonstrates that Isa 1 and 12 not only share themes and characters but also craft a rhetorical frame connecting the wealth of stories and oracles contained within the intervening chapters of Isa 2–11.

1. Introduction

As regards the question of unity, this study argues that the framework chapters (1, 12) along with the enclosed chapters (2–11) together present a preview in miniature of the whole book of Isaiah.

Marvin Sweeney's study also focuses upon the narrative feature of a character. He surveys the references to the character of Jacob and how it functions as a unifying motif across Isaiah. An intertextual study of three textual blocks (Isa 2–4; 5–12 and 40–54) concerning the status of Jerusalem/Judah crafts parallels with the elements of the Jacob story (punishment, exile, restoration) as narrated in the Pentateuchal texts (Gen 25–50 and Exodus–Deuteronomy), and thus attests to a synchronic unity of the book of Isaiah.

A critical review of a widespread opinion on the intricate relationship between Isaiah and Jeremiah is taken up in Georg Fischer's chapter. Two observations then follow: first, that there are many internal connections between the various parts of the book of Isaiah, thus pointing to a much stronger coherence than supposed before; and second, that the book of Jeremiah could pick up texts from the entire book of Isaiah. Five illustrations support the two-part proposal as well as bolster Fischer's pursuit of the whole book of Isaiah as a unity.

Finally, Boris Lazzaro employs cognitive metaphor approach to study the conceptual metaphor KNOWING IS SEEING and how it is *placed*, then *complicated*, *contradicted*, and finally *rehabilitated* in Isa 42–43. The pursued strategy not only helps in perceiving the collection of disparate data in a unified framework but also intercepts the links between the various linguistic modulations of the same metaphor, thereby strengthening cohesion and coherence of the entire book of Isaiah on a synchronic level.

The essays found in the third and final section investigate the matter of unity from either a contemporary grounding, a critical theory, or a reader-reception perspective. With recourse to critical spatial theory, Dominic Irudayaraj considers the interpretive potential of unexplored "desolate spaces" (*šmm* cognates) and their import for the pursuit of unity in Isaiah. To this end, the author traces two duets: first, a theological duet between Zion and the servant in Isa 49 and a disquieting lack of resolution therein; and second, a dialogic duet between the opening and closing entries, namely, the thematic patterning of "desolate" (*šmmh*) in 1:1–9 and 63:7–64:11 and how it discloses the intimate interconnection between the prospects of God, people, and land, which leads to a reiteration of unity *in* diversity.

Enlisting a feminist reading, Gina Hens-Piazza attends to the metaphoric depiction of Zion as woman in her varied forms, with a specific focus on the pronounced transformation in her portrait from the opening chapter of Isaiah to its conclusion in ch. 66. Further, the author suggests that this shift coheres with the required societal shift regarding women envisioned for the realization of Isaian eschatology. Further, Hens-Piazza considers how woman, as root of this metaphor, not only bears this revelatory significance but also may serve as one theological linchpin for a more holistic reading of the book of Isaiah.

Blaženka Scheuer explores the theme of suffering in the book of Isaiah using Albert Camus' concept of the absurd. Faced with persistent displacement and suffering, as well as a perception of YHWH's indifference to it, the authors/editors of the book of Isaiah accentuate a sense of absurdity of Israelite existence after the Babylonian exile. The author reads Isa 6, 53, 63–64 as illustrations of absurd protest in order to state that the book of Isaiah embraces suffering as the essence of Israelite existence. Further, she asserts that integrity and meaningful life are not acquired through a quiet acceptance of the destructive forces attributed to YHWH, but through an unyielding refusal to submit to such a theology.

Engaging trauma theory, Elizabeth Esterhuizen and Alphonso Groenewald bring together their individual disciplines of psychology and biblical studies to read Isa 1–12 and note that the concepts of remnant and the day of YHWH run as the common threads across these chapters. The remnant understood as a "we-group" appears as a category that expresses resilience. The motif is perceived to contribute significantly to the literary plotline of the book of Isaiah. The same holds true for the second "trauma marker": "the day of YHWH/in that day." These expressions indicate both a time of judgment but also a new dawn of hope. Resilient rebuilding strategies, when faced with trauma, are thus configured as possible connecting threads of Isa 1–12 and potentially of the entire book of Isaiah.

In the last essay of this third group, Attila Bodor highlights the important role of reception in the pursuit of unity across Isaiah. He presents how, in contradistinction to modern biblical scholars, ancient translations considered the Hebrew text of Isaiah in its entirety. To that end, the author enlists the Peshitta, with a specific focus on the motif "God as supporter/helper," which offers a rare insight into the early holistic reading of Isaiah. Informed by his reader-oriented interpretation, Bodor pleads for a need to distinguish between the unity of the original author(s)/editor(s) and the latter reception(s) of the book of Isaiah.

The exploration of the unity of Isaiah offered by this collection of essays can hardly be exhaustive and much less conclusive. It is hoped that each of the three reading perspectives (world behind the text, world of the text, world in front of the text) around which the chapters are organized, and yet which demonstrate considerable overlap across these perspectives, will elicit further exploration and research. Even today, unity in Isaiah is a valuable reading strategy to the book of Isaiah that can offer the interpreter not only enduring challenges but also promising rewards.

SECTION ONE

WORLD BEHIND THE TEXT

Chapter 2

THE "UNITY" OF THE BOOK OF ISAIAH:
A PERSONAL REVIEW AND OUTLOOK

Ulrich Berges

The aim of this contribution is not to give an overview over the many valuable exegetical publications on Isaiah of the last decades because there is no shortage of helpful bibliographical summaries,[1] and the attempts to come to terms with the complexity of the book of Isaiah are also numerous.[2] What this essay wants to present, however, is a review of twenty-five years of my own work on the book of Isaiah and a foresight of possible steps ahead with a focus on the so-called Trito-Isaiah.

---

1. Peter Höffken, *Jesaja. Der Stand der theologischen Diskussion* (Darmstadt: Wissenschaftliche Buchgesellschaft, 2004); Roy F. Melugin, "Isaiah 40–66 in Research: The 'Unity' Movement," in *Recent Research on the Major Prophets*, ed. A. J. Hauser (Sheffield: Sheffield Phoenix, 2008), 141–94; Uwe Becker, "Tendenzen der Jesajaforschung 1998–2007," *TRu* 74 (2009): 96–128; Christopher B. Hays, "The Book of Isaiah in Contemporary Research," *RC* 5 (2011): 549–66. For more information, see the online bibliography Charles Conroy, "Biblical Bibliographies and Related Material," May 28, 2022, https://www.cjconroy.net/bibliog.htm.

2. Ulrich Berges, *Isaiah: The Prophet and His Book* (Sheffield: Sheffield Phoenix, 2012; German original Leipzig: Evangelische Verlagsanstalt, 2010); Lena-Sofia Tiemeyer, ed., *The Oxford Handbook of Isaiah* (New York: Oxford University Press, 2020); Jacob Stromberg and J. Todd Hibbard, eds., *The History of Isaiah: The Formation of the Book and Its Presentation of the Past*, FAT 150 (Tübingen: Mohr Siebeck, 2021); Antti Laato, *Message and Composition of the Book of Isaiah: An Interpretation in the Light of Jewish Reception History*, DCLS 46 (Berlin: de Gruyter, 2022).

1. A Personal Look Back

With my habilitation thesis on the composition and final form of the book of Isaiah from 1998 I entered new territory because, up to then, there was no work that tried to bundle synchronic and diachronic considerations across all 66 chapters.[3] If today one even speaks of a "unity movement," the question of the unity of the book was by and large not an accepted research question in the exegetical guild until the mid-1980s. Rolf Rendtorff was still disappointed to find out that "the question of the composition of Isaiah in its present form does not belong to the universally recognized themes of Old Testament studies."[4] As a personal note, I would like to add that I owe my academic career to no small extent to him, because, after our fortuitous encounter at the IOSOT in Paris in 1992, he established the decisive contact with Erich Zenger, which eventually led to postdoctoral study in my city of birth, Münster.

Due to the exegetical tradition, Anglophone scholars pursue[d] the synchronic approach more easily, whereas the German colleagues employ[ed] predominantly diachronic methods. But over the years, a significant change took place, and the once heated debate about the prevalence of synchronic *or* diachronic methods gave way to the understanding that the validity and legitimacy of both approaches derive from the nature of the biblical books themselves. In the end, even die-hard redaction critics no longer considered the search for book compositional structures to be irrelevant, but they kept underlining that the quest for the oldest layers of the prophetic tradition should not be abandoned altogether. As Odil Hannes Steck stated, "The question concerning the prophets themselves, after differentiating earlier and later material in the prophetic books, has in no way been abandoned. But immediate access to the prophet and disparagement of the books are no longer self-evident positions. In fact, these books *may* also have a purpose as books. The present final structure of these books *could* also present a message that aspires to something and aims at something."[5] The conjunctural mode of expression is enlightening, because the fact that the book of Isaiah pursues its own goal is only recognized as a possibility. A further side note should be allowed: after Zenger instructed me to send my published habilitation to his friend in Zürich, a Bavarian like himself, Steck replied after a few weeks with a detailed letter, which I kept on my desk as an "eternal" reminder. In it, he expressed his astonishment that I had dared such an ambitious undertaking to examine the entire book of Isaiah. My book, in his view, came prematurely, because ultimately such a project would only be justifiable after all diachronic questions had been solved, but this could never be achieved by one person alone: "The mass of texts is too large, the

---

3. Ulrich Berges, *Das Buch Jesaja: Komposition und Endgestalt*, HBS 16 (Freiburg: Herder, 1998), published in English as *The Book of Isaiah: Its Composition and Final Form*, HBM 46 (Sheffield: Sheffield Phoenix, 2012).

4. Rolf Rendtorff, "Zur Komposition des Buches Jesaja," *VT* 34 (1984): 295–320 (295).

5. Odil Hannes Steck, *Die Prophetenbücher und ihr theologisches Zeugnis: Wege der Nachfrage und Fährten zur Antwort* (Tübingen: Mohr Siebeck, 1996), vi (emphasis mine).

secondary literature is too diverse, the discussion is still completely in flux with very different methodological approaches. What good is a hasty conclusion that has so little ground under its feet?"[6] Following his argument one might conclude that the fur can only be distributed when the bear is killed, that is, when the diachronic development of the whole book is completely resolved.

2. A New Paradigm: Unity in Complexity

After many years of working on the exegesis of the book of Isaiah, I think on the one hand that the diachrony of all chapters is still a long way off, but on the other that there can be little doubt that the theological intention(s) of the book of Isaiah can only be disclosed via an intensive inquiry of its literary-historical growth.[7] In this context, a certain reservation might also be in place with regard to the so-called *Fortschreibungen*. This idea figures very prominently in the exegesis of the prophetic writings in general and of Isaiah in particular. It is, however, not the master key for solving all the questions[8] because continuities and discontinuities are conspicuously co-existent in this book.[9] The search for harmony must be constantly interrupted by questions regarding the diachronic position of the singular elements.

And one of the central questions of the composition is not, in my opinion, resolved, perhaps not even addressed with the necessary vigor: Did the two main parts of the book (Isa 1–39 and 40–66) grow together by "expansion" (*Fortschreibungsthese*) or by "compilation" (*Vereinigungsthese*).[10] That the unity

---

6. From a letter dated August 5, 1998: "Die Textmasse ist zu groß, die Sekundärliteratur ist zu vielfältig, die Diskussion ist noch völlig im Fluss bei ganz unterschiedlichen methodischen Ansätzen. Was nützt da ein voreiliges Fazit, das so wenig Boden unter den Füßen hat."

7. Steck, *Prophetenbücher*, 17: "Also: Nicht wie ein Prophetenbuch damals wie heute gelesen werden kann—die Möglichkeiten sind Legion—, sondern wie es gegebenenfalls innerhalb seiner formativen Zeit nach dem Willen seiner Gestalter jeweils gelesen werden soll, muß uns beschäftigen, weil dies die Formation als historischen Vorgang zu seiner Zeit bestimmt."

8. Reinhard Gregor Kratz, "Die Redaktion der Prophetenbücher," in *Rezeption und Auslegung im Alten Testament und in seinem Umfeld: Ein Symposon aus Anlass des 60. Geburtstags von Odil Hannes Steck*, OBO 153, ed. Reinhard Gregor Kratz and Thomas Krüger (Freiburg/Schweiz: Universitätsverlag, 1997), 9–27 (15).

9. Lena-Sofia Tiemeyer and Hans M. Barstad, eds., *Continuity and Discontinuity: Chronological and Thematic Development in Isaiah 40–66*, FRLANT 255 (Göttingen: Vandenhoeck & Ruprecht, 2014).

10. Cf. Rüdiger Feuerstein, "Weshalb gibt es Deuterojesaja?," in *Ich bewirke das Heil und erschaffe das Unheil (Jes 45,7): Studien zur Botschaft der Propheten, Festschrift für L. Ruppert*, ed. Friedrich Diedrich and Bernd Willmes, FzB 88 (Würzburg: Echter Verlag, 1998), 93–134.

of the book of Isaiah cannot be established upon one author (Isaiah) is widely accepted. But the unity can neither be viewed as a result of two (Deutero-Isaiah) or three authors (Trito-Isaiah)[11] nor as the outcome of a final redaction of the whole scroll.[12] No one single group was responsible for the final shape of the scroll if there was a final editing at all.[13] Instead, one has to surmise partial compositions and different editorial attempts to structure the steadily growing scroll.[14]

As far as the synchronic research is concerned, there continue to appear very interesting monographs,[15] but nobody claims to have discovered the all-explanatory reading of the book in its final form. What Frederik Poulsen concludes as the result of his monograph applies *mutatis mutandis* to all other studies on the book of Isaiah, namely, they can illuminate just some aspects of a multifaceted *Gesamtkunstwerk*:

> To summarize, I believe I have demonstrated that exile constitutes a significant theme in the book of Isaiah. The black hole between Isa 39 and 40 forms an anti-climax—a center of destruction, darkness, and death—in the overall literary structure of the composition and several passages stress its importance by either pointing forward to it or looking back at it. Finally, exile constitutes a central element in the theological message of Isaiah and the concern for the fate of Zion.[16]

---

11. See recently David Davage, *How Isaiah Became an Author* (Minneapolis, MN: Fortress, 2022), who analyzes the concept of author and authorship in the Ancient World and in the Old Testament, especially in Isaiah.

12. H. G. M. Williamson, *The Book Called Isaiah: Deutero-Isaiah's Role in Composition and Redaction* (Oxford: Clarendon, 1994); Jacob Stromberg, *Isaiah After Exile: The Author of Third Isaiah as Reader and Redactor of the Book* (Oxford: Oxford University Press, 2011).

13. For a different view, see Joachim Becker, *Isaias, der Prophet und sein Buch*, SBS 30 (Stuttgart: Katholisches Bibelwerk, 1968), 36: "We postulate therefore one redaction responsible for the book in its present form and its unified theological concept."

14. See David M. Carr, "Reaching for Unity in Isaiah," *JSOT* 57 (1993): 61–80 (77): "It is clear that not just one, but several redactors have introduced their macrostructural conceptions into the book of Isaiah."

15. Andrew T. Abernethy, *The Book of Isaiah and God's Kingdom: A Thematic-Theological Approach*, NSBT 40 (Downers Grove, IL: IVP Academic, 2016); Miguel Angel Garzón Moreno, *La alegría en Isaías: la alegría como unidad y estructura del libro a partir de su epílogo (Is 65–66)* (Estella: Verbo Divino, 2011); Michael P. Maier, *Völkerwallfahrt im Jesajabuch*, BZAW 474 (Berlin: de Gruyter, 2016); Torsten Uhlig, *The Theme of Hardening in the Book of Isaiah: An Analysis of Communicative Action*, FAT II/39 (Tübingen: Mohr Siebeck, 2009); Archibald L. H. M. van Wieringen, *The Reader-Oriented Unity of the Book Isaiah*, ACEBTSup 6 (Vught: Skandalon, 2006).

16. Frederik Poulsen, *The Black Hole in Isaiah: A Study of Exile as a Literary Theme*, FAT 125 (Tübingen: Mohr Siebeck, 2019), 413.

The hardening-motif, the pilgrimage of the nations, as well as key concepts such as justice and holiness highlight important aspects, but the whole picture is much bigger and the perspective cannot be derived from them alone. In a smaller booklet mainly written for students, Willem Beuken and I refrained from a proposing a single perspective and presented instead some elements for a theology of the book by beginning with the different names of God that are used in the scroll ("Lord," "YHWH *ṣəḇāʾôṯ*," "the Holy one of Israel").[17] Subsequently we analyzed in a very condensed manner some major themes, such as the "glory" of God or "justice and righteousness." But this is certainly not the last word in the search for a theological understanding of this prophetic book. Another problem can only be approached: how does one come from the theologies *in* the book of Isaiah to an overall theology *of* the book?[18] It is certainly not sufficient to single out key words or similar phenomena and follow them throughout the 66 chapters, since the book of Isaiah is as complex on the synchronic as on the diachronic level. Everything taken together, it must be acknowledged that "Isaiah" is too diverse to be considered a unified whole and too united to be regarded as just a mere compilation of different parts. The main issue is not about unity *or* complexity, but about unity *in* complexity.

The guiding line of future research should not be "chaos or cosmos," but rather "controlled chaos." Methodologically, a "diachronically-reflected synchrony" is necessary, one which analyzes the existing textual fabric, keeping in mind the nearly four hundred years of development of this huge literary building. After decades of combat, the time is ripe not only for a cease-fire but for a common effort among synchronists and diachronists. They should mutually accept the restrictions of their approaches and recognize the strengths of each other's methodology. I call this approach a *"diachron reflektierte Synchronie."* It examines the final form in a synchronic way without, however, disregarding the stages of the literary growth of each section and of the book as a whole (chs. 1–12; 13–27; 28–35; 36–39; 40–48; 49–54; 55–66). The outcome might be that each of these sections represents the book of Isaiah in a nutshell under different aspects, but always from the perspective of Israel in the Persian period. It is no longer sufficient to place the synchronic divisions and the diachronic stratifications next to each other;[19] on the contrary, every synchronous observation must be accompanied by a redactional positioning.

---

17. Ulrich Berges and Willem A. M. Beuken, *Das Buch Jesaja: Eine Einführung*, UTB 4647 (Göttingen: Vandenhoek & Rupprecht, 2016), 35–49.

18. John Goldingay, *The Theology of the Book of Isaiah* (Downers Grove, IL: IVP Academic, 2014), 11.

19. See Marvin A. Sweeney, "Reading the Final Form of Isaiah as a Persian Period Text," in *The History of Isaiah: The Formation of the Book and its Presentation of the Past*, ed. Jacob Stromberg and J. Todd Hibbard, FAT 150 (Tübingen: Mohr Siebeck, 2021), 527–37 (527), who simply sets the two halves of the book of Isaiah (Isa 1–33; 34–66) and the four stages of formation (eighth, seventh, sixth, and fifth–fourth centuries BCE) next to each other.

Given the current state of research, one cannot continue to pretend that the book of Isaiah has grown more or less stringently from front to back so that the oldest texts stand at the beginning and the youngest at the end. It is true that the oldest parts are to be found in the first half, but not that one would have to look for the youngest portions at the end. Examples for this include texts such as Isa 19:16–25, but also Isa 24–27[20] and 34–35; in addition, Isa 36–39 was probably not inserted into the scroll until after Isa 66. If one takes all of this seriously, it has consequences for both the mostly English-speaking "synchronists" and the mostly German-speaking "diachronists"—and for everybody in between. The former should not fall into a history-forgetting reading of the final text (and which text is the final one?), and the latter should willingly include all the literary connections that arise from a synchronic perspective in their considerations and hypothesis formations. The requirements for the interpretation of Proto-Isaiah are particularly high in this respect, because not only in the first chapter,[21] but also in all others as well, the growth of the entire book must always be taken into account.[22]

3. Zion as the Center of Gravity of the Book of Isaiah

Working with the premise of a history of more than four centuries with a large number of writers and poets, is it possible at all to discover a red thread or rather a point of gravity that does justice to this polyphony? It is interesting to see that it is actually a proven redaction critic, Becker, who sees in Zion theology the thematic center of this prophetic book: "If one attempts to uncover a unifying bond, a common theme or leitmotif in the book of Isaiah, this tentative response could be offered: in every part of the book, from the first to the last chapter, Zion plays a pivotal role—its endangerment and protection."[23]

In my 25 years of study, a division of the 66 chapters into seven acts has proven to be quite useful. The term "act" means in this context a literary unit, not

---

20. See Donald C. Polaski, *Authorizing an End: The Isaiah Apocalypse and Intertextuality*, BIS 50 (Leiden: Brill, 2003).

21. See H. G. M. Williamson, *A Critical and Exegetical Commentary on Isaiah 1–27. Vol 1: Commentary on Isaiah 1–5*, ICC (London: T&T Clark, 2006), 10: "It [Chap. 1] was added at a late stage in the history of the growth of the book, by which time much of the remainder was already in an authoritative, and hence fixed, form."

22. Uwe Becker, "The Book of Isaiah: Its Composition History," in Tiemeyer, ed., *The Oxford Handbook of Isaiah*, 37–56 (51): "It is therefore no longer possible to understand the making of Proto-Isaiah without considering Isa 40–66. Despite all the differences, this may be the most important insight of contemporary scholarship."

23. Becker, "The Book of Isaiah," 38; cf. Ulrich Berges, "Die Zionstheologie des Buches Jesaja," *EstBib* 58 (2000): 167–98, and "Zion and the Kingship of YHWH in Isaiah 40–55," in *'Enlarge the Site of Your Tent': The City as Unifying Theme in Isaiah*, ed. Archibald L. H. M. van Wieringen and Annemarieke van der Woude, OTS 58 (Leiden: Brill, 2011), 95–119.

a section in a theatrical performance, for which there is no evidence in ancient Israel.[24] The book of Isaiah is therefore best considered as "the literary 'Drama of Zion' in which the readers or hearers witness the transformation of Jerusalem from a place of judgment into a place of eschatological salvation for both the righteous in Israel and the just ones from the nations."[25]

Act I	Isa 1–12: Zion and Jerusalem between judgment and salvation
Act II	Isa 13–27: Zion's enemies and friends—and YHWH's eternal kingship
Act III	Isa 28–35: The divine king and the congregation of Zion
Act IV	Isa 36–39: The threat and deliverance of Zion and Jerusalem
Act V	Isa 40–48: The Servant Jacob/Israel in Babylon and his way back home to Zion
Act VI	Isa 49–54: The Servant's struggle to persuade Zion about her restored future
Act VII	Isa 55–66: Zion/Jerusalem as YHWH's city for all believers and the servants' fate

In order not to simply repeat the results of my habilitation but to go one step further, the redaction critical processes in these literary acts would have to be examined, both with regard to the book of Isaiah as a whole and with regard to the cross-connections to all other parts of the Hebrew Bible, especially to the Pentateuch, other prophetic books, Ezra/Nehemiah and also the Psalms. The picture that has already emerged[26] and is likely to consolidate further is one of skilled literati, who creatively connected the Isaiah-tradition(s) with other currents of scribal activity in postexilic times. It would be a worthwhile and necessary task of the Isaiah research in the coming years to determine the possibly different circles of tradents who continued to build the literary cathedral of the book of Isaiah over more than four centuries. How did the center of gravity "Zion" affect the different literary acts of the drama? Which elements have been attracted by and attracted to this center of gravity in the course of the formative phase, such as the pilgrimage of the nations, the Exodus-, the Moses-, and the David-traditions. In the future, specialists of the Pentateuch, of the prophetic writings (especially the

---

24. See, differently, Klaus Baltzer, *Deutero-Jesaja*, KAT 10/2 (Gütersloh: Gütersloher Verlagshaus, 1999).

25. Ulrich Berges, "Isaiah: Structure, Themes, and Contested Issues," in *The Oxford Handbook of the Prophets*, ed. Carolyn J. Sharp (New York: Oxford University Press, 2016), 153–70 (157).

26. Ulrich Berges, "'Sing to the LORD a New Song': The Tradents of the Book of Isaiah and the Psalter," in Stromberg and Hibbard, eds., *The History of Isaiah*, 213–37; Ulrich Berges, "Isaiah 55–66 and the Psalms: Shared Viewpoints, Literary Similarities and Neighboring Authors," *JBL* 141 (2022): 277–99.

Twelve Minor Prophets[27]) and the Psalms have to be brought together in a long-term project. Without such a bigger academic endeavour, the research on the unity of Isaiah is in danger of perpetuating only the well-known positions without a literary-historical tracing of the origins and the stages of growth of the book with its partial compositions. The hypothetical nature of the expected results does not need to be frightening or deterring because this is the normal burden of any academic discipline.

4. Scribal Prophecy in the Background of the Formation of the Book of Isaiah

The above project should be firmly based on the premise that the texts of the Old Testament have increasingly taken on a self-referential character. At a certain point, biblical books were no longer written by adding new parts or by editorially linking originally independent texts. Rather, the creation of new texts builds upon an intensive engagement with already existing literature.[28] Thus, it is assumed that the authors of the Old Testament drew from a profound knowledge of previous texts and made this expertise a fruitful source of their exegetical imagination. Michael Fishbane's monography from 1985 is still illuminating since he underlines the two settings, one external and one internal, that stand at the origins of the biblical writings: "On the one hand, external historical determinants provide the social context for exegesis; on the other, exegesis arises from such purely internal factors as textual content and the 'issues' perceived therein by the tradents."[29]

Inner-biblical exegesis in general and scribal prophecy in particular are in vogue but the methodological problems are by no means solved. On the one hand, this concerns the criteria on which the determination of inner-biblical references is based. At what point can one speak of intentional references? Do we have to look for explicit quotations or implicit allusions in this regard? Or are extensive echoes or general terminological patterns sufficient?[30] Does one have to think of

---

27. Cf. James Nogalski, "The Role of Lady Zion in the Concluding Section of Zephaniah and Isaiah 40–66," in *Isaiah and the Twelve: Parallels, Similarities and Differences*, ed. Richard J. Bautch, Joachim Eck and Bernd M. Zapff, BZAW 527 (Berlin: de Gruyter 2020), 55–73.

28. Cf. Konrad Schmid, "Innerbiblische Schriftauslegung. Aspekte der Forschungsgeschichte," in *Schriftauslegung in der Schrift: Festschrift für O.H. Steck*, ed. Reinhard G. Kratz, Thomas Krüger and Konrad Schmid, BZAW 300 (Berlin: de Gruyter, 2000), 1–22, and *Schriftgelehrte Traditionsliteratur. Fallstudien zur innerbiblischen Schriftauslegung im Alten Testament*, FAT 77 (Tübingen: Mohr Siebeck, 2011).

29. Michael Fishbane, *Biblical Interpretation in Ancient Israel* (Oxford: Clarendon, 1985, reprint 2004), 18.

30. Benjamin D. Sommer, *A Prophet Reads Scripture: Allusion in Isaiah 40–66* (Stanford: Stanford University Press, 1998), 12–30; also Wolfgang Lau, *Schriftgelehrte Prophetie in Jes 56–66: Eine Untersuchung zu den literarischen Bezügen in den letzten elf Kapiteln des*

inner-biblical interpretation as a reflected and intentional process of forming and maintaining a tradition? Or was there simply a sufficiently large pool of forms of language and thought, which was more or less taken for granted and used for quite different purposes? Depending on the point of view, the assessments of the significance of inner-biblical quotations and allusions for textual pragmatics will differ considerably. Be that as it may, there were no longer charismatic individual figures and their disciples who appear as prophets and whose words are written down. Rather, the emergence of prophetic texts had shifted to the scribal guilds of the Second Temple with sometimes sharp criticism of its cult.[31]

Nevertheless, many details of the scribal work still remain unclear: Where were the centers of literary activity, since the *literati* of that time only made up a fraction of the population?[32] What did a biblical book look like?[33] How do we imagine the concrete work with such scrolls?[34] What were the social relationships between the different groups of scribes? From the religious-historical comparison with Syria and Mesopotamia, it is known that in the palace and temple archives of the ancient Near East there were collections of prophetic oracles, ones that had been written down and stored. However, the fact that such collections formed the starting point for further processes of transmission in the form of prophetic

---

Jesajabuches, BZAW 225 (Berlin: de Gruyter, 1994); Pancratius C. Beentjes, "Discovering a New Path of Intertextuality: Inverted Quotations and Their Dynamics," in *Literary Structure and Rhetorical Strategies in the Hebrew Bible*, ed. Lénart J. De Regt, Jan de Waard and Jan P. Fokkelman (Assen: Van Gorcum, 1996), 31–50; Richard L. Schultz, *Search for Quotation: Verbal Parallels in the Prophets*, JSOTSup 180 (Sheffield: Sheffield Academic, 1999); Risto Nurmela, *The Mouth of the Lord Has Spoken: Inner-Biblical Allusion in Second and Third Isaiah* (Lanham: University Press of America, 2006).

31. See Lena-Sofia Tiemeyer, *Priestly Rites and Prophetic Rage: Post-Exilic Prophetic Critique of the Priesthood*, FAT II/19 (Tübingen: Mohr Siebeck, 2006).

32. Ehud Ben Zvi, "Urban Center of Jerusalem and the Development of the Literature of the Hebrew Bible," in *Urbanism in Antiquity: From Mesopotomia to Crete*, JSOTSup 244, ed. Walter E. Aufrecht, Neil A. Mirau and Steven W. Gauley (Sheffield: Sheffield Academic Press, 1997), 194–209, and "Observations on Prophetic Characters, Prophetic Texts, Priests of Old, Persian Period Priests and Literati," in *The Priests in the Prophets: The Portrayal of Priests, Prophets and Other Religious Specialists in the Latter Prophets*, JSOTSup 408, ed. Lester L. Grabbe and Alice Ogden Bellis (London: Bloomsbury T&T Clark, 2004), 19–30.

33. Karel van der Toorn, *Scribal Culture and the Making of the Hebrew Bible* (Cambridge, MA: Harvard University Press, 2007); David M. Carr, *Writing on the Tablets of the Heart: Origins of Scripture and Literature* (Oxford: Oxford University Press, 2009).

34. See Hanne von Weissenberg, Juha Pakkala and Marko Marttila, eds., *Changes in Scripture: Rewriting and Interpreting Authoritative Traditions in the Second Temple Period*, BZAW 419 (Berlin: de Gruyter, 2011); William M. Schniedewind, *The Finger of the Scribe: How Scribes Learned to Write the Bible* (New York: Oxford University Press, 2019); H. G. M. Williamson, "Scribe and Scroll: Revisiting the Great Isaiah Scroll from Qumran," in *Making a Difference: Essays on the Bible and Judaism in Honor of Tamara Cohn Eskenazi*, ed. David J. A. Clines, Kent Harold Richards and Jacob L. Wright (Sheffield: Phoenix, 2012), 329–42.

books is, at least according to the current state of knowledge, a special feature of the Old Testament.[35] The result is a polyphony of voices, which brings Konrad Schmid to the following conclusion: "There is no reason to suppose that there was a homogenous milieu of Jerusalem scribes. Although the groups responsible for the origins of the Old Testament books were probably very limited and located mainly in Jerusalem, at least from the Persian period onward, they appear to have represented a relatively broad spectrum of theological ideas."[36]

5. Trito-Isaiah as Scribal Prophecy in the Book of Isaiah[37]

For the analysis of scribal activity, it makes perfect sense to look at the last main part of the book of Isaiah. The three guiding themes that characterize the composition of Isa 55–66 are specifically related to different biblical neighbors: "Zion" (Isa 60–62) is particularly found in the Psalms; the "prophetic critique" (Isa 56:9–59:21) leads to the Isaiah tradition itself; and the discussion about the "extent of the YHWH-community" (Isa 55:1–56:8; 66:18–24) is negotiated at about the same time in the priestly tradition, in Ezekiel and Ezra/Nehemiah.[38] The last theme comes to its climax in Isa 65–66, for the community of the believers that extends beyond Israel takes concrete form in the servants. These 'abadim are the descendants of the faithful servant (Isa 53:10) and the true children of mother Zion; their righteousness comes from YHWH, and they are protected against every hostility (Isa 54:17b).[39] These three lines of thought build on each other in diachronic terms,[40] because "Zion" in Isa 60–62 was followed first by the prophetic admonitions in Isa 56:9–59:21 and then by the separation into servants and opponents (Isa 65–66), triggered by the confrontation with Edom/Esau (Isa 63:1–6) and the prayer of the servants (Isa 63:7–64:11).

---

35. Manfred Weippert, "Aspekte israelitischer Prophetie im Lichte verwandter Erscheinungen des Alten Orients," in *Ad bene et fideliter seminandum: Festgabe für Karlheinz Deller zum 21. Februar 1987*, ed. Gerlinde Mauer and Ursula Magen, AOAT 220 (Neukirchen-Vluyn: Neukirchener Verlag, 1988), 287–319.
36. Konrad Schmid, *The Old Testament: A Literary History*, trans. Linda M. Malony (Minneapolis, MN: Fortress, 2012), 35.
37. See in more detail Ulrich Berges, *Jesaja 55–66*, HThKAT (Freiburg: Herder, 2022).
38. According to Andreas Schüle, "Third Isaiah: What's so Greek about It?," in *Prophecy and Hellenism*, ed. Hannes Bezzel and Stefan Pfeiffer, FAT/II 129 (Tübingen: Mohr Siebeck 2021), 97–110, Isa 56 and Isa 63–66 were written at the time of Ezra/Nehemiah; Uwe Becker, "Gibt es ein hellenistisches Jesajabuch?," in *Prophecy and Hellenism*, ed. Hannes Bezzel and Stefan Pfeiffer, FAT/II 129 (Tübingen: Mohr Siebeck, 2021), 83–96, pleads for Isa 19:18–25 and Isa 65–66 for the Hellenistic period.
39. For the extant of Trito-Isaiah, see Ulrich Berges, "Where Starts Trito-Isaiah?," in Tiemeyer and Barstad, eds., *Continuity and Discontinuity*, 63–76.
40. See Becker, "The Book of Isaiah," 46.

5.1. Zion

The guiding idea that Zion/Jerusalem is the place where the worldwide worship of YHWH by Israel and the nations takes place is most evident in Isa 60–62 ("Zion" in 60:14; 61:3; 62:1, 11; "Jerusalem" in 62:1, 6, 7). After YHWH had comforted his city and bride and asked her to rise from the dust (Isa 49:19; 51:3, 11, 16), he returned to her as the victorious king who directs the history of Israel and the nations (Isa 52:9–10). But why does it take so long in literary drama for Zion to reappear as the central figure in Isa 60–62? The reason for this lies in the delay of salvation, because, in view of the social and cultic grievances mentioned in Isa 56:9–59:21, God's light cannot possibly shine over his city and produce a positive effect on the nations. It is no coincidence, therefore, that just before Isa 60–62, the decisive condition is stated that YHWH will come only to those who repent from sin in Jacob (Isa 59:20). The arrival of divine salvation is linked to an ethical and cultic conduct without which there can be no future after the return from Babylon to Zion. Something similar can be observed at the beginning of the book of Isaiah, because in the two headings of 1:1 and 2:1, only Judah and Jerusalem are mentioned. When chaos rages in the city and the land, "Daughter Zion" stands abandoned (Isa 1:8). She is only to be redeemed by the righteousness of her inhabitants (Isa 1:27). The ideal of Zion as a place of salvation in the center of the world[41] can only be maintained if there are righteous people in her. Here is an overlap with all three parts of the book, since the pious remnant in Isa 1–39, the returnees from Babylon in Isa 40–54, and the servants in 55–66, for all their differences, are on a single line of argument. Without those who listen and trust in YHWH's word, there can be no salvation that shines forth from Zion, neither for Israel, nor for the nations. The focus on Zion is so central in the book of Isaiah that it has been inscribed several times in the so-called *Völkerspruch-Sammlung* in Isa 13–23.[42] In Isa 24–27, the global perspective is further expanded: YHWH is the worldwide king who reigns from Zion (Isa 24:23). The pre-exilic collection of oracles in Isa 28–32 was also revised in view of Zion, and this probably took place in the second half of the fifth century BCE.[43] This rule of Zion can only be realized if a congregation worthy of such a divine king is constituted there: "Highly exalted is YHWH. Because he lives in the heights. He fills Zion with law and justice" (Isa 33:5). This demand for justice and righteousness is in line with the accusations in Isa 56:9–59:21. In the final part of the book, it is YHWH's servants who form the congregation of the just, to which people from all nations have access (Isa 56:1–8).

---

41. Cf. Andrea Spans, *Die Stadtfrau Zion im Zentrum der Welt. Exegese und Theologie von Jes 60–62*, BBB 175 (Göttingen: Vandenhoeck & Ruprecht, 2015).

42. See Berges, *Das Buch Jesaja*, 159, cf. 13:2; 14:1–2; 16:1, 3–5; 18:3, 7; 23:17–18.

43. See Berges, *Das Buch Jesaja*, 221, cf. 28:5–6, 16–17a, 23–29; 29:11–12, 17–24; 30:9–11, 18–26; 32:1–8, 15–20.

5.2. Accusations and the Demand for Justice

The second line of thought, which defines the content of Isa 55–66 and is associated in many ways with the book of Isaiah as a whole, is the prophetic critic, the demand for justice. The ethical conduct is both the condition for the admission to the community of YHWH and for the arrival of salvation, which will also set the nations in motion. When the social duties towards the needy are ignored, there is no relationship with God worthy of this name: "*Moral behavior does not bring about salvation, but without moral behavior salvation cannot come either.*"[44] Especially in view of Zion as the globally visible center of divine salvation, the demand for justice is indispensable and the role of God's spirit for the liberation of the poor and the oppressed is specified (Isa 61:1–3, 10–11; cf. 60:17). The recourse to prophetic ethics in the first part of the book of Isaiah is palpable, because the lament about the city of justice, which has degenerated into a city of injustice (1:21), is countered by the hope of the final enforcement of social justice for the poor. The theme of justice runs like a red thread through all parts of the book of Isaiah,[45] but with significant shifts: Isa 1–39, Israel—with the exception of the faithful rest—fails because of the ethical demands, which the final verse of the Song of the Vineyard sums up in great poetic density: "For the vineyard of YHWH ṣəḇāōṯ is the house of Israel, and the people of Judah are his pleasant planting; he expected justice, but saw bloodshed; righteousness, but heard a cry!" (5:7). Divine punishment awaits especially the officials, as they have plundered the vineyard, filled their houses with looted goods from the poor (3:14), betrayed justice, acquitted the guilty for bribes and deprived the innocent of justice (5:23). There can only be a future with and through those who make law and justice the standard of their individual and political action: only in this way will the social desert become the life-giving garden of God (30:18; 32:1, 16–17; 33:5, 15). Conspicuously, in Isa 40–54, except in the last verse (54:17) as the opening of the theme of the "servants," the parallel use of justice/righteousness no longer occurs. This is because the entire people of God are considered poor and oppressed when they leave Babylon (Isa 40–48) and arrive at Zion (Isa 49–54). It is upon this people in deepest distress that YHWH exercises his justice, as he ensures Israel's liberation and return before the eyes of the nations. God enforces this righteousness of salvation through Cyrus (44:28; 45:1) and with the help of his faithful servant (42:1–7; 49:1–6). Israel can only accept this as proof of YHWH's incomparable uniqueness (43:10) or reject it (48:1–22). In the third part of the book, the justice to be practiced by Israel and believers from the nations is combined with God's righteousness (cf. 56:1). The salvation from Babylon and the repatriation to Zion is supposed to be the foundation of post-exilic Israel

---

44. Rainer Kessler, *Der Weg zum Leben: Ethik des Alten Testaments* (Gütersloh: Gütersloher Verlagshaus, 2017), 377: "*Das moralische Verhalten führt das Heil nicht herbei, aber ohne moralisches Verhalten kann das Heil auch nicht kommen*" (author's emphasis).

45. Cf. Thomas L. Leclerc, *Yahweh Is Exalted in Justice: Solidarity and Conflict in Isaiah* (Minneapolis, MN: Fortress, 2001).

committed to justice and solidarity.⁴⁶ But the reality in the fifth and fourth centuries BCE was quite different, as Isa 59:14–15 makes clear: "Justice is turned back, and righteousness stands at a distance; for truth stumbles in the public square, and uprightness cannot enter. Truth is lacking, and whoever turns from evil is despoiled. YHWH saw it, and it displeased him that there was no justice." There is no new judgment, but God will proceed with righteousness and anger against the unjust (59:17); he will come to Zion as a redeemer only for those in Jacob who renounce their sinful behavior (59:20; cf. 63:5). Part of this conversion is the confession of one's own guilt, as the servants do in their collective lament (63:7–64:11).⁴⁷ The separation between the servants and their opponents in Isa 65–66 makes it obvious that social and cultic transgressions continue to prevail in Jerusalem despite all prophetic preaching and exhortation.

5.3. The Extent of YHWH's Congregation and his Servants

The two aspects are so closely related that they can be treated together as a third line of thought. The plural "servants" is found for the first time in Isa 54:17b and continues until the end of the book (56:6; 63:17; 65:8, 9, 13, 14, 15; 66:14). They are YHWH's disciples (Isa 54:13) when they hear his word, as did the faithful servant (50:4). Like him, they can trust in divine protection against their enemies (50:8; 54:17). The servants continue the task of the exiled and returned servant (41:8–16; 44:1–5, 21; 45:4; 48:20), who is composed of those who understand themselves as worldwide heralds of YHWH's uniqueness, because he is the only liberating and saving God (42:8–17; 49:1–26). For this testimony, the servant comes under increasing pressure (50:4–11; 52:13–53:12), but YHWH guarantees his success especially in view of his apparent failure.⁴⁸ A people of God who have experienced the historical power of YHWH in contrast to the impotence of the Babylonian gods (cf. 46–47) cannot keep this to themselves, but must become the worldwide herald. As the redeemer of his people, the Holy One of Israel has proved to be powerful before the eyes of the whole world and is therefore called "God of the whole earth" (54:5). If this is so, it is not surprising that YHWH's invitation to enter into relationship with him is also accepted by non-Israelites (55:1–5). The mention of the servants in 54:17b indicates that it is they who take on the role of David and his house: "the case seems clear that a group, a community, whether large or small, is here taking

---

46. Cf. Andreas Schüle, "'Build Up, Pass Through': Isa 57:14–62:12 as the Core Composition of Third Isaiah," in *The Book of Isaiah: Enduring Questions Answered Anew: Festschrift für Joseph Blenkinsopp*, ed. Richard Bautch and J. Todd Hibbard (Grand Rapids, MI: Eerdmans, 2014), 83–112.

47. Cf. Richard Bautch, *Development in Genre between Post-Exilic Penitential Prayers and the Psalms of Communal Lament*, SBLAcBib 7 (Atlanta, GA: SBL, 2003).

48. Ulrich Berges, "The Servant(s) in Isaiah," in Tiemeyer, ed., *The Oxford Handbook of Isaiah*, 318–33.

the place in God's program that was once filled by David and his successors."[49] But not only the political function is transferred to them; they also receive the cultic-religious one, because the fact that they command the nations includes the Mosaic function of the mediator of God's will. The servants immediately take on this task and present the admission requirements for foreigners and eunuchs (56:1), so that the latter are recognized as YHWH believers and not eliminated from his congregation. The Ezra-Nehemiah faction, with its strong bounds to the Babylonian *golah*, and the servants got along well on some points, such as the uniqueness of YHWH and the rejection of foreign cults, but in the admission to the YHWH cult of non-Israelites, they parted ways: "The Repatriate leadership in Judah promoted narrower constructions of identity, such as we find in Ezra-Nehemiah, constructions that were pointedly opposed in Isa 56:1–8 with an inclusive vision of Sabbath observance."[50] The servants do not want to replace the Mosaic Torah, but they interpret it more openly. Nor do the believers from the nations displace Israel as the people of God; rather, the cult of YHWH should be accessible to "all flesh" (Isa 66:16, 23–24). The distinction between Israel and the nations, which is decisive in large parts of the book, is replaced by the distinction between the righteous and the wicked: "The nations are included in Israel's salvation, while the wicked suffer perdition."[51] The righteous, who act in social solidarity and do not engage in foreign cults (cf. Isa 57:3–13; 65:3–7; 66:3, 17), belong to YHWH's servants; those who do not meet or do not want to meet these requirements do not belong to Jacob, but to Edom, the descendants of the hated twin Esau (Isa 59:15b–21; 63:1–6). While it is true that neither in Isa 55–66 nor otherwise in the book of Isaiah is the problem of "mixed marriages" addressed, it cannot be inferred from this that the views of the servants and Ezra-Nehemiah on the "holy seed" were identical (Ezra 9:2; cf. Isa 6,13b). On the contrary, designations such as "holy seed" and "trembling" (Isa 66:2, 5; Ezra 9:4; 10:3), as well as the honorary title of "servants" (Neh 9:36), seem to have been contested concepts in post-exilic times.[52]

The Mosaic Torah was not only the frame of reference for Israel, but had to be interpreted with regard to worshippers from the nations. Thus, Isaiah's vision did not only serve to determine the relationship between Israel and the nations, but also concerned the inner essence of the people of God.[53] This is the only way

---

49. H. G. M. Williamson, "Davidic Kingship in Isaiah," in Tiemeyer, ed., *The Oxford Handbook of Isaiah*, 280–92 (288).

50. Mark G. Brett, "Postcolonial Readings of Isaiah," in Tiemeyer, ed., *The Oxford Handbook of Isaiah*, 621–36 (630).

51. Francis Landy, "The Poetic Vision of Isaiah," in Tiemeyer, ed., *The Oxford Handbook of Isaiah*, 393–408 (397).

52. Ulrich Berges, "Trito-Isaiah and the Reforms of Ezra/Nehemiah: Consent or Conflict?," *Bib* 98 (2017): 173–90; Brett, "Postcolonial Readings," 623.

53. Contrary to Marvin A. Sweeney, "The Book of Isaiah as Prophetic Torah," in *New Visions of Isaiah*, ed. Roy F. Melugin and Marvin A. Sweeney, JSOTSup 214 (Sheffield:

to explain the sharp separation of servants and opponents in Isa 65–66, in which the latter even appear to possess the authority of "excommunication" (Isa 66:5). The real point of contention lies in the self-understanding of Israel, not in a pure demarcation of relations to the outside. Unlike the Mosaic Torah, which had already included non-Israelites in the cult (cf. Exod 12:49; Lev 24:22), the Isaian Torah, which does not originate from Sinai but from Zion (Isa 2:3), embraces all nations in the cultic community of YHWH (Isa 66:18–21, 23–24). On a synchronic level, this was already indicated in some instances, such as Isa 2:2–5; 4:2–6; 11:10; 16:1; 18:7; 19:18–25. In the royal meal "on this mountain" (Isa 25:6, 7, 10), which undoubtedly means Zion, the relationship of God with all nations is sealed, just like his covenant with Israel was secured on Mount Sinai by the meal with the elders of the people (Exod 24:9–11): "Eating and drinking in communion gives meaning to life and creates togetherness. The meal that YHWH prepares as host brings together the peoples in the community with him."[54]

Even if the servants have failed in their strife for a broader interpretation of the Mosaic Torah, their scriptural prophecy, with its imagination of justice and redemption, has survived and continues to be influential: "Their cultural and religious influence apparently outstripped their political power during the Persian period."[55] According to them, this opening does not come at the expense of the special position of Israel, because the nations come to Jerusalem, bring their offerings to the temple and take over the festival calendar of the People of God (66:20–23). The book of Isaiah is the eloquent vision of Zion as the center of a worship that can only be achieved by the righteous of Israel and the nations, by all who place themselves under the primacy of ethics—not of ethnic origin—and thus make God's house the house of prayer for all nations (Isa 56:7).

Sheffield Academic Press, 1996), 50–67 (65): "In short, Mosaic Torah defines Israel's internal relations within its own community; the book of Isaiah defines Israel's relations among the nations."

54. Willem A. M. Beuken, *Jesaja 13–27*, HThKAT (Freiburg: Herder, 2007), 359.
55. Brett, "Postcolonial Readings," 632.

Chapter 3

TWO STEPS FORWARD, ONE STEP BACK:
METHODOLOGICAL REFLECTIONS ON READING
ISAIAH AS A UNITY

H. G. M. Williamson

However valuable Roy Melugin's 2008 article may be as a survey of research down to the time when he was writing, and however much we appreciate his great contribution to the study of Isaiah during the previous decades, it seems curious to somebody as old as me to trace back to his article the suggested starting point for a consideration of the so-called unity movement.[1] Some informal autobiographical remarks covering now more than half a century may help set the stage for an approach to our subject that seeks to differentiate separate aspects of the subject. It is against this background that we may come to appreciate more fully the confusion in which the subject currently finds itself.

When I was an undergraduate in Cambridge University in the late 1960s, the chief form of education was the individual supervision. Lectures were offered, of course, but attendance at those was entirely optional. What could not under any circumstances be missed was the weekly hour with a supervisor, for which one had written an essay based on a recommended reading list. One term I was privileged to have a course of weekly supervisions on the prophets with Ronald Clements, at that time one of the young upstarts in the Faculty. Although we did not have a textbook as such, the second volume of von Rad's *Theology* was always

---

1. Roy F. Melugin, "Isaiah 40–66 in Recent Research: The 'Unity' Movement," in *Recent Research on the Major Prophets*, Recent Research in Biblical Studies 1, ed. Alan J. Hauser (Sheffield: Sheffield Phoenix, 2008), 142–94. (Melugin's extensive survey allows him to include some works above and beyond those that I mention in the following.) This article was proposed as the starting point for contributions to the relevant session of the International SBL in Rome in 2019, for which the present paper was first prepared.

listed.² After essays on Amos and on Hosea, we then did two on Isa 1–39—one on Hezekiah and the other on the Immanuel prophecy. We next moved on to Jeremiah and Ezekiel, and then, just like von Rad's book, we turned to Isa 40–55. This was regarded as a separate composition from 1–39. The case for that was not argued but simply assumed as obvious. Not a single link with 1–39 was mentioned and the question of why those chapters appeared in the same book was not raised. Straw-in-the-wind articles by Jones and by Eaton or Becker's 1968 monograph were not listed,³ and if anyone went so far as to mention the fact that this was one book they were immediately dismissed as a totally bigoted fundamentalist. It is difficult now, perhaps, for younger scholars to appreciate what that world was like.

Purely from the point of view of the history of scholarship, the main change came first from the observation, collection and renewed appreciation of certain phraseological and thematic connections between the various parts of the book. From 1975 onwards, I myself gave 32 lectures each year on the Hebrew text of Isa 40–55 and began to note such connections as nowadays are a complete commonplace—the blind and the deaf, for instance, or the signal to the nations. Clements was also beginning to note these and we used to discuss them casually from time to time. Several feature in his seminal 1985 article,⁴ and this was preceded the year before by Rendtorff's longer but in some ways comparable article.⁵ Nor should I wish to undervalue the stimulus of the relevant chapter in Childs' 1979 volume,

---

2. We used the English translation, of course: Gerhard von Rad, *Old Testament Theology*, 2: *The Theology of Israel's Prophetic Traditions*, trans. David M. G. Stalker (London: Oliver & Boyd, 1965); trans. of *Theologie des Alten Testaments*, 2: *Theologie der prophetischen Überlieferungen Israels* (Munich: Chr. Kaiser, 1960).

3. Douglas R. Jones, "The Traditio of the Oracles of Isaiah of Jerusalem," *ZAW* 67 (1955): 226–46; John H. Eaton, "The Origin of the Book of Isaiah," *VT* 9 (1959): 138–57; Joachim Becker, *Isaias, der Prophet und sein Buch*, SBS 30 (Stuttgart: Katholisches Bibelwerk, 1968).

4. Ronald E. Clements, "Beyond Tradition-History: Deutero-Isaianic Development of First Isaiah's Themes," *JSOT* 31 (1985): 95–113; this was prefigured a little more impressionistically in "The Unity of the Book of Isaiah," *Int* 36 (1982): 117–29. Some other studies by Clements with relevance to our general topic have been collected in *Jerusalem and the Nations: Studies in the Book of Isaiah*, HBM 16 (Sheffield: Sheffield Phoenix, 2011), especially Part III.

5. Rolf Rendtorff, "Zur Komposition des Buches Jesaja," *VT* 34 (1984): 295–320; repr. in *Kanon und Theologie: Vorarbeiten zu einer Theologie des Alten Testaments* (Neukirchen-Vluyn: Neukirchener Verlag, 1991), 141–61; ET "The Composition of the Book of Isaiah," in *Canon and Theology: Overtures to an Old Testament Theology*, trans. Margaret Kohl (Edinburgh: T&T Clark, 1994), 146–69. This collection also includes two other articles of relevance to our topic, to which should further be added "The Book of Isaiah: A Complex Unity. Synchronic and Diachronic Reading," in *New Visions of Isaiah*, ed. Roy F. Melugin and Marvin A. Sweeney, JSOTSup 214 (Sheffield: Sheffield Academic, 1996), 32–49. (This latter volume also contains other articles of relevance to our present concern.)

though its approach was somewhat more discursive.⁶ Increasingly the force of these connections was refined in the direction of redaction-critical speculations. It was apparent that in fact the direction of influence was probably two-way, not just from the first part of the book to the second. How this was to be explained varied, some, like Berges, preferring what I should call a block method of composition, with the formal connections coming at a late stage,⁷ and others, such as myself, favouring rather a more integrated process of composition from the start, one part being deliberately added to the earlier and the redaction-critical joins being an integral part of that process.⁸ Others again, like Kustár, apply a rigorous literary and redaction-critical approach to the study of a given theme throughout the whole book.⁹ No matter which approach is preferred, the point to make is that this early work on the "unity" of Isaiah developed out of a better application of standard historical-critical methods than had previously prevailed. As I tried to suggest in a 1995 article, traditional diachronic analysis in fact led to and aided the increasingly fashionable synchronic analysis of the text.¹⁰

Following slightly behind this developing trend there came another whose epistemological basis was completely different. Conrad, Miscall, and others, though far from unaware of conventional analyses, approached the text from a completely different standpoint, namely that we are presented now with a book

---

6. Brevard S. Childs, *Introduction to the Old Testament as Scripture* (London: SCM, 1979), 311–38. Mention should also be made of his later commentary: *Isaiah*, OTL (Louisville, KY: Westminster John Knox, 2001). We may note that Christopher R. Seitz was a pupil of Childs and that he has developed his own distinctive approach to Isaiah in a development of his teacher's lead; *Isaiah 1–39*, Interpretation (Louisville, KY: John Knox, 1993); "The Book of Isaiah 40–66: Introduction, Commentary, and Reflections," in *NIB* 6 (Nashville, TN: Abingdon, 2001), 309–552.

7. Ulrich Berges, *Das Buch Jesaja: Komposition und Endgestalt*, HBS 16 (Freiburg: Herder, 1998); ET *The Book of Isaiah: Its Composition and Final Form*, HBM 46; trans. Millard C. Lind (Sheffield: Sheffield Phoenix, 2012). Odil Hannes Steck fits into this category as well, though his conclusions differ considerably; of his many relevant publications, see, for instance, *Bereitete Heimkehr: Jesaja 35 als redakionelle Brücke zwischen dem Ersten und dem Zweiten Jesaja*, SBS 121 (Stuttgart: Katholisches Bibelwerk, 1985); *Studien zu Tritojesaja*, BZAW 203 (Berlin: de Gruyter, 1991); *Gottesknecht und Zion: Gesammelte Aufsätze zu Deuterojesaja*, FAT 4 (Tübingen: Mohr Siebeck, 1992).

8. H. G. M. Williamson, *The Book Called Isaiah: Deutero-Isaiah's Role in Composition and Redaction* (Oxford: Clarendon, 1994); Jacob Stromberg, *Isaiah After Exile: The Author of Third Isaiah as Reader and Redactor of the Book*, OTM (Oxford: Oxford University Press, 2011).

9. Zoltán Kustár, *"Durch seine Wunden sind wir geheilt": eine Untersuchung zur Metaphorik von Israels Krankheit und Heilung im Jesajabuch*, BWANT 154 (Stuttgart: Kohlhammer, 2002).

10. H. G. M. Williamson, "Synchronic and Diachronic in Isaian Perspective," in *Synchronic or Diachronic? A Debate on Method in Old Testament Exegesis*, ed. Johannes C. de Moor, OTS 34 (Leiden: Brill, 1995), 211–26.

in 66 chapters, and literary criticism obliges us to treat it as such.[11] Of course, as with the historical-critical method, this does not lead to unanimity: some read sequentially, some thematically, and so on, but the different approaches nevertheless share that initial fundamental conviction in common.

My first point, therefore, is to stress that studies of the unity of Isaiah are divided by a deep methodological cleavage which persists to this day. It is usual to find in representatives of each that they pay respectful tribute to the validity of the other, taken on its own terms, but that they seldom make any effort to indicate how they have benefitted from the impact of the alternative. Melugin and others have recognized this too, of course, though I am not sure that many really do justice to the fundamental nature of this cleavage.

Let me now try to categorize the main approaches that scholars adopt to undertake a unity reading. First, in what looks like an attempt to retain diachronic responsibility, some take the presentation of a chosen topic as it appears in each of the three main parts of Isaiah and then in a concluding chapter or section try to combine them into one;[12] rather different in its aims but tending in the same direction is the earlier work of Lack, which in some ways was ahead of its time.[13]

There are two obvious problems with this approach, however. The first is that, with chs. 1–39 in particular, it is obvious that we have material included from all the main periods of the book's composition, so that, without introducing so many caveats and exceptions as to undermine the whole procedure, the approach is unable to overcome the problem it sets out to accommodate. And second, in the concluding chapter, it is by no means obvious by which method one may amalgamate material from different settings into a satisfying whole. Ma's monograph on God's Spirit in Isaiah[14] sensibly overcomes the first difficulty by labelling his first three chapters not according to the book's literary divisions but by chronology: pre-exilic, exilic, and post-exilic. That is fine so far as it goes, though of course there will be differences of opinion as to the appropriate setting of some, at least, of the material under examination. But more significantly, despite his methodological considerations which are critical of both canonical and redaction-critical approaches, it is not clear that he has managed to enunciate a method

---

11. Edgar W. Conrad, *Reading Isaiah*, OBT (Minneapolis, MN: Fortress, 1991); Peter D. Miscall, *Isaiah*, Readings (Sheffield: Sheffield Academic, 1993), and *Isaiah 34–35: A Nightmare/A Dream*, JSOTSup 281 (Sheffield: Sheffield Academic, 1999).

12. E.g., Antti Laato, *"About Zion I will not be silent": The Book of Isaiah as an Ideological Unity*, ConBOT 44 (Stockholm: Almqvist & Wiksell, 1998); Thomas L. Leclerc, *Yahweh Is Exalted in Justice: Solidarity and Conflict in Isaiah* (Minneapolis, MN: Fortress, 2001); Bohdan Hrobon, *Ethical Dimension of Cult in the Book of Isaiah*, BZAW 418 (Berlin: de Gruyter, 2010); Michael P. Maier, *Völkerwallfahrt im Jesajabuch*, BZAW 474 (Berlin: de Gruyter, 2016).

13. Rémi Lack, *La symbolique du livre d'Isaïe*, AnBib 59 (Rome: Pontifical Biblical Institute, 1973).

14. Wonsuk Ma, *Until the Spirit Comes: The Spirit of God in the Book of Isaiah*, JSOTSup 271 (Sheffield: Sheffield Academic, 1999).

which does justice both to the chronological variety as well as the literary unity of the book and its themes. Does the meaning of a passage vary between its historical and its final literary settings? That seems to me to be a simple but important question that nobody is asking.

An alternative way of trying to deal seriously with a different form of diachrony is to undertake a sequential reading which, after all, is how we generally read books in the modern world. This is not related to historical sequence, of course, but it equally takes seriously that one reads one chapter after another and so in principle the later builds up from the earlier. This was famously brought to the Isaianic table by Darr.[15] She is fully aware of the distinction in methods that I mentioned earlier and justifies her approach as a reader-orientated one. In this she traces two or three metaphors or images that are characteristic of the book, such as children and women, and seeks to show how they contribute to the wider themes of rebellion and future status. Her effort has been generally well received and in my opinion shows to best advantage how this approach works.

The dangers of pursuing this method in a more extreme fashion have been revealed more recently, however, by two monographs which expressly acknowledge their debt to Darr's first effort. In his study of *Eating in Isaiah*, Abernethy certainly succeeds in demonstrating that a theme one might have considered trivial or marginal in fact features at many of the significant literary turning points in the book and also that they are likely linked together by textual allusion in several cases.[16] At the same time, however, given Abernethy's stated intention to adopt a sequential-synchronic approach, it is not clear how his practice matches his intention. In his chapters on both Isa 40–55 and 56–66, for instance, he starts at the end and works backwards. This is illuminating and his exegetical observations are valuable; but it is hardly sequential. Equally, in dealing with Isa 2–35, he argues that the banquet in Isa 25:6–8 should be read in an imperial light, which follows well from his sequential reading, but also that it is "climactic," which is understandable in terms of a history of composition but which fits less well in terms of the fact that the reader then moves on to further unrelated references in the following chapters.

Kim's monograph treats a theme related to Darr's of Israel and Jerusalem as members of a household: sons/children, Zion as daughter, Zion as mother and wife, and servant(s).[17] The analysis moves through each passage in strictly canonical order and a final chapter tries to bring the whole together insofar as this can be done. The very strict synchronic method means that generally the outline of a story can be told as Kim works through the main sections of Isaiah, but there are exceptions where things do not fit so neatly, and she is honest in usually

---

15. Katherine Pfisterer Darr, *Isaiah's Vision and the Family of God*, LCBI (Louisville, KY: Westminster John Knox, 1994).

16. Andrew T. Abernethy, *Eating in Isaiah: Approaching the Role of Food and Drink in Isaiah's Structure and Message*, BIS 131 (Leiden: Brill, 2014).

17. Brittany Kim, *"Lengthen Your Tent-Cords": The Metaphorical World of Israel's Household in the Book of Isaiah*, Siphrut 23 (University Park, PA: Eisenbrauns, 2018).

acknowledging that fact. Perhaps at such points the synchronic stranglehold deconstructs itself. For instance, 3:16–4:6 cries out for separation, 3:16–4:1 being obviously disjointed with changes of person (not mentioned here) and 4:2–6 being almost universally recognized as a later and separate composition. Can a sensitive reader really ignore such obvious disjunctures in the text in favour of a reading blinkered by a predetermined commitment to unity come what may?

A final observation in relation to this method in general is that it has usually only been attempted in relation to some specific theme. (For the few exceptions to this rule, see below.) In other words, the method presupposes the book's unity for some other ulterior motive; it does not, therefore, contribute to the fundamental argument, nor can it be paraded as a satisfactory method for reading the book in all its parts as a whole.

A further difficulty that confronts readers who seek deliberately to bypass the results of historical-critical research in this way is that they either ignore much material which does not fit the line they have chosen to adopt or they make everything fit it in an unconvincing, because forced, manner. The former danger is obviously not relevant to those who, like the examples just given, have deliberately chosen one specific theme to study. It is more obvious, however, in what many regard as a ground-breaking contribution, namely Conrad's *Reading Isaiah*,[18] which claims to "understand the text as a whole by paying special attention to its structure."[19] Probably because of his previous research Conrad bases his analysis on the royal narratives and their echoes in other passages. In doing so he has made many observations of the greatest value which have since entered the mainstream. At the same time, however, it is bizarre that in a work which explicitly pays special attention to the structure of the book there is no reference, let alone discussion, of ch. 12, which on any showing is a major structural marker in the book, or of ch. 18, which opens three chapters on Egypt and Ethiopia, or, indeed, of chs. 60 and 62, which frame what is generally regarded as a united collection in 60–62. This does not detract from the value of what Conrad has given us, but it is clearly not tracing a pathway into the book as a whole in any recognizable form. One reader's response does not necessarily coincide with another's.

The complementary danger is well illustrated by the more recent monograph of Stulac.[20] He offers an agrarian reading of chs. 28–35 but in the course of this he has sections which explicitly relate his approach to most of the rest of the book as well. As I started to read my initial skepticism about the importance of agrarian readings was blown away not just by the initial methodological discussion but in particular by the possibilities that Stulac opened up of how this might help overcome the dilemma that I have set out earlier. Amidst all the changes in political and related circumstances which need to be taken into account, Stulac claims on the basis of archaeological, historical and anthropological evidence that agrarian

---

18. See n. 11 above.
19. Conrad, *Reading Isaiah*, 29.
20. Daniel John Stulac, *History and Hope: The Agrarian Wisdom of Isaiah 28–35*, Siphrut 24 (University Park, PA: Eisenbrauns, 2018).

practices changed very little during the centuries. This raises the expectation that we might here be embarking on a genuinely alternative contribution to the hermeneutical dilemma of how to hold together diachronic and synchronic readings, the independent value of each of which is not challenged. And as his analysis starts with ch. 28, which includes agricultural imagery in its first half and then the parable of the farmer in the second half, initial soundings look promising. As the analysis proceeds, however, it seems to me to become less convincing in its thesis. Of the variety of reasons for saying this I mention here just one, namely that Stulac tries to draw in far more material as relevant to an agrarian hermeneutic than I find plausible. While one might, at a stretch, allow its applicability to land issues in ch. 34 or to the way metaphor in ch. 35, the whole Zion theme and the application of *Torah* in several late passages cannot seriously be justified if the method as initially explained is to retain its integrity. All too often there is a danger that the material is made subject to the preferred method. The trouble with this is that the reader who wants to be sympathetic to the main thesis becomes disillusioned and then liable just to reject the whole. More caution is sometimes the better policy in persuasion.

It turns out, therefore, that many who appeal to the virtues of synchronic reading do so only in order to follow some alternative agenda, such as tracing a theme, which is therefore only a very partial reading, or claiming that everything contributes to the unified reading in a way which is patently misleading.

When I turn, then, finally to those very few who have seriously attempted a complete sequential reading that deals with all the material on the page in its present order I want on the one hand to commend them for their methodological purity while at the same time finding with regret that their work does not seem to me helpful to advance our understanding of the book.

O'Connell's presentation of a unified structure of the whole book, for example, is of an abstract nature that is not only complicated in its detail but also so intricate that one wonders whether his claim can really be upheld that this was achieved by design by an author in antiquity.[21] I may be presumptuous here, but what evidence is there to support the tacit claim that authors worked in anything like the manner which O'Connell supposes? And what is worse, he makes no claim that he is offering a reading in the usual sense of the word, that is to say one which communicates a coherent message. His proposals do not seem to have attracted any wider following. The same applies to Watts' attempt to read the whole book as a historical drama.[22] There have been two or three other attempts at "dramatic readings" of either smaller parts of Isaiah or, indeed, of other books, but again they have failed to convince anyone other than those who have proposed them. Miscall is therefore to be congratulated on offering the only example that I know (though I am probably just ignorant at this point) of a genuine synchronic

---

21. Robert H. O'Connell, *Concentricity and Continuity: The Literary Structure of Isaiah*, JSOTSup 188 (Sheffield: Sheffield Academic, 1994).

22. John D. W. Watts, *Isaiah 1–33* and *Isaiah 34–66*, WBC 24 and 25 (Waco, TX: Word Books, 1985 and 1987; rev. ed., 2005).

reading of the whole book in strictly literary terms in the form of a commentary in the Readings series.[23] It is brief (127 pages only on the whole book) and for the most part descriptive. It does not argue a thesis, but on the basis of obvious deep knowledge of the text its chief characteristic is to draw attention to many parallels and links with other passages in the book. Again, it does not try to get the text to tell a story, though links from one chapter to the next are often attempted. It works on a strict chapter by chapter basis, regardless of sense breaks that may differ from this. So it makes for an interesting, if sometimes quite dense, reading. Curiously, though, there are a few occasions where a latent historicism seems to override more strictly literary criteria. Miscall is rightly impressed by the reference to the death of Ahaz at the end of ch. 14 and suggests that this marks out chs. 7–14 as a major unit. Unusually, the heading in 13:1 is subordinated to this. From my perspective, however, this should be reversed. The close parallel between 6:1 and 14:28 seems most likely to me to be a remnant of the structure of the pre-exilic form of the book, with the headings in 2:1 and 13:1 clearly overriding this at a later time, and since this is also imitated at 1:1 it seems obvious that from a literary point of view it should be this form of heading which is decisive, not a historically earlier one. But such points are the exception rather than the rule in Miscall's thoughtful reading.

This brief survey of some of the major approaches to a synchronic reading of the book of Isaiah leads to the conclusion that they can often contribute to the understanding of one part of the book or another but that they fail almost universally as synchronic readings of the book as a whole. This suggests to me that in spite of all the incontrovertible claims that methodologically such readings may be justified (which I have no wish to deny) they ultimately fall down in practice. Why? In reader-response terms I suggest that part of the answer is that the book was never intended to be read as a whole but rather episodically, as it might be in the liturgy. Of course the reader, preacher or teacher might jump off from the given paragraph to others that might be related to it in a multitude of ways, and a "unity" approach means that this procedure can be defended. But it is completely spasmodic and piecemeal, not neat and tidy like a modern monograph. And equally, there will be as many possible readings as there are readers. What matters is the question each reader first brings to the text.

At the end, therefore, I return to the autobiographical narrative from which I started in order briefly to explain why I still maintain that diachronic considerations actually contribute positively to synchronic readings. And of course in saying that perhaps I may be allowed to dismiss the objection that there is no agreement between scholars about the details of composition history. That is no less true of any of the alternative approaches, as we have seen. It is a cheap form of argument that seeks a form of methodological high ground where none exists. If what I say attracts, well and good; if not, propose something better. I do not know of any other way to proceed, regardless of starting point.

---

23. See n. 11 above.

Continuing my research from those early days of beginning to accumulate lists of verbal and related connections across the various parts of the book, I came to be increasingly impressed by the fact that so far as dependence could be determined it ran in two directions, from earlier chapters in the book to later and also *vice versa*. In particular, very much in line with the directions of Rendtorff's work, I became impressed that chs. 40–55 were the literary heart of the book. Passages that are both ideologically and verbally very close to what we find in those chapters occur at the main turning points in the first half of the book (e.g. ch. 12) whereas 56–66 are equally clearly dependent on developing and reapplying the vision of those chapters after it. It is true, as Stromberg has shown,[24] that a similar conclusion might be drawn with regard to the last two chapters in the book and its links earlier on (e.g. at 1:29–31), and this needs to be taken into consideration, of course, but I do not find the relevant passages in 1–39 to be quite so formative; like 56–66 as a whole, they are more commentary than fundamental to the basic structure as a whole.

Given, as I have already said, that it seems to me most unlikely that the later chapters were originally written independently and without reference to those which precede, we have to ask, in relation to reading the book as a whole, how this model works out. In the most general of terms I offer three basic observations to serve as guidelines in a way which I hope will underline my conviction that the best way to a synchronic reading is through the diachronic.

First, the basic stance of chs. 40–55 may be characterized as stimulating faith in imminent deliverance. At this point I do not want to be distracted by questions of whether we have here the work of one writer or several, nor of whether he or they should be dated precisely in the late years of the Neo-Babylonian empire;[25] for the present purposes my point is of a purely literary nature.

Second, given that this applies equally to the related passages in the first half of the book and that they are strategically placed to govern an overall reading, it follows that the earlier material, which includes judgment as well as promise, has to be read as indicative of the situation from which deliverance is anticipated. Whatever we may think about the nature of the message of Isaiah of Jerusalem, the material has been arranged for us now as indicating that the destruction foretold has happened (and hints of an exile have been introduced by what I take to be a series of glosses rather than a full-scale redaction[26]) and that the reader should therefore look for the promised deliverance. I claim, therefore, that this approach allows the interpreter to do full justice to both main aspects of the first half of the book which commentators have sometimes had difficulty holding together. It also

---

24. See n. 8 above.

25. For the most recent and well-informed considerations, see the volumes of Ulrich Berges' commentary on Isa 40–66 in the HThKAT series (2008, 2015, 2022).

26. For my attempt to justify this distinction with examples drawn specifically in relation to this question, see "The Vindication of Redaction Criticism," in *Biblical Interpretation and Method: Essays in Honour of John Barton*, ed. Katharine J. Dell and Paul M. Joyce (Oxford: Oxford University Press, 2013), 26–36.

entails that themes in the first half have now to be read in the light of the second, not denying their older import, but interpreting them anew for the changed circumstances. My 1998 treatment of kingship illustrates how I see this working out in practice for one significant example.[27]

Finally, chs. 56–66 partially recap aspects of 40–55 and partially discuss why the vision has not yet been realized. They thus contribute to the reader the important consideration that, though delayed down to his or her own day, the deliverance remains available and imminent. Only with chs. 24–27 and related passages (e.g. 13:4–5, 9–13) is imminence replaced by a more fully eschatological perspective.

This is all presented in very broad-brush terms, I realize, and of course it needs to be worked out exegetically in each individual passage, as does the shape of the major sub-sections within each main part of the book.[28] My point, however, is that the history of recent scholarship has shown that attempts to go straight to a synchronic reading lead in almost every case to fundamental difficulties which the scholars in question tend either to ignore or to deny. Only a diachronic approach, which takes the untidy nature of the present form of the text fully into account, is able to arrive at a hermeneutically satisfying reading of the text in all its multifarious dimensions.

---

27. H. G. M. Williamson, *Variations on a Theme: King, Messiah and Servant in the Book of Isaiah* (Carlisle: Paternoster, 1998).

28. This, of course, is what I am attempting to do for chs. 1–27 in my ongoing work for the ICC series; the first two volumes appeared in 2006 and 2018. I should acknowledge here too the great contribution that Sweeney has made to this. Although I sometimes disagree with him in the diachronic placement of individual passages, I equally often find agreement and stimulus from his sustained attempt to relate redaction-critical and final form readings; of his many publications, see especially Marvin A. Sweeney, *Isaiah 1-4 and the Post-Exilic Understanding of the Isaianic Tradition*, BZAW 171 (Berlin: de Gruyter, 1988); *Isaiah 1-39 with an Introduction to Prophetic Literature*, FOTL 16 (Grand Rapids, MI: Eerdmans, 1996).

Chapter 4

E PLURIBUS UNUM: FINDING INTERTEXTUAL THREADS THAT UNITE THE BOOK OF ISAIAH

Hyun Chul Paul Kim

Through observing and analyzing the unifying, linked interconnections among many pieces of Isaiah, recent scholarship has contributed to the legitimacy of reading the book as a whole. Building on the works of pertinent scholars, the present study intends to probe and examine key catchwords and catchphrases that are considered key intertextual threads throughout the book of Isaiah. First, I will review key threads that have been suggested by scholars and also explore additional signposts and markers that are significant for the holistic reading. Then, I will investigate Isa 34 as a case study for its allusions to various passages within the book, as well as their interpretive implications.

1. *Brief Reviews*

The present topic has been generated by the Isaianic scholars who discovered that the author(s) and redactor(s) have deliberately constructed interconnected catchwords either as scribal glosses redactionally or key markers/signposts synchronically. Because Roy F. Melugin has trenchantly reviewed this issue as the "unity" movement, only a brief recap will suffice.[1]

---

1. Roy F. Melugin, "Isaiah 40–66 in Recent Research: The 'Unity' Movement," in *Recent Research on the Major Prophets*, ed. Alan J. Hauser (Sheffield: Sheffield Phoenix, 2008), 142–94.

First of all, notable catchwords in the bookending of Isa 1 and 65–66 have led many scholars to support the validity of reading the book of Isaiah as a unified whole.[2] This interpretive approach (re-)validates the importance of reading 1–66 as a unity, inasmuch as it has been read in separate segments, such as First Isaiah, Second Isaiah, Third Isaiah, oracles against/about the nations (= OAN), Isaiah apocalypse, historical appendix, servant songs, and the like. New interpretive insights have arisen through reading 1 and 65–66 as a literary inclusio, and also considering 1–4 as an overture to the entire book through multiple redactional transitions adumbrated by manifold inner-biblical allusions within Isaiah.[3]

Sporadic yet substantial and crucial echoes of catchwords have provided similar interpretive clues—whether for unity or not. H. G. M. Williamson's study of these features has led him to propose that Deutero-Isaiah's redactor must have been the essential redactor of Proto-Isaiah.[4] Jacob Stromberg further advanced this proposal, claiming that Trito-Isaiah's redactor(s) placed their editorial hands on the final formation of the entire book.[5] Such intertextual, inner-biblical allusions within Isaiah have produced rich scribal and rhetorical correlations that link themes across the book.[6] Concerning how those interconnections can help make visible both linear and reciprocal developments within the book, Willem A. M. Beuken's prolific studies on the intertextual correlations and developments have been exemplary for the unity-oriented reading.[7]

---

2. Anthony J. Tomasino, "Isaiah 1–2:4 and 63–66, and the Composition of the Isaianic Corpus," *JSOT* 57 (1993): 81–98.

3. Marvin A. Sweeney, *Isaiah 1–4 and the Post-Exilic Understanding of the Isaianic Tradition*, BZAW 171 (Berlin: de Gruyter, 1988).

4. H. G. M. Williamson, *The Book Called Isaiah: Deutero-Isaiah's Role in Composition and Redaction* (Oxford: Clarendon, 1994).

5. Jacob Stromberg, *Isaiah after Exile: The Author of Third Isaiah as Reader and Redactor of the Book* (Oxford: Oxford University Press, 2011).

6. Benjamin D. Sommer, *A Prophet Read Scripture: Allusion in Isaiah 40–66* (Stanford: Stanford University Press, 1998); Patricia T. Willey, *Remember the Former Things: The Recollection of Previous Texts in Second Isaiah*, SBLDS 161 (Atlanta, GA: Scholars Press, 1997). See also J. Todd Hibbard, *Intertextuality in Isaiah 24–27: The Reuse and Evocation of Earlier Texts and Traditions*, FAT/II 16 (Tübingen: Mohr Siebeck, 2006).

7. Willem A. M. Beuken, "The Prophet Leads the Readers into Praise: Isaiah 25:1–10 in Connection with Isaiah 24:14–23 Seen against the Background of Isaiah 12," in *Studies in Isaiah 24–27: The Isaiah Workshop—De Jesaja Werkplaats*, ed. H. Jan Bosman and Harm van Grol, OTS 43 (Leiden: Brill, 2000), 121–56, and "A Song of Gratitude and a Song of Malicious Delight: Is Their Consonance Unseemly? The Coherence of Isaiah Chs. 13–14 with Chs. 11–12 and Chs. 1–2," in *Das Manna fällt auch heute noch: Beiträge zur Geschichte und Theologie des Alten, Ersten Testaments: Festschrift für Erich Zenger*, ed. Frank-Lothar Hossfeld and Ludger Schwienhorst-Schönberger, HBS 44 (Freiburg: Herder, 2004), 96–114.

Additionally, scholars have paid closer attention to and appreciation for extensive sequential progressions of citations or allusions. Shalom Paul's commentary on 40–66 provides a valuable contribution. At the beginning of his exposition for each chapter, he enlists verbal links between the chapter and its immediately preceding chapter (e.g., 54//55, 55//56, 56//57, etc.).[8] Such features may not initially seem like something special, but the series of lexical chain links in sequential progress is stunning if we take the author to be the same—which in fact is what Shalom Paul asserts. In other words, when we read Isa 49 or 60, our reading would be incomplete if we did not read them in interaction with Isa 48 and 59, respectively.

2. Major and Minor Interconnections

2.1. Large-scale (Major) Threads

Numerous scholars have proposed to read or trace the book of Isaiah as a (unified) whole in light of key linguistic or thematic threads. First, the unique appellation, "the Holy One of Israel" (קדוש ישראל), occurs across the book (from 1:4 to 60:14), while it hardly occurs elsewhere in the entire Hebrew Bible: elsewhere only three times in the prophetic books (Jer 50:29; 51:5; Ezek 39:7); within the Enneateuch only in 2 Kgs 19:22 (= Isa 37:23); plus three times in the Psalter (Pss 71:22; 78:41; 89:18 [MT 89:19]).[9] Notably, those texts in Jer 50–51 and 2 Kgs 19 may insinuate their close correlations to Isaiah (e.g., Isa 13–14 and 36–38); conversely, this phrase is absent elsewhere in Jeremiah and 1–2 Kings.[10] J. J. M. Roberts takes this phrase as the "center" of Isaianic theology, that YHWH is the suzerain of the world and chose Zion as the divine habitation.[11] This uniquely Isaianic phrase encompasses the theme of the divine holiness innately associated with Israel. It also serves the literary (and compositional) functions of holding together or unifying the book. Read in intertextual correlation or contention

---

8. Shalom M. Paul, *Isaiah 40–66: Translation and Commentary* (Grand Rapids, MI: Eerdmans, 2012).

9. In Isa 1–39, this exact phrase קדוש ישראל occurs twelve times (1:4; 5:19, 24; 10:20; 12:6; 17:7; 29:19; 30:11, 12, 15; 31:1; 37:23; also cf. 10:17; 29:23 ["Holy One of Jacob"]) and in Isa 40–66 it occurs thirteen times (41:14, 16, 20; 43:3, 14; 45:11; 47:4; 48:17; 49:7; 54:5; 55:5; 60:9, 14; also cf. 40:25; 43:15).

10. Do these phenomena indicate that Jer 50–51 and 2 Kgs 18–20 may have been more related to the pertinent Isaianic texts than has been proposed? See Willem A. M. Beuken, "Common and Different Phrases for Babylon's Fall and Its Aftermath in Isaiah 13–14 and Jeremiah 50–51," in *Concerning the Nations: Essays on the Oracles against the Nations in Isaiah, Jeremiah and Ezekiel*, ed. Andrew Mein, Else K. Holt and Hyun Chul Paul Kim, LHBOTS 612 (London: Bloomsbury T&T Clark, 2014), 53–73.

11. J. J. M. Roberts, "Isaiah in Old Testament Theology," *Int* 36 (1982): 130–43; Klaus Baltzer, *Deutero-Isaiah*, trans. Margaret Kohl, Hermeneia (Minneapolis, MN: Fortress, 2001), 33–44.

with Leviticus and Ezra–Nehemiah, the concept of "holiness" (cf. "holy seed" in Isa 6:13; Ezra 9:2) may entail divergent implications regarding exclusivism or inclusivism.[12]

Second, the combined expression—"see" and "hear" (plus "know" and "understand")—in the call narrative (6:9-10; cf. Ezek 3:11), together with the theme of hardening the "heart," is another thread that occurs frequently, and uniquely, throughout Isaiah (from 6:9-10 to 66:19).[13] These catchphrases both interconnect and conjoin numerous passages, while presenting similar or shifted motifs. Though not the primary aim of this study, this motif occurs frequently in the New Testament (especially the Gospels)—"Let the one with ears to hear, hear" (Mt 11:15; 13:9, 43; Mk 4:9; Lk 8:8; 14:35; cf. Rev 3:13)—and supports the literary and theological importance of this Isaianic expression.

Third, the "servant(s) of YHWH" permeates as another uniquely Isaianic phrase and concept, although it occurs primarily in the second half of the book (from 41:8 to 66:14; cf. Jer 30:10; Ezek 28:25). Famously or notoriously, the clues for the identity of the "servant(s)" fluctuate throughout the book, baffling countless interpreters. Nevertheless, this figure, whether individual or communal, undoubtedly holds the Isaianic passages together. As Melugin's review elucidates, recent scholarly attention to the commands to bind up and seal the testimony for the prophet's "disciples" (8:16; 29:11) may provide a comparable thread in the first half of the book.[14] Although the book may not have intended direct ties between the prophet's disciples and the servant(s), the intricate correlations are intriguing for a holistic reading. Likewise, the "remnant(s)" motif (though this motif is not unique to the book of Isaiah) similarly connects the first half of the book, while the theme of the "righteous" versus the "wicked" prevails in the second. The tension between the "righteous" servant(s) and the "wicked" indeed may function as literary seams of 40–66 (48:22; 57:21; 66:24).

Fourth, as Ronald E. Clements delineates, the metaphorical and thematic roles of the motif of "light," over against darkness (cf. Gen 1:3), connects various dots in the book of Isaiah.[15] This unique motif occurs overwhelmingly and significantly

---

12. Consider Mark G. Brett, "Postcolonial Interpretation Unequal Terms: A Postcolonial Approach to Isaiah 61," in *Biblical Interpretation and Method: Essays in Honour of John Barton*, ed. Katharine J. Dell and Paul M. Joyce (Oxford: Oxford University Press, 2013), 243–56.

13. Craig A. Evans, *To See and Not Perceive: Isaiah 6.9–10 in Early Jewish and Christian Interpretation*, JSOTSup 64 (Sheffield: JSOT Press, 1989); Robert P. Carroll, "Blindsight and the Vision Thing: Blindness and Insight in the Book of Isaiah," in *Writing and Reading the Scroll of Isaiah: Studies of an Interpretive Tradition*, vol. 1, ed. Craig C. Broyles and Craig A. Evans (Leiden: Brill, 1997), 79–93; Torsten Uhlig, *The Theme of Hardening in the Book of Isaiah: An Analysis of Communicative Action*, FAT/II 39 (Tübingen: Mohr Siebeck, 2009).

14. Edgar W. Conrad, *Reading Isaiah*, OBT (Minneapolis, MN: Fortress, 1991).

15. Ronald E. Clements, "A Light to the Nations: A Central Theme of the Book of Isaiah," in *Forming Prophetic Literature: Essays on Isaiah and the Twelve in Honor of John*

in Isaiah, compared to Jeremiah or Ezekiel or the Twelve prophets. While the house of Jacob is exhorted to walk in the "light" of YHWH (2:5), it is ultimately YHWH who is to come as the everlasting "light" (60:20).[16] YHWH's divine sovereignty supersedes the ancient Near Eastern sun-god traditions, even over Cyrus (45:7; cf. Ps 19:4). On the contrary, the exile analogous to the black hole denotes darkness, captivity, and bereavement.[17] The motif of "light" is also closely associated with that of the "servant(s)," commissioned to become a "light to the nations" (42:6; 49:6; cf. Mt 5:14). The servant's (royal) task further concerns maintaining and carrying out "justice" and "righteousness" (e.g., 1:17, 21, 27; 42:1, 3–4; 56:1; 61:8; 64:4; 66:16).[18] The socioeconomic issues of justice and righteousness in (pre-exilic) Isaiah seem to have been influenced by Amos, among other earlier or contemporary prophets.[19] Likewise, this motif has continued to exert significant influence on later readers, including the Qumran community with their emphasis on the "Teacher of Righteousness."

Fifth, parallel to the servant(s) of YHWH, the book of Isaiah depicts key messages that are shared by both his sons and daughters. The three sons in the opening chapters—Shear-jashub, Immanuel, Maher-shalal-hash-baz—serve as symbolic messages that unfold in subsequent passages.[20] The royal son, "Wonderful Counselor" (9:5 [Eng. 9:6]), and the children in the peaceable kingdom (11:6–9) present essential theological implications as well. Katheryn Pfisterer Darr's study expounds the pertinent imagery of family and children in a sequential reading of the entire book.[21] Equally valuable, Chris Franke undertakes a literary study of Daughter Zion in comparative contrasts with Daughter

---

D. W. Watts, ed. James W. Watts and Paul R. House, JSOTSup 235 (Sheffield: Sheffield Academic, 1996), 57–69, and "'Arise, Shine; For Your Light Has Come': A Basic Theme of the Isaianic Tradition," in *Writing and Reading the Scroll of Isaiah: Studies of an Interpretive Tradition*, ed. Craig C. Broyles and Craig A. Evans, vol. 2. VTSup 70/2 (Leiden: Brill, 1997), 441–54.

16. Carol J. Dempsey, *Isaiah: God's Poet of Light* (St. Louis, MO: Chalice, 2009).

17. Frederik Poulsen, *The Black Hole in Isaiah: A Study of Exile as a Literary Theme*, FAT 125 (Tübingen: Mohr Siebeck, 2019).

18. Thomas L. Leclerc, *Yahweh Is Exalted in Justice: Solidarity and Conflict in Isaiah* (Minneapolis, MN: Fortress, 2001); H. G. M. Williamson, *Variations on a Theme: King, Messiah and Servant in the Book of Isaiah* (Carlisle: Paternoster, 1998).

19. Uwe Becker, "Sozialkritik in Jes 1–39 und im Amos–Buch," in *Isaiah and the Twelve: Parallels, Similarities and Differences*, ed. Richard J. Bautch, Joachim Eck, and Burkhard M. Zapff, BZAW 527 (Berlin: de Gruyter, 2020), 33–53.

20. Kay Weißflog, *Zeichen und Sinnbilder: Die Kinder der Propheten Jesaja und Hosea*, Arbeiten zur Bibel und ihrer Geschichte 36 (Leipzig: Evangelische Verlagsanstalt, 2011).

21. Katheryn Pfisterer Darr, *Isaiah's Vision and the Family of God*, LCBI (Louisville, KY: Westminster John Knox, 1994); Brittany Kim, *"Lengthen Your Tent-Cords": The Metaphorical World of Israel's Household in the Book of Isaiah* (University Park, PA: Eisenbrauns, 2018).

Babylon.²² The exile and restoration of Israel is elucidated by the metaphorical depictions of Daughter Zion.²³ The agonizing suffering and renewed call of the servant, Jacob-Israel, thus parallel the lament and renewal of Daughter Zion and her offspring.

Sixth, in addition to the children imagery, animals emerge as important symbols in Isaiah. Scholars have noted the compositional and thematic role both "ox" and "donkey" play in key places of the book (1:3; 30:24; 32:20; 34:7; 66:3).²⁴ Lions, birds, jackals, ostriches, and the like also play key functions, though these animals are more common in other prophetic books.²⁵ A recent study by Daniel J. Stulac on the agricultural depictions explicates the agrarian hermeneutic for a sequential unfolding of recurring motifs, cohesively flowing from destruction to hope.²⁶

Seventh, the divine planning of world events is another key motif that pervades Isaiah (e.g., 14:24–27; 41:26–28; 45:4–5; cf. Ps 33:10–11).²⁷ The subduing of the haughty and exalting of the lowly is a similar kind of thread that connects the book of Isaiah.²⁸ The prophetic concern for the poor alludes to the pentateuchal and deuteronomic legal ideology. Essentially related to these themes, the designated (domestic) kings and (international) empires likewise form substantial links within the book. Thus, the prose accounts of King Ahaz (ch. 7) and King Hezekiah (chs. 36–39) construct literary pillars for compositional and theological comparisons.²⁹ Similarly, the instrumental and derisive roles of Assyria (ch. 10),

---

22. Chris A. Franke, *Isaiah 46, 47, and 48: A New Literary-Critical Reading* (Winona Lake, IN: Eisenbrauns, 1994).

23. Sarah J. Dille, *Mixing Metaphors: God as Mother and Father in Deutero-Isaiah*, JSOTSup 398 (London: T&T Clark, 2004); Christl M. Maier, *Daughter Zion, Mother Zion: Gender, Space, and the Sacred in Ancient Israel* (Minneapolis, MN: Fortress, 2008).

24. Willem A. M. Beuken, "Women and the Spirit, the Ox and the Ass: The First Binders of the Booklet Isaiah 28–32," *ETL* 74 (1998): 5–26.

25. David H. Wenkel, "Wild Beasts in the Prophecy of Isaiah: The Loss of Dominion and Its Renewal through Israel as the New Humanity," *Journal of Theological Interpretation* 5 (2011): 251–64.

26. Daniel J. Stulac, *History and Hope: The Agrarian Wisdom of Isaiah 28–35* (University Park, PA: The Pennsylvania State University Press, 2018).

27. J. William Whedbee, *Isaiah and Wisdom* (Nashville, TN: Abingdon, 1971); Andrew T. Abernethy, "Wisdom in Isaiah," in *The Oxford Handbook of Isaiah*, ed. Lena-Sofia Tiemeyer (New York: Oxford University Press, 2020), 334–51.

28. Hyun Chul Paul Kim, "Little Highs, Little Lows: Tracing Key Themes in Isaiah," in *The Book of Isaiah: Enduring Questions Answered Anew: Essays Honoring Joseph Blenkinsopp and His Contribution to the Study of Isaiah*, ed. Richard J. Bautch and J. Todd Hibbard (Grand Rapids, MI: Eerdmans, 2014), 141–66.

29. Conrad, *Reading Isaiah*, 36–40. See also Willem A. M. Beuken, "The Unity of the Book of Isaiah: Another Attempt at Bridging the Gorge between Its Two Main Parts," in *Reading from Right to Left: Essays on the Hebrew Bible in Honour of David J. A. Clines*, ed.

Babylon (chs. 13–14; 21; 36–39), Persia (ch. 45), and Edom (chs. 34, 63) connect and coalesce in the thematic progress of the book.

2.2. Smaller (Minor) Catchwords, Markers, Signposts

In addition to the more explicit, or large-scale, threads reviewed above, there are minor symbols that run throughout Isaiah as well. First of all, nature is a common theme in the book. Hence, "trees" and pertinent lexemes are prevalent catchwords that provide literal or metaphorical messages.[30] The song of the vineyard, for example, sets the messages of both divine indictment (5:1–7) and divine restoration (27:2–5), together introducing their subsequent six oracles respectively in the present form (5:8–30 and chs. 28–33). Jerusalem is compared to a solitary, vulnerable booth in a cucumber field (1:9) but is also assured of restoration as the rebels are likened to the oaks, whose leaves wither (1:30). The divine declaration to humble the haughty cedars of Lebanon and oaks of Bashan (2:13; cf. 10:33–34) also presents an opening thesis. Pronouncing that all flesh is grass, the prophet proclaims that, over against the withering grass and fading flower, YHWH's word will stand forever (40:6–8). "Thorns and briers" (5:6; 7:23–25; 9:17 [Eng. 9:18]; 10:17; 27:4; 32:13) portray the devastation of the land, which can turn into a lush garden only by the divine work (55:13).[31] Likewise, while the "stump" of an oak (6:13) and the "dry tree" (56:3) bespeak the country's desolation and people's exile, the "shoot" from the root of Jesse (11:1) and the lifespan of "trees" (65:22) affirm the hope of renewal and restoration.

Second, fire and water are other themes related to nature. Fire consumes the sinners (9:1–7) and makes its way into YHWH's purifying fire (31:9), whereas the imperial idols are burned with fire (44:16, 19) and the wicked extinguished by YHWH's righteous fire (66:15–16, 24). The "way" in the desert that signals to the historical or metaphorical return from exile is represented by water.[32] Water as gushing rivers flood the region as punishment but also quenches thirst and ends famine.[33] These juxtapositions and recurrences of imageries of fauna and flora can suggest crucial insights toward reading from ancient (and contemporary) ecological perspectives.

J. Cheryl Exum and H. G. M. Williamson, JSOTSup 373 (London: Sheffield Academic, 2003), 50–62.

30. Kirsten Nielsen, *There Is Hope for a Tree: The Tree as Metaphor in Isaiah*, JSOTSup 65 (Sheffield: JSOT Press, 1989).

31. Andrew Abernethy, "The Ruined Vineyard Motif in Isaiah 1–39: Insights from Cognitive Linguistics," *Bib* 99 (2018): 334–50.

32. Bo H. Lim, *The 'Way of the Lord' in the Book of Isaiah*, LHBOTS 522 (London: T&T Clark, 2010); Øystein Lund, *Way Metaphors and Way Topics in Isaiah 40-55*, FAT/II 28 (Tübingen: Mohr Siebeck, 2007).

33. John T. Willis, *Images of Water in Isaiah* (Lanham, MD: Lexington Books, 2017).

Third, the city is another theme and is presented as both a space to dwell and a place of power.[34] It is also frequently used to denote the domineering empire's civilization and haughtiness. The inhabitants of city Zion hear the warnings of becoming vacant towns (5:3, 9; 6:11; 8:14). The inhabitants of "chaos city," representing cruel empires, will also be overthrown (chs. 24–27), while the penitent Daughter Zion will experience divine mercy (10:24).[35] The place and function of cities and empires throughout the book of Isaiah can thus be significant.[36]

Fourth, "woe" (הוי) oracles (1:4, 24; 5:8, 11, 18, 20–22; 10:1, 5; 17:12; 18:1; 28:1; 29:1, 15; 30:1; 31:1; 33:1; 45:9–10; 55:1), among others, function as unique threads that weave together the book of Isaiah. These "woe" (הוי or אוי) passages are quite unique to Isaiah, especially insofar as the six woe patterns in Isa 5 and 28–33, with their pertinent messages, are concerned. More study on these distinct features can generate further interpretive clues.

A fifth minor theme concerns human and divine body parts, which construct significant connections throughout Isaiah. The foundational metaphor appears in the prophet's call and the commissioning against the recalcitrant people, who "really hear" and "really see" but instead choose not to hear, see, or understand (6:9–10). They are blind and deaf to the righteous outcry of the people, indeed corrupted by sin from head to toe (1:5-6). The divine chastisement comes with the imagery of Assyria as YHWH's handy instrument (10:5–15). Eventually, the penitent people of God are inscribed in the divine palm (49:16). Whereas the obstinate rulers trample the divine temple courts (1:12), YHWH, whose footstool encompasses the earth, promises to uplift the humble and contrite (66:1-2). The miraculous restoration of the desert (exile) into streams (return and rebuilding) will usher in dramatic healings (39:7; 56:3–5), which beckons hermeneutical challenges and implications related to disability in the ancient and contemporary world (ch. 35).[37]

Sixth, food and drink make up another essential hermeneutical clue for understanding the book. Andrew T. Abernethy expounds on the motif of food and drink by positioning eating as a means for survival, punishment, and promise.

---

34. Hyun Chul Paul Kim, "City, Earth, and Empire in Isaiah 24–27," in *Formation and Intertextuality in Isaiah 24–27*, ed. J. Todd Hibbard and Hyun Chul Paul Kim, SBLAIL 17 (Atlanta, GA: SBL Press, 2013), 25–48.

35. Archibald L. H. M. van Wieringen and Annemarieke van der Woude, eds., *'Enlarge the Site of Your Tent': The City as Unifying Theme in Isaiah: The Isaiah Workshop—De Jesaja Werkplaats*, OTS 58 (Leiden: Brill, 2011). See also Mary Mills, "Wasteland and Pastoral Idyll as Images of the Biblical City," in *The City in the Hebrew Bible: Critical, Literary and Exegetical Approaches*, ed. James K. Aitken and Hilary F. Marlow, LHBOTS 672 (London: T&T Clark, 2018), 105–22.

36. Shawn Zelig Aster, *Reflections of Empire in Isaiah 1–39: Response to Assyrian Ideology*, SBLANEM 19 (Atlanta, GA: SBL Press, 2017).

37. Consider Jeremy Schipper, *Disability and Isaiah's Suffering Servant* (Oxford: Oxford University Press, 2011).

Abernethy explicates how this motif holds the whole book together, through the three key themes of retribution, sovereignty, and repentance.³⁸

Such fine-grained examination may require the use of digital textual analysis tools and filters, which can make far more detailed searches than using a concordance. Uses of similar catchwords or altered expressions (e.g., the name "David" occurs in Isaiah, Jeremiah, and Ezekiel but "Jesse" occurs only in Isa 11:1, 10) can suggest various interpretive clues. As for now, the list of these (smaller) threads can increase, as numerous related monographs have been published. The validity of these features notwithstanding, we will now look at one text for a sample case study toward the unity of Isaiah.

3. Isaiah 34 as a Sample Case

3.1. A Close Look at Isaiah 34 via Inner-biblical Allusions

It is worthwhile to discover the threads of a key catchword or theme and then trace all the occurrences throughout the book to investigate the redactional stages and/or intertextual implications. Many scholars have done this task, and new monographs are being published. At the same time, however, it can be equally significant to examine a single text/chapter and inspect (in a kind of panoramic view) its interconnections to other parts of Isaiah, thereby exploring the implications toward their unity. Hence, as a case analysis of literary development and inner-biblical correlations in the book, we will examine Isa 34. Scholars have identified countless citations both within and outside the book. Next is an examination of some of those echoes and considerations of the pertinent issues of both diachronic and synchronic implications regarding the unity of Isaiah:

33:13 Hear (שמע), you [2mp] who are far away, what I have done, and you who are near (קרוב), acknowledge my might.	34:1 Draw near (קרוב), O nations, to hear (שמע); O peoples, give heed! Let the earth hear and all that fills it, the world and all that comes from it.
24:4 The earth dries up and withers, the world languishes and withers (נבל); the heavens languish together with the earth. 7 The wine dries up, the vine languishes; all the merry-hearted sigh.	4 All the host of the heavens shall rot away, and the skies will roll up like a scroll; All their host will wither (נבל), like a leaf withering (נבל) on a vine, or fruit withering (נבל) on a fig tree.
1:11 "What to me is the multitude of your sacrifices (זבח)?" says the LORD; I have had enough of burnt offerings of *rams* and the fat (חלב) of fed beasts; I do not delight in the blood (דם) of bulls or of *lambs* or of *goats*.	6 The LORD has a sword; it is sated with blood (דם); it is gorged with fat (חלב), with the blood (דם) of *lambs* and *goats*, with the fat (חלב) of the kidneys of *rams*. For the LORD has a sacrifice (זבח) in Bozrah, a great slaughter in the land of Edom.

---

38. Andrew T. Abernethy, *Eating in Isaiah: Approaching the Role of Food and Drink in Isaiah's Structure and Message*, BIS 131 (Leiden: Brill, 2014).

13:6 Wail, for *the day of the LORD is near*; it will come like destruction from the Almighty! 61:2 to proclaim the year of the LORD's favor (שנת־רצון), and the day of vengeance (יום נקם) of our God, to comfort all who mourn. 63:4 For the day of vengeance (יום נקם) was in my mind, and the year for my redeeming work (שנת גלואי) has come.	8 For the LORD *has a day* of vengeance (יום נקם), a year of vindication (שנת שלומים) for Zion's cause. 9 And the streams of Edom shall be turned (הפך) into pitch, and her soil into sulfur (גפרית); her land shall become burning pitch.
13:19 And Babylon, the glory of kingdoms (ממלכה), the splendor and pride of the Chaldeans, will be like Sodom and Gomorrah when God overthrew (הפך) them. [// 1:7, 9–10] [Gen 19:24 Then the LORD rained on Sodom and Gomorrah sulfur (גפרית) and fire from the LORD out of heaven.] Isa 13:20 It will never (לא) be inhabited (שכן) or lived in *for all generations*; Arab will not (לא) pitch their tents *there*; shepherds will not (לא) make their flocks lie down *there*. [Isa 24:10 The city of chaos (קרית־תהו) is broken down; every house is shut up so that no one can enter.] [cf. 40:23; 41:29] [28:10, 13 line upon line (קו־לקו) ...] [32:18 My people will abide in a peaceful habitation (משכן), in secure dwellings, and in quiet resting places.]	10 Night and day it shall not (לא) be quenched; its smoke shall go up forever. *From generation to generation* it shall lie waste, no (אין) one shall pass through it forever and ever. 11 But the desert owl and screech owl shall possess it; the great owl and the raven shall live (שכן) in it. He shall stretch the line of confusion (קו־תהו) and the plummet of chaos (אבני־בהו) over it. 12 They shall call its nobles No (אין) Kingdom (מלוכה) *There*, and all its princes shall be nothing (אפס). [40:17 All the nations are as nothing (אין) before him; they are accounted by him as less than nothing and emptiness (אפס ותהו).] [45:6 ...there is no one (אפס) besides me; I am the LORD, and there is no other (אין).]
13:21 But wild animals will lie down *there* (שם), and its houses will be full of howling creatures; there ostriches (בנות יענה) will live, and there goat-demons (שעיר) will dance (שם). 22 Hyenas (איים) will cry ["dwell"] (שכן) in its towers (אלמנות) and jackals (תנים) in the pleasant palaces; its ["Babylon's"] time is close at hand; and its days will not be prolonged. [cf. 33:21 ...*there*... (שם)]	13 Thorns shall grow over its strongholds (ארמנת), nettles and thistles in its fortresses. It shall be the haunt of jackals (תנים), An abode for ostriches (לבנות יענה). 14 Wildcats shall meet with hyenas (איים); goat-demons (שעיר) shall call to each other; there (שם) also Lilith shall repose and find a place to rest. 15 *There* (שם)... *there* (שם)... *there* (שם)...
40:26 ... Who created these? ... because he is great in strength, mighty in power, not one is missing (איש לא נעדר).	16 Seek and read from the book of the LORD: Not one of these shall be missing; none shall be without its mate (לא נעדרה אשה רעותה) ...
	17 He has cast the lot for them; his hand has portioned it out to them with the line (קו).[39]

39. English translations of this chart are from NRSVue (New Revised Standard Version Updated Edition).

Diachronically, Isa 34 is a composite unit that many scholars consider having been inserted at a later redactional stage, if not by the final redactor.[40] At the outset, a key question lingers: was ch. 34 intended to be the conclusion of 1–33 or an introduction to 35–66? Ulrich F. Berges sums up the recent regnant theory that first we had chs. 1–33 (where 33 previously joined as its conclusion, and a bridge for chs. 40–52), to which 34 was added, and then 35 was conjoined to present a contrasting theme, anticipating 40–66.[41] Without belaboring all the detailed redactional theories thus far, which Berges has reviewed, the present study will focus on several features pertaining to the issues of unity.

Whether verbatim citations or indirect catchword(s), ch. 34 certainly belongs to a text that connects with many other parts of the book. Admittedly, there are numerous other texts in Isaiah that do not share inner-biblical correlations with 34. The text includes more than one isolated segment across substantially diverse sections of the book which serve as evidence that the intertextuality may be *intentional*. Likewise, because 34 is considered a very late text redactionally (likely in the so-called Trito-Isaianic setting), we can reasonably presume that our text is *aware of* and dependent on most (if not all) of the echoed texts. We will explore the allusions in the order of chapters that echo Isa 34.

First of all, 34:6 may echo 1:11. Although we may not find unequivocal verbatim phrases, the collocation of numerous similar or related words makes it possible that our text alludes to the opening chapter. For example, the catchwords of "blood" and "fat" in both texts describe pertinent animals—"rams" along with "lambs and goats"—that are an inverted chiasm, if read together. Both texts address the issue of "sacrifice." Furthermore, if the day of YHWH (34:8) has an allusion to the pertinent texts (13:6; 61:2; 63:4), it also alludes to Sodom and Gomorrah (13:19)—see the discussion below. Strikingly, 1:11, too, is addressed to the rulers of Sodom and the people of Gomorrah (1:10).

Read intertextually, in 1:11 YHWH rebukes the duplicitous rituals of the Judeans. Now, in 34:6, such offerings and sacrifices are not condemned but complimented. It is because the subject of sacrifices is no longer the human of 1:11, but instead YHWH, associated with the sword of YHWH the divine warrior. The location of the ritual is shifted from Jerusalem to Bozrah as well. Whereas YHWH was fed up with the stacks of slaughtered animals in the land of Judah, now YHWH is to be sated with a great slaughter in the land of Edom. Through the lexical allusions, our text presents an intensified condemnation on Judah's enemy, Edom.

---

40. Many scholars consider vv. 5–15 to be the initial subunit (with v. 8 a possible later insertion), to which v. 1 and vv. 2–4 (where the name "Edom" is absent, or replaced by "nations") were added later, and vv. 16–17 the work of a final redactor or "scribe." See Willem A. M. Beuken, *Isaiah 28–39*, trans. Brian Doyle, HCOT (Leuven: Peeters, 2000), 283–304.

41. Ulrich Berges, *The Book of Isaiah: Its Composition and Final Form*, trans. Millard C. Lind (Sheffield: Sheffield Phoenix Press, 2012), 229–31, 242–4. See also Bert Dicou, "Literary Function and Literary History of Isaiah 34," *BN* 58 (1991): 30–45.

Second, the explicit allusions next jump to Isa 13. Scholars have discovered and delineated these allusions to be deliberate, to the point that ch. 34 (against Edom) alluded to and adapted Isa 13 (against Babylon).[42] Notably, 34:10-15 shares numerous catchwords with 13:19-22. Interestingly, both passages progress in roughly similar order, as though mirroring each other. Even in terms of related motifs, the day of YHWH may connect 34:8 to 13:6, just as Edom's rivers "overthrown" into pitch and brimstone (34:9) relates to Babylon's beauty "overthrown" into Sodom and Gomorrah (13:19)—both passages hearkening back to Gen 19:24.

The dethroning of the Babylonian "kingdom" (13:19) recurs in the disappearance of "kingship" in Edom (34:12). The repeated negation ("no") of shepherds or merchants in Babylon (13:20) likewise recurs in the nullification of Edom's nobles or princes (34:12). Another repeated expression ("there") connects these two texts (13:20-21 and 34:12, 14-15), as though distancing and renouncing the locality of Babylon or Edom (cf. Ps 137:1, 3). Distinct catchwords of wild animals (ostriches, goat-demons, hyenas, and jackals) uniquely correlate these texts (13:21-22 and 34:13-14; cf. Jer 50:39), with a pertinent theme: just as Babylon became a deserted place of wild animals, so Edom is to become a lush habitat for the animals—with Isa 34 adding the metaphorical nuance of animals as the disenfranchised, oppressed group. The closing passage of the reversed portrayal (34:16-17) further accentuates the thematic development. Whereas Babylon is denounced with no one to "dwell...from generation to generation" (13:20), the restored, penitent community as wild animals are to "dwell" and possess the land "from generation to generation" (34:17).[43]

Third, following the OAN section (with another potential interconnection between 22:2 and 34:3 through the motif of the dismissal of the "slain"), we find possible echoes to ch. 24. The cosmic demolition of the earth (or the "land" for the lexical double meaning) causes the earth to weep, weaken, and "wither" (24:4). In 34:4, even the armies of the heavens are to rot and "wither." Moreover, the land of ruined Edom where pelican and porcupine will possess and dwell, there will be the "line of chaos" and "stones of void" (34:11). Albeit lacking explicit verbatim expressions, the cumulative effect of key catchwords—"line," "chaos," and "void"—may allude to the "chaos city" (24:10), all referring to the earth in the status of a "formless void" in Gen 1:2. Accordingly, the chaos city in Isa 24-27, which is commonly identified with Babylon, is now extended to signal to Edom, whose status too will revert to that of void and darkness.

---

42. Jacques Vermeylen, *Du Prophéte Isaïe à l'Apocalyptic, Isaïe I-XXXV, miroir d'un demi-millénaire d'expérience religieuse en Israël*, vol. 1 (Paris: Gabalda, 1977), 440-1; Burkard M. Zapff, *Schriftgelehrte Prophetie: Jes 13 und die Komposition des Jesajabuches: ein Beitrag zur Erforschung der Redaktionsgeschichte des Jesajabuches* (Würzburg: Echter, 1995), 249-54.

43. Jacob Stromberg, *An Introduction to the Study of Isaiah* (London: T&T Clark, 2011), 15.

Fourth, distinct allusions to the six woe-oracles in Isa 28–33 seem to be missing. Nevertheless, though not quite explicit, we may find several inner-biblical allusions reciprocally. The motif of the "line" uniquely recurs in our text, which may allude to the gibberish babble, "line to line" (28:10, 13). In 28:10–11, the prophet's oracles are deemed incomprehensible to the hard-hearted "this people" (cf. 6:9–10). While the enigmatic phrase "line to line" may indicate a mere wordplay, its hidden implication is insinuated as justice for the line and righteousness for the level (28:17). If the literary pun is intended, Isa 34 presents a comparative motif that the "line upon line" of obduracy of the Samaritan and Jerusalemite leaders (28:10, 13), opposite the expected "line of justice" (28:17), is now expanded as the "line of chaos" together with the "stones of void" over Edom (34:11; cf. 34:17), thereby turning Edom into a formless void (Gen 1:2).[44] The combination of the phrase, "a little *there*, a little *there*," adds the likelihood of literary allusion to 28:10, 13 in the repetitive occurrences of "there" in 34:12, 14–15. Additionally, as briefly discussed above, the theme of dwelling as "inhabitants" is a noteworthy signpost. In 32:18, contrary to recalcitrant "this people" (e.g., 28:11, 14; 29:13–14), "my people" are assured to dwell in a peaceful "habitation" (32:18); contrarily, pelican, porcupine, owl, and raven will become the "inhabitants" of Edom (34:11). As Reinhard G. Kratz explicates the intentional *Fortschreibung* of preceding passages evident in 28–31, therefore, we can also detect the kind of *relecture* of 28–33 extant in 34.[45]

Within the six woe-oracle section of Isa 28–33, ch. 33 has been considered an earlier conclusion of the first half of the book of Isaiah. Again, the lexical correlations are not explicit. However, given the compositional likelihood that 34 expands on 33 (along with 1–32), the linguistic and thematic interconnections can be significant. The imperative admonition to "hear" has continued in its preceding texts (e.g., 28:14, 23; 32:9; 33:13), which is now extended to the command toward nations and peoples to "hear" (34:1; cf. 1:2, 10). Also, the catchwords—"earth" and "world"—as the addressees may allude to the inhabitants of the "world" and dwellers of the "earth" addressed in the previous sections (13:11; 14:17, 21; 18:3; 24:4; 26:9, 18; 27:6). Furthermore, the dwelling place designated as "there" connects 34 not only with 13 (see the discussion above) but also with 33:20–24. In 33:21, "there," in the restored city Zion, peace and stability are assured as the devout acknowledge YHWH as their judge, king, and savior.

Fifth, if the allusions of 34 to 28–33 (especially to 33) are notable, then it is important to note that 34 shares many apparent catchwords with 35 as well. Indeed, 35 is considered a redactional counterpart to 34, and the two chapters form a diptych, at the center of the whole book. Because scholars have expounded on the correlations of 34 and 35 in extensive studies, particularly by Odil Hannes

---

44. The description of Cush as a nation "menacing (קו־קו) and conquering" (18:2, 7), with its possible double meaning for "line-line," may also be alluded to in 34:11.

45. Reinhard G. Kratz, "Rewriting Isaiah: The Case of Isaiah 28–31," in *Prophecy and Prophets in Ancient Israel: Proceedings of the Oxford Old Testament Seminar*, ed. John Day, LHBOTS 531 (New York: T&T Clark, 2010), 245–66.

Steck and Claire R. Mathews, it will suffice to discuss a few pertinent observations.[46] Undoubtedly, in addition to the cumulative result of numerous catchwords that tie the two chapters, 34 and 35 present a dual theme—both the divine judgment on Edom, plus comparable enemy nations, and the divine restoration of Judah with its reversal of fortune, respectively.

Significantly, concerning the issue of the book's unity, we note the reversal of Edom's burned "rivers" (נהלים) (34:9), against the outpouring "rivers" (נהלים) in the desert around Zion (35:6). Contrary to Edom, where (arrogant) humans will "not pass through it" (אין עבר) (34:10), in the sanctified Zion it is the unclean who will "not pass through it" (לא־עבר) (35:8). Comparable to the removal of the tyrannical nobles, kings, and princes "there" (שם) in Edom (34:12), no lion or violent creatures will enter "there" (שם) in Zion (35:9).[47] Whereas deserted Edom will become an abode (חציר) of jackals (נוה תנים) and ostriches (34:13), such an abode of jackals (נוה תנים), like grass (חציר), will become a tranquil resting place in Zion (35:7).[48] All in all, the verbal and thematic interconnections between 34 and 35 must be considered purposeful, providing additional clues concerning the unity of the book of Isaiah.

Sixth, as scholars have discovered many verbal links between 35 and 40, 34 too may reverberate select passages in the so-called Deutero-Isaiah.[49] The negation of the nations and empires as "nothing" (אין) and "empty chaos" (אפס ותהו) in 40:17 may provide an important template for the repetitive expressions of "no" (אין), "line of chaos" (קו־תהו), and "nothing" (אפס) in 34 (34:10–12). These descriptions of the emptiness of idols, as opposed to the incomparable YHWH (40:23; 41:11–12, 29; 45:6, 14; 46:9), thus may have functioned to intensify the nullification of Edom.

The unique phrase that "no one is missing" (איש לא נעדר) (40:26) may further have been a *Vorlage* for the concluding statement about the surety of the divine word (34:16–17), as the verb "to be lacking" (עדר) occurs only in three passages (34:16; 40:26; 59:15) in the book: "not one of these will be missing" (אחת מהנה לא נעדרה), "no female will be lacking her mate" (אשה רעותה לא פקדו) (34:16). In 40:26, YHWH exhorts the dejected Jacob-Israel (40:27) that YHWH is the true creator under whose protection no one is missing. In 34:16, the promise of surety highlights the constant and trustworthy word of YHWH, that not one will be

---

46. Odil Hannes Steck, *Bereitete Heimkehr: Jesaja 35 als redaktionelle Brücke zwischen dem Ersten und dem Zweiten Jesaja*, SBS 121 (Stuttgart: Katholisches Bibelwerk, 1985); Claire R. Mathews, *Defending Zion: Edom's Desolation and Jacob's Restoration (Isaiah 34–35) in Context*, BZAW 236 (Berlin: de Gruyter, 1995), esp. 116–19, 158–70.

47. Beuken, *Isaiah 28–39*, 283: "a threefold 'there' in 34:14f. and 35:8f."

48. Perhaps, the lexeme for "home" (חציר) in parallel with "an abode of jackals" in 34:13 may have been intended in the "grass" (חציר) in parallel with "an abode of jackals" in 35:7.

49. Hyun Chul Paul Kim, "The Spider-Poet: Signs and Symbols in Isaiah 41," in *The Desert Will Bloom: Poetic Visions in Isaiah*, ed. A. Joseph Everson and Hyun Chul Paul Kim, SBLAIL 4 (Atlanta, GA: SBL Press, 2009), 159–79.

missing. This promise then includes the thoroughgoing restoration of the wild animals—also as metaphors for the downtrodden, exploited exiles—each member with their mate (cf. 34:15), hence no widows in the restored community.

Seventh, the interconnections between ch. 34 and the so-called Trito-Isaiah are significant not only due to the thematic link concerning Edom in 34 and 63:1–6 but also because of the possible stage of the common final redaction (cf. 66:16). Beyond the theme of Edom, many pertinent words construct the likelihood of mutual correspondence—e.g., divine anger/wrath (63:3, 6; 34:2), blood (63:3, 6; 34:3, 6), no one existent (63:5; 34:10, 12).[50] The most explicit, almost verbatim, expressions concern the "day of vengeance" and the "year of retribution" (63:4; 34:8). Scholars conjecture that 61:2 (the "favorable year" and the "day of vengeance") is reformulated in 63:4, with inverted chiasm—year + day // day + year. Our latest text in 34:8 then alludes to these passages, with thematic extension (cf. 13:6). Whereas the day and year of YHWH accompany comfort of the mourners (61:2), the year of YHWH's "redemption" ushers in the destruction of Edom (63:4). Now our text reasserts these notions as the year of "retribution," when not only Edom will be doomed (34:9) but also Zion is to be delivered (34:8).

3.2. What Can These Allusions Do (or Not Do) for the "Unity" Reading?

It seems evident that ch. 34 was composed with the awareness of a great majority of the book. This chapter, however, does not allude to or echo every verse of every chapter of the book of Isaiah. Yet, it does correlate to select texts of each major section or subdivision of the book, in terms of key terms or motifs. Those texts include chs. 1, 13, 22, 24–27, 28–33, 40, and 63, among others. Again, we still wonder how much of the entire scroll of Isaiah would have been available to the editor of ch. 34. It is nonetheless notable that, albeit not extensively, the echoes of ch. 34 seem consistent and spread out.

Moreover, many of the catchword allusions seem more than haphazard, and thus we may say those were "intentional" (a term Melugin was often cautious accepting, and reasonably so). By intentional, I mean that whenever these allusions are established or identified (though difficult to confirm), the editor of ch. 34 seems to assume and invite readers to be aware of those alluded to texts (even trusting that we readers do read the texts carefully). This to me is substantial and valuable evidence of the editorial intention toward the unity of the book of Isaiah. Put another way, in light of those allusions, we readers are expected not merely to discover that those catchwords in ch. 34 recur and echo other texts, but rather to explore what those allusions intend for composition, how they reaffirm or reconceptualize the related themes or theologies, and what implications such (dialogical) interconnections make for interpreting the entire book.

---

50. Dominic S. Irudayaraj, *Violence, Otherness and Identity in Isaiah 63:1–6: The Trampling One Coming from Edom*, LHBOTS 633 (London: Bloomsbury T&T Clark, 2018), esp. 32–5.

This does not mean that, in searching for unity via catchwords, we should only look at the whole, and thus aspire to read the entire book holistically, on a macro-level. Holistic reading through tracing key semantic or thematic threads is one of the most revolutionary and rewarding approaches of the unity movement on the study of Isaiah. Yet, at the same time, it can be equally legitimate to examine parts and parcels of minute allusions, on a micro-level. Again, when we read "Let the one with ears to hear, hear" (Mt 11:15), even though it is a brief catchphrase, it may have the "Isaianic" language, flavor, and theology. From my HB-oriented reading of this New Testament-phrase, I would be reminded of the obduracy passage (Isa 6:9–10) and all the prophetic reprimands toward the Jerusalem rulers and leaders blinded by sins and deafened to outcries of the powerless. Likewise, when we read the catchwords, "blood" and "fat," occurring no fewer than a total of four times in 34:6, they correlate not only to the stains of wine-press and blood on the garments of the divine warrior (63:3, 6)—which echo the vineyard song with the motif of "trampling" in 5 and 27—but also the adulterated sacrifices and offerings of the people of Judah (1:11). It is now Edom where the bloodshed and slaughter will be rampant, as YHWH put them to the ban, the holy war (34:2). Other examples can include distinct verbatim allusions of the day and year of YHWH (13:6; 34:8; 61:2; 63:4), as well as the wild animals (13:21–22; 34:13–14; 35:7; cf. Jer 50:39–40).

Questions persist, however. How "Isaianic" are these allusions? Put differently, do these catchwords, as markers or signposts, have to be "Isaianic" in order to make the unity a legitimate phenomenon and reading approach? Considering the past and present scholarship thus far, I would have to say both yes and no.

On the one hand, to take these allusions as clues for unity, it would be best if they are uniquely "Isaianic." In analogy, our comparison of the Synoptic Gospels in the New Testament can help identify what is uniquely Matthean, Markan, Lukan, or even Johannine. Similarly, many of the key threads or catchwords can be considered uniquely "Isaianic." For example, some catchphrases, such as "pluck up…pull down" (e.g., Jer 1:10; 24:6), "sword, famine, and pestilence" (e.g., Jer 14:12; 21:9; 24:10), and the like, can be regarded uniquely "Jeremianic." Phrases like "son of man" (or "human one" CEB; e.g., Ezek 2:1; 3:1) are uniquely "Ezekelian." Scholars have proposed comparable threads for the Twelve prophetic literature (e.g., the day of YHWH) or for the Psalter (e.g., the poor and the righteous).[51] By the same token, several features have made the candidates to be uniquely "Isaianic": for example, the obduracy passage (hear, see, know, understand), the servant(s) of YHWH, the "light" over darkness, the "Holy One of Israel," and so on. When we find these threads, they build the uniquely "Isaianic" compositions, implying that redactor(s) may have intended to concatenate those dots and that readers want to trace as many pieces together as possible from the unified whole.

---

51. H. G. M. Williamson, "The Day of the Lord in the Book of Isaiah and the Book of the Twelve," in *Isaiah and the Twelve: Parallels, Similarities and Differences,* ed. Richard J. Bautch, Joachim Eck, and Burkhard M. Zapff, BZAW 527 (Berlin: de Gruyter, 2020), 223–42.

On the other hand, such catchwords do not have to be "Isaianic" and can still function to connect a few dots, or webs, within the book of Isaiah as a whole. For example, we note that while the intricate parallels between chs. 1–2 and 65–66 form an inclusio as framing bookends, those outermost edge chapters do not necessarily stipulate that all the internal chapters resemble similar affinity. Put simply, bookends are just bookends, and what remains inside may be quite different. Nonetheless, though catchwords may not be unique to Isaiah, the collocation of several key lexemes (such as "blood-fat-ram-lambs-goat" between 1:11 and 34:6 or "line-chaos-dwell/inhabit-there" between 13:19–20; 24:10; 28:10 and 34:11–12) can establish legitimate allusions. Such cases of rare occurrences and their cumulative effects within Isa 34 can make the correlations substantially noteworthy, thereby contributing toward unity.

4. Conclusion

The famous catchphrase, *E pluribus unum* ("out of many, one"), is known as the motto concerning the initial thirteen small colonies of the United States which when joined together formed a greater unity. These states then grew, became expanded and boundaries were redrawn. We may regard the book of Isaiah analogously, with regard to both diachrony (redaction) and synchrony (final form), both parts and the whole. The present study yields an analogous observation: on the one hand, not all states may be equal (e.g., portion, catchwords, and themes of each chapter of the book); on the other hand, each state is distinct, valuable, and important (e.g., each text, chapter, and section of the book).

Concerning the unifying threads or united catchwords, our study of Isaiah has much to do with both *continuity* and *discontinuity* as well.[52] Fascinatingly, both of these features can contribute to the unity and help provide clues to comprehend it. The (holistic) continuity contains recurring words or themes, theories of why they do so, and for what compositional or theological purposes. The (redactional) discontinuity displays what differences are employed, how those switches or insertions came to be, and for what resultant outcomes.[53] Continuity, via interconnections, links various parts of the book together. Discontinuity, via disjoints, also exhibits shifts and changes, which can also illumine how those disjoints eventually

---

52. Lena-Sofia Tiemeyer and Hans M. Barstad, eds., *Continuity and Discontinuity: Chronological and Thematic Development in Isaiah 40–66*, FRLANT 255 (Göttingen: Vandenhoeck & Ruprecht, 2014).

53. Francis Landy, "Ancestral Voices and Disavowal: Poetic Innovation and Intertextuality in the Eighth-Century Prophets," in *Second Wave Intertextuality and the Hebrew Bible*, ed. Marianne Grohmann and Hyun Chul Paul Kim, SBL Resources for Biblical Study 93 (Atlanta, GA: SBL Press, 2019), 79: "The new text may coexist uneasily with the old one. This is evidently an issue with major collections such as Isaiah. The more one writes, the more difficult it will be to achieve poetic unity. The text is fundamentally heterogenous."

came together toward unity. Both continuity and discontinuity matter for our understanding of unity.

For example, the distinct phrase, the "house of Jacob" (along with the "house of Israel," the "house of David," the "house of Judah," etc.), evidences both continuity and discontinuity within the book. The phrase can mean one group (continually and steadily), but at the same time it can refer to various entities (disjointedly and differently). Such a feature of both clarity and complexity can make it difficult to dissect, retrieve, and reconstruct all the processes prior to unity—although someone may have gotten it right (like winning a lottery in which "all" the numbers, or redactional strata and procedures, are accurate).

Melugin's concluding remark opens with the assessment: "This essay has shown that those who see 'unity' in the book of Isaiah represent a diverse group indeed."[54] Just as some see some optical illusions and others do not, finding and interpreting unity in the book of Isaiah remains a matter of dispute and disagreement. Yet, like many of his colleagues and successors, including this indebted mentee, Melugin's appraisal and call for the "new movement" in reading Isaiah holistically has been prolific and rewarding. It still remains our humble tasks both to distinguish the parts and parcels of the texts (like disassembling LEGO pieces) and to appreciate the conglomeration of the whole. Like so many small functions of the iPhone, parts can be as invaluable as the whole, and vice versa. It is no coincidence that our focus text, Isa 34, concludes with the assertion, "Seek from the scroll of YHWH and proclaim, not one of these will be missing" (34:16). Therefore, let there be ongoing efforts treasure-hunting and analyzing the catchwords (*Stichwörter*) and similar markers/signposts for *Fortschreibung* or *relecture*. Let's continue to seek, let the study evolve, let the eureka inform and inspire. "Let the one with ears to hear, hear" (Mt 11:15).

---

54. Melugin, "Isaiah 40–66," 194.

Chapter 5

TRACKING THE SCRIBAL TRAILS
IN THE BOOK OF ISAIAH: THE SABBATH AFFAIR

Benedetta Rossi

The Sabbath in Isaiah presents characteristics that are unique in the Hebrew Bible: in addition to the gradual extension of the Sabbath to marginal categories of eunuch and foreigner (56:3–8) and to each individual (56:1–2; 66:23), Isa 56:1–2 identifies the Sabbath with the practice of justice. Observing the distribution of the occurrences of the Sabbath in Isaiah, Hans Barstad maintains that reflection on the Sabbath—together with that on justice—is a distinctive characteristic of the ideological agenda of Third Isaiah.[1] The predominant presence of references to the Sabbath in Isa 56–66 is undeniable. However, the mention of the Sabbath in Isa 1:13, but, above all, the placing of references to the Sabbath in framework texts of a redactional and composite character leads to review this judgment. In fact, the references to the Sabbath seem to be attributable to scribal contributions which presuppose the presence of the whole of Isa 1–66, and whose purpose is to set reflection on the Sabbath within the book of Isaiah as a whole, placing it, at the same time, in dialogue with the Torah. Thus, the texts concerning the Sabbath in Isaiah offer a chance to understand the nature of scribal processes at work within the entire collection, providing, at the same time, some clues for identifying the context of these developments.

I shall show that the unique representation of the Sabbath in Isa 56:1–2 (1) is shaped as a response to the Isaian debate on the relation between the observance of the Sabbath and the practice of justice (2). The reprise and transformation of

---

1. See Hans Barstad, "Isaiah 56–66 in Relation to Isaiah 40–55: Why a New Reading is Necessary," in *Continuity and Discontinuity: Chronological and Thematic Development in Isaiah 40–66*, ed. Lena-Sofia Tiemeyer and Hans Barstad, FRLANT 255 (Göttingen: Vandenhoeck & Ruprecht, 2014), 41–62 (61).

the traditions of Exodus, placed at the service of the interaction between Israel and the nations, offer an authoritative point of reference for the innovation proposed (3). The negotiation of Israel's identity in changed social and political contexts (i.e. the Persian and Hellenistic contexts) acts as a background to the dialogue with the Torah and the innovative representation of the Sabbath (4). This is what emerges from a comparison with other biblical witnesses relating to Sabbath observance together with some extra-biblical evidence. Tracking the scribal trails in Isaiah, starting out from the representation of the Sabbath, can offer an insight into the unity of Isaiah, showing how this unity is perceived and constructed.

1. *Observe the Sabbath and Practice Justice: Isaiah 56:1–8*

Isaiah 56:1–8 can be ascribed to two successive scribal contributions which mark at the same time a development in the conception of the Sabbath.[2] Verses 3–8 represent the first stage of composition, to which were added subsequently, vv. 1–2 which extend the reflection on the Sabbath.[3]

כה אמר יהוה שמרו משפט ועשו צדקה כי־קרובה ישועתי לבוא וצדקתי להגלות	1	Thus says Yhwh: Observe righteousness, do justice, for my salvation is about to come, my justice, about to be revealed.
אשרי אנוש יעשה־זאת ובן־אדם יחזיק בה שמר שבת מחללו ושמר ידו מעשות כל־רע	2	Blessed the mortal who does this, and the human being who holds fast to it; the one who keeps the Sabbath without profaning it, the one who keeps his hand from doing any evil.

---

2. Differently, Jacob Stromberg, *Isaiah after Exile: The Author of Third Isaiah as Reader and Redactor of The Book* (Oxford: Oxford University Press, 2011), 39–42, reviews the various theories and concludes in favour of the unity of 56:1–8. See also Ulrich Berges, *Das Buch Jesaja: Komposition und Endgestalt*, HBS 16 (Freiburg: Herder, 1998), 509–11; Paul A. Smith, *Rhetoric and Redaction in Trito-Isaiah: The Structure, Growth and Authorship of Isaiah 56–66*, VTSup 62 (Leiden: Brill, 1995), 50–66; Joseph Blenkinsopp, *Isaiah 56–66: A New Translation with Introduction and Commentary*, AB 19B (New York: Doubleday, 2008), 131; Jan Leunis Koole, *Isaiah. Part III: Volume 3. Isaiah 56–66*, HCOT (Leuven: Peeters, 2001), 3. However, as Joachim Schaper declares, the number of positions with regard to the history of the redaction of Isa 56:1–8 is almost endless; see Joachim Schaper, "Rereading the Law: Inner-Biblical Exegesis of Divine Oracles in Ezekiel 44 and Isaiah 56," in *Recht und Ethik im Alten Testament: Beiträge des Symposiums „Das Alte Testament und die Kultur der Moderne" anlässlich des 100. Geburtstags Gerhard von Rads (1901 - 1971), Heidelberg, 18. - 21. Oktober 2001*, ed. Bernard M. Levinson and Eckart Otto, Altes Testament und Moderne 13 (Münster: LIT, 2004), 125–44.

3. For this arrangement of the text, see among others Claus Westermann, *Das Buch Jesaja: Kapitel 40-66*, ATD 19 (Göttingen: Vandenhoeck & Ruprecht, 1986), 244.

ואל־יאמר בן־הנכר הנלוה אל־יהוה לאמר הבדל יבדילני יהוה מעל עמו ואל־יאמר הסריס הן אני עץ יבש:	3	The foreigner joined to Yhwh should not say: Yhwh will surely separate me from his people; and the eunuch should not say: Behold, I am a dried tree.
כי־כה אמר יהוה לסריסים אשר ישמרו את־שבתותי ובחרו באשר חפצתי ומחזיקים בבריתי	4	For thus says Yhwh: to the eunuchs who keep my sabbath, and choose what pleases me, and hold fast to my covenant.
ונתתי להם בביתי ובחומתי יד ושם טוב מבנים ומבנות שם עולם אתן־לו אשר לא יכרת	5	I shall give them in my house and within my walls a position and a name better than sons and daughters, an everlasting name I shall give them,[4] which will not be cut off.
ובני הנכר הנלוים על־יהוה לשרתו ולאהבה את־שם יהוה להיות לו לעבדים כל־שמר שבת מחללו ומחזיקים בבריתי	6	And the foreigners joined to Yhwh to serve him and to love Yhwh's name and to be his servants, everyone who keeps the Sabbath without profaning it and those who hold fast to my covenant.
והביאותים אל־הר קדשי ושמחתים בבית תפלתי עולתיהם וזבחיהם לרצון על־מזבחי כי ביתי בית־תפלה יקרא לכל־העמים	7	I shall bring them to my holy mountain, I shall make them rejoice in my house of prayer; their holocausts and sacrifices (will be) a pleasure on my altar; for my house shall be called house of prayer for all peoples.
נאם אדני יהוה מקבץ נדחי ישראל עוד אקבץ עליו לנקבציו	8	Oracle of the Lord Yhwh who gathers the scattered ones of Israel; others I will gather to him besides those already gathered.

Verses 3–8 are arranged around a specular scheme of citation of the direct speech of the foreigners and the eunuchs (introduced by אל ימאר, vv. 3 and 4), and the subsequent response addressed first to the eunuchs (vv. 4–5) and then to the foreigners (vv. 6–7). Verse 8 closes the composition: a reference to the action of Yhwh (קבץ 3×) comes into view. The structure indicates vv. 3–7 as a cohesive textual unit. Some lexical and thematic references link 56:3–7 to the close of Isa 55.[5]

In 55:13, Yhwh's work is described as a "name" (שם) and an eternal sign (אות עולם) for Yhwh which cannot be cancelled (לא יכרת). The syntagma לא יכרת returns in 56:5 with reference to the "eternal name" (שם עולם) Yhwh promises to the eunuchs.[6]

From the thematic point of view: the reference to the Exodus traditions, represented, in particular, by the *motif* of going-out, closes Deutero-Isaiah (hereafter DI) in 55:12–13. According to Willem A. M. Beuken, Isa 56:7-8 is linked to this theme, providing answers to the questions left open. Isaiah 55:12–13 does not specify the goal of the New Exodus; besides, the verb in the passive in 55:12 ("you shall be brought back") leaves open the question as to the identity of the one who

---

4. With the LXX αὐτοῖς.
5. In this regard, see also Stromberg, *Isaiah after Exile*, 77–9.
6. Stromberg, *Isaiah after Exile*, 79: Isa 56:5 takes up 55:13 and transforms it into a promise of access to the temple for the obedient eunuch.

leads those going out.⁷ Isaiah 56:7 specifies that the goal of the New Exodus is the house of Yhwh on his holy mountain. As for the leader: Yhwh himself brings back and gathers those who take part in this movement (v. 8).

If, on the one hand, Isa 56:3–8 is linked to the close of DI, on the other hand, it shows new features. Access to the house of Yhwh is permitted also to marginal categories and those otherwise excluded: the eunuch (56:5) and the foreigner (v. 7), who will be led (בוא hi.) on to his holy mountain by God himself. Moreover, in 56:8, Yhwh presents himself as the one who not only gathers the "scattered ones of Israel" (v. 8a) but will continue to gather others too: "Others (עוד)⁸ I will gather to him (i.e. Israel),⁹ to those who are (already) gathered." Thus, the gathering of the dispersed is not limited to Israel but includes non-Israelites also.¹⁰ Therefore, participation in the movement of the New Exodus, which begins in 55:12–13 (יצא; יבל ho.) and reaches its goal in 56:7 (בוא hi.), is extended also to marginal categories ("eunuch," סרים, v. 4),¹¹ and expanded beyond the borders of the people of Israel ("foreigners," בני הנכר, v. 6; "others I will gather to him," עוד אקבץ עלו, v. 8). The role assigned to observance of the Sabbath in 56:3–7 is crucial for this expansion. Sabbath observance becomes a kind of summary of the provisions of the covenant, ending up as the necessary condition to be able to enter and become part of the people of Yhwh.

Isa 56:1–2 can be considered an addition to the previous unit (vv. 3–6): the expression שמר שבת מחללו (v. 2) links up with the following v. 6, but vocabulary and themes indicate a discontinuity with what follows.

Whereas Isa 58:3–7 is focused on the בית יהוה and on cultic practices, 56:1–2 are focused from the beginning on the practice of justice (v. 1: "observe righteousness, do justice," שמרו משפט ועשו צדקה; "my justice," צדקתי; v. 2: "keep his hand away from doing any evil," ושמר ידו מעשות כל־רע). In vv. 1–2, the verb שמר, reserved in vv. 2, 4, 6 to the observance of the Sabbath, refers, in addition, to the

---

7. Willem A. M. Beuken, *Jesaja. Deel IIIB*, POuT (Nijkerk: G. F. Callenbach, 1989), 37.

8. The temporal interpretation of עוד is possible and could indicate a gradual and continuous movement with which Yhwh gathers Israel. However, in view of the inclusion of eunuchs and foreigners in the movement towards the house of Yhwh, it is probable that עוד refers here to others gathered by Yhwh in addition to Israel. Koole, *Isaiah 56–66*, 27; *DCH*, s.v. עוד, 291–2.

9. For a summary of the debate about the referent of the 3rd m. sing suffix and the plausibility of its reference to Israel, see Koole, *Isaiah 56–66*, 26.

10. See Koole, *Isaiah 56–66*, 27, who underlines the reprise of this vision in Isa 66:18.

11. If the eunuch is identified with the person "with crushed testicles" of Deut 23:2, the סריס (eunuch) should be considered a category excluded from the assembly of Yhwh (קהל יהוה). For the relation between Isa 56:1–8 and Deut 23:2–9, see among others Schaper, "Rereading the Law," 128–36; Christoph Nihan, "Ethnicity and Identity in Isaiah 56–66," in *Judah and the Judeans in the Achaemenid Period: Negotiating Identity in an International Context*, ed. Oded Lipschits, Gary N. Knoppers, and Manfred Oeming (Winona Lake, IN: Eisenbrauns, 2011), 67–104 (75–6).

keeping of justice and the need to guard oneself from evil. The cultic emphasis becomes less central compared to the ethical one.

Isaiah 56:3–7 guarantees to marginal categories access to the "house of Yhwh." The latter becomes the goal of a centripetal movement: even eunuchs and foreigners will be included in what will be a "house of prayer for all the peoples" (v. 7). In Isa 56:1, by contrast, the justice of Yhwh and his salvation move and draw near to the addresses of the prophetic message ("my salvation is about to come, my justice, about to be revealed," קרובה ישועתי לבוא וצדקתי להגלות).

Isaiah 56:3–7 give central place to the dialectic between the people of the covenant and some marginal categories (eunuchs and sons of foreigners) who find a way of inclusion and access to the community of the covenant. Isaiah 56:1–2 invites every human being without any reference to Israel or to those included in it. This is, therefore, a move from a perspective that aims at inclusion in Israel to a decidedly universal one where there is no mention of any inclusion in the people of the covenant.

As we have already shown, Isa 56:3–7, 8 take up the vocabulary and themes of 55:12–13 and also provide answers to some open questions. Isaiah 56:1–2 take the form of a subsequent insertion, which expands the reflection on the Sabbath, opening it to a new perspective.

Two elements mark the change of perspective: a) the identification between Sabbath observance and the practice of justice; b) the universalisation of the Sabbath.

1.1. *The Sabbath and the Practice of Justice*

Isaiah 56:1–2 identifies observance of the Sabbath with the practice of justice; elements of a lexical and syntactical nature favour this interpretation.

As for vocabulary: the exhortation to practise justice, expressed by the hendiadys, שמרו משפט ("observe righteousness") and עשו צדקה ("do justice") opens Isa 56:1–2. Verse 2a proclaims the blessed state of the human being who "does this" (אשרי אנוש יעשה־זאת); the repetition of the verb עשה and the pronoun זאת (object of the verb) with anaphoric value[12] enables us to read this beatitude with reference to the practice of justice (v. 1).

Having called blessed the individual (בן אדם; אנוש) who practises justice assiduously (חזק), the proclamation of the beatitude continues for "the one who keeps the Sabbath without profaning it" (שמר שבת מחללו), and "the one who keeps his hand from doing any evil" (ושמר ידו מעשות כל־רע). The triple repetition of the verb שמר, referring to the practice of justice (v. 1), the observance of the Sabbath (v. 2c) and the refraining from evil (v. 2d) underlines a relation between these attitudes. The connection is further confirmed by the combination of the verbs שמר and עשה in vv. 1 and 2d. In 56:1, the verbs express the practice of justice (שמרו משפט ועשו צדקה); in v. 2d, they also signify refraining from evil (ושמר ידו מעשות כל־רע).

---

12. See *IBHS* §17.4.3a: the pronoun זה (in the feminine form, זאת) specifies an antecedent that is otherwise vague. See also Koole, *Isaiah 56–66*, 9.

As for syntax: v. 2cd is constructed by a sequence of two main clauses coordinated by *waw*: שמר שבת מחללו ושמר ידו מעשות כל־רע ("the one who keeps the Sabbath without profaning it, and the one who keeps his hand from doing any evil"). From the stylistic point of view, such a structure is typically considered synonymous parallelism.[13] However, this interpretation makes it difficult to understand the reference to Sabbath observance. As Joseph Blenkinsopp declares: "It will seem somewhat surprising that the quite general injunction to avoid evil-doing is linked with the very specific point of Sabbath observance."[14] The relation of synonymy, the hermeneutical key of parallelism, does not manage to explain the juxtaposition of Sabbath observance and abstention from evil. The difficulty in considering parallelism as a purely semantic and stylistic phenomenon comes here into view.

In a contribution of 2019, Robert D. Holmstedt proposes analyzing parallelism as a syntactic phenomenon based on apposition,[15] a phenomenon not only attested with noun phrases (or participles), but also with verbal clauses introduced by *waw*.[16] The use of *waw* in such contexts is typically described as coordination or as epexegetical (*IBHS* §39.2.4, §33.2.2), which introduces a clarification and specification of what precedes it. The function of clarification and specification is precisely the semantic function of non-restrictive apposition.[17] This syntactic category enables Holmstedt to reconsider parallelism.

Non-restrictive apposition does not provide information necessary to identify the anchor but reformulates it by offering additional description, more precise information or corrections of the anchor itself.[18] From the syntactic point of view, non-restrictive apposition is marked by non-subordinate syntax.

In Isa 56:2cd, the syntagma שמר שבת מחללו ("the one who keeps the sabbath without profaning it") is the anchor; the following v. 2d (ושמר ידו מעשות כל־רע, "and keeps his hand from doing any evil") can be considered a non-restrictive apposition, which provides more precise information about v. 2c: observing the Sabbath signifies refraining from doing what is evil. This is not just a relation of synonymy but a clarification of what is meant by Sabbath observance.[19]

---

13. E.g. Koole, *Isaiah*, 10; John Goldingay, *A Critical and Exegetical Commentary on Isaiah 55–66*, ICC (London: Bloomsbury, 2014), 69.

14. Blenkinsopp, *Isaiah 56–66*, 135. Also Koole, *Isaiah 56–66*, 11, considers the transition surprising.

15. Robert D. Holmstedt, "Hebrew Poetry and the Appositive Style: Parallelism, *Requiescat in pace*," *VT* 69 (2019): 617–48.

16. Holmstedt, "Hebrew Poetry," 627–9.

17. Holmstedt, "Hebrew Poetry," 629.

18. Holmstedt, "Hebrew Poetry," 625.

19. Holmstedt summarizes it thus: "The nature of the additional or alternative description provided by a non-restrictive appositive is formally speaking a subset relationship: the second is semantically a logical subset of the first (X_1, "that is," X_2)"; see Holmstedt, "Hebrew Poetry," 626.

1.2. The Universalization of the Sabbath

This is marked by two elements: the referent of the discourse, the one "who observes" the Sabbath (v. 2c), has been identified previously as אנוש ("mortal," v. 2a) and בן־אדם ("human being," v. 2b). Both lexemes refer to human beings in their universal and mortal dimension,[20] without any specific reference to Israel. In addition, the connection between one who observes the Sabbath (v. 2c) and v. 2a links the observance of the Sabbath with a macarism: אשרי [...] שמר שבת מחללו ("blessed [...] the one who keeps the Sabbath without profaning it").[21] This connection between respect for the Sabbath and blessedness is unique in the Hebrew Bible. In the prescriptions regarding Sabbath observance there is no indication of any reward for the one who observes it; on the contrary, Exod 31:12–17 specifies that whoever does not observe the Sabbath and profanes it will be put to death and separated from the people. A positive promise is linked to observance of the Sabbath day in Jer 17:24–26, and matches the threat of judgment for those continuing to disregard the Sabbath rest (v. 27). Here the promise bound up with the observance of the Sabbath by individuals has a collective significance that reflects on the very welfare of Jerusalem. In Isa 56:2, Sabbath observance is possible for each individual (אנוש; בן־אדם), not necessarily an Israelite; in addition, the blessedness destined for those who observe it has a distinctly personal character and does not have any consequence for the community.

An analogous tendency to the universalization of the Sabbath occurs at the close of Trito-Isaiah, in Isa 66:23: "From new moon to new moon, from Sabbath to Sabbath, all flesh (כל בשר) will come to worship before me, says Yhwh." The syntagma כל בשר recalls closely the references to the human being (אנוש and בן אדם) of Isa 56:2. However, the perspective delineated by 66:23 does not match that of Isa 56:1–2. In fact, the Sabbath is portrayed in 66:23 as a movement towards Yhwh; there is no reference to the ethical dimension of the Sabbath. On the contrary, the predominant image is that of a cultic act of prostration before Yhwh, the universal sovereign.

To recap: the representation of the Sabbath in Isa 56:1–2 appears as a development of 56:3–8. The Sabbath is no longer bound up with the cult but is identified with the ethical case of the practice of justice. It is precisely this that enables each individual, Israelite or not, to practise the Sabbath and enjoy the

---

20. The majority of the occurrences of the substantive אנוש ("mortal") in Isaiah implies precisely the condition of fragility and transience of the human being (e.g. 13:7; 24:6; 51:12); Koole, *Isaiah 56-66*, 9. The pair of substantive אנוש and the phrase בן־אדם ("human being") in the Hebrew Bible confirms that (e.g. Isa 51:12; Ps 8:5; Job 25:6). The two terms reinforce the condition of mortality and inferiority of the human being *vis-à-vis* the divinity. In Isa 56:2, fragility and mortality emphasize the universality of the human condition.

21. The coordination between the 3rd m. sing suffix (מחללו) and the feminine שבת can be resolved by considering implicit the expression יום השבת (see Koole, *Isaiah 56-66*, 10 with further bibliography).

promise of blessedness. Practising the Sabbath as the realization of justice means participating in the actualization of justice and divine salvation (see 56:1), almost preparing the way for them. Thus, each human being can participate in the work of Yhwh. The unique representation of the Sabbath in Isa 56:1–2 offers a solution to the dialectic between Sabbath and justice present in the other occurrences of the Sabbath in Isaiah.

2. Sabbath and Justice: Tracking the Scribal Trails in Isaiah

The Sabbath appears for the first time in Isaiah in 1:13 alongside the new moon (חדש ושבת, "new moon and Sabbath"), beside cultic practices displeasing to Yhwh. The rejection of these cultic practices is motivated by the wicked actions performed alongside them: "I cannot endure wickedness and assembly" (v. 13). In order that the cult may be pleasing, Yhwh invites the people and their rulers (v. 10) to practise justice: "seek justice (דרשו משפט), put right the oppressor (אשרו חמוץ),[22] give justice for the orphan, plead for the widow" (v. 17). On the one hand, the dispositions required for the observance of the Sabbath are not specified; nevertheless, its practice is associated with the requisite justice. Failure of justice renders the Sabbath abominable to Yhwh.

Although, according to Beuken, the references to the injustices perpetrated and to the justice that is necessary can be ascribed to the environment of the prophet Isaiah,[23] it is possible to consider Isa 1:1–20 as a scribal composition placed as a prologue to the entire book. Some elements lean towards this interpretation: the combination of different literary genres in sequence indicates the text as a scribal production; the formula "hear the word of Yhwh" (שמעו דבר יהוה; 1:10) occurs elsewhere only in Isa 66:5, and represents a framing element for the whole Isaian corpus.[24]

As for v. 13: the Sabbath is mentioned along with a series of cultic practices and usages expressed in a language which can be detected in P and post-exilic texts.[25]

---

22. The correction of the oppressor is mentioned among the works of justice. See H. G. M. Williamson, *Isaiah 1-5: A Critical and Exegetical Commentary*, ICC (London: T&T Clark, 2014), 101: the oppressor must not only be punished but, even more, corrected so as to push him into changing his conduct. *BHS* proposes reading חמוץ, following the LXX (ἀδικούμενον), and interprets: "rescue the oppressed."

23. Willem A. M. Beuken, *Jesaja 1-12*, HThKAT (Freiburg: Herder, 2003), 69. Other authors refer this text to the pre-exilic practice of the Sabbath; the connection between the Sabbath and the new moon would stress this interpretation. However, this argument does not seem convincing since both are mentioned, for example, in Isa 66:23, a text that is clearly post-exilic.

24. Berges, *Jesaja*, 58. According him, the composer of the addition relates the Sabbath to the post-exilic practice of the fast. However, the dominant ethical imperative in 58:1–12 remains ignored (ibid., 477).

25. See Williamson, *Isaiah 1-5*, 92–5.

The scarcity of the cultic language relating to sacrifice and offerings in Isaiah confirms the secondary nature of the unit.[26] The mention of the Sabbath beside the new moon (חדש ושבת) is not a decisive criterion for being able to maintain a pre-exilic dating for the text. In fact, the two substantives occur together also in post-exilic texts (e.g. Isa 66:23).[27]

The connection between Sabbath and justice in 58:13-14 is debated. Verses 13-14 represent a scribal addition set between the previous vv. 1-12 and the following ch. 59 where the theme of justice becomes prominent.[28] As a holy day to be venerated through a series of practices (58:13-14), the Sabbath seems to be separated from the theme of social justice which dominates vv. 1-12 and continues in Isaiah 59. In 58:13-14, the Sabbath is repeatedly described in relation to Yhwh: "a holy day for me" (יום קדשי), "holy for Yhwh" (קדוש יהוה). The observance of the Sabbath would enable the worshipper to enter into relation with Yhwh even without the practice of justice in his dealings with his neighbour.[29] Moreover, the ethical imperative at the centre of 58:1-12 is ignored by the prescriptions regarding the Sabbath day in vv. 13-14. According to a widespread interpretation, the observing of the Sabbath prescribed in 58:13 would envisage the abstaining from journeys (אם־תשיב משבת רגלך, "if you restrain your foot on the Sabbath day," i.e. if you abstain from journeying on the Sabbath day).[30] Along the same lines we should interpret the expression וכבדתו מעשות דרכיך, "[if] you honour it by refraining from journeys." To this we should add the prohibition from looking after one's own affairs as expressed by the syntagmas עשות חפציך ("doing your business") and ממצוא חפצך ("pursue your affair"). This vision of the Sabbath, as a day to be venerated through a series of practices, would be completely jettisoned from the attention to social justice predominant in the preceding 58:1-12.

If, on the one hand, the separation between Sabbath and justice indicates the redactional nature of vv. 13-14, on the other hand, it does not succeed in explaining the purpose of the addition of vv. 13-14 between two units that are

---

26. E.g. עתודים, which is typical of Numbers, only 2× in Isaiah; עלה 7× in Isaiah vs. 59× in Leviticus and 53× in Number; זבח 7× in Isaiah vs. 32× Leviticus and 20× Numbers.

27. See Williamson, *Isaiah 1-5*, 94.

28. The distance of vv. 13-14 from what precedes it finds confirmation also from the manuscript tradition: in 1QIsa\u1d43, vv. 13-14 are clearly separated from the previous ones. The preceding line ends with the last two words of v. 12, thus remaining almost completely empty. See Donald W. Parry and Elisha Qimron, eds., *The Great Isaiah Scroll (1Q Isaᵃ): A New Edition*, STDJ 32 (Leiden: Brill, 1999), 96-7.

29. Berges, *Jesaja*, 476-7.

30. In this case, the preposition מן, "from," would have a locative value (משבת, "on the Sabbath"), similar to ב. See Mitchell Dahood, "Hebrew–Ugaritic Lexicography V," *Bib* 48 (1967): 427, on the basis of comparison with the Ugaritic. The Old Latin (*si averteris in sabbatis pedem tuum*) confirms this interpretation. The rendering *in sabbatis* (< gr. *ἐν; vs. MT: משבת; LXX: ἀπὸ τῶν σαββάτων) understands the Sabbath as the day in which to restrain one's own foot so as not to handle one's own business (OL: *ut non facias voluntates tuas in die sancta*; LXX: τοῦ μὴ ποιεῖν τὰ θελήματά σου ἐν τῇ ἡμέρᾳ τῇ ἁγίᾳ).

well connected. Berges summarizes this difficulty: "it is not clear why the authors of 58, who are also behind 59, should have weakened the connection between their texts by inserting 58:13–14" (my translation).³¹ In my opinion, the relation between the Sabbath and the practice of justice can be reconsidered in a positive light.

The Sabbath practice as abstention from journeys and from business (v. 13) is not the only possible reading of the text. The expression אם־תשיב משבת רגלך can be interpreted as "if you restrain your foot far from (מן) the Sabbath," understanding the preposition מן as "far from." The expression would be a warning not to enter with one's feet into the sacred space of the Sabbath, treading on it and abusing it. Thus, the text does not refer to the prohibition of travelling.³² As the exclusive possession of Yhwh and the expression of his holiness, the Sabbath must not be abused and infringed. The potential abuse is specified by the continuation of the text which can be understood thus: "[if] you call the Sabbath 'delight' (וקראת לשבת ענג), the holiness of Yhwh 'glorified' (לקדוש יהוה מכבד),³³ and glorify it more than going your own ways, more than following your own business/obtaining what you desire,³⁴ and carrying out negotiations." With regard to the most common interpretation which understands מן as "without," to introduce what is prohibited,³⁵ the syntagma וכבדתו מעשות [...] ממצוא + מן + כבד can have a comparative value ("glorify it more than").³⁶ Therefore, v. 13 would not be indicating what is prohibited on the Sabbath day; rather, it contains a warning to subordinate one's own interests to the holiness of the Sabbath, without offering further clarifications.

---

31. See Berges, *Jesaja*, 476–7.

32. See *DCH* s.v. מן, "restrain from trampling/defiling." See also Goldingay, *Isaiah 56–66*, 184.

33. I understand the expression לקדוש יהוה as parallel to the previous לשבת. Both are object of the verb קרא (introduced by ל). In this case, the epithet קדוש יהוה refers to the Sabbath: the Sabbath itself, "holiness of Yhwh," must be called "honoured." In this direction, see the interpretation of Koole, *Isaiah 56–66*, 155, 157 ("and call the Sabbath a delight, the holy [day] of Yhwh honourable").

34. For this possible interpretation of the syntagma מצא + obj. חפץ, cf. 4Q416 2 ii 8. The expression ואז תמצא חפצכה is interpreted by John Strugnell and Daniel J. Harrington as "and then thou wilt attain thy wish"; see John Strugnell, Daniel J. Harrington and Torleif Elgvin, *Qumran Cave 4. XXIV Sapiential Texts, Part 2: 4QInstruction (Mûsār lĕ Mēvîn)*, DJD 34 (Oxford: Clarendon, 1999), 93. However, the authors underline the multiple semantic possibilities of חפץ (ibid., 99). A double interpretation for Isa 58:13 can be left open: on the one hand, the substantive חפץ could refer to "affairs/business" (מצוא חפצך, "pursue your business"), or, on the other, to desire (מצוא חפצך, "obtain what you desire"). In any case, the pursuit of a personal interest comes clearly into view.

35. See Koole, *Isaiah 56–66*, 155.

36. See also Job 3:6 (*DCH* s.v. מן). Closer to this reading is Goldingay, *Isaiah 56–66*, 183, who interprets מן as "instead of."

If this is the case, the connection between the Sabbath and the practice of justice desired in the previous vv. 1–12 is not excluded. On the contrary, some lexical and stylistic connections between Isa 58:1–12 and 58:13–14 support this connection.

The phrase חפץ + מצא occurs in the Hebrew Bible only in Isa 58:3 and 58:13, establishing a clear connection between vv. 1–12 and 13–14. In 58:3, the syntagma is part of an accusation addressed to the people about their attitudes on the day of fasting: "on your fast day, you serve your own interest (תמצאו־חפץ), and oppress all your workers (וכל־עצביכם תנגשו)." The quest for one's own interest or the carrying out of one's own business is paralleled to the injustice practised at the expense of ones' dependants. In the light of the connection with 58:3, the expression ממצוא חפצך in 58:13 does not exclude a reference to the injustice perpetrated in the pursuit of one's interests.

The syntactic structure of vv. 13–14, based on the sequence of protasis (אם, v. 13) and apodosis (אז, v. 14), takes up the preceding vv. 8–9 in inverted form:

v. 13: <u>if</u> (אם) you restrain your foot far from the Sabbath [...]	vv. 8–9: <u>then</u> (אז) your light shall break forth like the dawn [...] then (אז) you shall call and Yhwh will answer [...]
v. 14: <u>then</u> (אז) you shall delight in Yhwh [...]	v. 9: <u>if</u> (אם) you remove the yoke from among you [...]

After the denunciation of the injustice practised at the expense of the weaker brethren (vv. 1–5), the following verses indicate the path of justice, showing the positive consequences for those who wish to follow it. Through the reprise of the same syntactic structure, the reflection on the Sabbath aims at being a sequel to the preceding reflection on injustice.

In Isa 58:14, Yhwh closes the series of promises made to those who honour the Sabbath with these words: "I will feed you[37] with the heritage of Jacob, your father." Clearly metaphorical, the language represents Yhwh as one who nourishes those who honour the Sabbath. The same image is present in Isa 58:11: "Yhwh will fill you in dry regions (והשביע בצחצחות נפשך)." The verbs אכל and שבע belong to the same semantic field and can be considered synonyms. In Isa 58:11, Yhwh fills those who practice justice; an analogous reward ("I will feed you," v. 14) is reserved for those who honour the Sabbath day.

Together with the insertion of the reflection on the Sabbath (58:13–14) within two larger portions of text devoted to the theme of justice (58:11–12 and 59), the abovementioned connections reveal an open debate on the relation between Sabbath and justice.[38] It is not a question of honouring the Sabbath by refraining

---

37. I read אכל hi. with 1QIsa[a] and LXX.

38. Berges, *Jesaja*, 477, does not exclude that the insertion of vv. 13–14 about the Sabbath could be attributed to the same layer which concerns the observance of the Sabbath for foreigners and proselytes in 56:1–8. In fact, vv. 13–14 are linked with 56:2, 4, 6 and presuppose 66:23–24 (see p. 476).

from business and not travelling, cultic practices which are detached from any ethical nuance. Rather, it is a matter of warning that Yhwh's sacred day is to be put before the pursuit of one's own interest (v. 13), obtained through unjust practices (see the connection between v. 13 and v. 3).

To recap: both Isa 1:13 and 58:13–14 relate observance of the Sabbath and the practice of justice. Explicitly in Isa 1:13 and through an addition in 58:13–14, the dichotomy between the injustice practised and the cultic observance of the Sabbath is brought into focus. The horizon of this denunciation is that of the community of Israel and of the relations between oppressors and oppressed within it. The unprecedented developments on the Sabbath in Isa 56:3–7 and 56:1–2 take place within an open debate. It is precisely in the search for a possible solution that one understands the quest for an authoritative point of reference, identified within the traditions of the Pentateuch.

3. Developing the Sabbath: Transformations of Exodus in Isa 56:1–8

Typically, the gradual extension of Sabbath observance to marginal categories in Israel and subsequently to every creature is ascribed to P's tradition of the creation.[39] Every individual, *qua* creature, can enter into relation with the Creator God by observing the Sabbath. This presupposes the idea of the observance of the Sabbath as abstention from work and from every activity on the seventh day. However, Isa 56:3–7 does not specify in detail what Sabbath observance consists of; in the same way, Isa 56:1–8 makes no mention of the creation tradition.[40] Thus, the idea of the Sabbath as abstention from all activity does not appear in the text. Furthermore, hypothesizing the connection with the creation traditions does not explain the identification of the Sabbath with the practice of justice.

Instead, it is the Exodus traditions that offer a point of reference. The singular conception of the Sabbath in Isaiah takes up and transforms Exod 31:12–17: on the one hand, the Sabbath, as exclusive sign of the covenant between Yhwh and Israel is extended to every human being; at the same time, the mode of Sabbath observance is redefined.

---

39. See among others Judith Gärtner, "'Keep Justice!' (Isaiah 56.1): Thoughts Regarding the Concept and Redaction History of a Universal Understanding of Ṣedaqa," in *Ṣedaqa and Torah in Post-Exilic Discourse*, ed. Susanne Gillmayr-Bucher and Maria Häusl, LHBOTS 640 (London: Bloomsbury T&T Clark, 2017), 86–100. For the importance of the creation in the process of universalization and inclusion of other peoples, see also Daniela Scialabba, *Creation and Salvation: Models of Relationship Between the God of Israel and the Nations in the Book of Jonah, in Psalm 33 (MT and LXX) and in the Novel "Joseph and Aseneth,"* FAT/II 106 (Tübingen: Mohr Siebeck, 2019), esp. 309–18.

40. However, the references to the creation and the rest of the seventh day are also absent in Isa 1:13 and 58:13–14. By contrast, the Creator God is mentioned in 66:22, which precedes the final mention of the Sabbath in Isaiah, in v. 23. In this case, however, there is no mention of the connection between the Sabbath and the practice of justice.

Observance of the Sabbath, expressed by the syntagma שמר + obj. שבת, occurs in the Hebrew Bible, other than in Isa 56:2, 4, 6, only in Exod 31:14, 16, within the pericope on the institution of the Sabbath on Sinai (Exod 31:12–17) and in Deut 5:12, within the Decalogue (Deut 5:6–21). With the plural form of the substantive ("my sabbaths," שבתותי), the syntagma occurs in Exod 31:13; Lev 19:3, 30; 26:2 and Isa 56:4.[41]

The connection between Isa 56:2, 4, 6 and Exod 31:12–17 is further marked by the occurrence of the combination of the verbs חלל and שמר in relation to the Sabbath. The combination, attested in Isa 56:2, 6, occurs in Exod 31:14: "you shall keep (ושמרתם) the Sabbath [...] the one who profanes it (מחלליה) shall be put to death."

The connection between Isa 56:3–8 and Exod 31:12–17 is reinforced additionally by the singular and plural alternation of the substantive שבת. Whereas Isa 56:4 records the plural form (ישמרו את־שבתותי, "they observe my Sabbaths"), in v. 6, the singular form of the noun comes into view in the syntagma כל־שמר שבת מחללו, "whoever observes the Sabbath without profaning it."

This alternation does not appear in the LXX, where the plural σάββατα comes into view both in v. 4 (ὅσοι ἂν φυλάξωνται τὰ σάββατά μου, "those who keep my sabbaths") and in v. 6 (καὶ πάντας τοὺς φυλασσομένους τὰ σάββατά μου μὴ βεβηλοῦν, "and all those who keep my sabbaths without profaning them"). The translator is harmonizing the joint presence of singular and plural. He probably perceived this as an anomaly and preferred the typical plural form of the LXX. Sometimes, the strangeness of the singular/plural alternation in 56:4, 6 is explained as a reflection of different conceptions of the Sabbath: the singular (v. 6) would reflect a monthly Sabbath, associated with the new moon and belonging to a pre-exilic legacy. By contrast, the plural (v. 4) would indicate a restatement of the feast which can then probably be ascribed to the practice of the weekly Sabbath.[42] However, it is difficult to think that a text, brief and cohesive and so ascribable to a single scribal hand (vv. 3–8), has preserved traces of two divergent conceptions of the Sabbath.

In my opinion, the alternation of the singular and plural forms of the substantive שבת is a marker that signals the reference to Exod 31:12–17. In Exod 31:13, the plural form (שבתתי, "my sabbaths") occurs as object of the verb שמר (אך את־שבתתי תשמרו, "you shall keep my sabbaths"); the singular form appears in the following v. 14 in the context of the possibility of a profanation (חלל) of the Sabbath: "you shall observe the Sabbath (ושמרתם את השבת) [...] whoever profanes it (מחלליה) will be put to death." An analogous alternation returns in Isa 56:3–7: v. 4 uses the plural, "my sabbaths" as object of the verb שמר (ישמרו את־שבתות, "you shall observe my Sabbaths"). When the

---

41. In Lev 19:3, 30; 26:2, the observance of the Sabbath is accompanied by the fear (ירא) of Yhwh or his sanctuary.

42. See, in this regard, Leszek Ruszkowski, "Der Sabbat bei Tritojesaja," in *Prophetie und Psalmen: Festschrift für Klaus Seybold zum 65. Geburtstag*, ed. Beat Huwyler, Hans Peter Mathys, and Beat Weber, AOAT 280 (Münster: Ugarit Verlag, 2001), 61–74 (73).

possible profanation of the Sabbath is involved (חלל, v. 6), the singular appears (כל־שמר שבת מחללו, "everyone who keeps my sabbath without profaning it").

Considered a scribal addition, Isa 56:1–2 is linked to vv. 3–8 by the expression שמר שבת מחללו (v. 2c). The connection which marks the reprise of Exod 31:12–17 in vv. 4, 6 acts as a scribal "hook" between the two units. Isaiah 56:1–2 even seems to be a polemical rereading of the idea of abstaining from "doing" work on the Sabbath day. Not doing any work (Exod 31:14, 15) is replaced by "not doing any evil." The lexical parallels indicated show an intentional reference in Isa 56:2, 4, 6 to Exod 31:12–17, the foundational text of the institution of the Sabbath.[43]

Set at the conclusion of the instructions for the construction of the Tent of Meeting, the instructions regarding the observing of the Sabbath signal the institution of a sacred time; repeated in 35:1–3 before the account of the construction of the Tabernacle, they mark the precedence of sacred time over sacred space.[44] Right from 31:14, the profanation (חלל) of sacred time is explicitly identified with doing any kind of work (עשה + מלאכה). The same expression is repeated in v. 15 and linked to the observance of rest on the seventh day in the face of the six days in which to carry out one's own works (ששת ימים יעשה מלאכה, "during six days shall work be done"). The alternation of six days of work and one—the seventh— of cessation from work is repeated in v. 17 and linked with a causal connection (כי) to the P account of the creation: "for in six days Yhwh made heaven and earth (ששת ימים עשה יהוה את־השמים ואת־הארץ), and on the seventh day he rested (וביום השביעי שבת), and took breath."

Thus described and accounted for the Sabbath is a perennial sign between Yhwh and Israel (v. 13: "that is the sign between me and you throughout your generations," אות הוא ביני וביניכם לדרתיכם; v. 17: "between me and the people of Israel that is a sign forever," ביני ובין בני ישראל אות הוא לעלם), and an "eternal covenant" (v. 16: ברית עולם). The Sabbath is, therefore, a sign of the foundational identity of Israel, established in the covenant on Sinai,[45] an identity that involves every generation of Israelites along with the generation that came out of Egypt. The profanation (חלל) of the Sabbath is punished by death (vv. 14, 15), the extreme sign of the separation of the individual from the community (v. 14: "that one shall be cut off from among his people," ונכרתה הנפש ההוא מקרב עמיה). Thus, to profane the Sabbath means no longer belonging to Israel.

---

43. If the repetition of a foundational text in Is 56:1–8 is plausible, the opposite direction of dependence does not find equally convincing explanations. The deliberate nature of the reference is underlined both by the exclusive lexical relations and by the *marker* of the sg./pl. alternation of the substantive שבת.

44. See Cornelis Houtmann, *Exodus: Volume 3. Chapters 20–40*, HCOT (Leuven: Peeters, 1999), 588.

45. Dominik Markl and Georg Fischer, *Das Buch Exodus*, NSK.AT 2 (Stuttgart: Katholisches Bibelwerk, 2009), 318: the eternal covenant is none other than the covenant at Sinai.

Isaiah 56:1–8 takes up Exod 31:12–17, relating to the institution of the Sabbath, and places it at the service of a new message: on the one hand, the Sabbath (a) is no longer the exclusive property of Israel; on the other hand, the Sabbath (b) is no longer identified with the seventh day rest but is gradually bound up with the practice of justice.

(a) In Isa 56:4–6, Sabbath observance makes possible the inclusion of eunuchs and strangers in the community of Israel assembled in the "house of Yhwh." They can come to the temple (vv. 5, 7) and offer sacrifices and holocausts. Eunuchs and foreigners, categories otherwise marginalized and excluded from the community, can enter the temple by means of the practice of the Sabbath.[46] The involvement of foreigners in the observance of the Sabbath was contemplated in Deut 5:14. In the observance of the Sabbath rest, the *pater familias* is required to involve also the foreigner who is "in your gates" (וגרך אשר בשעריך). The perspective outlined in Isa 56:3–8 is decidedly broader. Deuteronomy 5:14 does not envisage any inclusion in the community for the resident foreigner who observes the Sabbath; on the contrary, this is what is envisaged in Isa 56:6–7. In Isa 56:1–2, in a still more singular way, the observance of the Sabbath is destined for every human being without any further reference to membership of the chosen people.

(b) Isaiah 56:2 takes up the syntagma שמר שבת מחללו (v. 7) to refer to the observance of the Sabbath, thus signalling the reference to Exod 31:12–17. The vocabulary and the syntax indicate that the practice of the Sabbath in 56:2c is being identified with that of the justice which is expressed in v. 2d by the clause ושמר ידו מעשות כל־רע (see §1). This expression presents vocabulary and syntax that are unique within the Hebrew Bible. The syntagma שמר + obj. יד is *hapax*; the pair of verbs שמר and עשה is attested only twice in Isaiah (56:1, 2). Characteristic of the Deuteronomistic vocabulary, it is typically employed in the Hebrew Bible for the observing of the commandments; or else to indicate the practice of justice (e.g. Ps 106:3; Isa 56:1). The use of the verbs שמר (+ obj. יד) and עשה in 56:2 is a *unicum* in the Hebrew Bible. The singularity of the expression ושמר ידו מעשות כל־רע ("and the one who keeps his hand from doing any evil," 56:2d) can be explained

---

46. See the possible reference to Deut 23:2–10. The concern with the exclusion of these categories from the community appears also in the words of the foreigners and eunuchs in Isa 56:3. The foreigners fear to be separated (בדל, hi.) from the people of Yhwh. The eunuch fears to be a "dried tree" (עץ יבש). The expression is certainly referring to his concern for his own sterility and the lack of descendants. However, Yhwh's response indicates the overcoming of the eunuch's marginal position. In fact, Yhwh does not promise descendants but "a place and a name" (v. 5) within the sacred (בביתי) and civil (בחומתי) space destined for the people who belong to him. Although the syntagma כרת ni. + subj. שם can indicate the permanence of the name of the dead person in the community (e.g. Ruth 4:10), an interpretative suggestion is possible. The same verb כרת *niphal*, employed in Exod 31:14 to indicate the separation from the community of the Israelite who does not observe the Sabbath (ונכרתה הנפש ההוא מקרב עמיה), indicates in Isa 56:5 the inclusion in the community of the eunuch who observes it: his memory will not fail within the community (לא יכרת).

as a deliberate syntactical calque of the preceding v. 2c: שמר שבת מחללו ("the one who keeps the Sabbath without profaning it").

The connection with Exod 31:12–17 provides an additional suggestion: the prohibition of doing any work (see the phrase עשה + מלאכה), which summarizes the Sabbath observance required in Exod 31:14, 15, seems to find a singular *relecture* in Isa 56:2d. From not "doing any work," there is a movement to not doing any evil (phrase השע + רע): in Isa 56:1–2, the observance of the Sabbath finds a new form of actualization.

To sum up: Isa 56:3–7 and, subsequently, vv. 1–2 refer to the foundational text on the institution of the Sabbath (Exod 31:12–17). However, neither in 56:2 nor in 56:7 is there any reference to the rest of the seventh day envisaged in Exod 31:12–17. By contrast, in Isa 56:1–2, the Sabbath comes to be identified with the practice of justice. This identification is accompanied by a kind of universalization of the Sabbath: any human being (Israelite and not) can observe the Sabbath and so be proclaimed blessed. It remains to find a plausible background for this singular interpretation of the Sabbath.

4. The Background and the Stakes

The connection between Sabbath and justice, like the gradual universalization of the Sabbath attested in Isaiah, are unique in the Hebrew Bible. In the attempt to account for this singular development, Hartenstein calls on the eschatological nuance of the Sabbath.[47] Not only Israel but also the peoples will be judged on the basis of their observance of the Sabbath. In particular, Isa 56:1–2 should be read as a reversal of Isa 1:10–17: cultic and social solidarity is what establishes the peoples' belonging to Yhwh. The eschatological perspective characterizes the mention of the Sabbath in Isa 66:23;[48] it is not present, however, in the other Isaian occurrences of the Sabbath (Isa 1:13; 56:1–8 and 58:13–14).

The redefinition of the observance of the Sabbath as the practice of justice leads to the supposition of problems relating to the observance of the abstention from work on the seventh day.[49] Furthermore, the gradual extension of the

---

47. See Friedhelm Hartenstein, "Der Sabbat als Zeichen und heilige Zeit. Zur Theologie des Ruhetages im Alten Testament," in *Das Fest: Jenseits des Alltags*, ed. Martin Ebner, JBTh 18 (Neukirchen-Vluyn: Neukirchener Verlag, 2004), 83–102 (129–30).

48. Ibid. 130.

49. Thus Yigal Bloch, "Judean Identity during the Exile: Concluding Deals on a Sabbath in Babylonia and Egypt under the Neo-Babylonian and the Achaemenid Empires," in *A Question of Identity: Social, Political, and Historical Aspects of Identity Dynamics in Jewish and Other Contexts*, ed. Dikla Rivkin Katz et al. (Berlin: de Gruyter Oldenbourg, 2019), 43–69 (45): "The overall impression received from the prophetic books (except Amos) and from Nehemiah's narrative is that the Judeans, both before and after the Babylonian exile, were not enthusiastic about refraining from at least some of the activities forbidden on the Sabbath."

Sabbath outside the borders of Israel brings on stage a context of international relations in which Israel negotiates her own identity.⁵⁰

The biblical texts already attest difficulties in the observance of the Sabbath as abstention from work; it is what appears in Neh 13:15–22. The problems of Sabbath observance which are behind Nehemiah's provisions (vv. 20–22) are connected with the agricultural harvest and trade.⁵¹ The violations of the Sabbath rest include the trading of the grape, the transport of mounds of cereal (or fruit), and of wine and figs made to arrive in Jerusalem (v. 15), including the import of fish by the inhabitants of Tyre who were resident in Jerusalem. The opposition to Nehemiah's provisions lets us understand the disadvantages deriving from it: inactivity on the Sabbath favours the spoiling of foodstuffs. Moreover, if, on the one hand, closing the gates of Jerusalem preserves its identity, it, on the other hand, cuts the city off from the regular flow of commercial transactions and from interaction with foreign traders (e.g. Phoenician merchants coming from Tyre).

Evidence from Elephantine and Āl-Yāḫūdu confirms a certain flexibility with regard to observance of the Sabbath rest. The Sabbath is mentioned only sporadically at Elephantine, in *ostraka* containing private communications, dated to the first half of the fifth century BCE.⁵²

The *ostrakon* TAD D 7.16 (= CG 152),⁵³ written on a Friday, announces a consignment of vegetables for the following day, i.e. the Sabbath; Islaḥ, the woman to whom the message is addressed (שלם יסלח, l. 1), is urged to look after the arrival of the load on the Sabbath:

> Legumes I shall dispatch tomorrow. Meet the boat tomorrow on Sabbath (ערקי אלפא מחר בשבה, l. 2)
>
> Lest, if they get lost (הן יאבד, l. 3), by the life of YHH (היליהה), if not (= surely) yo[ur] life I shall take [...]

---

50. On Trito-Isaiah's being a privileged text to explore the question of the identity of Israel, see Andreas Schuele, "Who is the True Israel? Community, Identity, and Religious Commitment in Third Isaiah (Isaiah 56–66)," *Int* 73 (2019): 174–84.

51. A similar criticism of Sabbath observance pertinent to trade is attested in Jer 17:19–27.

52. See Bezalel Porten, *Archives from Elephantine: The Life of an Ancient Jewish Military Colony* (Berkeley/Los Angeles, CA: University of California Press, 1968), 126, and "The Religion of the Jews of Elephantine," *JNES* 28 (1969): 116–18. For an overview of Sabbath practice in Elephantine, see Luz Doering, *Schabbat: Sabbathalacha und -praxis im antiken Judentum und Urchristentum*, TSAJ 78 (Tübingen: Mohr Siebeck, 1999), 23–42.

53. Bezalel Porten and Ada Yardeni, eds., *Textbook of Aramaic Documents from Ancient Egypt. Volume IV. Ostraca & Assorted Inscriptions* (Winona Lake, IN: Eisenbrauns, 1999). For the edition of the collection Clermont-Ganneau, see Hélène Lozachmeur, *La Collection Clermont-Ganneau: Ostraca, épigraphes sur Jarre étiquettes de bois*. Vol. 1, Mémoires de L'académie des Inscriptions et Belles-Lettres 35 (Paris: De Boccard, 2006).

According to a common interpretation, the violation of the Sabbath rest attested by this *ostrakon* is a wholly exceptional occurrence.[54] This is indicated by the expression, "by the life of YHH (הילידה)" (l. 3), which underlines the urgency of the appeal and the exceptional nature of the situation. Furthermore, according to Pablo Díez Herrera, the syntagma בשבה (l. 2) should be interpreted "before the Sabbath": the sender knows that it is forbidden to transport goods on the Sabbath and so urges that the business is concluded before the evening of the Preparation Day.[55] This interpretation cannot be deduced from the text: the expression "by the life of YHH" is common in the *ostraka*, and indicates simply a desire, an oath or a serious warning.[56] Additionally, the expression "before the Sabbath" is attested elsewhere in the *ostraka* in the form עד יום שבה (e.g. CG 186 = TAD D 7.35, l. 7). It is not clear, therefore, why בשבה (CG 152 l. 2) should have been used with this meaning instead of the normal phrase, עד יום שבה.

TAD D 7.48 also attests the request of a consignment of food ("a little bread," זעיר לחמא, ll. 2–3) on the Sabbath day:

> Dispatch to me… that day
> Dispatch to me a little (זעיר, l. 2)
> Bread this day (לחמא יומא זנה, l. 3)
> And now bring (or: they brought) (וכענת היתיו, l. 4)
> To me on the Sabbath (לי בש תא, l. 5).

Differently, according to TAD D 7.35 (= CG 186), consignment of salt and fish must be carried out before the Sabbath:

> Dispatch to me (l. 4)
> … and salt
> Until (= before) the Sabbath day (עד יום שבה, l. 7)
> In the hand of (= with) Meshullam 3 fishes and […] (l. 8).

The examples reveal a fluid situation:[57] on the one hand, the Sabbath rest is observed (e.g. CG 186 = TAD D 7.35); on the other, there appears a flexibility in

---

54. Thus, among others, Porten, *Archives*, 127; Bloch, "Judean Identity," 57.

55. Pablo Díez Herrera, "Clermont-Ganneau 152. El sábado en Elefantina ¿Una observancia laxa?," *EstBib* 77 (2019): 315–44 (338).

56. See Lozachmeur, *Collection*, 529–8. See also André Lemaire, "Judean Identity in Elephantine: Everyday Life according to the Ostraca," in *Judah and the Judeans in the Achaemenid Period: Negotiating Identity in an International Context*, ed. Oded Lipschits, Gary N. Knoppers, and Manfred Oeming (Winona Lake, IN: Eisenbrauns, 2011), 365–73 (366).

57. To the examples that mention the Sabbath, we can add the studies relating to the dating of the papyrus contracts originating from Elephantine. The conversion of the dates appended to the contracts has enabled the identification of some contracts that were drafted on the Sabbath day; see Bloch, "Judean Identity," 57–64.

this regard (CG 152 = TAD D7.16; TAD D 7.48). Such flexibility can be ascribed to circumstances relating to commerce and transport, especially of perishable goods.[58] As Reinhard Achenbach summarizes: "The religion of the merchants [...] stands in some tension to the religion of a priestly dominated temple community."[59]

Similar flexibility emerges from the contracts originating from the colony of Āl-Yāḫūdu, as well as from those of the Murašû archive.[60] The study of the dating recorded on the tablets has enabled the identification of some contracts drafted on the Sabbath day (three tablets from the Murašû archive and eight coming from Āl-Yāḫūdu and its surroundings). These documents indicate that abstention from work and from business was not perceived as binding on the Sabbath day; in particular, according to Yigal Bloch, there is no trace of a "conscious effort on the part of ethnic Judeans in Babylonia to refrain from participating in transactions concluded on a Sabbath."[61]

The fluidity in the observance of the Sabbath rest attested by the biblical and extra-biblical evidence offers some insights for understanding the peculiar presentation of the Sabbath in Isa 56:1–8. That Isa 56:1–8 is antecedent to the definition of the Sabbath rest on the seventh day is to be excluded. Hints to Exod 31:12–17 in Isa 56:1–8 indicate that the Sabbath observance as prescribed in Exod 31:12–17 was known and transformed as to the content of the observance and to its extension. The Sabbath is identified with the practice of justice and is no longer the exclusive marker of the identity of Israel.

Against the background of the extra-biblical evidence, the need to redefine the Sabbath in new and more inclusive terms can be a response to the fluidity of the observance of the Sabbath rest. In the face of the difficulty of keeping the Sabbath rest as a sign of identity, the scribes at work in the text of Isaiah reformulate the Sabbath. In Isa 56:1–2, the Sabbath, identified with the practice of justice, calls for the openness of Israel to the nations: each individual who observes the Sabbath is not included in the community of the people of Yhwh nor, even less, in his sanctuary (see v. 5). Rather, they are simply proclaimed blessed (v. 2), a condition which does not imply membership of Israel nor entry into the covenant with Yhwh. In this perspective, the transformation of the Sabbath into something ethical becomes common ground on which Israel can be open to relation with the nations. Each person, Israelite and non-Israelite, can be blessed by practising justice. This is what it means to honour the Sabbath.

---

58. With regard to CG 152, Lozachmeur (*Collection*, 93) underlines that the consignment of fresh vegetables is not incompatible with the demands of the Sabbath.

59. See Reinhard Achenbach, "*Lex Sacra* and Sabbath in the Pentateuch," *ZAR* 22 (2016): 101–9 (108).

60. For a presentation and discussion of the material, see Bloch, "Judean Identity," 46–55, and "Was the Sabbath Observed in Āl-Yāḫūdu in the Early Decades of the Babylonian Exile? Reply to Oded Tammuz, 'The Sabbath as the Seventh Day of the Week and a Day of Rest: Since When?,' *ZAW* 131 (2019) 287–294," *ZAW* 132 (2020): 117–20.

61. See Bloch, "Judean Identity," 55.

5. Some Concluding Remarks

In the late Persian and/or Hellenistic period, at a time when Israel was negotiating its own identity with the nations, transforming the Sabbath into a purely ethical phenomenon offered the possibility to overcome the difficulties in observing the rest of the seventh day. At the same time, the emphasis on the ethical at the expense of the cult transformed the Sabbath into something of a universal value, a ground of encounter with the nations. The biblical and extra-biblical evidence help to shed light on the possible *Sitz im Leben* of Isa 56:1–8. However, one question remains open: what was the authority behind the revision of Exod 31:12–17 and this intervention on such a crucial point for the identity of Israel?

If it is true that the first principle of authority comes from the divine word invoked right from v. 1 (כה אמר יהוה), perhaps it is possible to add another element. The study of the texts that mention the Sabbath in Isaiah has highlighted how Isa 56:1–8 is situated against the background of the tension between Sabbath and justice attested elsewhere in the book, in framing texts (1:13 in 1:2–20) and in secondary additions (Isa 58:13–14). The scribes responsible for 56:3–8 and its subsequent expansion (vv. 1–2) take up and enrich the thread of the connection between Sabbath and justice. Therefore, the unity of Isaiah is on the one hand presupposed; but at the same time, it is pursued by the scribes working on the texts. Indeed, several cross-references connect the new texts to the more extensive collection. It is possible, therefore that the unity of the prophetic book, presupposed by the scribal work, offers the scribes an authoritative point of reference for rereading and transforming the traditions of the Torah. At the same time, scribal expertise in the more extensive collection offers the scribe the chance of expressing new ideas by employing textual material already available. Reference to the figure of an authoritative prophet is replaced by the reference to a prophetic book that is equally authoritative. It seems that mastering the prophetic book and its compositional threads endows the scribes with the authority needed to support an unprecedented Sabbath development.

Chapter 6

CONCEPT OF HISTORY IN THE BOOK OF ISAIAH

Peter Dubovský

This paper studies direct references to historical events and persons in the book of Isaiah (the BoI).[1] To this aim, I gather and analyze all the direct references. Based on this analysis I suggest that the scribes, editors, and final redactor(s) of the BoI[2] made an effort to present an alternative vision of human history. The fact that these references were inserted into the BoI at later stages of its redaction betrays the redactor's strategy in structuring the book. This conclusion leads us to the key question of the present volume: Are the direct historical references spread out through the BoI a sign of the redactor's intent to create a unified vision of human history? In other words, did the direct references support the impression that the BoI should be ultimately read as a unity?

1. *Direct References*

It is reasonable to assume that, beside other devices, the redactor of the BoI used these references to convey his concept of history and to create overarching links among passages that are otherwise vaguely connected. There are six direct references that can be divided into two types.

---

1. There are numerous indirect references to historical events, such as the conquest of Egypt (20:4–6), the fall of Assyria (14:25), the fall of Babylon (43:14), the return from the exile (14:2–3), etc. However, I will not analyze these references for two reasons. First, many of the allusions and references are too vague and allow multiple interpretations; secondly, a similar analysis would go far beyond the page limit of this paper.

2. In this paper I will use the term "the redactor" to refer to the scribes responsible for the final editorial process of the BoI.

1.1. Type I: "In the days of..." (PR + בימי)

This expression occurs in 1:1 (Uzziah to Hezekiah; 767–687 BCE)[3] and in 7:1 (Ahaz; 732/31–716/15 BCE). In the Bible, it refers to a broad span of time. Nevertheless, the period to which the expression PR +בימי refers is distinctly defined by the point of reference (PR), which can be a person or an event.[4]

Thus, the expression PR + בימי is not a peculiarity of the BoI, but it occurs in the works of other prophets.[5] Striking similarities between the superscriptions in the BoI and in other prophetic books suggest that there was a redactor who used stereotyped formulae to link the prophecies with historical figures.[6] Consequently, the expression בימי in Isa 1:1 and 7:1 can rightly be considered an intervention of later redactor(s) who likewise edited other prophetic books.[7] The redactor's intervention can be noticed when 7:1 is compared with 2 Kgs 16:5:[8]

---

3. The expression, for stylistic reasons, is not repeated before each name. H. G. M. Williamson, *A Critical and Exegetical Commentary on Isaiah 1–27. I. Isaiah 1–5*, ICC (London: T&T Clark, 2006), 13.

4. It can be linked with kings (Gen 14:1; Saul in 1 Sam 17:12, cf. also 1 Chr 13:3; David in 2 Sam 21:1, cf. also 1 Chr 7:2; Solomon in 1 Kgs 10:21, cf. 2 Chr 9:20; Asa in 1 Kgs 22:47; Pekah in 2 Kgs 15:29; Hezekiah in 2 Kgs 20:19/Isa 39:8/2 Chr 32:26, cf. also 1 Chr 4:41; Uzziah in Zech 14:5; Jotham in 1 Chr 5:17; Ahasuerus in Esth 1:1) and with an important person (Abraham in Gen 26:1, 15, 18; Shamgar and Jael in Judg 5:6, Gideon in Judg 8:28; Jeshua in Neh 12:7, Eliashib, Joiada, Johanan and Jaddua in Neh 12:22; Joiakim in Neh 12:26, King David as a singer in Neh 12:46, Zerubbabel in Neh 12:47; Abijah in 2 Chr 13:20; Zechariah in 2 Chr 26:5). Rarely it can have a metaphoric meaning, thus a season (wheat harvest in Gen 30:14; Judg 15:1, cf. also 2 Sam 21:9). However, the point of reference can also be a specific period in Israelite history (the sojourn of Jacob's sons in Egypt in Gen 47:9; Philistine occupation in Judg 15:20; the period of Judges in Ruth 1:1).

5. The expression occurs as a superscription linking the prophetic collection with kings; see Hos 1:1; Amos 1:1; Mic 1:1; Jer 1:1–2; Zeph 1:1; this is called "synchronistic royal date"; see Gene M. Tucker, "Prophetic Superscriptions and the Growth of a Canon," in *Canon and Authority: Essays in Old Testament Religion and Theology*, ed. George W. Coats and Burke O. Long (Philadelphia, PA: Fortress, 1977), 60.1977 However, it also introduces a section of a prophetic collection (Isa 6:1; Jer 3:6; 26:18; 35:1).

6. David Noel Freedman, "Headings in the Books of the Eighth-Century Prophets," in *Divine Commitment and Human Obligation: Selected Writings of David Noel Freedman*, ed. John R. Huddlestun (Grand Rapids, MI: Eerdmans, 1997), 380–1.

7. Hans Wildberger, *Isaiah 1–12: A Continental Commentary*, trans. Thomas H. Trapp (Minneapolis, MN: Fortress, 1991), 3; Joseph Blenkinsopp, *Isaiah 1–39: A New Translation with Introduction and Commentary*, AB 19 (New York: Doubleday, 2000), 174–5; Willem A. M. Beuken, *Jesaja 1–12*, HThKAT (Freiburg: Herder, 2003), 59; Williamson, *Isaiah 1–5*, 15–17.

8. For the review of scholarly opinions on the mutual dependence of 2 Kgs 16 and Isa 7 see Blenkinsopp, *Isaiah 1–39*, 229–30; John D. W. Watts, *Isaiah 1–33*, WBC 24 (Nashville, TN: Thomas Nelson, 2005), 6–16.

אז	יעלה	רצין	(2 Kgs 16:5)
ויהי בימי אחז...	עלה	רצין	(Isa 7:1)

Even though this expression appears in other parts of the Bible, it becomes a hallmark of the post-exilic intervention.[9] This observation allows us to conclude that the Type I formula is the hallmark of a post-exilic redactional intervention that aimed at structuring the BoI according to historical periods.[10] Consequently, Isa 1:1 situates Isa 1–39 into the reign of four kings,[11] and Isa 7:1 links the oracles in Isa 7–9 with Ahaz.

1.2. Type II: "In the year" (בשנת)

These expressions point to a concrete event and use the word שנה. They can be divided into two subgroups:

a. בשנת followed by an infinitive construct

There are three formulae in this subgroup. The first two refer to the death of a king (Isa 6:1 and 14:28) and the third one to the campaign of Sargon's officials against Ashdod (20:1[12]). The first two expressions read בשנת־מות המלך (MT). It can be translated "in the year of king (Uzziah)'s death" (6:1)[13] or "in the year when the king (Ahaz) died" (14:28).[14] The former interprets מות as a construct form of the noun מָוֶת. The latter understands מות as an alternative form of the infinitive construct מוּת (cf. Num 16:29; 2 Kgs 3:5; Qoh 3:19[15]). Indeed, all occurrences of בשנת followed by a verb have the infinitive in the construct form (Isa 20:1; 2 Kgs 25:27 // Jer 52:31). Moreover, this reading is supported by LXX and the Old Latin manuscripts. Given the overwhelming textual evidence and since the superscriptions in 6:1; 14:28 and 20:1 (בשנת בא תרתן) were most likely done by the same

---

9. Thus, Nehemiah (12:7, 22, 26, 46, 47) and the Chronicles (1 Chr 4:41; 5:17; 7:2; 13:3; 2 Chr 9:20; 13:20; 26:5; 32:26).

10. It has been suggested that the intent to link the prophetic corpora with historical periods corresponds to the Deuteronomistic mind set; see Tucker, "Prophetic Superscriptions and the Growth of a Canon," 68–70. The occurrences presented above suggest that it is more reasonable to link the date part of the superscriptions with the post-exilic scribal mindset as reflected in Neh 12 and in the Chronicles.

11. For the superscription introducing chs. 1–39, see Beuken, *Jesaja 1–12*, 56–7. Some scholars think that the superscription is intended for the whole book of Isaiah Wildberger, *Isaiah 1–12*, 3; Williamson, *Isaiah 1–5*, 14–15.

12. Contrary to 6:1 and 14:28, this verse uses a foreign king as a point of reference; cf. 2 Kgs 25:8 that refers to Nebuchadnezzar.

13. Beuken, *Jesaja 1–12*, 160; Williamson, *Isaiah 6–12*, 11.

14. Cf. NRSV, JPS, NKJV.

15. *HALOT*, 563; *DCH* V, 192. The form of the infinitive construct would be thus identical with the infinitive absolute.

hand, I prefer interpreting מות as an infinitive construct, i.e. "in the year when the king (Uzziah/Ahaz) died."

These two expressions (6:1 and 14:28) have, as a point of reference, the death of a king. This is in striking contrast with similar expressions that refer to a year of the king's reign or to the moment of his enthronement (the first regnal year of Merodach-baladan in 2 Kgs 25:27/Jer 52:31; the accession of Cyrus in Isa 44:28–45:25). Beside Isa 38:1 // 2 Kgs 20:1, which refers to Hezekiah's demise, the death as a point of reference appears only in 2 Kgs 3:5 (Ahab) and 14:7 (probably Joash[16]). These two occurrences may suggest that taking the death of a king as a point of reference was a northern way of synchronizing the kings. The redactor, probably by means of the northern style, recalls the death of three major kings: Uzziah, Ahaz, and Hezekiah. In this way, the reign of the kings from Uzziah to Hezekiah in Isa 1:1[17] is overshadowed by the immediate or incumbent death of these other kings (6:1; 14:28; 20:1).

b. שנה preceded by a number

This is the most common way of dating the events in the Bible and it occurs in Isa 36:1.[18] Despite the complex discussion regarding Hezekiah's 14th year, this event is dated by the Neo-Assyrian annals to Sennacherib's campaign in his third regnal year (701 BCE). This formula introduces the last section of First Isaiah (chs. 36–39).

1.3. *Implications*

This analysis suggests that the redactor inserted the direct references in six places in the First Isaiah. Even an approximate linking of the direct references with an absolute chronology shows that these references are organized in the correct chronological order:

1:1 In the days of (Type I)	(767–687)
6:1 In the year when Uzziah died (Type IIa)	(739)
7:1 In the days of Ahaz (Type I)	(743–716/15)
14:28 In the year when Ahaz died (Type IIa)	(716/15)
20:1 In the year when Tartan came (Type IIa)	(713/711)
36:1 In the 14th year of Hezekiah (Type IIb)	(701)

---

16. For the analysis of this unusual formula, see Peter Dubovský, "Usual and Unusual Concluding Formulas in 2 Kings 13–14: A Reconstruction of the Old Greek and its Implication for the Literary History," *Bib* 101 (2020): 321–39.

17. Jotham is mentioned only in Isa 1:1. Isa 7:1 has Jotham as the father of Ahaz.

18. For the synchronization using ויהי, cf. 2 Kgs 12:2; 18:1; 25:1, 27; Zech 7:1.

2. Indirect References

The second way of connecting the oracles with historical periods is a reference to kings whose reign can be identified from extra-biblical sources.

2.1. Levantine Kings

The first reference to non-Judahite kings surfaces in Isa 7–9, namely, Rezin king of Aram (7:1, 4, 8; 8:6; 9:10) and Pekah, king of Israel (7:1; as son of Remaliah in 7:4, 5, 9; 8:6). The Bible presents the military conflict known as the Syro-Ephraimite war (734–732 BCE) in four versions: 2 Kgs 15:28–30; 2 Kgs 16:5–9; 2 Chr 28:5–15, and Isa 7–9. A comparison of the versions shows that the redactors exclude the siege of Jerusalem (cf. 2 Kgs 16:5–9) and its conquest (cf. 2 Chr 28:5–15). Moreover, Isaiah 7–9 has some additions. The addition, 7:2–9, gives the impression that the redactor wants to present the early stage of the conflict, namely, the pressure of two local powers upon Ahaz, their intention to substitute him, and Ahaz's fear. Isaiah's critique in 7:10–17 implies that Ahaz did not follow Isaiah's advice. Moreover, the Hebrew and Greek versions of 8:6 imply that Judah entered into a discussion with Pekah and Rezin and joined the anti-Assyrian coalition. Even though this interpretation does not correspond to the Judahite version (2 Kgs 16:5–9), it fits Isaiah's critique in 7:10–17 and 8:6.[19] Finally, the redactors present the conflict as a local skirmish and not primarily as an Assyrian campaign (contrary to 2 Kgs 15:28–30 and Tiglath-pileser III's annals). Assyria's role was to punish Judah for its unfaithfulness (contrary to 2 Kgs 15:28–30).

In sum, the reference to Tiglath-pileser III narrows down "in the days of Ahaz" to 734–732 BCE. The military conflict is presented as a local war in which Judah is attacked by the Israelites and the Arameans. This crisis would be resolved by a foreign king, the king of Assyria.

---

19. The *crux interpretum* is the expression "this people has refused the waters of Shiloah" (8:6). Roberts has suggested that "this people" should refer to Israel, the northern kingdom; see Roberts, *First Isaiah*, 133. Most scholars, including the author, also agree that Ahaz did not join the anti-Assyrian coalition; see Peter Dubovský, "Tiglath-pileser III's Campaigns in 734–732 B.C.: Historical Background of Isa 7, 2 Kgs 15–16 and 2 Chr 27–28," *Bib* 87 (2006): 153–70. Even though this is the most reasonable interpretation, we must be humble in our conclusions. This reconstruction is based on 2 Kgs 16:5–9, which assumes a particular literary genre (1 Kgs 15:16–22). This obviously raises the question about the historical reliability of 2 Kgs 16:5–9. On the other hand, the Assyrian sources list (Jehu)ahaz among the tribute-bearers (RINAP 1 47 r. 6'–13'). Since among the listed are kings who willingly collaborated (Panammu of Sam'al) as well as those who rebelled against Assyria (Mittinti of Ashqelon), we must admit that the Assyrian sources allow both the interpretation of the books of Kings and Isaiah.

2.2. Assyrian Kings

The BoI has the highest concentration of references to Assyria in the whole Hebrew Bible.[20] The BoI mentions by name only Sargon (20:1), Sennacherib (36:1, 17, 21, 37), and Esarhaddon (37:38). The BoI also refers to Assyrian kings that are not named (7:17, 20; 8:4, 7; 10:12; 38:6):

Unnamed Assyrian kings (7:17, 20; 8:4, 7; 10:12)	(859–722)
Sargon (20:1)	(713/711)
Sennacherib (36:1, 17, 21, 37[21])	(705–681)
Esarhaddon became king (37:38)	(681)
An unnamed Assyrian king (38:6)	(669–609)

The redactor leaves the Assyrian king in 7:17, 20; 8:4, 7 without a name, even though according to 2 Kgs 15–16 he is identified as Tiglath-pileser III.[22] Moreover, the redactor skips Shalmaneser V who is mentioned in 2 Kgs 17:1–6.[23] The fact that the last Assyrian king in the BoI is Esarhaddon implies that the redactor omits Ashurbanipal, even though the authors of the First Isaiah had to be familiar with his propaganda.[24] Furthermore, 2 Kgs 23:29 refers indirectly to the end of Assyrian empire that is also omitted in Isaiah.

To summarize, the redactor of the First Isaiah skips the Assyrian kings from Shalmaneser III to Shalmaneser V (859–722 BCE), even though the Israelites and the Judahite scribes were familiar with some of these kings. Similarly, the redactor passes over the last Assyrian kings from Ashurbanipal through Ashur-uballit II (669–609 BCE). The whole Assyrian history is, thus, reduced to three kings: Sargon, Sennacherib, and Esarhaddon. The kings before and after are conflated into unnamed individuals. The choice of these three kings might have been motivated by their ignominious ends.[25] If this supposition is correct, then the redactor

---

20. All the references are in the First Isaiah, cf. Isa 7:18, 20; 8:4, 7; 10:5, 12, 24; 11:11, 16; 14:25; 19:23–25; 20:1, 4, 6; 23:13; 27:13; 30:31; 36–38 (19×); except 52:4 that refers to the Assyrian oppression as a past event. For studies, see Peter Machinist, "Assyria and its Image in the First Isaiah," *JAOS* 103 (1983): 719–22; Shawn Zelig Aster, *Reflections of Empire in Isaiah 1–39: Responses to Assyrian Ideology* (Atlanta, GA: SBL Press, 2017).

21. See also 36:14; 37:9.

22. The reference in Isa 10:12 does not have an equivalent in 2 Kgs 15–16. It is part of the dirge regarding Assyria (10:5–19). If viewed in the context of chs. 7–12, the unnamed king of Assyria might have been the same as the one mentioned in chs. 7–8.

23. In addition, the First Isaiah does not mention the Chronicler's episode on Assyrian deportation of Manasseh (2 Chr 33:10–13).

24. Peter Dubovský, *Hezekiah and the Assyrian Spies: Reconstruction of the Neo-Assyrian Intelligence Services and its Significance for 2 Kings 18–19*, BibOr 49 (Rome: Pontificio Istituto Biblico, 2006), 189–238.

25. Sargon died in battle and was not properly buried. Sennacherib was assassinated by his sons. Esarhaddon suffered from illness and died at Haran *en route* to Egypt. I express my deep gratitude for this observation to my colleague Anthony SooHoo.

of BoI follows similar logic as when he referred to the death of the kings (see above).

Among these three Assyrian kings in the First Isaiah Sennacherib stands out. Sargon is mentioned as a background figure to describe the Assyrian invasion of Ashdod. Similarly, Esarhaddon in 37:8 is mentioned only as a successor of Sennacherib. Sennacherib's letters sent to Hezekiah refer to the glorious actions of his predecessors, "kings of Assyria" (37:11, 18). A comparison of 37:8–13 with 36:18–20 shows that Sennacherib's propaganda used the expression "kings of Assyria" (37:11), a phrase that betrays Sennacherib's perception of history. He presents all the kings of Assyria before him as unnamed kings. Thus, Sennacherib emerges from the biblical texts as the apex not only of Assyrian military history but also of its propaganda.[26] Consequently, the angel's annihilation of the Assyrian troops at the gate of Jerusalem and the murder of Sennacherib prefigures the end of the Assyrian empire, its military power and propaganda, even though the empire continued through Esarhaddon (37:38) and an unnamed king (38:6).[27]

Another particularity of the First Isaiah is the reference to the Assyrian conquest of Ashdod in Isa 20:1, dated to Sargon's 11th (RINAP 2 1:234–255) or 9th (RINAP 2 82 vi 13'–8") regnal year, 713 and 711 BCE respectively.[28] The annals attribute it directly to Sargon II, not to his officials, as the BoI does. It is quite reasonable to assume that the Isaianic version is more plausible since Assyrian royal scribes gladly attributed to the Assyrian kings even the victories that were accomplished by their military officials.[29] However, Isa 20:1 is the only reference to Sargon in the entire Bible. The particularity of this reference can be grasped when compared to the references to other Assyrian kings.

Canonical books					
Source	Tiglath-pileser/Pul	Shalmaneser	Sargon	Sennacherib	Esarhaddon
Kings	2 Kgs 15:19, 29; 16:7, 10	2 Kgs 17:3; 18:9		2 Kgs 18:13; 19:16, 20, 36	2 Kgs 19:37
Chronicles	1 Chr 5:6, 26; 2 Chr 28:20			2 Chr 32:1, 2, 9, 10, 22	
Ezra					Ezra 4:2
Isaiah	Isa 66:19		Isa 20:1	Isa 36:1; 37:17, 21, 37	Isa 37:38

26. See Peter Dubovský, "Inverting Assyrian Propaganda in Isaiah's Historiography: Writing the Hezekiah–Sennacherib Conflict in the Light of the Ashurbanipal–Teumman War," in *The History of Isaiah: The Formation of the Book and Its Presentation of the Past*, ed. Jacob Stromberg and J. Todd Hibbard, FAT 150 (Tübingen: Mohr Siebeck, 2021), 365–406.

27. Peter Dubovský, "Assyrian Downfall through Isaiah's Eyes (2 Kings 15–23): The Historiography of Representation," *Bib* 89 (2008): 1–16.

28. See Andreas Fuchs, *Die Annalen des Jahres 711 v. Chr. nach Prismenfragmenten aus Ninive und Assur*, SAAS 8 (Helsinki: The Neo-Assyrian Text Corpus Project, 1998), 1–17.

29. See also Eckart Frahm, "Samaria, Hamath, and Assyria's Conquests in the Levant in the Late 720s BCE: The Testimony of Sargon II's Inscriptions," in *The Last Days of the Kingdom of Israel*, ed. Shuichi Hasegawa et al. BZAW 511 (Berlin: de Gruyter, 2018), 55–86.

Apocrypha					
Source	Tiglath-pileser/Pul	Shalmaneser	Sargon	Sennacherib	Esarhaddon
Tobit		Tob 1:2, 13, 15, 16		Tob 1:15, 18, 22	Tob 1:21, 22; 2:1
Esdras		4 Esd 13:40		4 Esd 7:110	1 Esd 5:69
Sirach				Sir 48:18	
Maccabees				2 Macc 8:19; 15:22; 3 Macc 6:5	
Other writings					
Source	Tiglath-pileser/Pul	Shalmaneser	Sargon	Sennacherib	Esarhaddon
Herodotus				*Histories* 2.141	
Aristotle				*Rhetoric* 2.24	
Josephus	*Ant.* 9:232, 235, 252	*Ant.* 9:259, 277, (284), 287; 10:184; 11:19, 85		*Ant.* 10:1, 2, 6, 14, 18, 20, 21, 23; *J.W.* 3:447; 5:387	*Ant.* 10:23
Baruch		2 Bar 62:6		2 Bar 63:2, 4	
Ahiqar				Ahiqar 3, 4, 5, 7, 15, 27, 47, 50, 51, 55	Ahiqar 5, 7, 10, 11, 13, 14, 19, 23, 28, 32, 47, 53, 60, 64, 65, 70, 75, 76, 78
Hellenistic prayers				*AposCon* 7.37.3	
Clement of Alexandria				*Strom.* 1.141.1	
Rabbinic writings				*Meg.* 11b; *Sanh.* 95a–b; *Exod.R.* 18:5; *Git.* 57b	

In contrast to the numerous references to Sargon's campaigns and building activities which have been preserved in the Assyrian and Babylonian royal inscriptions and letters, it is surprising that Sargon fell out of the Greek and Levantine narratives.[30] This raises the question of whether the omission of Sargon's name was intentional. Whatever could have been the reason for omitting Sargon, it seems that the redactor of the First Isaiah does not conform to this historiographic trend and saves Sargon from falling into oblivion.[31]

---

30. The author of Tobit skipped Sargon also that Shalmaneser's successor is not Sargon but Sennacherib. Josephus, who must have been aware of Isa 20:1, nonetheless omits Sargon.

31. The omission of Sargon might have been intentional due to his death. Ann M. Weaver, "The 'Sin of Sargon' and Esarhaddon's Reconception of Sennacherib: A Study in Divine Will, Human Politics and Royal Ideology," *Iraq* 66 (2004): 61–6; Josette Elayi, *Sargon II, King of Assyria*, SBL Archaeology and Biblical Studies 22 (Atlanta, GA: SBL, 2017).

This evidence points to an Isaianic perception of Assyria. According to the Isaianic worldview, the history of Assyria is divided into three periods: unnamed oppressors–three Assyrian kings (Sargon, Sennacherib, Esarhaddon)–unnamed oppressors. The Assyrian kings, thus, represent direct historical references that link together the First Isaiah and partially the First and the Second Isaiah by means of 52:4, which refer to Assyria as to a past event.

Moreover, the redactor does not follow the general historiographic tendency that tended to put aside Sargon. By doing so, he makes his selection of three Assyrian kings unique. The chosen Assyrian kings are organized in the correct chronological order: Sargon II–Sennacherib–Esarhaddon. Isaiah attributes the conquest of Ashdod to Sargon II's officials, not to Sargon II, as does Assyrian propaganda. The number of references to Sennacherib shows that the redactor wants to present Sennacherib as the prototypical Assyrian oppressor. Because of his *hubris* he is killed in Nineveh. Esarhaddon, according to Isaiah, does not wage any campaign and, thus, Isaiah portrays him as a militarily ineffective king, even though the contrary was true.

2.3. Babylonian Kings

References to Babylonian kings in Isaiah, 2 Kings, Jeremiah, and Ezekiel show that the redactors of the BoI made a clear choice.[32] Even though the Babylonian conquest was traumatic for the Judeans,[33] the redactor omitted the conqueror of Jerusalem, King Nebuchadnezzar. As a result, the BoI, adopting 2 Kgs 20:12–19, concludes the presentation of pre-exilic Judah with Hezekiah and the Babylonian king Merodach-baladan (39:1–8).[34] Hence, the only Babylonian king mentioned by name in the BoI is Merodach-baladan (39:1). Besides him, unnamed Babylonian kings appear in 14:4 and 39:7.

The order of the Babylonian kings in the First Isaiah follows that of the Assyrian kings: unnamed–named–unnamed kings. However, the Babylonian kings are not presented in chronological order. The presentation starts with the end of the Neo-Babylonian kingdom (ca. 539 BCE), moves to Babylonia during the Assyrian period (ca. 700 BCE), and concludes with the prophecy on the looting of Jerusalem (596–586 BCE).

The downfall of an *unnamed Babylonian king* (14:4)	(539)
Merodach-baladan (39:1)	(ca. 700)
The looting of Jerusalem by an *unnamed Babylonian king* (39:7)	(596–586)

---

32. Babylonia appears in 13:1–14:23; 21:1–10; 43:14; 47:1; 48:14, 20; see also 45:20–25.
33. See Dominik Markl, "The Babylonian Exile as the Birth Trauma of Monotheism," *Bib* 101 (2020): 1–25.
34. The Chronicler significantly changed Merodach-baladan's story (2 Chr 32:31).

In sum, while the books of Kings, Jeremiah, Ezekiel, Daniel, Chronicles, Ezra, Esther, and Judith present Nebuchadnezzar as the most important Babylonian king, the BoI gives primacy to Merodach-baladan.

2.3.1. *Why Merodach-baladan?* The following historical review of his reign can provide insights about why this redactor highlights Merodach-baladan.[35] When Tiglath-pileser III conducted his campaign against the Babylonian king Mukinzeri, Merodach-Baladan together with other Chaldean chieftains submitted to Assyria in 728 BCE. However, after Shalmaneser V's death (722 BCE), Merodach-baladan gained the support of Elam and accomplished an unprecedented feat—he unified the Chaldean and Aramean tribes into an anti-Assyrian coalition (*ABC* 1 i 27–32). Sargon II considered Merodach-baladan's revolt unacceptable. He conducted a campaign against the Babylonian–Elamite coalition but was defeated at Der in 720 BCE. In 710 BCE Sargon II conducted another campaign against Babylonia and finally defeated Merodach-baladan who went into exile. After Sargon II's death Merodach-baladan returned from exile and became king in Babylon for nine months in 703 BCE. Sennacherib defeated Merodach-baladan, who once again escaped. In 700 BCE Merodach-baladan and Mušezib-Marduk regained control over Babylonia. Sennacherib conducted another punishing campaign and Merodach-baladan again escaped to Elam. After this campaign Merodach-baladan disappeared from the political scene.

In sum, Merodach-baladan was the first Chaldean ruler who unified Babylonia and fought against Assyria until the last drop of his blood. Even though it was Nabopolassar and Nebuchadnezzar who defeated Assyria, Merodach-baladan became the Babylonian icon of anti-Assyrian resistance.

To this argument we can add other elements that can further enlighten the choice of Merodach-baladan and his connection with Hezekiah. Both Hezekiah and Merodach-baladan referred to their illustrious predecessors, David[36] and Eriba-Marduk[37] respectively. Both collaborated with Assyria at certain moments during their reigns.[38] After Sargon II's death, both rebelled against Assyria.[39]

---

35. J. A. Brinkman, "Merodach-Baladan II," in *Studies presented to A. Leo Oppenheim: June 7, 1964* (Chicago: University of Chicago Press, 1964), 6–53; Marvin A. Powell, "Merodach-Baladan at Dur-Jakin: A Note on the Defense of Babylonian Cities," *JCS* 34 (1982): 59–61; Daniel T. Potts, *The Archaeology of Elam: Formation and Transformation of an Ancient Iranian State* (Cambridge: Cambridge University Press, 1999), 263–88.

36. Hezekiah is linked with David in 2 Kgs 18:3 (similarly only Abijam in 1 Kgs 15:3–5; Asa in 1 Kgs 15:11; Amaziah 2 Kgs 14:3).

37. RIMB 2 B.6.21.1:13.

38. Merodach-baladan submitted to Assyria in 728 BCE; Brinkman, "Merodach-Baladan," 9–10. Hezekiah rebelled against Assyria (2 Kgs 18:7; RINAP 3/1 22 iii 18), while his predecessor Ahaz was loyal to Assyria.

39. Merodach-baladan organized the anti-Assyrian coalition immediately after Sargon II's death but it was defeated in Sennacherib's first regnal year. Sennacherib had to pacify

During moments of their independence from Assyria, both kings significantly enlarged their territory.[40] Both kings used rather harsh methods to deal with their opponents—they put them in prison and kept them as hostages.[41] Both centralized their regions around their capitals.[42] The resistance of both kings was supported directly or indirectly by bigger political powers; Egypt supported the Levantine rebels,[43] and Elam supported the Babylonian resistance.[44] Both kings became the target of Assyrian propaganda and the Assyrian intelligence services closely watched them.[45] Before the Assyrians intervened, they sent messengers to Merodach-baladan and Hezekiah.[46] While the provincial governors were fighting against Merodach-baladan, Sennacherib was involved in fighting Cutha.[47] Similarly Sennacherib was laying siege against Lachish while his commanders were engaging Hezekiah.[48] The Assyrians intervened militarily against both kings. Both were defeated, even though the local sources do not admit the defeat. In both cases, Sennacherib destroyed several cities and took great booty, including nobles.[49]

---

a rebellion in the Zagros Mountains (his 2nd regnal year) and in Syria-Palestine (his 3rd regnal year), giving Merodach-baladan enough time to reorganize the resistance. Similarly, Hezekiah after the death of Sargon II, took advantage of the seeming destabilization of the Assyrian Empire and encouraged by the fact Sennacherib was busy in Babylonia and the Zagros region, joined the Levantine anti-Assyrian coalition.

40. Hezekiah attacked Philistia (2 Kgs 18:8) and Merodach-baladan controlled almost all of Babylonia in 721–710, 703 BCE and the territory of Bit-Yakin in 700 BCE (*PNAE 2/II*, 706).

41. Hezekiah kept Padi, king of Ekron, in prison in Jerusalem (RINAP 3/1 4:48), and Merodach-baladan kept hostages in Dur-Yakin during his first period of rule. Both groups of hostages were liberated by the Assyrian kings, Sennacherib and Sargon II respectively. Brinkman, "Merodach-Baladan," 13–14.

42. Cf. 2 Kgs 18:3–4, 22; Merodach-baladan's scribes expressed it more poetically citing Marduk: "This is indeed the shepherd who will gather the scattered (people)" (RIMB 2 B.6.21.1:14).

43. Sennacherib's envoys interpreted Hezekiah's reform as a rebellion (2 Kgs 18:19–25).

44. RINAP 3/1 1:5–7.

45. Guo Honggeng, "The Assyrian Intelligence Activities during the Assyrian Empire," *JAAS* 18 (2004): 59–71; Peter Dubovský, "Sennacherib's Invasion of the Levant through the Eyes of Assyrian Intelligence Services," in *Sennacherib at the Gates of Jerusalem: Story, History and Historiography*, ed. Isaac Kalimi and Seth Richardson, CHANE 71 (Leiden: Brill, 2014), 249–91.

46. RINAP 3/1 1:20 and 2 Kgs 18:17–19:13.

47. RINAP 3/1 1:23–24.

48. 2 Kgs 19:8.

49. For the accounts, cf. RINAP 3/1, 10–11. Neo-Assyrian archives mention that Sennacherib emptied the treasuries of Babylon and deported nobles (RINAP 3/1 3:8–9). A similar prophecy was uttered by Isaiah (Isa 39:6–8).

Even though it is not clear how many of these details could have been known to the Judahite scribes, recent studies have shown that the Assyrians made a great effort to disseminate their propaganda and ideology (see above). In each case, the choice of Merodach-baladan seems to draw on his ferocious anti-Assyrian resistance and similarities he shared with Hezekiah.

2.3.2. *Textual variants in Isaiah 39:1 and 2 Kings 20:12.* Merodach-baladan appears in Isa 39:1, whose wording contrasts with that of 2 Kgs 20:12:

כי שמע   כי חלה חזקיהו (2 Kgs 20:12)
וישמע   כי חלה ויחזק (Isa 38:1, MT)
וישמע   כיא חלה ויחיה (Isa 38:1; 1QIsa)
(LXX Isa 38:1) ἤκουσεν γὰρ ὅτι ἐμαλακίσθη ἕως θανάτου καὶ ἀνέστη[50]

The textual variants suggest that the redactor of the BoI wanted to present a partially different motive for Merodach-baladan's embassy. In both the books of Kings and Isaiah, the embassy takes place after Hezekiah has recovered from his sickness (LXX and 1QIsa). However, the MT of Isaiah reads ויחזק, while 2 Kgs 20:12 has a proper name חזקיהו. The root חזק in *qal* allows two possible interpretations. First, it could recount that Hezekiah once again became strong, that is, he recovered physically from his sickness, as in LXX and 1QIsa.[51] Secondly, it could mean that he became powerful once again, both economically and militarily (cf. Deut 11:8; Josh 17:13; Judg 1:28; in *hiphil* 2 Kgs 15:19). The latter interpretation is further supported by the riches that Hezekiah accumulates after the Assyrian invasion (Isa 39:2–3). This interpretation suggests that, according to Isaiah, Hezekiah recovered not only physically from his sickness but also that he regained his previous glory and power after Sennacherib's destructive campaign. Thus, Isaiah depicts Merodach-baladan's embassy as a plea for Hezekiah's support.[52]

2.3.3. *Isaianic dating of Merodach-baladan's embassy.* The previous paragraphs imply that the redactor of the BoI made three important choices. First, he refers to only one Babylonian king, Merodach-baladan, by name and excludes all other Babylonian kings. Secondly, he changes the wording of 2 Kgs 20:12 and presents

---

50. Some mss add εκ της μαλακιας (αρρωστιας αυτου); see Joseph Ziegler, *Isaias*, sVtg 14 (Göttingen: Vandenhoeck & Ruprecht, 1939), 265.

51. *HALOT*, 303.

52. Scholars have presented three motifs for this visit: (1) because Hezekiah was sick and recovered; (2) because the Babylonians were interested in astronomic signs; (3) because the Babylonians wanted to establish a political alliance with Judah. The last interpretation was proposed by Josephus (*Ant.* 10:29–32) and followed by most scholars, including James A. Montgomery, *A Critical and Exegetical Commentary on the Books of Kings*, ICC (Edinburgh: T&T Clark, 1951), 509; John Gray, *I & II Kings: A Commentary*, OTL (Philadelphia, PA: Westminster Press, 1976), 701–2; Shemu'el Vargon, "The Time of Hezekiah's Illness and the Visit of the Babylonian Delegation," *Maarav* 21 (2014): 37–56.

Hezekiah *redivivus*. Thirdly, he adopts the sequence of events of 2 Kgs 20 and, thus, situates Merodach-baladan's embassy after Sennacherib's invasion of Judah.

Let us, now, address the problem of dating Merodach-baladan's embassy. Scholars have argued for two possible dates: ca. 703 BCE and ca. 711 BC. Both dates are derived from the Babylonian king list:

> 5 Ululayu, dynasty of Ashur
> 12 *Marduk-apla-iddina*, dynasty of the Sea-Land
> 5 Sargon
> 2 Sennacherib, dynasty of Habigal[8]
> 1 month Marduk-zakir-shumi, son of Ardu
> 9 months *Marduk-apla-iddina*, Habi soldier
> 3 years Bel-ibni, dynasty of Babylon
> 6 Aššur-nadin-šumi, dynasty of Habigal (*COS* I, 134)

Thus, the Babylonian embassy would correspond to Merodach-baladan's first (721–710 BCE) or second (703 BCE) period of rule. Shemu'el Vargon has reasonably argued that Merodach-baladan's visit took place during Sargon II's conquest of Ashdod, ca. 713/711 BCE.[53] Most scholars, however, prefer dating Merodach-baladan's visit to 703 BCE.[54]

Even though these two dates are plausible from the historical viewpoint, this is not the idea that the redactor of the First Isaiah wanted to convey. To arrive at these dates, whether 711 or 703 BCE, we must reorganize the biblical text. On the other hand, if we accept the chronology of Isa 36–39, then we must date Merodach-baladan's embassy between 700 BCE and before ca. 694 BCE (Merodach-baladan's death). The latter hypothesis raises the eyebrows of many scholars who, in order to justify their dating, have asserted that the chapters in Isa 36–39 // 2 Kgs 18–20 are not in chronological order.[55] Given the excellent knowledge of Assyrian realia and history in the Isaianic text, it seems reasonable to ask what concept of history the redactor of the BoI conveyed when he placed Merodach-baladan's embassy after Sennacherib's invasion of Judah (701 BCE).

Even though the Babylonian king list makes Merodach-baladan's second reign coincide with Sennacherib's first campaign (703 BCE), this does not mean that Merodach-baladan disappeared from the political scene after 703 BCE. In response to Sennacherib's troops, Merodach-baladan escaped to Guzummanu, the swampland in southern Iraq (RINAP 3/1 1:26). Sennacherib sent his soldier to search for Merodach-baladan, but they did not find him (RINAP 3/1 1:34–35). Once the Assyrian troops had left Babylonia, the Chaldeans and Arameans revolted against the Assyrian regime. Bel-ibni, a king appointed by Sennacherib to reign over Babylonia, was removed from power in 700 BCE by Mušezib-Marduk, who

---

53. Vargon, "Hezekiah's Illness," 47–50.
54. Brinkman, "Merodach-Baladan," 33; Roberts, *First Isaiah*, 488.
55. Roberts, *First Isaiah*, 488. However, this proposal was raised already by Rashi, Rabbi David Kimhi, Isaac ben Judah Abrahanel, etc.

ruled in Babylon. In the same year Merodach-baladan reappeared and regained control over southern Babylonia. Thus, Mušezib-Marduk and Merodach-baladan once again ousted the Assyrians. Sennacherib did not delay with his intervention. During his campaign in 700 BCE, he defeated Mušezib-Marduk and marched against Bit-Yakin, Merodach-baladan's seat of power. Merodach-baladan escaped to Elam. When Sennacherib intervened against the Babylonian exiles in Elam in 694 BCE, Merodach-baladan had no longer been active (RINAP 3/1 22 iv 32–53). Therefore, it can be concluded that Merodach-baladan died shortly after 700 BCE but before 694 BCE.

Taking into consideration this historical background, we can argue that the BoI linked Merodach-baladan's embassy with Sennacherib's second invasion of Babylonia (700 BCE) or shortly after it, namely, while Merodach-baladan escaped and looked for refuge in Elam (700–694 BCE). Nonetheless, the Bible identifies Merodach-baladan as king of Babylon, even though the Babylonian king list attributes this title in this period to two pro-Assyrian leaders (Bel-ibni and Aššur-nadin-šumi). The fact that Mušezib-Marduk is not listed among the kings of Babylonia, even though he still ruled in Babylon around 700 BCE, shows that the Babylonian king list omitted some kings after 703 BCE. Thus, Mušezib-Marduk and Merodach-baladan could rightly claim this title, even though they are not listed in the Babylonian king list. In sum, Merodach-baladan had real political power in 700 BCE and could be truly called king.[56] Theoretically he could still claim this title while he was in exile (700–694 BCE), but without having real political power.

Let us draw some implications from this analysis. First, the redactional choice to explicitly name Merodach-baladan seems to have a good reason, since he was a symbol of anti-Assyrian resistance. This choice and the omission of major Babylonian kings suggest that the redactor presented Babylonian history through Assyrian eyes and not through a Babylonian perspective. Furthermore, placing Merodach-baladan's embassy around 700 BCE, the redactor depicts Merodach-baladan as a king in decline. He had lost several battles against Assyria, was forced to escape from Babylonia, lived as a refugee in Elam without having any real power, and finally died in exile. On the contrary, the Isaianic version of the story presents Hezekiah as the king who recovers not only physically from his sickness but also economically and militarily from the destructive Assyrian campaign. The redactor, thus, creates a contrast between Hezekiah, who recovers from Assyrian invasion, on the one hand, and Merodach-baladan, whose reign is ruined by multiple Assyrian invasions, on the other hand.

2.3.4. Conclusions. The Babylonian kings are not presented in chronological order. The first occurrence of Babylonia and its king speaks about their downfall. This introduction to Babylonia gives a clue as to how the redactor wants to

---

56. John A. Brinkman, "Elamite Military Aid to Merodach-Baladan," *JNES* 24 (1965): 161–5 (165).

portray Babylonia. From the very beginning, this kingdom was doomed to fall. Thus, we might ask who is the Babylonian king who threatened Jerusalem (Isa 39:7). First, he was a predecessor of an unnamed Babylonian king who had been destined to be utterly destroyed (Isa 13:1–14:23). Secondly, he was a successor of Merodach-baladan (Isa 39:1–3) who, even though being a symbol of Assyrian resistance, was defeated, forced to live in exile, and asked Hezekiah *redivivus* for help. Finally, the "victorious" Babylonian king (Isa 39:7) is able only to loot the city and to deport a few people (contrary to 2 Kgs 25). Thus, the Isaianic redactor conveys his own presentation of Babylonian "success" in the following sequence:

Unnamed Babylonian king   completely destroyed (Isa 13:1–14:23)
  Merodach-baladan partially destroyed (Isa 39:1–3)
  "Victorious Babylonian looter" (Isa 39:7)

2.4. Cyrus

While the chapters of the First Isaiah are populated with references to historical events and proper names that can be associated with historical events and persons, the Second Isaiah contains only one reference of this type. Verses 44:28–45:1 mention King Cyrus twice and the suffix in 45:13 too refers to him.[57] Similar to the case of the Assyrian and Babylonian kings, the redactor makes a clear choice. He chose Cyrus and omitted all other Persian kings such as Darius, Cambyses, Xerxes, Artaxerxes, who would also have been familiar to the biblical audience.

The choice of Cyrus also seems to be well motivated. By defeating the Babylonian and Median kingdoms, Cyrus created one of the largest empires in the ancient world. Its geographical extension almost tripled the extent of the Assyrian empire and Cyrus' Empire lasted for more than two hundred years. Only Alexander the Great conquered more territory, but his kingdom crumbled in a few years after his death.[58]

Despite Cyrus' success, the Second Isaiah did not praise him for his strategic genius nor for his and his successors' administrative capabilities. Instead, he blurred Persian royal propaganda[59] with Israelite theological concepts, as stated by B. Childs:

---

57. There are other possible indirect references to Cyrus: Isa 41:1–4, (5–7), 21–29; (42:5–9); 44:24–28; 45:1–7(8), 9–13; 46:(5)9–11; 48:12–15(16a); *OHI*, 181. See also the expression "the bird of prey" in Isa 46:11; Michael J. Chan, "Cyrus, Yhwh's Bird of Prey (Isa. 46.11): Echoes of an Ancient Near Eastern Metaphor," *JSOT* 35 (2010): 113–27.

58. Another motivation for choosing Cyrus might be a word play in Greek. His name is Κυρος, which resembles Κυριος, "the Lord/the lord." The Church Fathers changed κυρω in κυριω. They probably followed some minor mss (534); Joseph Ziegler, *Isaias* (Würzburg: Echter, 1948), 290.

59. Gian Pietro Basello, "Il Cilindro di Ciro tradotto dal testo babilonese," *RSB* 25 (2013): 249–59.

the references to the historical events associated with Cyrus are minimal. Cyrus has become such a theological projection, an instrument in the hand of God, that his role blurs into the description of Abraham, who was also chosen…called from the ends of the earth…called from its farthest concerns…and upheld with a victorious right hand."[60]

In other words, the biblical poets envisioned a historical Cyrus into a theological Cyrus.

The theological portrait of Cyrus emerges even more when we compare the references to Cyrus and other Persian kings in the BoI and in the rest of the Bible. Isaiah 44:28–45:13 display noticeable similarity with 2 Chr 36:22–23 // Ezra 1:1–4: (1) Cyrus is chosen by the Lord to accomplish his mission;[61] (2) both texts use the verb עיר in *hiphil* to describe the vocation of Cyrus (Isa 45:13[62] and 2 Chr 36:22 // Ezra 1:1); (3) rebuilding Jerusalem and the Lord's temple constitutes the most important part of Cyrus' mission (Isa 44:28b and 2 Chr 36:23).[63] This image of Cyrus significantly differs from the presentation of the Persian kings in Daniel, Esther, Ezekiel, Judith, 1–2 Maccabees.

Moreover, the Second Isaiah does not call Cyrus the king of "Persia" or "the Persian" (מלך פרס cf. Ezra 1:1; Dan 10:1; פרסיא cf. Dan 6:29). Thus, Cyrus is presented as a ruler who is not strictly bound to a nation (Isa 45:1–13).

Finally, the Second Isaiah does not call Cyrus king (as in 2 Chr 36:22; Ezra 1:7; Dan 1:21), but his titles are "shepherd" and "anointed."[64] He rules over the kings (Isa 45:1) but he is not called king. These titles point to Cyrus' special role in Israelite history: "David was chosen to subdue nations within the territory assigned to Israel and thus to establish YHWH's sovereignty over Canaan. Now that task is being assigned to Cyrus. This must have been a shock to Israel… As the Assyrian

---

60. Brevard S. Childs, *Isaiah: A Commentary*, OTL (Louisville, KY: Westminster John Knox, 2001), 418.

61. Both texts state that the initiative comes from God (roots אמר and חזק in Isa 44:28; 45:1 and פקד in 2 Chr 36:23).

62. See also Isa 41:2 that most likely refers to Cyrus; Joseph Blenkinsopp, *Isaiah 40–55: A New Translation with Introduction and Commentary*, AB 19A (New York: Doubleday, 2002), 92.

63. The connection with Ezra is further buttressed by the use of the verb יסד, "to lay foundation," for rebuilding the temple (Isa 44:28 and Ezra 3:10–12).

64. Lisbeth S. Fried illuminated the background of these titles. An Egyptian priest Udjahorresnet claimed: "I composed his (Cambyses') titulary, to wit his name of King of Upper and Lower Egypt, Mesuti-Re (Offspring of Re)." She concluded that as Udjahorresnet in Egypt and the priests of Marduk in Babylon, so the Second Isaiah handed over to Cyrus the royal Judean titles; see Lisbeth S. Fried, "Cyrus the Messiah? The Historical Background to Isaiah 45:1," *HTR* 95 (2002): 373–93.

was summoned to destroy (10:5–6), so now the Persian is called to perform the military and political tasks necessary to rebuild Jerusalem."[65]

In conclusion, the only ruler mentioned by name in the Second Isaiah is Cyrus. This choice seems to accentuate the birth of the largest empire in the known world, the inauguration of a new type of kingship, and the beginning of the liberation process for the Israelites.[66] Cyrus is not called king but "the shepherd" and "the anointed one." He is directly stirred up by the Lord and he is entrusted with a special mission to rebuild the temple and the city of Jerusalem. His reign concludes the age of exile and marks the beginning of a new future for Israel.

3. Unity: To Be or Not to Be?

Let us now put all the references in one table:

1:1 In the days of Uzziah, Jotham, Ahaz, and Hezekiah	767–687
6:1 In the year when Uzziah died	739
7:1 In the days of Ahaz	743–716/15
7–9 Pekah and Rezin	734–732
7:17, 20; 8:4, 7; 10:12 Unnamed Assyrian king(s)	734–732
14:4 Unnamed Babylonian king	539
14:28 In the year when Ahaz died	716/15
20:1 In the year when Tartan came (Sargon II)	713/711
36:1 In the 14th year of Hezekiah	701
37:38 Esarhaddon became king	681
38:6 Unnamed Assyrian king	669–609
39:1 *Merodach-baladan*	700
39:7 Unnamed Babylonian king	596/586
44:28–45:1, 13 Cyrus	600/539–530
56–66 no reference	

This table shows that the redactor makes great effort to put the references in the correct chronological order. The only exception is Babylonia. The reversed chronological order and the choice of Merodach-baladan as the only Babylonian king mentioned by name suggest that the redactor intentionally downplays the Babylonian conquest and domination. Babylonia is presented through Assyrian eyes and the linking of Merodach-baladan with Hezekiah *redivivus* suggests that Babylonia was even asking Judah for help.

---

65. John D. W. Watts, *Isaiah 34–66*, WBC 25 (Nashville, TN: Thomas Nelson, 2005), 700.

66. Cyrus became a symbol of a positive and merciful king. Thus, the sixteenth-century tapestry in the Museo Bagatti Valsecchi in Milan depicts the life of Cyrus and under the scenes is embroidered "war brings fame, but a kingdom is founded on justice and liberality."

All direct references, except 44:28–45:1, 13, appear in the First Isaiah. There are no historically datable direct references in the Third Isaiah. There are eleven references to the Neo-Assyrian period (859–612 BCE), two to the Neo-Babylonian period (612–539 BCE), and one to the Persian period (539–330 BCE; the Second Isaiah). As a result, this choice of the redactor indicates that the Isaianic world is divided into three historical periods: Neo-Assyrian, Neo-Babylonian, and Persian. The Neo-Assyrian period is the most important one. The Neo-Babylonian is only marginally mentioned and linked to the Neo-Assyrian Empire via Merodach-baladan. Similarly, Pekah and Rezin are also part of the Neo-Assyrian world. All four Judahite kings are active during the Neo-Assyrian period. A peculiarity of the First Isaiah is that several references are linked with death and downfall, reinforcing the idea that the Neo-Assyrian period is the world of oppression, doomed to end in disaster. This empire symbolically finishes with the death of Sennacherib, the biblical icon of oppression and propaganda.

An unconventional presentation of Cyrus underlines the difference between the Neo-Assyrian / Neo-Babylonian and Persian portrayals of rule and, thus, between the First and the Second Isaiah. Cyrus becomes the anointed one, the shepherd of the nations. He is linked with life and creation, inaugurating a new age in human history. Third Isaiah is left without any direct references to historically datable persons and events. The world of these chapters grows out of the new age heralded by Cyrus' accession to power and assumes eschatological features that is beyond history.

These conclusions point to the redactor's intent to organize the history of the world into three stages:

1. The period of Neo-Assyrian (and marginally also Neo-Babylonian) domination
2. The period of a new age inaugurated by Cyrus
3. The eschatological period that goes beyond the human history

This division of history in the BoI resembles the oppression–liberation pattern known in the book of Judges, but especially in the narrative of the exodus. Phraseology involving the exodus appears in Isa 63:11–12. Therefore, it can be proposed that the redactor, by organizing the direct references in a particular way, may have intended to present a new exodus model in the BoI. The role of Egypt and the Pharaoh is assumed by Assyria and Sennacherib. However, the liberation is not accomplished by an Israelite hero, but happens thanks to a foreigner Cyrus, who assumes the role of a new Moses. Both were chosen by the Lord to accomplish the divine plan. The return from the exile becomes a parallel to liberation from slavery in Egypt and the taking possession of the Promised Land. Finally, the promised land is sketched in an eschatological prospective. This might lead us to a conclusion that the redactor's insertion of the direct references betrays his vision of history that aims at organizing the otherwise disconnected prophecies into a unity that at the same time offers a new interpretation of the history of humanity.

Chapter 7

THE REMNANTS OF A FIGURAL PAST: SYMMETRY, ANALOGY, AND THE SEARCH FOR A HOLY SEED IN THE BOOK OF ISAIAH

Jacob Stromberg

1. *Introduction*

The book of Isaiah is big, but exquisitely made. To the historian of ancient Israelite literature, the complexity of this book discloses a massive literary competence in antiquity, a competence which modern scholars have probably only just begun to understand. It is no surprise, then, that its unity (or lack thereof) remains a matter of debate: some see it as a drama,[1] others as a loose anthology,[2] some as an imperfectly unified work,[3] and still others think the question of Isaiah's unity is itself anachronistic.[4] All such assessments assume the modern critic has mastered that literary competence in antiquity which produced Isaiah. In the space allotted to this essay, I hope to make a modest contribution to our understanding of such competence. More specifically, I hope to illuminate such competence as it was employed to enable a comparison between the two halves of the book by the ancient reader.

---

1. Christopher R. Seitz, "Isaiah 1–66: Making Sense of the Whole," in *Reading and Preaching the Book of Isaiah*, ed. Christopher R. Seitz (Philadelphia, PA: Fortress, 1988), 105–26 (122).

2. E.g., Blake Couey, *Reading the Poetry of First Isaiah: The Most Perfect Model of the Prophetic Poetry* (Oxford: Oxford University Press, 2015), 13; Nathan Mastnjak, "The Book of Isaiah and the Anthological Genre," *HS* 61 (2020): 49–72.

3. David Carr, "Reaching for Unity in Isaiah," *JSOT* 57 (1993): 61–80.

4. J. J. M. Roberts, *First Isaiah: A Commentary*, Hermeneia (Minneapolis, MN: Fortress, 2015), 2.

2. Unity and Structure

By at least the 1980s, the term "unity" found utility as many scholars began to question the supposed independent status of chs. 40–66 as a book separate from chs. 1–39.[5] On its own, the word is inadequate for the purposes of the present essay, but not because it was employed to challenge a view now no longer widely held (that Isaiah is two books, rather than one). Rather, the word by itself is inadequate because it is insufficiently specific, being applied by some to authorship, by others to literary features, and by still others to the phenomenological conditions necessary for reading of any kind to take place.[6] Instead, I will address the problem from the standpoint of textual *structure*. The notion of "structure" has an oblique relationship to authorial unity because textual structure can be the product of multiple authors or a single hand. However, because textual structure here refers to that set of operations given to the reader, namely, the text itself, it directly entails the relationship between the latter two uses of "unity": the relationship between literary features and the phenomenological unity necessary for reading to occur.[7]

What, then, is structure? As intended here, "structure" is a "purposeful arrangement of parts within a whole" (*OED*). Because texts consist of parts (e.g., words, sentences) purposefully arranged into wholes (e.g., words into sentences, and sentences into paragraphs), they have structure, or, perhaps better, they are themselves structure, linguistic structure. As parts purposefully arranged into wholes for consumers, texts require their readers to perceive both the parts and the wholes to activate them in a manner commensurate with their design. To do this, textual structure enables the reader to segment the whole into parts (e.g., a sentence into words) and coordinate the parts into a whole (e.g., words into a sentence). While these procedures of segmentation and coordination are reasonably well understood at the level of the Hebrew sentence or line (in the case of poetry), they are not grasped nearly as well (or so easily) at levels above this. In what follows, we will see that these two procedures are consistently controlled by elements of symmetry and analogy which have been woven into Isaiah's textual tapestry every bit as much as they have been worked into the wording of the Hebrew Bible elsewhere.[8]

---

5. See especially Ronald E. Clements, "The Unity of the Book of Isaiah," *Int* 36 (1982): 117–29.

6. D. Andrew Teeter and William A. Tooman, "Standards of (In)coherence in Ancient Jewish Literature," *HBAI* 9 (2020): 101–3.

7. Alexander Samely, "How Coherence Works: Reading, Re-Reading and Inner-Biblical Exegesis," *HBAI* 9 (2020): 130–82; Teeter and Tooman, "Standards," 102–3.

8. On symmetry, see (with further bibliography): Emmylou J. Grosser, "What Symmetry Can Do that Parallelism Can't: Line Perception and Poetic Effects in the Song of Deborah (Judges 5:2–31)," *VT* 71 (2021): 175–204; idem, *Unparalleled Poetry: A Cognitive Approach to the Free-Rhythm Verse of the Hebrew Bible* (Oxford: Oxford University Press, 2023); Andrew Teeter, "Biblical Symmetry and Its Modern Detractors," in *Congress Volume:*

3. Overview of Texts

The book of Isaiah preserves narrative remnants from the past of the prophet. Recounting snippets of the life and times of Isaiah, these narratives have a figural quality in the book whereby the past portends the future. This quality is achieved by means of an historiography wherein the events of the future are portrayed on analogy to those of the past. For the purposes of this essay, I draw attention to two sets of texts which employ this analogical strategy as has been widely recognized. First, the narrative of Hezekiah has been set on analogy to the account of his father, Ahaz, as well as the chapters which follow immediately after this (7:1–9:6 // 36–39). Second, the commission scene in Isa 40:1–11 has been patterned on the call of the prophet in ch. 6. So far as I am aware, scholars have not observed that the former strategy has been sandwiched by the latter, that on either side of the two royal narratives has been placed one of the two commission scenes (see Figure 7.1 below).

Figure 7.1 The Prophetic Commission and the Royal Narrative

First Half of Isaiah (chs. 1–39)				Second Half of Isaiah (chs. 40–66)
Isaiah 6	Isaiah 7:1–9:6	Isaiah 36–39	Isaiah 40:1–11	
Commission	Royal Narrative + 7:18–9:6	Royal Narrative	Commission	
Divine King	Human Kings	Human Kings	Divine King	

In what follows, I examine what the one has to do with the other, how the commission scenes have been related to the royal narratives in between. Moreover, because the second of these commission scenes introduces the second half of the book (40:1–11), I consider how these obviously interrelated narrative

---

Aberdeen 2019, ed. by Grant Macaskill, Christl M. Maier, and Joachim Schaper, VTSup 192 (Leiden: Brill, 2022), 435–73. On analogy, see (with further bibliography): Joshua A. Berman, *Narrative Analogy in the Hebrew Bible: Battle Stories and Their Equivalent Non-battle Narratives*, VTSup 103 (Leiden: Brill, 2004); Jacob Stromberg, "Figural History in the Book of Isaiah: The Prospective Significance of Hezekiah's Deliverance from Assyria and Death," in *Imperial Visions: The Prophet and the Book of Isaiah in an Age of Empires*, ed. by Reinhard Kratz and Joachim Schaper, FRLANT 227 (Göttingen: Vandenhoeck & Ruprecht, 2020), 81–102; D. Andrew Teeter and Michael A. Lyons, "The One and the Many, the Past and the Future, and the Dynamics of Prospective Analogy," in *Isaiah's Servants in Early Judaism and Christianity*, ed. Michael A. Lyons and Jacob Stromberg, WUNT II/554 (Tübingen: Mohr Siebeck, 2021), 15–44; Yair Zakovitch, מקראות בארץ המראות (*Through the Looking Glass: Reflection Stories in the Bible*) (Tel Aviv: Hakibbutz Hameuchad, 1995).

strategies were to be brought to bear on the second half of the book by the reader of the whole. I will argue that the past recounted in the first half of the book has been assigned a prospective significance for its second half. Imparting a figural quality to the history recounted therein, this prospective significance emerges for the reader attuned to the use of analogy and symmetry throughout the book.

4. The First Half of Isaiah

Beginning with the first half of Isaiah, I will examine the following in order: (1) the relationship between the call of the prophet in ch. 6 and the narrative of Ahaz in ch. 7 along with the closely related material in 8:1–9:6; (2) the structure of ch. 6, as this relates to the subsequent material; and (3) the relationship between 7:1–9:6 and 36–39, the account of Hezekiah.

4.1. *Isaiah 6 and 7:1–9:6*

Aspects of Isa 7:1–9:6 have been set on analogy to the narrative recounting the commission of the prophet in ch. 6. An important part of this analogy is the comparison between Isaiah and Ahaz. Because this presupposes an understanding of the portrayal of the prophet's commission, I will begin there.

4.1.1. *The Past of the Prophet and the Future of the People (Isaiah 6).* The structure of ch. 6 compares the past of the prophet with the future of the people, the one being presented as a prospective model for the other. In response to seeing (רא״ה) a vision of the One who is "holy" (קדוש), the prophet confesses that he is "unclean of lips" (טמא שפתים [vv. 1–5]). After confessing this, a burning creature takes a burning coal,[9] applying this to Isaiah's unclean "lips" so that his sin is atoned for, the implication being that with this he has moved from the state of "unclean" to that of "holy" (vv. 6–7). Only then does the prophet "hear" (שמ״ע) and obey the divine voice (v. 8). The prophet is then given a mission whose effect would be to prevent the people of "unclean lips" (טמא שפתים) from seeing (רא״ה) or hearing (שמ״ע), lest they repent, and God heal them (vv. 5, 10).

Despite what they have in common ("unclean lips"), the people's future will not be like the prophet's past: he heard, saw, and repented; they will not—at least not initially. As soon as the Seraph applies the coal to Isaiah's mouth and lips (so that he hears), the prophet is commissioned to apply a salve to their eyes and ears (so that they do not see, hear, repent, and enjoy healing like the prophet). Here, the contrast manifests both in the material applied (a burning coal versus salve) and in the body part to which it is applied (the organs of speech [mouth and lips] versus the organs of perception [eyes and ears] and discernment [heart]). The latter contrast underscores the point that as soon as the prophet could speak God's word to the people, they would not be able to perceive it. The former underscores

---

9. Observe the wordplay between שרף and רצפה here.

the difficult path to the prophet's own healing, not through the usual method of applying salve (as was to be done with the people), but by a hot coal.

While the prophet's mission would deny the people the sensory experience granted to himself (which led to his confession and the burning away of his uncleanness), the consequences of this denial for the history of the people were calculated, nonetheless, to achieve the same effect (a burning that would leave a holy remnant). In response to the assignment of this negative mission, Isaiah asks "how long" would the people not hear or see and so not be healed (v. 11). God answers that this condition would last until the land lay waste, emptied out, and that which remained in it would itself be "burned," leaving only a remnant that was "holy" (קדש [vv. 11–13]). Just as Isaiah ("unclean of lips") endured a burning to remove his sin and enable him to hear the voice of the Holy One, so the people ("unclean of lips" like the prophet) would also endure a burning that would produce a holy remnant, which (it is implied by the analogy) would hear God's voice, understand, and know. Thus, the prophet's own burning by the Seraph and coal to purify him from uncleanness prefigures the future burning that was to fashion a holy remnant out of the people. Like the prophet's own healing, theirs was to be accomplished not by salve, but by fire.

As for the agent who would carry out the actual destruction to come, its identity remains only implicit. This agent would lay waste their cities and houses, devastate their ground, exile the inhabitants, and (on analogy to the Seraph) burn the remainder, so that only a holy remnant remained (vv. 11–13). Because the Assyrians go on to do all these things in the subsequent career of the prophet, it is instructive that the oracle against Philistia (14:28–32), patterned on the prophet's commission in ch. 6, describes the Assyrian threat as a "flying Seraph" (שרף מעופף)—a form of usage found otherwise only in 6:1-2 and 30:6 in the whole Hebrew Bible.[10]

Finally, if the path of the people towards healing would follow that of the prophet to whom was applied the coal, why was the prophet himself told to apply to the people salve instead? A small number of scholars have observed the potentially positive connotations of the verbs describing Isaiah's task (השע, הכבד, השמן [v. 10a]).[11] The first of these—השמן ("to apply oil")[12]—is perhaps the most notable in this respect, as elsewhere "oil" overwhelmingly appears in a positive sense.

---

10. Jacob Stromberg, "Hezekiah and the Oracles Against the Nations in Isaiah," in *The History of Isaiah: The Formation of the Book and its Presentation of the Past*, ed. Jacob Stromberg and J. Todd Hibbard, FAT 150 (Tübingen: Mohr Siebeck, 2021), 299–302.

11. Edgar Kellenberger, "Heil und Verstockung: Zu Jes 6,9f. bei Jesaja und im Neuen Testament," *TZ* 48 (1992): 268–75; H. G. M. Williamson, "Isaiah: Prophet of Weal or Woe?," in *"Thus Speaks Ishtar of Arbela": Prophecy in Israel, Assyria, and Egypt in the Neo-Assyrian Period*, ed. Robert P. Gordon and Hans M. Barstad (Winona Lake, IN: Eisenbrauns, 2013), 293–4; cf. idem, *A Critical and Exegetical Commentary on Isaiah 1–27. II. Isaiah 6–12*, ICC (London: Bloomsbury T&T Clark, 2018), 76–82.

12. The verb שמ״ן occurs in *hiphil* only one other time, where (unlike here) it has an internal sense (Neh 9:25).

Even in those cases where the enjoyment of superabundance (described with שׁמ״ן) is followed by rebellion, the superabundance itself is a gift from God and not something negative (Deut 32:13, 15; Neh 9:25). Having become fat on divine blessing, the people forgot God. According to Edgar Kellenberger, none of the many passages employing "oil" (שׁמן) ever assign it a negative quality.[13] Quite the opposite: "Oil (שׁמן) and incense make the heart (לב) glad," according to Prov 27:9, which, as far as I can see, is the only other passage in the Hebrew Bible positing a direct relationship between the two.[14]

In fact, the application of oil has a medicinal purpose in the first chapter of the book, a chapter clearly related to the prophet's commission in Isa 6, as is widely recognized.[15] Here, the metaphorical body of the people—beaten and with an ill "heart" (לבב)—is covered with wounds that are not treated, "not softened with oil (בשׁמן)" (1:5–6). This describes the condition of the people after the ravages of the Assyrians in 701 (1:3, 7–9).[16] As we shall see, this devastation of the people by the Assyrians (which had already happened to the audience of ch. 1) is something the commission of the prophet foresees for the future of the people: what God foretells the prophet in ch. 6 (האדמה תשאה שממה) had already come to pass for the audience of ch. 1 (ארצכם שממה).[17] According to 6:9-10, this destruction would result from the people's lack of knowledge (יד״ע) and discernment (בי״ן), precisely how they are described by ch. 1 after the Assyrian ravages had taken place (v. 3).

In the light of this close relationship between ch. 6 and ch. 1 (where שׁמן has a medicinal function), the formulation of 6:10 is highly conspicuous. This command to the prophet is formulated as an inverse symmetry, forcing a comparison between השׁמן ("apply oil") and רפא ("to heal"): (a) השׁמן; (b) לב; (c) אזניו; (d) עיניו; (c') עיניו; (b') אזניו; (a') לבבו; ורפא. This suggests an awareness of the medicinal use of oil, as at 1:6. Accordingly, the symmetry of the command sharpens the question: if the application of oil had medicinal value (as in 1:6), why would it lead to the opposite result here, the prevention of healing?

For Kellenberger (who does not note the symmetrical design of v. 10), the positive valence of these verbs points towards the conclusion: "Es ist Jahwes Heilsbotschaft, womit Jesaja die Verstockung bewirken soll."[18] H. G. M. Williamson offers a similar explanation:

---

13. Kellenberger, "Heil und Verstockung," 269.
14. Kellenberger, "Heil und Verstockung," 269.
15. Compare the following: 1:3, 10 // 6:9–10; 1:4 // 6:7; 1:4, 31 // 6:13; 1:7 // 6:6, 11, 13. See, for instance, Uwe Becker, *Jesaja—von der Botschaft zum Buch*, FRLANT 178 (Göttingen: Vandenhoeck & Ruprecht, 1997), 182–3.
16. For a summary and bibliography on 701 as the background to 1:5–9, see H. G. M. Williamson, *A Critical and Exegetical Commentary on Isaiah 1–27. I. Isaiah 1–5*, ICC (London: Bloomsbury T&T Clark, 2006), 59.
17. Isaiah 1:7; 6:11.
18. Kellenberger, "Heil und Verstockung," 268.

> For all the uncertainties that attend such data, it seems that, although 6:10 is clearly seriously negative in its current formulation, the vocabulary chosen is in itself ambiguous, so that there may be an indication here that it was precisely in the proclamation of deliverance that Isaiah's message, being rejected, could be turned to judgment.[19]

In support of this, I would observe that even the imperative to "make heavy" (הכבד) its ears lest "it hears" (ישמע)—which in the present form of the book cannot but belong to an echo of God's dealing with Pharaoh[20]—fits this interpretation surprisingly well. In the usage closest to this one,[21] Pharaoh is said to have made his heart heavy (הכבד את לבו) and not listened (לא ישמע) to Moses and Aaron, precisely in line with the result in Isa 6:10.[22] Importantly, this was Pharaoh's response to *seeing* the *deliverance* from the plague that had been inflicted upon him and his people: "when Pharaoh *saw* there was a relief, he *made his heart heavy*, and he would *not listen* to them" (Exod 8:11; cf. Isa 6:9, "*see*, but do not *know*"). The second instance of this comes in Exod 8:28, where Pharaoh again makes his *heart heavy* in response to deliverance (from the swarm of flies), not sending the people away. Here, as in other places in the Exodus narrative, God sends the plague on Pharaoh "so that you may *know* that I am the Lord" (8:18)—a goal Pharaoh consistently resists by making his heart (mind) heavy. After one further instance of Pharaoh making his heart heavy in response to deliverance (Exod 9:34),[23] God vows to be the one to do this to the king's heart, "so that I may place my signs in their midst" and "you may *know* that I am the Lord" (10:1–2).

Underscoring the potential ambiguity of the phrase הכבד את לבו in Exodus (and therefore possibly the parallel to this in Isa 6:10), one could conceivably read this as "he honored his heart," that is, himself.[24] If only a potential meaning with Pharaoh, this possibility ends up being exploited by the finale of this theme in Exod 14:4: "I will harden Pharaoh's *heart* (לב) and he will pursue after them, *so that I may win glory* (ואכבדה) over[25] Pharaoh and all his army and the Egyptians

---

19. Williamson, "Isaiah: Prophet of Weal or Woe?," 294.

20. It will have to suffice here to draw attention to Ethan Schwartz, "Mirrors of Moses in Isaiah 1–12," in Stromberg and Hibbard, eds., *The History of Isaiah*, 269–96.

21. In addition to this, there are several instances where Pharaoh's "heart" is "hardened" (חז"ק).

22. Cf. Exod 7:14, where Pharaoh's "heavy heart" is no doubt to be compared back to 4:10, where Moses objects to his commission to speak on the grounds that he is "heavy of mouth," taken in relation to a disability—which God can overcome—by the next verse.

23. Exod 9:7 is similar in that Pharaoh responds this way to the deliverance of Israel's livestock.

24. Cf. Jer 30:19, where כבד in Hebrew Bible means "to honor," and especially 2 Chr 25:19, where לב is used with כב"ד in the sense of self-glorification. On הכביד in Isa 8:23, where it probably means "to honor," see Williamson, *Isaiah 6–12*, 383–4.

25. Graham I. Davies translates the force of the ב preposition on analogy to its hostile use, as in נלחם ב, "so that I may win glory *over* Pharaoh" (*A Critical and Exegetical*

will know that I am the Lord" (cf. 14:17-18). Where Pharaoh made his *heart heavy* in response to deliverance from the plagues, God would *be honored* when the people were delivered from Pharaoh, whose final pursuit of them began with a divine hardening of his *heart*.

Besides the other important parallels here between Exodus and Isa 6, the point is that in both cases the transformation would come *as a response to deliverance*. In response to deliverance from the plagues, Pharaoh makes *his heart heavy*, thereby resisting the divine goal that he should *know*. This pattern in Exodus fits well the proposed reading of Isa 6:10. In response to the announcement of deliverance, their ears (thereby *made heavy*) would not hear, and their *heart* (thereby treated with salve) would not understand, so that they would not *know*. Understood this way, the potentially positive verbs describing the prophet's task have a negative effect because they relate to the prophet's preaching, first, a message of deliverance, but then, once this is rejected by the people, a message of judgment. The prophet was to apply salve to their *heart* and *honor* their ears with words of deliverance, with the result that they would neither hear nor understand, leading to judgment.

Besides the findings mentioned here, the comparison between the past of the prophet and the future of the people in ch. 6 suggests that the reader will encounter at least four things in what follows this visionary account: (1) a contrast between the prophet and the people (the prophet "heard" God's voice, but the people will not); (2) the people's inability to hear (the negative side of this contrast) will lead to the destruction aimed at producing a remnant, which itself was to be holy, with understanding and knowing; (3) if the oracle against Philistia is any guide, the destruction to come upon the people (including the burning that was to leave a holy remnant) would involve the Assyrians, as the people's counterpart to the prophet's own experience with the Seraph and its coal; and (4) if Kellenberger and Williamson are on the right track, the prophet will preach deliverance, which will be rejected, leading to a message of judgment; and in this connection, if the parallel with Exodus is to be taken seriously, this judgment will involve "signs," leading to an Exodus style deliverance. All these points are present in the telling of the Ahaz narrative as this has been patterned back on the commission of the prophet in ch. 6. For obvious reasons, the one exception is an Exodus style deliverance, which is, in fact, promised later for the other side of the Assyrian consequences caused (in part) by the failure of this Judean king.[26]

Commentary on Exodus 1–18. II. *Exodus 11–18*, ICC [London: Bloomsbury T&T Clark, 2020], 229, 232–3). The fulfillment of this in v. 25 (e.g., כבדת) may support Davies' reading since the recognition formula there finds expression in their realization that "the Lord is fighting (נלחם) for them *against* Egypt (במצרים)." Alternatively, one may translate it, "*through* Pharaoh," which would offer up a contrast as well, but with a different emphasis.

26. Chapter 10 describes the Assyrian oppressor and his overthrow, which is immediately followed in chs. 11–12 by a restoration of royal rule in Judah accompanied by the return of exiles. Both passages are portrayed as a new exodus: (1) 10:24–26 describes the Assyrian threat to Jerusalem as "in the manner of Egypt," promising a deliverance "in the

4.1.2. *Isaiah versus Ahaz: Two Responses to Two Different Kinds of Kingship (Isaiah 6–7).* The future revealed to the prophet in ch. 6 begins to unfold immediately in the following narrative, where the situation confronting King Ahaz has been set on analogy to those circumstances which faced the prophet Isaiah in the prior episode.[27] Where Isaiah faced the terrifying presence of the one divine king in the year of Uzziah's death, a menacing plan of two human kings confronted Ahaz (his grandson), whom they sought to dethrone. In these circumstances, the response of Ahaz to the two human kings (Rezin and Pekah) in the third-person narrative (ch. 7) offers up a contrast to the reaction of Isaiah to the one divine king in the preceding first-person account (ch. 6). This narrative repeats all the following elements from ch. 6 in nearly exact order, urging the reader into a comparison of the two accounts.

The threatening presence of the two human kings confronting Ahaz has been patterned on Isaiah's fearful encounter with the one divine king. In "the year king Uzziah (עזיהו) died," Isaiah saw the Lord "*high and lifted up*" on a throne, in which vision the "doorposts of the threshold *shook* (וינעו)" and "*the temple* (הבית) was filled with *smoke* (עשן)" from the Seraphim, the fiery beings in attendance (6:1–4).[28] Because Isaiah was a man of unclean lips living *in the midst of* (בתוך) a people of unclean lips, he responded in fear to this vision of the divine *king* (המלך [6:5]) in his throne room. As a result, the prophet's sin was removed by the Seraph. Each of these items is echoed in the Ahaz account. In the days of Ahaz, "the son of Jotham, the son of *Uzziah* (עזיהו),"[29] the Aramean *king* (מלך) and the Israelite *king* (מלך) "*went up*" to fight against Jerusalem. When their alliance was made known "to *the house* (בית) of David,[30] his heart and the heart of his people *shook* (וינע) like

---

manner of Egypt" (v. 24 // v. 26); (2) the echoes of the Exodus in chs. 11–12 are well known (e.g., 11:15-16; 12:2b // Exod 15:2); see Williamson, *Isaiah 6–12,* 677–740; Schwartz, "Mirrors of Moses in Isaiah 1–12."

27. Cf. Jörg Barthel, *Prophetenwort und Geschichte: Die Jesajaüberlieferung in Jes 6–8 und 28–31,* FAT 19 (Tübingen: Mohr Siebeck, 1997), 151–3; Becker, *Jesaja,* 57–9; Willem A. M. Beuken, *Jesaja 1–12,* HThKAT (Freiburg: Herder, 2003), 194, 206; Williamson, *Isaiah 6–12,* 89–172.

28. By means of semantics combined with assonance, the שרף is associated with the רצפה which it takes from upon the altar (v. 6), so that if the altar produced smoke, then so (the reader was probably to infer) did the Seraph. This is clearly assumed by Isa 14:28–32, where the שרף is equated with עשן from the north. As discussed above, Isa 14:28–32 has been modeled on ch. 6.

29. It is generally agreed that the note in 7:1, "the son of Uzziah," functions to link the line to 6:1, so that both accounts begin with a reference to Uzziah. This conclusion tends to be supported by the fact that 2 Kgs 16:1-5 (which many scholars suppose is the source of 7:1) introduces Ahaz simply as "the son of Jotham" (16:1), raising the question as to why the Isaiah editor would have added the note "the son of Uzziah" in 7:1. Cf. Barthel, *Prophetenwort und Geschichte,* 132–3; Becker, *Jesaja,* 35–6; Williamson, *Isaiah 6–12,* 112.

30. This parallel (house of God // house of David) is developed in 2 Sam 7 and is active in the parallel between Isa 7 and 36–39. See Stromberg, "Figural History," 88–91.

7. The Remnants of a Figural Past

the *shaking* (כנוע) of the trees of the forest before the wind" (7:1–2). Then Isaiah is sent to Ahaz with the message: "do not be afraid" before "these two stumps of *smoking* (העשנים) firebrands" who plan to place a *king* (מלך) of their own "*in the middle of* it (בתוכה) [Judah]" (7:3). In response to this threat, God tells Isaiah to assure Ahaz of deliverance, that their planned invasion would fail (7:7–9).

The consequences of Ahaz's rejection of this assurance are patterned on the consequences of the prophet's commission. Isaiah was commissioned to tell the people to "*listen carefully* (שמעו שמוע)…but do not *know* (תדעו)," which condition would last until judgment came on the people, leaving "the ground" (האדמה) desolate with a great "forsakenness" (העזובה) in the land, sparing only a *remnant*, who—as was seen above—would know and be holy (6:7, 11–13). Again, each of these items is echoed in the remainder of the Ahaz account. Ahaz rejects the prophet's message which assures deliverance from the enemy as well as the "sign" offered in confirmation of it. Ahaz is then told, "listen" (שמעו). In what follows, he is given the "sign" of Immanuel, whose diet of "curds and honey" signaled the fact that, "before the lad *knows* (ידע) how to reject evil and choose good, *the ground* [of these two hostile kings] *will be forsaken* (תעזב האדמה)." The king of Assyria would then turn against Judah itself, leaving only a remnant in the land, a remnant foreshadowed by the sign of Immanuel (7:10–17, 22).

The analogy between these two narrative accounts is more complex than can be elaborated here, including the presence of structures concurrent with this one (e.g. the role of לבב in both stories). Nevertheless, the above analysis seems sufficient to establish the case in at least a preliminary way. Not only are the listed items found together exclusively in these two chapters of the Hebrew Bible, but they follow nearly the same sequence in each case. Moreover, each of the repeated items in ch. 7 functions as a meaningful analogue to its corresponding element in ch. 6: the chronographic introduction (עזיהו [the *year Uzziah* died // the *days* of Ahaz, grandson of *Uzziah*]); the object of fear (מלך [the divine and human *kings*]); the location chosen by the divine and human kings (*high and lifted up* // *they went up*);[31] the description of the presence of these kings (ע"שן [*smoke* fills the temple // two stumps of *smoldering* firebrands]); the response to their royal presence (+ בית נו"ע [the *shaking* of the doors of the *temple* // the *shaking* of the *house* of David]); the imperative to the judged (שמעו); a period of judgment before knowing (ע"ד); and the judgment itself (ע"ז + אדמה) that will leave a remnant. Most importantly, the distribution of these items into a larger whole follows a definite strategy with a clearly discernible message: while a fearful response to the divine king in his house leads to the forgiveness of sins (as in the case of Isaiah the prophet), a fearful response to human kings against the divine command leads to judgment on the house of David (as in the case of Ahaz the king).

---

31. The words עלי"ה, נש"א, רו"ם are used *together* for the haughty pride of the Assyrian king against "the Holy One of Israel" in Isa 37:23–24. As we shall see below, the king of Assyria in ch. 37 finds his analogical correspondents in the Aramean and Israelite kings of ch. 7 (e.g., 7:1 // 36:1). Cf. 14:13–14.

Both passages envision the destruction leading to a remnant. In Isa 6:13, this remnant (like the prophet before it) becomes holy through burning. In Isa 7, the question whether the remnant will be holy is bound up with the sign of Immanuel. In the present form of the text, the diet of Immanuel points forward to the poetic elaboration of a remnant that will remain in the land of Judah after this judgment takes place (7:22–23).

Isaiah 6	Isaiah 7
"*The ground* (האדמה) will be left a wasteland…and great will be *the forsakenness in the midst of the land* (העזובה בקרב הארץ)…holy seed" (6:11b–13).	"*Curds and honey he shall eat* (חמאה ודבש יאכל)…for before the child knows how to reject the evil and choose the good, *the land will be forsaken* (תעזב האדמה)" (7:15–16). ↑ When the king of Assyria wreaks havoc on the land (v. 20), "everyone left over *in the midst of the land* (בקרב הארץ) will eat curds and honey (חמאה ודבש יאכל)" (7:22–23).

As this suggests, all three passages point to the same reality. Isaiah 7:22–23 combines a reference back to the child's ominous diet (7:15–16 [חמאה ודבש יאכל]) with an echo of the corresponding judgment announced in the visionary account (6:12 [בקרב הארץ]). Because the sign of Immanuel in 7:15–16 itself elaborates that judgment brought by the prophet's mission in 6:11–13 (האדמה + עז"ב), both texts serve as background to the description of the remnant in 7:22–23, the reality to which the child's diet points. The remnant left "in the midst of the land" after the Assyrian ravages will "eat curds and honey" like Immanuel.

But would this remnant be holy, like the one in 6:13? According to Isa 6:10–13, the people would not attain knowledge (יד"ע) until they had been reduced to a holy remnant. According to Isa 7:15–16, Immanuel—who was a sign of the remnant to come—would eat "curds and honey" in order to attain the knowledge (יד"ע) of how to "reject evil and choose good."[32] Because the remnant would also eat "curds and honey" as a consequence of invasion, the implication seems to be that, through their degradation at the hands of the Assyrians, they were to learn to know how to reject evil and choose good like Immanuel himself. In this way, both passages portray the period of judgment as a process that was to produce a remnant acceptable to God, whose holiness could not tolerate the unjust speech of "unclean lips."[33]

32. 7:15 has לדעתו. 7.16 has בטרם ידע.

33. In part, the moral significance of rejecting evil and choosing good in 7:15 derives from its relationship to 5:18–20, the center two of six woes in that chapter dealing with justice and righteousness. These two woes are developed in the frame of the invasion oracle at 5:26–30 (5:19 // 5:26; 5:20 // 5:30). Accordingly, each of these two woes finds an inversion on the other side of the Assyrian invasion with the royal restoration announced in the two royal oracles (9:1–6; 11), on which see Stromberg, "Hezekiah and the Oracles Against the

If they were to become a *holy* remnant after the Assyrian destruction, they would need to follow in the footsteps of the prophet himself, who, realizing that he was unclean of lips and had seen the divine king, responded in a fearful confession of this, thereby attaining a state of holiness after his experience with the burning coal. According to 6:10, repentance was necessary for healing. So, the remnant, which would become holy only after a burning like that of the prophet, would need to repent and be healed. This is the inescapable implication of the pattern of holiness in ch. 6.

In sum, all four expectations that arose in our analysis of ch. 6 are fulfilled in the narrative pattern of ch. 7: (1) there is a contrast between the prophet in ch. 6 and Ahaz in ch. 7, the former fearing the divine king, the latter fearing the human kings—with opposite consequences (forgiveness vs. judgment); (2) the refusal of Ahaz to hear the divine word caused a destruction aimed at producing a remnant that was to embrace righteousness; (3) the agent of the people's destruction, parallel to the Seraph in ch. 6, is identified as Assyria, portrayed elsewhere as a Seraph; (4) in line with the reading of 6:10 proposed by Kellenberger and Williamson, the prophet initially announces deliverance to Ahaz, who rejects the message, so that an announcement of judgment for the future follows; and, in fulfillment of the Exodus-like mission of 6:10 to apply salve to the *heart* and make the ears *heavy* (so that they do not listen or perceive), the refusal of Ahaz to listen to the divine voice leads to the multiplication of "signs" in judgment, precisely the consequence of Pharaoh's *heart* being made *heavy* in the Exodus account (7:14; 8:1–4, 18; Exod 7:3; 10:1–2; cf. 4:41).

4.1.3. The Prophet's Response to Threat (Isaiah 6–7 and 8:1–9:6). Building on this analogy between the commission of the prophet and the account of Ahaz, Isa 8:1–9:6 develops the comparison further, only some aspects of which may be mentioned here.[34] The first comes in Isa 8:5–10. Here, God tells Isaiah of the judgment to come on Judah (vv. 5–8), and then the prophet responds with an expression of confidence (vv. 9–10). There is wide agreement that ch. 8 has been deliberately coordinated with chs. 6–7. In the present instance, the announcement

---

Nations in Isaiah," 311–13. But before these two royal oracles, the two woes from ch. 5 are developed in the two portents of the Assyrian invasion, namely, the Immanuel sign (5:19 // 7:15) and the Maher-shalal-hash-baz sign (5:19, 26 // 8:1, 3). Moreover, because these two woes deal with "those who say," their linkage to ch. 6 (5:19 // 6:3, 9) probably serves as the background to the accusation that the people are unclean of "lips" in 6:4 with an eye towards the invasion to come (5:9 // 6:11–13). Chapter 1 also serves as important background here. In 1:2–20 (which looks back on the devastation wrought by the Assyrians in fulfillment of 6:10–13), the people, who neglect justice (vv. 16–17), who neither "know" nor "understand" (v. 3), spurn "the *Holy One* of Israel" (v. 4). Thus, holiness and justice are not only compatible in Isaiah, but one cannot have the former without the latter.

34. The links between chs. 6–7 and 8:1–9:6 are widely recognized, though there is much debate regarding the diachrony of this material. See, for instance, Barthel, *Prophetenwort und Geschichte*, 37–242; Becker, *Jesaja*, 21–123.

of judgment echoes the commission of the prophet (6:1–9 // 8:6–8). Also, the prophet's confident response echoes his earlier message to Ahaz (7:4–8 // 8:9–10). Above, we saw that the account of Ahaz had been patterned on the commission of the prophet to enable a contrast: where Isaiah feared the divine king (leading to forgiveness), Ahaz feared the human kings (leading to judgment). This suggests that a similar contrast will emerge in 8:5–10, which echoes both texts.

I would start by noting that 8:5–10 unfolds as a two-part elaboration of the significance of the Immanuel child in ch. 7. In 7:14–17, Immanuel initially represents an assurance to Judah (the land of the two hostile kings will be devastated) and then a threat against Judah (God would bring against it the king of Assyria [את מלך אשור]). The two-part elaboration of this Immanuel prophecy in 8:5–10 reverses this order (from assurance–threat to threat–assurance). First, God tells Isaiah how the people had sinned in relation to the two hostile kings, sentencing the people to a future judgment by the king of Assyria (8:5–8). The judgment here echoes the Immanuel prophecy in ch. 7: God was sending the king of Assyria (את מלך אשור [7:17; 8:7]) to inundate Judah, "your land, O Immanuel" (עמנו אל [7:14; 8:8]). Second, the prophet responds with confidence to the announcement of this menacing future (8:9–10). Like the announcement of judgment, his confidence echoes the Immanuel prophecy in ch. 7: the plans of the nations (including Assyria) will not prevail, "because God is with us" (עמנו אל [8:10; cf. 7:14]). Both parts conclude with a reference to Immanuel (8:8, 10), sharpening the contrast between the Assyrian threat and the prophet's confident theological response to it.

Alongside this development of the Immanuel prophecy, 8:5–10 first echoes the prophet's message to Ahaz and then his experience in the divine throne room. But what do these echoes achieve? To begin with the judgment God reveals to the prophet, 8:5–8 portrays the coming Assyrian threat and its cause on analogy to the commissioning of the prophet and his vision of the divine throne room (6:1–9). In his vision, the prophet sees the following: "the king" (המלך), the Lord of hosts; his skirts "filling" (מלאים) the temple; Seraphim with six "wings" (כנפים) each, proclaiming that "the fullness of all the land is his glory" (מלא כל הארץ כבודו); and the temple "filling" (ימלא) with smoke. After the prophet decries his wretched state, a Seraph *touches* (ויגע) his lips with a hot coal, removing his sin. Then the prophet is commissioned (את מי אשלח ומי ילך לנו) with his task *vis-à-vis* "this people" (לעם הזה): they would not listen to the prophet leading to a devastation of their land.

Alluding to this scene, 8:5–8 works its way backwards from the prophet's commission to his vision of the throne room. Echoing the prophet's commission, God accuses "this people" (העם הזה) of rejecting "*the waters of Shiloh that flow* (את מי השלח ההלכים) *gently.*" Because this rejection entailed a refusal to listen to Isaiah (the one sent [של״ח] by God), it was a fulfillment of his commission wherein the people would not listen and become subject to judgment. In line with the goal of that commission, this rejection of "the waters of Shiloh" results in a threat to the land of Judah: a human *king* (מלך), the king of Assyria, with his army would inundate the land like a flood. This flood would not *touch* (נג״ע) the lips (as with the prophet), but the neck. Whether this watery threat would have the same effect as the fiery coal is yet to be seen, though the analogical implication seems to be that such was the desired result. In line with this, the Assyrian king and his army are set on analogy to the divine king and his Seraphim: the Assyrian king and "his glory" (כבודו) will inundate Judah, so that the full outspreading of "his wings" (כנפיו) will be "the fullness of the breadth of your land (מלא רחב ארצך), O Immanuel" (8:8).

The inversion in sequence here underscores two things. First, their rejection of the gently flowing waters of Shiloh (השלח)—an image of reassurance that stands in contrast to the raging waters of Assyria that would take their place—was a rejection of the prophet sent (שלח) by God.[35] This follows the pattern seen earlier of an initial message of reassurance, having been rejected, being replaced by a message of judgment. Second, the judgment they would endure as a result would be like the experience of the prophet, both encountering a king and his glory, being touched painfully by the winged thing attending his presence. Once again, the Seraphim of Isaiah's earlier experience find their analogical counterparts in Assyria. In line with ch. 7, both points echo the expectations created by the pattern of ch. 6 itself, where the people would not receive the message of the prophet whose experience in the divine throne room with the Seraph, nevertheless, ultimately portended their own future.

Where God reveals the threat to the prophet in 8:5–8, the prophet responds to this confidently in 8:9–10. Because 8:5–8 portrays the threat from the king of Assyria on analogy to the prophet's vision of the divine king in 6:1–9, the reader is compelled to compare the response of the prophet to each. In ch. 6, Isaiah responds to the divine king in fear. Here, the prophet responds to the human king—the king of Assyria portrayed on analogy to the divine king—not with fear, but confidence. Indeed, his expression of confidence in the face of threat from the Assyrian king draws directly on the divine word he delivered to, but which was rejected by, Ahaz when confronted by the kings of Aram and Ephraim (7:4–8 // 8:9–10). Though Aram and Ephraim plotted evil (יעץ רעה) against Judah, it would not stand (לא תקום), and Ephraim would be shattered (יחת). Ahaz rejected this divine word, leading to the future threat by the Assyrian king. In response to the impending Assyrian deluge into Judah, the prophet proclaims: "Be evil (רעו), O peoples, and be shattered (וחתו)... Plan a plan (עצו עצה), and it will not stand (ולא יקום)."

---

35. At 8:6, 1QIsaᵃ reads שולח: "this people rejected the gently flowing waters of *the one sending*." LXX has Σιλωαμ, a name ("Siloam") understood in relation to "sending" by at least one early interpreter. In John 9:7, Jesus sends a blind man to the pool of Siloam, which the reader is told "means 'sent.'" Because Isa 8:5–10 is a development of the prophet's commission in ch. 6 (where he was to prevent the people from seeing), it is noteworthy that here in John the blind man receives his sight after washing in the pool of "sent," which then leads to a broader debate about metaphorical sight and blindness between Jesus and the Pharisees in which allusion is made to Isa 6:9 (John 9:39). Here, Jesus' deliverance of the blind man is called a "sign" (9:16), whose reception (unbelief) is later explained by a citation of Isa 6:9 (John 12:37–40).

Immediately after expressing this confidence, the prophet justifies his words ("for the Lord said to me"), recounting how God disciplined him not to fear what this people fears, but to fear God instead (vv. 11–13). The prophet's justification for his confidence explicitly articulates the principle governing all of the above contrasts: (1) the contrast between Isaiah (who feared the divine king in ch. 6) and Ahaz (who feared the human kings in ch. 7); (2) the contrast between Ahaz (who feared the human kings in ch. 7) and Isaiah (who did not fear the human king in ch. 8); and (3) Isaiah (who feared the divine king in ch. 6) and Isaiah (who did not fear the human king in ch. 8). Because this whole series of comparisons begins in ch. 6 itself where the prophet's experience (his transition from a state of unclean to holy through the agency of the Seraph) portends the future of the people (when they will be transformed into a holy [קדש] remnant through judgment), it is surely significant that the prophet is admonished not to follow the people in proclaiming conspiracy (קשר) and fearing man, but to "sanctify" (תקדישו) the Lord, for "he is your object of fear" (8:12–13). The portrait of the prophet from the past is a model for the remnant in the future, a remnant that was to embrace holiness, rejecting the fear of mere mortals.

This leads to a brief consideration of the royal oracle which follows (9:1–6). Instead of fearing the divine king like Isaiah (ch. 6), Ahaz feared the two human kings of the Syro-Ephraimite coalition (ch. 7). By contrast, Isaiah—fearing the divine king (ch. 6)—did not respond in fear to the human king of Assyria, who had taken the place of the Syro-Ephraimite coalition as the next threat to Judah (8). The nature of that threat emerges from the analogical structure of the Ahaz account itself: because of Ahaz's failure, the coalition's plan to install a king (מלך) in Judah, Ben Tabal (את בן טבאל), gives way to the divine plan to send days against Judah, namely, the king of Assyria (את מלך אשור). The repetition of את marking the second direct object of a verb in *hiphil* comes precisely at the conclusion of each of two parallel units[36] to underscore the point: where the Syro-Ephraimite coalition had no right to decide the king over Judah (את בן טבאל), the parallel conclusion impels the reader to accept that God did (את מלך אשור). Whether God had actually intended the Assyrian king to take the place of the Judean king because of the failure of Ahaz, the comparison forces the reader to contemplate this possibility. And such was Sennacherib's objective when he showed up in Jerusalem. Having conquered all the fortified cities of Judah, Sennacherib attempted to compel the remaining inhabitants of Jerusalem to abandon Hezekiah as their king and to submit to his rule instead, the rule of "the great king, the king of Assyria" (36:13–17).

---

36. By means of a forward symmetry, vv. 10–17 are patterned on vv. 1–6, with vv. 7–9 as a center piece having its own inverse symmetrical organization. For instance, consider the following: העלמה // העליונה, תעלת, בן, לקראת (vv. 2, 13); בית דוד (vv. 1, 20); למעלה // עלה, וקראת בן (vv. 3, 14 [each son is a sign]); קו"ץ, משני שני מפני/משני, עליך, אפרים (vv. 4–5, 16–17 [forcing a division in it // splitting of Ephraim from Judah]); // נמליך מלך...את בן טבאל יביא...את מלך אשור (vv. 6, 17).

Because the fearful response of Ahaz to the Syro-Ephraimite plan led to potential rule under the Assyrian (rather than Davidic) king, one might expect Isaiah's confident response to the Assyrian threat to lead down the opposite path: future rule under a Davidic (rather than Assyrian) king. This, I suspect, is the point of presenting the prophet as a model for hope under judgment in the remainder of ch. 8,[37] which leads directly to an expression of renewed rule on the Davidic throne after the foreign yoke would be removed (9:1–6). Indeed, this royal renewal is contrasted with the failure of Ahaz. Where King Ahaz—the first person we are told who responded to Isaiah after his commission—is contrasted negatively with Gideon,[38] the royal renewal in 9:1–6 is compared positively with the success of this judge, as a time after the Assyrian yoke would be removed (9:3; cf. 10:26–27; 14:24–27). And the fact that this royal oracle concludes in 9:6 with what sounds like an echo of 6:1 suggests that, with this, the argument has come full circle: in the year of the death of the Davidic king, Isaiah sees the divine king sitting on his throne (על כסא) from where he announces a period of judgment at the end of which there will again be rule on the throne (על כסא) of David.[39] This too relates divine kingship to that of men, in this case, the descendants of David, who ruled only at the pleasure of the One whom Isaiah saw in the throne room, *the* king, the Lord of hosts (6:5).

4.2. *Ahaz and Hezekiah (Isaiah 7:1–9:6 and 36–39)*

Turning from father to son, I note first that the account of Hezekiah has been set on analogy to that of Ahaz, as has long been recognized. I have developed this case at length elsewhere, so I give only a summary here along with a few new items related to the present argument.[40] This analogy begins with a contrast between the response of Ahaz to the Syro-Ephraimite threat and that of Hezekiah to the Assyrian threat.

Both accounts have a similar narrative introduction, underscoring an important contrast between the two situations (7:1 // 36:1): "It happened in (ויהי ב)" the time of Ahaz/Hezekiah, *king* of Judah, that a foreign *king(s)* went up (עלה) to do battle against Jerusalem/the fortified cities of Judah. In each case the sentence concludes with the outcome, the one contrasting with the other: "they were not able to do battle against it" vs. "and he captured them."

In response to each situation, a messenger is sent, one by the divine king, the Lord, and the other by the human king, Sennacherib (7:3 // 36:2–3). In the case of Ahaz, "the Lord commanded Isaiah, 'Go out (צא) to meet Ahaz, you and your son

---

37. On this, but in relation to chs. 40–55, see H. G. M. Williamson, *The Book Called Isaiah: Deutero-Isaiah's Role in Composition and Redaction* (Oxford: Clarendon, 1994), 94–110.

38. See Stromberg, "Hezekiah and the Oracles against the Nations in Isaiah," 318 n. 42.

39. Barthel, *Propheten und Geschichte*, 113 n. 208: "Das Motiv des Thrones (כסא) in 6,1 und 9,6 bildet (jetzt) einen Rahmen um Jes 6,1–9,6."

40. Stromberg, "Figural History in the Book of Isaiah."

Shear-yashuv at the end of *the conduit of the upper pool along the highway to the fuller's field* (קצה תעלת הברכה העליונה אל מסלת שדה כובס)." In the case of Hezekiah, "the king of Assyria sent the Rav-shakeh with a great army from Lachish to Jerusalem, to the king, Hezekiah, and he stood *at the conduit of the upper pool along the highway to the fuller's field* (בתעלת הברכה העליונה במסלת שדה כובס)." And Elyakim and others "*went out* (ויצא) to him."

The message to Ahaz was reassuring, whereas the dispatch to Hezekiah was threatening. Isaiah was to tell Ahaz: "do not fear" (אל תירא [7:4]). By contrast, the Assyrian messenger carried a threatening message (36:4–20), to which Isaiah responded, after Hezekiah beseeched him to pray: "do not fear" (אל תירא [36:6]). In both cases, this imperative is followed by an assurance that the foe will not succeed in conquering Jerusalem.

Where Ahaz rejects the assurance from the divine king resulting in the promise of judgment on Judah (7:16–17), Hezekiah responds to the threatening words of the human king by turning to the Lord resulting in the promise of deliverance and renewal for the remnant in Judah (37:10–35).

To these contrasts between the two kings, I would add that Hezekiah is compared positively with the prophet. The description of the Assyrian threat in 36:1–3 evokes the same threat promised in ch. 8. In 8:7, "the Lord will *bring up against them* (מעלה עליהם)...the *king of Assyria and all of his glory* (כבודו); and *he will go up* (ועלה) *over all* (על כל) its channels and pass *over all* (על כל) its banks." In 36:1–3, "the *king of Assyria*, Sennacherib, *went up against all* (עלה על כל) of the fortified cities of Judah...the *king of Assyria* sent the Rav-shakeh with a *great* (כבד) army." Regarding the former, Isaiah responds to the threat of the glory (כבוד) of the Assyrian king with confidence in God (8:9–10). Regarding the latter, Hezekiah responds to the great (כבד) army of the Assyrian king by going to the "house" of God in prayer, precisely the location of the prophet's call account (37:11). In the former, Isaiah's expression of confidence leads to the hope of a renewal of the Davidic throne after the Assyrian aggression (9:1–6). In the latter, Hezekiah's pious action (set on analogy to that of the prophet) leads to an assurance that the remnant of the house of Judah would come forth from Jerusalem (after God saw the Assyrians off) for a renewal. This promise concludes with the last line of the royal oracle in 9:1–6: "the zeal of the Lord of hosts will do this (קנאת יהוה צבאות תעשה זאת)" (9:6; 37:32). What the prophet modeled (hope under judgment), the king enacted, resulting in the same hope, the hope of a righteous renewal of the remnant under rule of the Davidic throne, characterized by justice within society.

If the above analysis of chs. 6–7 is correct, so that the remnant-sign of Immanuel evokes the holy remnant revealed in the prophet's commission (6:13), then one should expect the same for the sign given to Hezekiah for the renewal of a remnant that would survive the Assyrian onslaught. The question then becomes: would this remnant which survived the Seraph-like devastation of the Assyrians become the holy remnant revealed to the prophet at his call?

This question appears to govern the sign given to Hezekiah regarding this remnant, as it evokes the Immanuel sign given to Ahaz regarding the remnant (7:11, 14 // 37:30–32). To reassure Ahaz, God tells him, "Ask *for yourself a sign*

(לך אות) from the Lord your God, making it *as deep as Sheol or as high as above* (למעלה)." But, after Ahaz refuses, he is told "therefore the Lord himself will give *you a sign* (לכם אות), behold *the young woman* (העלמה)...[the lad] *shall eat* (יאכל) curds and honey." Echoing this passage, a sign of assurance is given to Hezekiah, "This shall be *for you the sign* (לך אות)...in the third-year sow and reap, plant vineyards and *eat* (אכלו) their fruit; for the remnant of the house of Judah left over will take root *downwards* and make fruit *upwards* (למעלה), because from Jerusalem shall go forth a remnant and escapees from Mount Zion."

In both cases, the sign—especially the reference to eating (אכ"ל)– pertains to a remnant that survives the Assyrian onslaught. Because the remnant-sign given to Ahaz portended the remnant in 6:13, one expects the remnant-sign given Hezekiah to do the same.[41] In this light, it is significant that, where the remnant in 6:13 is called a "holy *seed* (זרע)," the sign given to Hezekiah involved "*sowing seed*" (זרעו) and harvesting, planting vineyards and eating their "fruit" (37:30). This was a sign that the remnant of the house of Judah would take "root downward and bear fruit upward" (v. 31). What this renewal of the remnant entailed is not elaborated here beyond the given metaphor.

However, the passage is highly evocative, as is widely recognized, suggesting the renewal would have to involve the embrace of God's will for society (37:30–32). We have already seen that it evokes the remnant-sign of Immanuel (who points toward a time after judgment of rejecting evil and choosing good) as well as the royal oracle in 9:1–6 (a time after judgment characterized by justice and righteousness). The sign given to Hezekiah probably also evokes a set of related passages: (1) the vision of Jerusalem's exaltation when it would be so characterized by justice that the nations would to go there to learn the word of the Lord and find justice (2:3 // 37:32);[42] (2) the royal restoration in ch. 11 after the threat of Assyria (a period of restoration characterized by justice and righteousness);[43] and, (3) by way of inversion, the "vineyard" that produced bad fruit for God (bloodshed and outcry instead of justice and righteousness), thereby incurring diving wrath, the "thorns and thistles" later developed in relation to the Assyrian devastation of their land (5:1–7; compare 5:5–6 with 7:23–25 and, as an inversion of this, 10:17).

All of this indicates that the renewal of the remnant of the house of Judah under the leadership of Hezekiah was to be a fulfillment of that righteous remnant revealed to the prophet in 6:13, one characterized by righteousness. This expectation is suggested by both the Hezekiah narrative (with the sign given to the king) and the earlier narratives in chs. 6–7 to which it is related. That the remnant left in Jerusalem by the Assyrians would not be automatically holy is clear from ch. 1, which addresses itself to just this remnant (1:2–9) to persuade it to embrace justice and, with that, a better future (1:10–20).

---

41. On the relationship between 6:11–13; 7:14–15, 22, see above.
42. Marvin Sweeney, *Isaiah 1–4 and the Post-Exilic Understanding of the Isaianic Tradition*, BZAW 171 (Berlin: de Gruyter, 1988), 170–1; Williamson, *Isaiah 1–5*, 177.
43. Stromberg, "Hezekiah and the Oracles Against the Nations in Isaiah."

In the sign given to Hezekiah, the success of this remnant went hand in hand with that of the Judean leadership. The future of the remnant takes a turn for the worse, then, when Hezekiah, the king of Judah, fails at the end of the narrative. This suggests that the post-Assyrian remnant of Hezekiah's day did not ultimately enjoy the righteous renewal anticipated by the sign of Immanuel and the holy remnant, revealed to the prophet.

In Isa 39, Hezekiah's failure at the visit of the Babylonian delegation brings consequences that echo those caused by the sin of Ahaz, his father, starting the cycle of judgment all over again (7:17 // 39:6–7). In response to the sin of Ahaz, the prophet says, "The Lord *will bring* (יביא) upon you, upon your people, and upon *the house of your father* (בית אביך) *days* (ימים) which have not *come* (באו) since *the day* (למיום) when Ephraim split from Judah, namely, *the king of Assyria* (מלך אשור)." In response to the sin of Hezekiah, the prophet says, "Behold, *days are coming* (ימים באים) when everything in *your house* (בביתך) and everything which *your fathers* (אבתיך) stored up to *this day* (עד היום) will be carried away to Babylon…and some of your sons…will become eunuchs in the palace of *the king of Babylon* (מלך בבל)." The former judgment spares a remnant: "all who *are left* (הנותר) in the land" (7:22 → 7:15). By contrast, the latter envisions a total emptying of the palace: "not a thing *will be left* (לא יותר)" (39:6). Those left in the land were to learn to reject evil and choose good like Immanuel. Because Hezekiah fails in this respect, nothing would be left in his house.

Just as God told Isaiah of a holy remnant (זר"ע) while in the Lord's house (בית), so he told Hezekiah of the renewal (זר"ע) of a remnant while in the Lord's house (בית).[44] But just as Ahaz brought judgment on the house (בית) of his father leaving (ית"ר) only a remnant, so Hezekiah caused judgment on his house (בית)—where his fathers had stored their treasure—leaving (ית"ר) nothing.[45] First promised that a remnant of "the house of Judah" would "go forth from Jerusalem (מירושלם תצא)" to bear the fruit of renewal (37:32), Hezekiah is now told that some of the sons "which come forth from you (אשר יצאו ממך)" will be taken as eunuchs into the palace of the king of Babylon (39:7). The former echoes the hopes for a renewed establishment (כו"ן) of the Davidic throne (כסא) and kingdom (ממלכה) forever (עד עולם) in 9:1–6 (9:6 // 37:32). The latter contrasts with that future promised to David when, "I will raise up your seed (זרעך) after you, which comes forth from your loins (אשר יצא ממעיך)…and I will establish the throne of his kingdom forever (וכננתי את כסא ממלכתו)" (2 Sam 7:12–13). With Hezekiah's sin, the hopes for a new Solomonic kingdom for the post-Assyrian remnant (זרע) fade away.

The prophet's last words to Hezekiah (מלך בבל [39:7]) echo his last words to Ahaz (מלך אשור [7:17]). In each narrative, these come as the last two words of the prophet to the Judean king. According to the analogical shape of these narratives, the future Babylonian oppression would be like a repetition of the past

---

44. 6:4, 13; 37:14, 30–32.
45. 7:2, 13, 17, 22; 39:6.

Assyrian destruction. As with the survivors of the Assyrian destruction, we may anticipate that the remnant of the Babylonian catastrophe will receive the same call to embrace holiness.

5. The Second Half of the Book

If the judgment under Assyria becomes an analogy for that under Babylon (so that we are to expect a holy remnant after the latter as we did after the former), then we may anticipate that the second half of Isaiah will present its message on analogy to these earlier passages in the first half of the book to precisely this end. The punishment under Babylon (like that under Assyria) had as its aim the creation of a holy remnant, as was revealed to the prophet at his commission in Isa 6. This expectation finds a partial fulfillment in the opening of the second half of the book, which, announcing the dawn of a new day for the Babylonian captives, initiates its message by means of analogies to both the Assyrian threat and the commission of the prophet.

5.1. The Prophet's Commission and the Opening of the Book's Second Half (Isaiah 6 and 40:1-11)

Immediately after the Hezekiah narrative, the second half of the book begins with a clear evocation of the prophet's original commission, as is widely recognized (6 // 40:1–11).[46] To understand this allusion, one must first perceive the structure of Isa 40:1–11, which consists of four parts governed by an inverse symmetry (A [vv. 1–2]; B [vv. 3–5]; B' [vv. 6–8]; A' [vv. 9–11]). Respectively, the outer units (A // A') mention "Jerusalem" and "our God," followed by "her work" // "his wage,"[47] followed by "her punishment" // "his recompense,"[48] followed by the "hand" // "arm" of the Lord, the one acting in judgment in the past and the other in salvation for the future. Respectively, the inner units (B // B') begin with "a voice proclaiming" // "a voice saying, 'proclaim'" and end with "the mouth of the Lord has spoken (דבר)" // "the word (דבר) of our God." While the coordination of these parts involves more than this (such as an additional forward symmetry in B // B'[49]), this analysis is sufficient for the purpose here. Among other things, this four-part structure invites a comparison between A // A', between the past punishment

---

46. Peter R. Ackroyd, *Studies in the Religious Tradition of the Old Testament* (London: SCM, 1987), 106–7; Friedhelm Hartenstein, *Das Archiv des verborgenen Gottes: Studien zur Unheilsprophetie Jesajas und zur Zionstheologie der Psalmen in assyrischer Zeit*, BThSt 71 (Neukirchener-Vluyn: Neukirchener Verlag, 2011), 119–25; Christopher R. Seitz, "The Divine Council: Temporal Transition and New Prophecy in the Book of Isaiah," *JBL* 109 (1990): 229–47; Williamson, *The Book Called Isaiah*, 37–8.
47. For the parallel between צבא and שׂכ"ר, see Job 7:1.
48. For the close relationship between עון and פעלה, see Isa 65:7.
49. "Our God," "all flesh," "all the flesh," "our God."

of Jerusalem and its future role as the herald of salvation.[50] This comparison enables the reader to perceive the strategy behind the echoes of ch. 6 here, which are distributed among all four parts.

Isaiah 6	Isaiah 40:1–11
Isaiah sees (רא"ה) a vision of God the king, during which a voice is crying out (קול קורא) that all the earth is God's glory (כבוד). The prophet responds, "I am undone" (vv. 1–5).	(A) "'Comfort, comfort my people,' says your God, 'Speak to the heart of Jerusalem, proclaim to her that her hard service is finished, that her punishment (עונה) is paid, that she has received from the hand (לקחה מיד) of the Lord double for all her sins (חטאתיה)'" (vv. 1–2).
In response, one of the Seraphim flies to the prophet with a coal in his hand (בידו), which he had taken with tongs from upon (במלקחים לקח מעל) the altar. Having touched the prophet's mouth with this, the Seraph says: "your iniquity and your sin (עונך וחטאתך) are removed" (vv. 6–7).	(B) "A voice cries out (קול קורא): prepare the way of the Lord…the glory (כבוד) of the Lord will be revealed and all flesh together will see (וראו) it" (vv. 3–5).
Then: "I heard the voice (קול) of the Lord speaking (אמר), 'Who will I send and who will go for us?' And I said (ואמר), 'Here I am, send me.' And he said, 'Go and say to this people'" (vv. 8–9).	(B') "A voice speaking (קול אמר), 'proclaim'. And one said (ואמר), 'what shall I proclaim?'" (v. 6).
Like the prophet, the people would face a burning away of their uncleanness so that a holy seed (זרע) remained. (vv. 9–13)	(A') Jerusalem is commissioned to announce restoration now that judgment is complete: "Behold the Lord God is coming with strength, his arm (זרעו) ruling for him… with his arm (בזרעו) he will gather lambs." (vv. 9–11)

I am able to offer only a partial analysis here. I begin by observing that the sequence in ch. 40 is very close to that in ch. 6, except for the first two units (A and B) which invert the order of the corresponding parallels in the account of the prophet's commission. This inversion is coordinated with the structure of 40:1–11, wherein the commission of Jerusalem in the future (A') is brought into relation with the punishment of Jerusalem in the past (A). Essential to understanding how the allusion to the commission of the prophet functions within this four-part context (wherein A' is compared to A) is, as observed above: the structure of ch. 6 assigns a prospective significance to the prophet's experience, the burning of the prophet in the past foreshadows the burning of the people in the future. The allusion follows the figural logic of ch. 6. God's agent, the Seraph, took

---

50. On the translation "herald of good tidings, Jerusalem" (rather than "herald of good tidings *to* Jerusalem"), see most recently, H. G. M. Williamson, "Good News To or From Zion? A Reconsideration of Isaiah 40.9," in *Herald of Good Tidings: Essays on the Bible, Prophecy and the Hope of Israel in Honour of Antti Laato,* ed. Pekka Lindqvist and Lotta Valve, HBM 97 (Sheffield: Sheffield Phoenix, 2021), 13–22.

(לק״ח) in his hand (יד) the hot coal and touched the lips of the prophet with it, removing his עון and חטאת. Likewise, Jerusalem, "my people," had been punished, taking (לק״ח) from the hand (יד) of God her punishment, removing her עון and חטאת (A [vv. 1–2]). And just as this led to the commission of the prophet which was aimed at producing a seed (זרע) after judgment, so the parallel experience of Jerusalem led to her commission to proclaim a restoration involving the divine arm (זרוע) after judgment (A' [vv. 9–11]).

Since this opening of the second half of the book evokes the commission of the prophet (to whom was revealed a holy seed [זרע קדש] after destruction), we can expect the survivors of the Babylonian captivity addressed in what follows to be called to holiness. And based on the specific parallel at the end of this passage, we might expect this call to holiness to involve the holy arm (זרוע קדש) of the Lord.

5.2. The Hezekiah Narrative and the Opening of the Book's Second Half (Isaiah 36–39 and 40:1–11)

While the opening of the second half of the book evokes the commission of the prophet in this way, it also exhibits an analogy with the Assyrian period of destruction emanating from this commission and portrayed in the first half of the book. Thus far, I have argued that (1) chs. 36–39 have been coordinated with 7:1–9:6 and (2) these two narratives have been framed by the commission of the prophet on one end (ch. 6) and the commission scene parallel to this on the other (40:1–11). Since the transition from ch. 6 to ch. 7 involves an analogy of inversion (*divine* king // *human* king), we can anticipate the comparable transition from chs. 36–39 to ch. 40 to make use of a similar analogy, but one that runs in the opposite direction (*human* king // *divine* king). Following immediately on the Hezekiah account, Isaiah 40:1–11 presents an analogical inversion of that narrative to precisely this effect.

Both accounts involve the sending of a messenger (36:1–2 // 40:9). After Sennacherib captures all "the fortified cities of Judah" (ערי יהודה הבצרות), he sends a messenger from one of these (Lachish) "to Jerusalem" (ירושלמה). In ch. 40, God commissions "the herald of good tidings, Jerusalem" (מבשרת ירושלם) to deliver a message to "the cities of Judah" (ערי יהודה). In the former, a messenger from one of the cities of Judah brings a message to Jerusalem, whereas in the latter a messenger, Jerusalem, is to bring a message to the cities of Judah. The direction of travel is inverted, as is the sender (human → divine). Underscoring this inversion is a possible wordplay between the descriptions of the respective locations from which the message is sent: the cities of Judah as "fortified" (בצ״ר+ת) and Jerusalem as "herald" (בש״ר+ת).

The action of the messengers involves a contrast (37:23–24; cf. 36:13 // 40:9). As a mouthpiece for the Assyrian king, the Assyrian messenger to Jerusalem *lifted his voice* (הרימותה קול) *against* (על) God, saying, "I [Sennacherib] have *gone up* (עליתי) to *the height of the mountains* (הרים)." On behalf of the divine king, the messenger, Jerusalem, was told to "*ascend a high hill*" (על הר גבה עלי) and *lift her voice* (הרימי בכח קולך). Instead of a messenger for the king of Assyria, there is a herald for the divine king. Instead of criticizing the Assyrian king for boasting through his messenger that he had ascended to the height of the mountains, the divine king commands his own herald to ascend a high mountain, presumably as a reflection of God's own exalted status (cf. 6:1; 14:13–15).

The messages to Jerusalem and the cities of Judah are contrasted (37:17, 29, 34 // 40:11). In the former message, the king of Assyria is *coming* (בו״א) to take them to a land like their own. In the latter, the divine king is *coming* (בו״א) to gather the sheep and carry them to their own land. Here God would return the people to the promised land, whereas earlier Sennacherib would take them from it. To sharpen the comparison, the Assyrian king would take them from it to "a land *like your land*," which is then described in terms reminiscent of the promised land, as "a land of grain and new wine" (36:17; cf. Deut 33:28).

The description of the route of the king of Assyria and the divine king is the same (36:2; 37:29, 34 // 40:3–5). In preparation for the coming of the Assyrian king on a "path" (דרך), the messenger is sent to a "highway" (מסלה) with "a great army" (חיל כבד). In preparation for the coming of the divine king, one is to prepare "a path" (דרך) and "a highway" (מסלה) because all flesh will see his "glory" (כבוד). As seen above and from this contrast, the latter echoes the revelation of the divine glory in 6:3, whereas the former fulfills the sentence of judgment in 8:7, itself an echo of 6:3 by way of inversion (6:3 = the glory of the divine king; 8:7 = the glory of the Assyrian king).

In both accounts, the same assurance goes to Jerusalem (36:6 // 40:9). The head of Jerusalem, Hezekiah, is told: "do not fear" (אל תירא). Here, Jerusalem is told: "do not fear" (אל תיראי).

The highly specific locutions, meaningful parallels in subject matter, and consistent strategy of inversion (cities of Judah → Jerusalem // Jerusalem → cities of Judah; *human* king // *divine* king) all suggest that this is a deliberate strategy. The commission in 40:1–11 signaled not only the end of judgment; it also marked a reversal in the direction of Israel's history from one of judgment to one of salvation. This reversal is precisely what one would expect from everything seen up to this point. Where the *divine* king in ch. 6 becomes the point of comparison for the *human* kings in chs. 7–8, the *human* king in chs. 36–37 becomes the point of comparison for the *divine* king in ch. 40. And where the former transition signals the beginning of judgment, the latter signals the beginning of salvation. Where ch. 6 initiated a period when the eyes and ears of the people would not see or hear, which leads to a lack of understanding, ch. 40 initiated the opposite: from this point, the eyes and ears of the people were to see and hear, leading to understanding.

I would parenthetically add that ch. 35 strengthens the perception of the relationship between chs. 36–37 and 40:1–11. As is widely recognized, Isa 35 and 40:1–11 exhibit an entire sequence of deliberate parallels involving some of the same locutions mentioned above in relation to chs. 36–37. For the present argument, it will have to suffice to observe that the Hezekiah narrative has been sandwiched by these two parallel texts. This suggests a deliberate strategy in which the outer "frame" has been related to the narrative in between (see Figure 7.2).

Figure 7.2 The Desert and the Highway

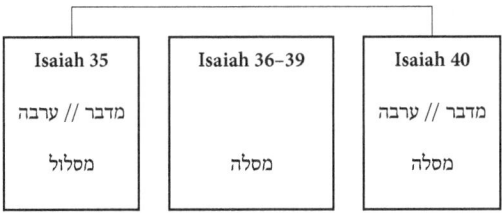

While this strengthens the case, the parallels between chs. 36–37 and 40:1–11 are sufficiently striking on their own as to merit attention. With a perceptive eye on many of these parallels, Matthew Seufert has argued that the scene portrayed in Isa 40:1–11 was to be read in the light of chs. 36–37.[51] For him, Isa 40:1–11 inverts the scenario portrayed in chs. 36–37, because it announces the deliverance by marking the end of that judgment on Judah and Jerusalem enacted through the Assyrian king. Accordingly, the setting for this announcement of deliverance in 40:1–11 comes just after God sent the angel to smite the 185,000 Assyrian troops, which in the narrative results in the retreat of Sennacherib from Jerusalem back to Nineveh (37:36–37). This moment marked the end of the Assyrian threat described in chs. 36–37. It would be fitting, then, for the subsequent announcement of deliverance from the Assyrian king (40:1–11) to invert the earlier narrative pattern portraying that threat.

Indeed, as Seufert notes, the word describing Jerusalem as "herald" (בש״ר) is used most often elsewhere in relation to a messenger sent to report the outcome of a battle in which (usually) the enemy has been defeated.[52] In his analysis, the herald brings news of Assyrian defeat. This usage is at least partially consistent with the development of 40:1–11 in 52:7–10. The latter passage begins with a herald (מבשר) proclaiming "salvation" and concludes with a call to "go out from there," almost universally understood as Babylon (not Assyria) whom God would defeat through Cyrus (vv. 7, 11; cf. 48:14, 20). But to Seufert's point (though not noted by him), it is important that 52:7 finds an unmistakable parallel in Nah 2:1. With a slightly different introduction in each passage, the exact phrase על ההרים רגלי מבשר משמיע שלום occurs in both texts to describe the herald of salvation. In Nah 2:1, this phrase is followed by a close parallel to Isa 52:1, stating that the enemy will no longer (כי לא יוסיף עוד) pass through. These parallels with Nah 2:1 come precisely at the beginnings of what we will see below are the two halves of 52:1–12 (vv. 1–6, 7–12). Some have concluded from these two parallels that Nahum is borrowing from Isaiah,[53] though the distribution of these phrases in Isa

---

51. Matthew Seufert, "Reading Isaiah 40:1–11 in Light of Isaiah 36–39," *JETS* 58 (2015): 269–81.

52. 1 Sam 4:17; 31:9; 2 Sam 1:20; 4:10; 18:19–20, 26, 31; Nah 2:1; Pss 40:10; 68:12; 1 Chr 10:9.

53. Cf. Joseph Blenkinsopp, *Isaiah 40–55*, AB 19A (New York: Doubleday, 2000), 342.

52:1, 7 (at the head of each half of the passage) may indicate the opposite direction of referencing. In either case, a relationship of some sort seems likely. It is significant, then, that the herald in Nah 2:1 announces salvation for Judah with the defeat, not of the Babylonians (as in Isa 52:7), but of the Assyrians, precisely the foe whose defeat in Isa 37 occasioned the announcement of salvation in 40:1-11, according to Seufert.[54]

While all of this suggests that Seufert has put his finger on a critical component of the strategy behind 40:1-11 as this relates to Jerusalem and the Assyrians, his analysis omits ch. 39, which announces the future destruction of the royal apparatus in Jerusalem by the Babylonians. Many scholars have sensed the significance of ending the first half of the book with this announcement in ch. 39. Immediately juxtaposed with this announcement, Isa 40:1-11 begins the second half of the book with the proclamation of consolation for Jerusalem who is said to have received her punishment. Rightly, then, scholars have read the latter passage in the light of the former, the announcement of judgment by the Babylonians being presupposed in all that follows.[55] This is probably the significance of the long debated כפלים in 40:2, which, according to Joseph Blenkinsopp, conveys the idea that "two bad things have happened to" Jerusalem.[56] Thus, Isa 40:1-11 announces that Jerusalem had "taken from the hand of the Lord *double* for all of her sins," being punished once under the Assyrians and later a second time under the Babylonians (v. 2).

Importantly, Seufert's analysis also overlooks the prospective function of the Ahaz account which serves as the analogical background to the Hezekiah narrative patterned on it (see above). As one aspect of this analogical patterning, the announcement of the Babylonian threat to come (39:6-7) echoes the earlier proclamation of the Assyrian devastation to be wrought on Judah in the days of the prophet (7:17). Together, the two announcements enable a narrative rhythm in which the threat posed by the Assyrian king prefigures that represented by the Babylonian king. The Babylonian threat is not merely an extension of that period of judgment which the people were made to endure under the Assyrians. It is a kind of repetition in history: the shape of the future is set on analogy to that of the past because the past had prospective significance. Thus, it is not just that "two bad things have happened to" Jerusalem, but also that the second was like the first. Seen this way, Isa 40:1-11 can invert the narrative pattern of chs. 36-37 to signal the end of the later judgment under Babylon, because it echoed the earlier judgment under Assyria portrayed there.

---

54. Seufert does not mention Nah 2:1 in this connection. Nah 2:1 applies to the downfall of Nineveh rather than to the defeat of the Assyrian army in Jerusalem as recounted in Isa 37 (and announced in 40:1-11, according to Seufert). But, whatever its precise significance, Nahum's close parallel to Isa 52 and its link to Assyria should not be dismissed too easily, especially since Isa 52 contains the only explicit reference to "Assyria" in chs. 40-66.

55. E.g. Ackroyd, *Religious Traditions*, 119-20, and many since.

56. Blenkinsopp, *Isaiah 40-55*, 181, refers these two things to "famine and military defeat," though he does not say why.

I conclude, therefore, that Isa 40:1–11 introduces the second half of Isaiah in a way that evokes those literary strategies and attendant expectations that are developed in the first half of the book. As an introduction to the second half of the book, Isa 40:1–11 creates two expectations for what follows, both precisely in line with the strategy in the first half of the book examined above. First, we can expect that in what follows the deliverance from Babylon will be portrayed on analogy to the deliverance from Assyria. Second, just as we were led to expect a holy remnant after the Assyrian threat (in fulfillment of the words spoken to the prophet in ch. 6), so we are led to expect the same after the later Babylonian threat.

5.3. Isaiah 40–55: Further Exilic Development

If the latter half of the book begins in 40:1–11 with an inversion of that threat portrayed in chs. 36–37, then one can expect the chapters following this introduction further to develop this same comparison. By way of a brief example, consider the contrasting fates of Jerusalem and Babylon in chs. 40–55 against the background of chs. 36–39.

5.3.1. Isaiah 40–48. In the Hezekiah narrative, the messenger from the cities of Judah tells the inhabitants of Jerusalem that the Assyrian king was coming to them. In the light of this, they are told to "come out" (צא) from there and make a deal with him, their God being unable to "deliver" them from "his hand" (נצ״ל +מיד [37:16–20]). After confessing that the Lord "alone" is God, Hezekiah is told that "the virgin daughter Zion" (בתולת בת ציון) mocks the Assyrian king, who would not be allowed to enter her because God would repel him (37:16, 22, 29, 34). Precisely the opposite situation is presented to the reader of chs. 40–48. At the beginning of these chapters, Jerusalem is to tell the cities of Judah that the divine king was coming to them (40:1–11). After announcing that God would support Cyrus, he declares that "I am God and there is no other," raising up the Persian king for his purpose (45; 46:9–11). Then, "the virgin daughter Babylon" (בתולת בת בבל) is told that her nakedness will be exposed and that none of her astrologers will be able to "deliver" her "from the hand" of the flame (נצ״ל + מיד [47:1, 13–14]). In the light of this, the divine king tells his people, "come out (צא) from Babylon" (48:20; cf. v. 14). This analogy contrasts the fate of Jerusalem in the past days of Hezekiah with that of Babylon in the exilic future, assigning to God the role which was earlier given to Sennacherib in telling the people to "come out" of the city under threat, a city called a "virgin daughter." Where Sennacherib would have taken the people to a land like their own, God will take them to their own land. Where Sennacherib claimed to work a new Exodus (37:25),[57] God will work for them something better than a new Exodus (48:21).[58]

---

57. See Stromberg, "Hezekiah and the Oracles Against the Nations in Isaiah," 322 n. 50.

58. In addition to n. 60 below, see Michael Fishbane, *Biblical Interpretation in Ancient Israel* (Oxford: Clarendon, 1985), 364.

5.3.2. Isaiah 52:1–12.

A similar contrast is at play in Isa 52:1–12. Besides being a clear evocation of 40:1–11, this passage begins and ends with references to just these passages in chs. 47–48. Beginning 52:1–12 with a contrast, Jerusalem is told to clothe herself and, as a "captive,"[59] to "rise from the dust" (מעפר קומי שבי [52:1–2]), whereas earlier the "virgin daughter Babylon" is told to "sit in the dust (שבי על עפר) and remove her clothes, as her nakedness would be exposed (47:1–3). Concluding 52:1–12, the people are told "come out (צאו) from there" (v. 11), which most scholars recognize as a reference back to 48:20, "come out (צאו) from Babylon."[60]

All of this suggests that a consideration of 52:1–12 will be productive for the purposes of the present argument. Indeed, 52:7–10 forms a widely recognized parallel with 40:1–11. In both texts, there is a "herald upon the mountains" (על ההרים + מבשר // על הר + מבשרת [v. 7 // 40:9]); there are two mentions of a "voice" that will sound forth (קול + קול [v. 8 // 40:3, 9]); with the arrival of "our God" "all will see" his manifestation (וראו כל + אלהינו [vv. 8, 10 // 40:3–4]); God has "comforted" his "people," namely "Jerusalem" (ירושלם + עם + נח״ם [v. 9 // 40:1–2]); and finally, when he comes, his "arm" will do the work (זרוע קדשו // זרעו [v. 10 // 40:10–11]). Unsurprisingly, both passages together have played a major role in redaction-critical theories dealing with the development of "Deutero-Isaiah."[61]

To understand the significance of 52:1–12 to the present argument, we must first consider its structure. Without going into detail on the smaller subdivisions, I note that the passage consists of two main halves, the second half being systematically coordinated with the first (vv. 1–6, 7–12). This coordination follows two concurrent paths, one an inverse symmetry and the other a forward symmetry.[62]

5.3.2.1. Forward symmetry of the two halves (Isaiah 52:1–6 // 52:7–12)

First Half (vv. 1–6)	Second Half (vv. 7–12)
לב״ש + עיר הקדש 2.f.s pronouns Zion—Jerusalem—Jerusalem—Zion	חש״ף + זרוע קדשו 2.f.s. pronouns Zion—Zion—Jerusalem—Jerusalem
שם + אפס Sojourn in Egypt in the beginning 2.m.p. pronouns	משם + אס״ף New Exodus 2.m.p. pronouns

---

59. Some read שבי as an imperative ("sit"); e.g. LXX. The contrast with Babylon would then be that where Babylon sits in the dust without a throne, Jerusalem rises from the dust to sit on her throne; cf. Blenkinsopp, *Isaiah 40–55*, 340.

60. See, e.g., Blenkinsopp, *Isaiah 40–55*, 343. Strengthening the connection, both statements are immediately followed by echoes of the Mosaic deliverance of the people: the water from the rock (48:21 [// Exod 17:6]) and the flight from Egypt "in haste" together with divine protection along the way (52:12 [// Exod 12:11; Deut 16:3; Exod 13:21]).

61. See the partial survey of opinions in Hartenstein, *Das Archiv*, 101; Lena-Sofia Tiemeyer, *The Comfort of Zion: The Geographical and Theological Location of Isaiah 40–55*, VTSup 139 (Leiden: Brill, 2011), 341–3.

62. On concurrence in structure, see Teeter, "Symmetry," 466.

Both halves begin with an explicit address to Zion (vv. 1–2 // vv. 7–10). In vv. 1–2, the name of the city, addressed with 2.f.s. pronouns, is mentioned four times, twice called "Zion" and twice "Jerusalem." Here, Jerusalem, called "the holy city" (עיר הקדש), is told to "clothe herself" (לב״ש) in anticipation of the deliverance to come. Each of these points finds its counterpart in the beginning of the second half. In vv. 7–10, again the name of the city, addressed with 2.f.s. pronouns, is mentioned four times, twice called "Zion" and twice "Jerusalem." Here, in the deliverance of Jerusalem, the Lord has "uncovered" (חש״ף) "his holy arm" (זרוע קדשו). In line with the use of חש״ף elsewhere,[63] here the baring of the holy arm of God (by pulling back the sleeve of his metaphorical garment) to act in deliverance pairs with the imperative to the holy city to clothe herself in anticipation of this deliverance (again, also in contrast to the removal of Babylon's clothing to expose her shame [47:1–3]). The reader has already been prepared to perceive this parallel between Jerusalem (v. 1) and the arm of the Lord (v. 10), as it is signaled right at the beginning of the passage with a reference to an earlier verse (52:1 → 51:9): in these two texts, both the city and the arm are told to awake (עורי עורי) and to put on strength (לבשי עז).

Each half of the passage then moves on to the promise of a deliverance that would be like the Exodus from Egypt (vv. 3–6 // 11–12). In vv. 3–6, the people are addressed with 2.m.p. pronouns. Here, their current captivity is compared to former times when they went down to "Egypt" to dwell "there" (שם) and when Assyria oppressed them "at the price of nothing" (באפס).[64] When God acts again, his people will "know" his "name" (cf. Exod 3:4), as he will be the one saying "here I am" (הנני; cf. Exod 3:13). Each of these items finds a pair in the continuation of the second half of the passage. In Isa 52:11–12, the people are again addressed with 2.m.p. pronouns. Here, their deliverance from captivity will be like the Exodus from Egypt, but better, as they will not go forth "from there" (משם) in haste.[65] To this, the text adds that God is the one who "gathers you" (מאספכם). In these parallels, one observes a wordplay (Assyria oppressed them at no price [אפס], but God gathers them [אס״ף]), the repetition of שם (first as the place they *went to*, and then as the place they *will go from*), and the accompanying allusions to their time in Egypt (their descent there in the beginning and now their new Exodus from Babylon). Through these features, vv. 11–12 signal the end of the present captivity of the people by referencing the two past periods of oppression mentioned in vv. 3–6, which are both presented there as past analogies to their present bondage.

---

63. Compare this parallel with Jer 13:26 where חש״ף is used for the removal of Jerusalem's cover of clothing to expose her shame underneath.

64. Apart from this passage, באפס is always followed by a noun (X) meaning "without X" (Job 7:6 ["without hope"]; Prov 14:28 ["without people"]; 26:20 ["without wood"]; Dan 8:25 ["without hand"]; cf. 1 Sam 17:1). Here, it is taken to mean "at the price of nothing," the meaning of the ב preposition being dependent on the relationship between 52:4 (באפס) and the parallelism of v. 3 (חנם // לא בכסף).

65. See nn. 58, 60.

For the argument of this essay, I would emphasize that here the present bondage from which they are to be delivered (vv. 11–12) has been set on analogy to the past oppression they suffered under Egypt *and Assyria* (vv. 3–6).[66] This point is made in a different way by the inverse symmetrical structure of the passage.

5.3.2.2. Inverse Symmetry of the Two Halves (Isaiah 52:1-6 // 52:7-12). One can also trace an inverse symmetry through the whole of this passage, which pivots at the precise location where the second half of the unit began in the forward symmetry traced above.

> (A) Jerusalem, the *holy* city, is told to clothe herself, "*because no* (כי לא) longer will the uncircumcised and *unclean* (טמא) *go into* (יבא) *you*" (vv. 1–2).
>> (B) God says: "*without cost* (חנם) you were sold, and without money *you will be redeemed* (תגאלו)…(to) Egypt, *my people* went down in the beginning to dwell there; and Assyria *for nothing* (באפס) oppressed him" (vv. 3–4).
>>> (C) God exclaims: "'*What* (מה) am I doing here,' saying of the Lord, 'that my people have been taken without cost, its *rulers howl*,' saying of the Lord…my people will *know*" (v. 5).
>>> (C') The exclamation goes forth: "*how* (מה) pleasant on the mountains are the feet of the herald of good news…who says to Zion, 'your God *reigns as king*…they will *rejoice*…they will *see* when the Lord returns to Zion" (vv. 7–8).
>> (B') The imperative to rejoice goes forth, "because the Lord *has comforted* (נחם) *his people*, he *has redeemed* (גאל) Jerusalem…and all of the *ends* (אספי) of the earth will see the salvation of our God" (vv. 9–10).
> (A') The people are told "go out from there, do not touch anything *unclean* (טמא)…*purify yourselves*…*because not* (כי לא) in haste will *you go out* (תצאו)" (vv. 11–12).

Each part in the second half involves elements of both continuity and contrast with its corresponding parallel in the first half.

A // A' (continuity): unclean (טמא) vs. holy // unclean (טמא) vs. purify.
A // A' (contrast): enter (בו"א) into Jerusalem // come out (יצ"א) from Babylon.
B // B' (continuity): redeem (גא"ל) // redeem (גא"ל).
B // B' (contrast): sold without cost (חנם) and oppressed for nothing (באפס) // God comforts (נחם) his people and "all of the ends (אספי) of the earth will see the salvation of our God."
C // C' (continuity): they will *know* // they will *see*.
C // C' (contrast): מה in response to oppression, in which their *rulers howl* // מה in response to deliverance, when they *rejoice* that their God *reigns as king*.

---

66. Also note the reference to the "bonds of your neck" in 52:2, the word "neck" occurring in Isaiah otherwise only in relation to Assyrian oppression (10:27; cf. 8:8; 30:28).

For the sake of the argument here, I would emphasize that once again the reader is forced to compare the current distress of the people from which they will be delivered (vv. 9–10) to their past oppression at the hands of the Egyptians *and the Assyrians* (vv. 3–4), a comparison made already within vv. 3–6.[67] This analogy—their current oppression under Babylon is like their past oppression under Assyria—comes in just this passage (52:7–10) which most scholars acknowledge serves as an obvious counterpart to 40:1–11.

In sum, both the forward and inverse symmetries of 52:1–12 present the past Assyrian oppression as an analogy to their current situation under the Babylonian rule from which they will be freed, a strategy precisely in line with the expectations created by the first half of the book as well as the opening of its second half, 40:1–11, which is set on analogy to Sennacherib's attempted assault on Jerusalem.

But what of the expectation for a holy remnant? If the judgment under Assyria becomes an analogy for that under Babylon, then we should expect a holy remnant after the latter as we did after the former. This expectation—encouraged as much by the structure of allusion in 40:1–11 (which echoes ch. 6) as by the analogical structure of the first half of the book (where Assyria prefigures Babylon)—is woven also into the structure of 52:1–12 itself, being present in both the forward and inverse symmetrical patterns examined above.

The inverse symmetry forces a comparison between the imperative to Jerusalem (A [vv. 1–2]) and that to the people (A′ [vv. 11–12]). In A, Jerusalem, "the holy city," is commanded to clothe herself, "*because no longer* (כי לא) will the uncircumcised and *unclean* (טמא) *go into* (יבא) you." In A′, the people are told, "come out from there, touch *no unclean thing* (טמא), come out from it, purify yourselves…*because not* (כי לא) in haste will *you go forth* (תצאו)." The people were not to make themselves "unclean," but to "purify" themselves, as they came out of Babylon in order to enter Jerusalem, "the holy city," into which no "unclean thing" would enter again. With their deliverance from Babylon, the people are to embrace holiness for their entrance into Jerusalem. This call to embrace "holiness," rather than "uncleanness," after judgment echoes that future foreseen in ch. 6: by destruction and exile, the people of "unclean (טמא) lips" would be transformed into a "holy (קדש) seed" (6:5, 13).

---

67. In vv. 3–4, the comparison is enabled by the parallelism of v. 3 ("without cost [חנם] you were sold // without money [לא בכסף] you will be redeemed"), which is then exploited by v. 4 ("first my people went down to Egypt // then Assyria oppressed them at the price of nothing [באפס]"). In this way, the past oppression by Assyria (באפס) is made to stand in contrast with the future promise of deliverance (לא בכסף) via its parallelism with their past sale (חנם). Then, the oppression of the past (ראשנה + שם [v. 4]) is contrasted with God's perception of the present (עתה + פה [v. 5]), leading to a vow to intervene (v. 6), which ties back into the initial promise of redemption (vv. 3, 5–6 [חנם]). This passage may be compared to chs. 13–14, which present Assyria as a type for later Babylon. See Marvin A. Sweeney, *Isaiah 40–66*, FOTL 19 (Grand Rapids, MI: Eerdmans, 2016), 205; cf. Stromberg, "Hezekiah and the Oracles Against the Nations in Isaiah," 302–27.

Complementing this argument from the inverse symmetry of 52:1–12, the forward symmetry of this passage forces a comparison between the imperative to Jerusalem (v. 1) and the deliverance of God (v. 10). In light of the imminent deliverance, Jerusalem is commanded, "*clothe yourself*, with your garments of beauty, O Jerusalem, *holy city* (עיר הקדש)." About to act in deliverance, "the Lord has *bared* (made naked) *his holy arm* (זרוע קדשו) in the sight of all nations." The call to embrace holiness is predicated on the imminent deliverance wrought by the "holy arm." Considering all the foregoing analysis, it is striking that here the holy arm (זרוע קדשו) echoes the arm (זרוע) of the Lord about to act in deliverance after judgment in 40:10–11, which itself alludes to the holy seed (זרע קדש) to emerge after judgment in 6:13. In this line of development, the holy seed (זרע קדש) would be the work of his holy arm (זרוע קדשו).

5.4. *Isaiah 56–66: Post-Exilic Development*

Just as the post-Assyrian remnant was to become a holy seed, so too was the post-Babylonian remnant. Exhorting the soon-to-be-released captives to embrace a holy identity after their exilic punishment in Babylon, Isa 52:1–12 echoes the future revealed to the prophet in ch. 6[68] as refracted through 40:1–11. It is not surprising, then, that the "holy seed" (זרע קדש) of 6:13 has been coordinated with Ezra's description of the Babylonian returnees to the land.[69] In fulfillment of 6:13 (but probably in violation of 52:1–12), the returnees from Babylon, the "holy seed" (זרע הקדש), had failed to separate themselves from the unclean abominations of the nations. This was, at any rate, the opinion reported to Ezra by the leaders of the day (Ezra 9:1–2). Calling these abominations "unclean" (9:11), Ezra responded by confessing their "iniquities" (9:6; cf. Isa 40:2) and admitting God's favor in leaving them a "remnant" in his "holy place" (Ezra 9:8)—all in the hopes that he would not destroy that "remnant" (9:14). From this vantage point, one might conclude that just as the post-Assyrian remnant failed to embrace its calling to be a holy seed, so too did the returnees from Babylon.

Like Ezra 9 (and describing the righteous in language found otherwise only there), the last eleven chapters of Isaiah also level accusations of sin against the post-exilic generation (chs. 56–59, 65–66).[70] If the past is any indication of the future (which seems like much of the point of the shape of the book), then we can expect the whole process to repeat itself in a still further distant future. As I have argued elsewhere, this is precisely the point of the last eleven chapters of the

---

68. For further parallels between Isa 6 and 52:1–12, compare 6:5, 9–10 // 52:6, 8, 10 ("see" with "eyes" and "know"), 6:4, 8 // 52:8 ("voice" [2×]) 6:8 // 52:6 ("behold, I"), and 6:5 // 52:7 (the divine "king"). Note also that 52:13, which follows our passage, echoes 6:1.

69. Elsewhere I have argued that the "holy seed" in Isa 6:13 is a development secondary to Ezra 9:1–2 which itself derives the phrase on the basis of a reading of Deuteronomy; see Jacob Stromberg, *Isaiah After Exile: The Author of Third Isaiah as Reader and Redactor of the Book*, OTM (Oxford: Oxford University Press, 2011), 160–74.

70. Stromberg, *Isaiah After Exile*, 160–74.

book. Here, the accusations made against the post-exilic generation become the basis for yet another judgment on the people, a judgment deliberately patterned on that devastation wrought by Assyria in the past.⁷¹ Like 6:13, this future judgment would produce a righteous remnant called a "seed" (זרע [65:9]). And like the remnant spared in the days of Hezekiah (whose sign was sowing [ז"רע]), this seed would be like the fruit of the vine, spared to offer up its blessing for a new day (37:30–32; 65:8–9; cf. 5:1–7).

6. Conclusion

The book of Isaiah employs symmetry and analogy to portray a history wherein the past portends the future. In this figural history, the remnants of the past—those survivors of the Assyrian and Babylonian eras—were to carry a lesson for the holy seed of the future.

---

71. On the parallel between chs. 34–39 and 63–66 (wherein the events involving Assyria in the Hezekiah narrative become a model for the eschatological judgment portrayed in chs. 65–66), see Stromberg, "The Book of Isaiah," 33–4. On the patterning of the eschatological judgment and salvation in ch. 66 on the initial announcement of Assyrian invasion into Judah (8:5–9) and its reversal in God's defense of Jerusalem (30:27–33), see Stromberg, "A Covenantal Community," 83–7; Cf. Judith Gärtner, "The Kabod of YHWH: A Key Isaianic Theme from the Assyrian Empire to the Eschaton," in Stromberg and Hibbard, eds., *The History of Isaiah*, 431–46.

SECTION TWO

WORLD OF THE TEXT

Chapter 8

THE UNITY OF THE BOOK OF ISAIAH: MORE THAN A MEMORY GAME OR A FATA MORGANA?

Willem A. M. Beuken

1. *Introduction*

Research of the book of Isaiah oscillates for almost a century between two light sources. On the one hand, thematic and lexical agreements between passages are projected against the vicissitudes of a twofold nation, Judah and Israel, and a city, Jerusalem, during the rise and rule of the successive empires of Assur, Babylon, and Persia. On the other hand, all that substance is reduced to the mind-set of a prophetic movement that would have developed its self-image in a literary tradition of its own. These two approaches to the book occur independently or in a more or less harmonious mixture. In both ways, attention is paid to passages in which real or imaginarily distinct speakers discuss the same issue. The mission of the prophet in Isa 6 and 40:1–11 can serve as an example.

The methodological alternative, however, does not suffice for passages where, *in successive episodes of the text course, speakers discuss matters pertaining to their relationship while they take their preceding talk into account*. The concept of a "fly-over" seems to suit that sort of composites. Different autonomous scenes with different effects are connected by *lexis* and *opsis* in a coordinating event (*meta-plot*), in which the same actants develop their relation in a dynamic way. Moreover, this occurs in front of a text-immanent audience which, in second instance, can even perform as actant. It is essential that the interaction proceeds. A clear example is the change of speakers and audience in Isa 50–51 (cf. the commentaries). This sort of literary construction differs from a combination of various prophetic performances with the same actants who speak on similar themes, neither in on-going activity nor in front of the same audience (cf. the complicated constellation of Hos 1–3).

The present study aims at showing that Isa 1 and Isa 12 do not only share themes and even characters, but at the same time, create a rhetorical frame in which the conversation produces a specific activity and brings this into effect by stages. Since this frame connects the wealth of stories and oracles in between them (Isa 2–11), it earns the characterization "dramatic." For a long time already, the qualities of the literary genre "drama," established by the antique literary theory, have been recognized in biblical, even non-narrative texts.[1] The specific quality which, according to Aristotle, is fundamental for drama, i.e. the unity of action, occurs in various biblical texts in a composed manner, less strict than in classical literature (Greek, Latin, Renaissance). In that derived case, the course of action is often related to the development of the axes space and time, so much so that these are more than a steady décor. We try to prove in three sections that Isa 1 and 12 together operate as an encompassing frame of dramatic quality with an open-end to the rest of book. We conclude that this literary structure contributes to the unity of the book of Isaiah insofar as it presents chs. 1–12 as a preview of the whole book.

2. Isaiah 1: Vision Turned Word

Isaiah 1:2–31 presents itself as an introduction to the whole book.[2] Consequently, the book title of 1:1 is resumed in a different form in 2:1.[3] Moreover, the verse next to this one (2:2a: "It shall come to pass at the moment of time beyond the days"[4]) situates the subsequent oracle on "the mountain of YHWH's house" (vv. 2b–5) in

---

1. Reference to some first studies on the book of Isaiah from this angle should suffice here: Stefan Ark Nitsche, *Jesaja 24–27: ein dramatischer Text: Die Frage nach den Genres prophetischer Literatur des Alten Testaments und die Textgraphik der großen Jesajarolle aus Qumran*, BWANT 166 (Stuttgart: Kohlhammer, 2006); Helmut Utzschneider, *Gottes Vorstellung: Untersuchungen zur literarischen Ästhetik und ästhetischen Theologie des Alten Testaments*, BWANT 175 (Stuttgart: Kohlhammer, 2007); with regard to coherent communicative action throughout the book of Isaiah: Torsten Uhlig, *The Theme of Hardening in the Book of Isaiah: An Analysis of Communicative Action*, FAT II/39 (Tübingen: Mohr Siebeck, 2009); regarding the book of Psalms, cf. Matthias Hopf, "Die Psalmen als 'verbale Bühnen'. Ein experimenteller Blick auf die dramatisch-performativen Strukturen der Psalmen," *BZ* 65 (2021): 1–27.

2. A great many, if not the majority of commentators recognize this function of Isa 1. It has extensively been argued by H. G. M. Williamson, *Isaiah 1–27. I. Commentary on Isaiah 1–5*, ICC (London: T&T Clark, 2006), 7–11; cf. Hyun Chul Paul Kim, *Reading Isaiah: A Literary and Theological Commentary* (Macon, GA: Smyth & Helwys, 2016), 77–82.

3. For the diachronical relation of the two "book headings," cf. Joachim Eck, *Jesaja 1— Eine Exegese der Eröffnung des Jesaja-Buches: Die Präsentation Jesajas und JHWHs, Israels und der Tochter Zion*, BZAW 473 (Berlin: de Gruyter, 2015), 28–79.

4. The Scriptures are quoted according to the New Revised Standard Version (adapted).

another period than that of Isaiah 1 (v. 1: "the days of Uzziah... Hezekiah"). In the final text form, Isa 1 consists of three sections marked by incitements to listen to YHWH's word (vv. 2, 10) or an appeal to that (vv. 20 [closure], 24 [to continue: "Therefore"]).[5] Each of the three sections contains a discursive unity *with a time moment of its own*: how the present situation has risen (vv. 2–9), into what it can be changed (vv. 10–20), and finally, how it will eventually look (vv. 21–31). The three sections are integrated into an on-going discussion between YHWH and the other characters on their mutual activity, by which the axis time is given a narrative course. The title of John L. Austin's book, *How To Do Things With Words* (1962), could be applied here as "How to make visions come true with words."

2.1. Three Discursive Units

(a) In *the first discursive unit, vv. 2–9*, a lawsuit is presented.[6] The narrator summons the audience to listen to God's word, introduces "heaven and earth" as the jury and YHWH as the prosecutor, and quotes the latter's charge against his people (vv. 2–3). He elaborates the gravity of the defendant's offence ("Woe," הוי)[7] while he appeals to the jurisdiction of the prosecutor as "the Holy One of Israel" (v. 4). Little by little, the text-immanent audience appears as an actant. They may feel themselves focused on in "Israel/my people" (v. 3), yet in particular in the change of person from v. 4 to v. 5a, i.e. from "children who deal corruptly..." (3rd person pl.) to "Why do you seek further beatings? Why do you continue to rebel?" (2nd person pl.). Since an address by name is lacking, readers at first will interpret these sentences as directed to the defendant. Finally, they must feel themselves to be standing alongside the defendant in the dock. The charge regards them (vv. 5b–6) when they are confronted with the collapse of both the country (v. 7) and the daughter Zion (v. 8). In the end, they identify with the defendant who in the meantime has appeared as the punished party in the "we" of the confession: "If YHWH of hosts had not left us a few survivors, we would have been like Sodom, and become like Gomorrah" (v. 9). Readers are now faced with a question that guarantees the rhetorical progress: Why has YHWH indeed left some survivors?

Thus the stage setting of Isa 1 provides a dramatic set-up. First, the text-immanent speaker makes his audience into a co-actant of the argument. In terms of literary theory, the so-called fourth wall between actants and audience outside the text falls down in vv. 4–7. This is a minor example of the largely recognized literary phenomenon that lyric and epic texts can break open into dramatic passages and vice versa. With regard to the Scriptures, the symptom notably has been attested

---

5. What follows is based on the speech-act analysis of Isa 1 by Archibald L. H. M. van Wieringen, *The Reader-Oriented Unity of the Book of Isaiah*, ACEBTSup 6 (Vught: Skandalon, 2006), 172–89.
6. For related, mainly diachronical questions of this section, cf. Eck, *Jesaja 1*, 81–365.
7. The interjection expresses both dismay and disaster (*DCH* 2:503–4).

in Psalms and the Song of Songs.[8] In the Isaianic context at stake here, the décor of the ravaged country, the subject matter of the argument, develops into a quality of the audience with whom, moreover, the speaker identifies. From now on, space can no longer be dissociated from the actants.

(b) In *the second discursive unit, vv. 10–20*, the speaker legitimizes his action again: "Hear the word of YHWH // listen to the torah of our God" (v. 10). He zeroes in on the preceding scene by addressing the audience as "rulers of Sodom, people of Gomorrah" (v. 10), a characteristic which they themselves, just before, have called inapplicable to them because of God's intervention ("If YHWH of hosts had not left us a few survivors, we would have been like Sodom…," v. 9). In v. 10, the possessive pronoun "we" in "our God" comprehends both the speaker and the audience; in this way, the rhetorical constellation of the previous unit is extended and refined. Together, the prophetic speaker and the people are now standing before God ("when you [pl.] come to be seen before me," v. 12).

God's relationship with the people is the subject matter of reproach and reform. The audience carries the guilt of their almost complete ruin by means of a cult which God not only rejects but personally wards off ("I will hide my eyes from you… I will not listen," vv. 11–15). At the same time, the charge contains a series of imperatives by which God links up with the speaker's confession "our God" (v. 10). This series runs from "Bring no more vain oblations" (v. 13) to "Wash yourselves // remove the evil of your doings from before my eyes… cease to do evil / learn to do good" (vv. 16–17). It turns into a proposal of agreement: "Come now, let us argue it out," says YHWH: "Though your sins are like scarlet, they ought to become white like snow[9]… If you are willing and obedient, you shall eat the good of the land; but if you refuse and rebel, you shall be devoured by the sword" (vv. 18–20). The proposal produces ambiguity about the future that awaits resolution, not within the narrated time of the discussion, but at any time later. In this way, the dialogue helps readers suspecting that YHWH's dealing with his people somehow goes on.

(c) The third discursive unit, vv. 21–31, contains a prophetic oracle (vv. 21–26) and an exhortation (vv. 27–31). The oracle is structured according to the literary genre of an indictment by the prophet, i.e., a dirge on the city (vv. 21–23), and a verdict of God himself (vv. 24–27 in twofold form: God's action in vv. 24–26a and its effect in v. 26b). The whole oracle is enclosed by the catchword צדק, "righteousness" (vv. 21, 26).

The oracle's rhetorical pattern continues that of the two preceding discussions (vv. 2–9 and 10–20). The speaker marks the verdict proper to an act of YHWH by the frame formula: "Therefore YHWH says" (v. 24). He changes the charge from

---

8. Literature to the problem of the borders between these foundational literary genres and their interaction is extensive. For the theory of drama, see the classical work of Manfred Pfister, *Das Drama: Theorie und Analyse*, UTB 580 (Munich: W. Fink Verlag, 11th ed., 2001). For the phenomenon at stake here, see the study of Hopf, "Psalmen."

9. For the interpretation "they ought to become like snow," cf. Andrew R. Hay, "An Exegetical Reflection on Isaiah 1.18," *BiTr* 20 (2016): 288–91.

the 3rd person ("the faithful city has become a whore" v. 21) to the 2nd person ("your silver… your princes… they…," vv. 22–23). In this way, the rhetorical pattern of the two preceding units (vv. 2–9, 10–20) is extended. Before this, "the daughter Zion," home of all sorts of malefactors, was the subject of discussion (v. 8; hereafter from v. 22 on, she herself is addressed (vv. 21–27: forms in fem., 2nd person sg.), and she becomes an actant in YHWH's discussion with his people (cf. the same phenomenon in vv. 5, 9). As such, she is somehow split up. The accused wrongdoers in her, the city, stay on as subject matter: God will destroy them (vv. 23–25). In this way, she herself, the primarily addressed defendant, can be imagined as returning to her original status: "Afterward you shall be called the city of righteousness, the faithful city" (v. 26). The exhortation characteristically combines admonition and incitement (vv. 27–31).[10] The speaker is no longer YHWH (1st person in vv. 24b–26, 3rd person in v. 28), but the prophetic implied speaker of vv. 21–24a.[11] A step further in the narrated time is taken by means of a description of the city's situation "afterward." The direction of speech oscillates. On the one hand, there is a sketch of the contrast between Zion as "redeemed" (3rd person sg. in v. 27) and the sinners as "destroyed" (3rd person pl. in vv. 28–29a), on the other hand, the city functions as an actant, directly addressed in an attempt to convert her: "For you shall be ashamed on the oaks in which you delighted/ you shall blush… for you shall be like an oak whose leaf withers" (2nd person pl. in vv. 29b–30). Verse 31 elaborates the preceding verse by applying the metaphor of "oaks/ gardens" in decay to "the strong and his work" and by rhetorically closing the section with a *litotes*: "no one to quench them."

2.2. A Plot Analogous

The three discursive units of Isa 1 are more than a series of distinct discussions, more even than a treatise on the same subject matter. According to how they develop by changes of the person(s) speaking, and link up to each other, they activate a coherent narrative in three successive episodes, which we can acknowledge as a meta-plot on top of their own dynamics or plots. Not unity of action but concatenation of actions is perceptible and effective by the fact that the series consists of "words of YHWH" which have resulted so far and, moreover, will result in some happening (vv. 2, 10, 20, 24). It leads from YHWH's complaint against the people and the actual chastising of Israel and Zion to God's offering a trustworthy choice to him and his conversion of Zion. The narrator has put the three discussions in an epic compound of successive scenes. It looks back on a process whose purpose is yet to be discerned.

(a) Pattern of Actants. The actants of the three rhetorical units in Isa 1 maintain their identity in relation to each other while they develop as speakers (*lexis*). In the first scene, within the comprehensive appeal of the text-immanent speaker

---

10. Marvin A. Sweeney, *Isaiah 1–39 with an Introduction to Prophetic Literature*, FOTL 16 (Grand Rapids, MI: Eerdmans, 1996), 527.
11. Van Wieringen, *Unity*, 181–2.

to heavens and earth, the actant God changes from the person present, yet misunderstood (vv. 2–3), to the speaker to Israel (vv. 4–8, on the subject matter of country and Zion), whereupon Israel joins as "we" without introduction and in monologue (v. 9). Precisely this rhetorical entrance of the plural actant "we" enables the narrator in the second scene to address them on behalf of YHWH: "Rulers of Sodom // people of Gomorrah, hear the word of YHWH" (v. 10). This address leads to a new "we" by which YHWH the audience and himself encompasses: "Come now, let us argue it out... If you... if you..." (vv. 18–19). Thereupon, the narrator introduces YHWH's adversary as a "city full of injustice" (v. 21). Separating "murderers... your princes" from it, God addresses this location as "you" (v. 23), while "they" disappear from the discussion of the actants (vv. 24–25, 28). At this point, YHWH announces his intention to "turn" Zion (v. 26a), yet does not implement that purpose within this speech act itself. Although it comes into view, "Afterward you shall be called the city of righteousness... Zion shall be redeemed" (vv. 26b–27), it is not realized in the present of the narrated time. For Zion, another time will precede: one of "shame/blushing" in which its earlier abominable pleasure and preferences will be assessed (v. 29).[12] At that time, the *lexis* and *opsis* of the three combined discussions will reach their final momentum, one beyond the actuality.

In sum, the rhetorical cohesion of ch. 1 relies on three "fly-overs," switches in the speech pattern, one in each of the three discursive units: from "they" to "you" and "we" in vv. 2–9, from "you" to "we" and "I" in vv. 10–20, from "she (the city)" to "you" and "I" in vv. 21–31.

(b) Space and Time as Compliant Coulisses of the Meta-plot. In function of the series' purpose, the axes of time and space in Isa 1 develop. The beginning situates Isaiah's vision in space ("concerning Judah and Jerusalem," v. 1) and in time, while the latter is first viewed historically ("in the days of... kings of Judah"), next metahistorically ("Hear and listen, heavens and earth, YHWH has spoken [*qatal*]," v. 2). The evaluation of space and time in this first chapter is subsequently determined by semantemes which serve the plot of the three discursive units. Time shapes up from the mention of Israel's origin from God ("I reared children," v. 2) and their departure from God ("Children who have forsaken YHWH," v. 4) along a confrontation with YHWH ("Come now, let us argue it out," v. 18) to an opposite future ("Afterward you shall be called the faithful city," v. 26).

Space shapes up from "your desolate country" (v. 7) and "Zion, the booth" (v. 8), by the likeness with "Sodom/Gomorrah" (vv. 9, 10) and the confrontation with God ("to appear before me," vv. 12–20) to its destiny as "city of righteousness/ the faithful city" (v. 26).

---

12. Ombretta Pettigiani, "Il motivo della vergogna come conclusione di Is 1," in *La profezia tra l'uno e l'altro Testamento: Studi in onore del prof. Pietro Bovati in occasione del suo settantacinquesimo compleanno*, ed. Guido Benzi, Donatella Scaiola and Marco Bonarini, AnBib Studia 4 (Rome: Gregorian and Biblical Press, 2015), 89–91.

(c) Conclusion. The title of the book of Isaiah mentions its genre, its author, and its content in one draught ("The vision of Isaiah, son of Amoz, which he saw concerning Judah and Jerusalem, in the days of…kings of Judah," v. 1). Its discursive opening ("Hear, O heavens// give ear, O earth. Truly, YHWH has spoken," v. 2) makes the vision audible as a word of YHWH which creates a story. The first rhetorical composite, Isa 1, determines its course and purpose. At its closure, the goal of the book has not yet been reached, but in a pragmatic way, the first chapter moves readers to undertake the journey to that end.

3. Isaiah 12: Word Coming True

Opinions concerning the compositional unity of the book of Isaiah diverge, but there is a general agreement that at the level of the final text, Isa 12 presents a major closure and a prospect as well. Intratextual connections with Isa 1–11 and the rest of the book (13–39 and 40–66) abound. This fosters the surmise that the chapter has been shaped in view of the whole prophetic writing.[13] This background comes first to light in the fact that the next part of the book opens with a new title: "The oracle concerning Babylon that Isaiah son of Amoz saw" (13:1). Since our research so far conveys the impression that Isa 1 contains the report of a composed speech act in three scenes, which bridges different points of time and space, the question arises whether and how Isa 12, as the closure of the first part of the prophetic book, corresponds to the set-up of the introduction. Therefore, an analysis of the speech act in Isa 12 is recommended.[14]

(1) The first question concerns *the subject* of the clause: "You will say on that day" (v. 1a). From this point on, ambiguity rules the chapter. The speaker splits his argument for the sake of pragmatics: he entrusts his song of gratitude to a single figure in vv. 1b–2 and he commits a double charge to a plural figure in vv. 3–5. *From outside the text-syntactical context,* the two figures can be identified as king and people, for they are central characters in Isaiah's preceding oracles. *From within the text-syntactical context,* the answer differs. The command of v. 1, "You will say (ואמרת, *wᵉqatal*) on that day," results from God's saving action in 11:11–16.[15] It lines up with the subject therein: "On that day YHWH will extend his hand yet a second time to recover the remnant that is left of his people… He will raise

---

13. Gérard Nissim Amzallag, "The Paradoxical Source of Hope in Isaiah 12," *RB* 123 (2016): 357–77; H. G. M. Williamson, "Isaiah 12 and the Composition of the Book of Isaiah," *HBAI* 6 (2017): 101–19; idem, *Isaiah 1-27. II. Commentary on Isaiah 6-12*, ICC (London: T&T Clark, 2018), 705–40, esp. 712–15.

14. Cf. Archibald L. H. M. van Wieringen, *The Implied Reader in Isaiah 6-12*, BIS 34 (Leiden: Brill, 1998), 228–41.

15. For the position of Isa 11:11–16 within ch. 11 and their connection with ch. 12, cf. Eric Ortlund, "Reversed (Chrono-)Logical Sequence in Isaiah 1–39: Some Implications for Theories of Redaction," *JSOT* 35 (2010): 209–24, esp. 210–13.

a signal for the nations, and will assemble the outcasts of Israel... YHWH will utterly destroy the tongue of the sea of Egypt...and make a way to cross on foot. So, there shall be a highway from Assur for the remnant that is left of his people... and you will say on that day....". The adjunct of time, "on that day," too, connects 12:1 with the beginning of the quoted passage in 11:11. In this larger context, it is YHWH who *procul a conspectu* issues the admonition of v. 1a to bring him thanks. In continuation of his intervention against Assur, as against Egypt in old times, moreover in favour of Israel, God engages both a single (12:1b-2) and a plural figure (12:3-5) to speak and to act.

Thus, in the clause "you will say," YHWH addresses those whom "he causes to march over dryshod" (11:15), i.e. "the remnant of his people for whom there is a highway from Assur" (v. 16a) as a single person, exactly like he speaks about Israel in v. 16b ("on the day that he came up from Egypt"). He proposes that the people give him thanks with words borrowed from the song after the passage through the Sea of Reeds ("I will sing to YHWH... YHWH is my strength and my song, he has become my salvation," Exod 15:2). The next clause, too, suits the mouth of the remnant: "You were angry with me. Let your anger turn away, so that you comfort me (ותנחמני)" (12:1b). The optative mode of the second clause continues the announcement of 11:16. It does not surprise that the command to praise YHWH in 12:1-2 syntactically links up with Isa 11, for vv. 11-16 of that chapter deal with YHWH's recovering the remnant of his people from Assur.[16] The preceding does not mean that the song of Isa 12 is presented to the returning exiles as a group of its own, to the exclusion of those who have stayed behind in the land and Jerusalem. The paradigm of the rescue from Egypt precludes such anachronistic distinction (cf. 11:15-16). Moreover, the context situates "the remnant of his people" in the surrounding countries and peoples, even in "the corners of the earth" (11:11-12), while the enmity between Ephraim and Judah has ceased (11:13-14). Briefly, the address "You will say on that day" (12:1) is directed to "the remnant of his people" in an exemplary sense, i.e. the people of YHWH.[17] Thus the literary phenomenon which we have called "ambiguity" is better characterized as a dramatic effect. In the command "You will say" (12:1a), the text-immanent speaker (the prophet) addresses a figure in the preceding story, "the remnant of his people" (11:16), and he has that figure subsequently address the main actant of the story, YHWH: "I will give thanks to you" (12:1b). The shift of address involves a pragmatic move. By his incitement, the speaker charges the newly appearing actant with a twofold assignment: he/they will act as an interpreter of gratitude for rescue (12:1-2) and will proceed this acknowledgment as a messenger of YHWH's name and great deeds among the nations (12:4-5).

---

16. For the historical setting of Isa 11:1-12:6 in the Josiah era, cf. Sweeney, *Isaiah 1-39*, 203-11.

17. Cf. extensively Franz Delitzsch, *Commentar über das Buch Jesaja*, BCAT III/1 (Leipzig: Dörffling & Franke, ⁴1889), 199; Sweeney, *Isaiah 1-39* (n. 9), 203.

(2) *The second question* concerns *the figure to whom* the subject of the opening clause ("You will say in that day" v. 1a), in our view "the remnant of his people," addresses himself after his act of gratitude to YHWH and his prayer for comfort (v. 1b). He proceeds, along with the mention of his rescue and a confession of confidence ("he"—"me," v. 2), to a twofold task for a plural audience: "You will draw water // You will say on that day" (vv. 3–4). Since the thanksgiving and the embedded message regard the same issue, i.e. "salvation," commentators in general identify the single speaker of thanks and trust ("you" → "me/I" [sg.], vv. 1–2) with the prophet Isaiah, who has spoken to and in the name of his people in Isa 1–11.[18] Consequently, the plural "you" of the message ("you shall draw water // you shall say," vv. 3–4) regards the people in the same chapters. An allusion to the name of the prophet Isaiah ("YHWH brings salvation") is thought to be effective therein. It might plead against this explanation that nowhere in chs. 1–11 is YHWH "angry" with the prophet; however, this argument has little weight, for the prophet is closely involved in God's "anger" with his people (אף: 5:25; 9:11, 16, 20; 10:4, 5, 25).

On the basis of these two questions, we conclude that the prophetic speaker calls upon his audience to achieve two actions that will, next to their likeness to the prophet, further determine their identity: "You will draw water with joy // you will say in that day" (vv. 3–4, both verbs pl.). The first instruction concerns the supply of water, in sequel to the passage through the "Egyptian Sea/River" in 11:15. Reference to the paradigm of water supply for Israel in the desert is evident, yet the literary style gives only slight and indirect reference to this image. As in 11:15–16, without semantic analogies (the terms "to draw water" [שאב מים] and "wells" [מעינים] do not occur in Exod 15:22–27; 17:2–11 or Num 20:2–13).[19] Reference by means of only some key words confirms the comparability of the audience with "the remnant of his people" (11:11). At the same time, readers may anticipate the rest of the book of Isaiah, for, therein the term "in joy" (בששון) characterizes the return from exile and the restoration of Jerusalem (22:13; 35:1, 10; 51:3, 11; 61:3, 10; 62:5; 64:4; 65:18–19; 66:10, 14; Jer 33:9–11).[20] In this way, the text-immanent speaker uses the name Isaiah, "YHWH brings salvation," in order to refer his audience to the prophet's oracles before and later on in the book as "wells of salvation."

---

18. Joseph Addison Alexander, *Commentary on the Prophecies of Isaiah* (Grand Rapids, MI: Zondervan, 2nd ed. 1875, 7th ed. 1976), 263: "The prophet now puts into the mouth of Israel a song analogous to that of Moses, from which some of the expressions are directly borrowed."

19. Without entering the issue, I presume that the difference between audible and written biblical intertextuality may play a role here; cf. Cynthia Edenburg, "Intertextuality, Literary Competence and the Question of Readership: Some Preliminary Observations," *JSOT* 35 (2010): 131–48.

20. The root שוש neither occurs in analogous application in the Pentateuch nor in other prophetic books.

The content of the second instruction connects the plural audience with the single person of the first instruction: "You will say in that day: 'Give thanks to YHWH, call on his name. Make known his deeds among the nations, proclaim that his name is exalted, sing praises to YHWH'" (vv. 4–5; all verbs in pl.). The people addressed will take up the praise of YHWH by the first single addressed person ("I will give thanks to YHWH," v. 1), moreover, in the form of a call on other people. The laudation of YHWH should propagate as a sound wave, carried on by successive imperatives (pl.): "Give thanks / call / make known / proclaim / sing praises." This praise, starting from the prophet and the saved remnant of Israel (vv. 1–2), will reach to "the nations" and culminate in the recognition of YHWH by "all the earth" (vv. 4–5). Whereas the praise of the remnant focuses on the theologoumenon of YHWH's "strength" (v. 2: עז), the praise of the audience should focus on God's "name" (twice in v. 4: שם) and his "glorious deeds" (v. 4: עלילת; v. 5: גאות).

While the remnant's praise of YHWH should resound to all the earth, one character in particular is invited to share its propagation: "Shout aloud and sing for joy, O inhabitant Zion! Truly, great in your midst is the Holy One of Israel" (v. 6). Zion, the place which had accommodated malefactors (1:21–23) but should become the place of YHWH's intervention (1:24–26), now indeed turns into an actant.[21] Her hymn counters God's complaint on his repudiation at the beginning of Isaiah: "Children who deal corruptly, who have forsaken YHWH, who have despised the Holy One of Israel" (1:4). Their misbehaviour has turned "the daughter Zion" into an abandoned booth (1:8). The mountain Zion remains, nevertheless, YHWH's domain, where he dwells and works for people who are left or come from elsewhere (2:3; 4:3–5; 8:18; 10:12, 24, 32). In the second half of the book too, Zion will react with "singing for joy" (רנה) on the arrival of salvation (35:10; 51:11; 52:8–9), when "the Holy One of Israel" shows himself to be its saviour (54:5; 60:9, 14).

The analysis of the speech direction in Isa 12 clarifies that the chapter forms a composed act of successive encomiasts, i.e. of the prophet *alias* the remnant of Israel, which embodies God's people as a whole, and the inhabitant Zion. The encompassing praise emanates from YHWH's acting, which is announced at the end of Isa 11:11–16: the liberation of God's people from Assur and the creation of a highway. The laudation opens a perspective on the worldwide recognition of YHWH's authority and power by all the nations among whom the remnant was dispersed (vv. 11–12).

---

21. Cf. Christl M. Maier, "Daughter Zion as a Gendered Space in the Book of Isaiah," in *Constructions of Ancient Space Seminar*, ed. Jon L. Berquist (AAR/SBL Seminar Papers 2003), 1–20; Brittany Kim, *"Lengthen Your Tent-cords": The Metaphorical World of Israel's Household in the Book of Isaiah*, Siphrut 23 (University Park, PA: Eisenbrauns, 2018), 51–85.

4. Isaiah 1 and 12: A Dramatic Frame

Putting Isa 1 and 12 side by side, we shall establish connections that help comprehend the chapters as forming a rhetorical frame with a special realization of the time axis.

(1) As for *literary genre and structure*, the implied speaker, the prophet of Isa 1, reports a complaint of YHWH on Israel's rebellion and Zion's iniquity, in which God refers to his actual punishment and opens a prospect for his corrective intervention, i.e. Zion's restoration. The complaint develops in a series of three discussions of YHWH with an accused party that appears as different figures. In Isa 12, the implied speaker, again the prophet, calls on two successive characters, i.e. the remnant of Israel and the inhabitant Zion, to give thanks to YHWH for his saving action against Assur and the production of a highway out from there (11:16–12:2). In view of structure across the two chapters (Isa 1 and 12), the complaint and the call forms a composite of distinct speech acts with alternating speakers. YHWH, the principal actant of the complaint, presents himself as "the Holy One of Israel" in the beginning of the first composite (1:4). At the end of the second composite, the call, his name is proclaimed by the summoned party (12:4–5), even explicitly under the same title by the inhabitant Zion (12:6).

(2) As for *narrated time*, the two composites, each by itself, extend over a larger period. Taken absolutely, it is the same event: Isa 1 runs from "rebellion" (v. 2: פשע) to God's "redemption" (v. 27: פדה) and Isa 12 extends from God's "anger" (v. 1: אף) to Israel's "salvation" (vv. 2–3: ישועה). The agreement in time connects the characters involved in a comparable way. In both composites, they develop with regard to their relation with YHWH, due to his initiative. In Isa 1, the implied speaker describes this process in anticipation of God's rescue; in 11:16–12:6, he does so in view of the aftermath, i.e. YHWH's worldwide fame. *The different perspective turns the latter composite into the sequel of the former.* In this way, there is a narrative connection between God's announcement that he will intervene in 1:25 ("I will turn my hand against you and smelt away your dross as with lye"), and the prophet's call to praise him in 12:4–5 ("Make known his deeds among the nations… he has done gloriously"). The announcement is based on God's previous initiative "to leave a few survivors (הותיר שריד)"[22] (1:9) and the laudation elaborates the prophecy coming true. "On that day YHWH will extend his hand yet a second time (*i.e. after the exodus from Egypt*) to recover the remnant (לקנות שאר)[23] that is left of his people… He will wave his hand over the

---

22. For הותר, cf. Tryggve Kronholm, "יתר," *ThWAT* 3:1082–6; for שריד, cf. Benjamin Kedar-Kopfstein, "שריד," *ThWAT* 7:879–82.

23. For שאר, cf. Ronald E. Clements, "שאר," *ThWAT* 7:942–3. With regard to 11:11, 16: "Beide Verse behaupten, daß der Rest alle zerstreuten Gemeinschaften Israels, die ins Exil getrieben worden sind, einschließt." The variance of terminology for "survivors" (1:9) and "remnant" (11:11, 16) may have a diachronical background, but does have a semantic value as well. The former includes the aspect of useless waste, the latter that of retrievable stuff (cf. the literature mentioned in n. 21).

river... there shall be a highway" (11:11-16; text syntactically seen, this flows over into in Isa 12).

(3) As for Isa 2-11, if chs. 1 and 12 together form a rhetorical frame around the enclosed text block while the end of Isa 11 and the opening of Isa 12 are connected in the manner of a fly-over, the question arises whether the performance of the actants in the composite in-between, namely Isa 2-11, supports that connection. It cannot be anticipated that the characters therein would develop in relation to each other as is customary in classical drama. The sizeable textual block of Isa 2-11 contains self-reliant stories and oracles. The characters therein are YHWH, Isaiah, and the king, Israel and Zion, and subservient to these, the adherents of YHWH's plan and the evil-minded unbelievers. All these figures function primarily in the context of the successive episodes. Next to that, as we have pointed out here, they play a role in the frame of Isa 1 and 12. Consequently, it has to be found out how the actions in which they are involved as subject or object in Isa 2-11, lie as to their function in the frame of Isa 1 and 12. The next survey serves that question (a more detailed definition is outside our scope).

Excursus

(a) With regard to YHWH, his activity in chs. 2-11 concerns the following paradigms:

- "he teaches his ways" from his house on the mountain (2:2-5)
- "his terror on his day" is directed against all haughtiness (3:10-26)
- "his work on his vineyard" is unavailing and calls for his counter-action (ch. 5)
- "he appears in holiness" and "sends" the prophet to his people (ch. 6)
- "he sets the sign of Immanuel" ("with us God") for the house of David, Israel and Jerusalem (7:1-9:6)
- "his anger/hand" strikes his enemies, climaxing against Assur (9:7-10:24)
- "his spirit rests upon the shoot from Jesse's stump" (11:1-11)
- "he sets up an ensign for the nations" and "creates a highway out of Assur" (11:12-16)

In sum, the range of YHWH's activity regards the restoration of Israel with the house of David and the gathering of the exiles from Assur.

(b) With regard to Israel, Judah, and Zion, their names occur in a variety of grammatical functions but hardly indicate an independent activity:

- The name "Israel" occurs in construct state with a title of YHWH (1:4, 24; 5:19, 24; 10:17), moreover, as object of God's action (5:7; 8:14, 18; 9:7, 11, 13; in connection with the remnant or exiles in 4:2; 10:20, 22; 11:12, 16). The name "Israel" is subject of an action with regard to YHWH on just two places: "Israel does not know... They have forsaken YHWH // they have despised the Holy One of Israel" (1:3-4); and "The remnant of Israel...will lean upon YHWH, the Holy One of Israel" (10:20). These occurrences comply with the extent of the frame.

- The name "Judah" has an ethnic or geographical meaning (1:1; 2:1; 7:1, 6, 17) and serves as object of God's actions (3:1, 8; 5:7; 8:8; 9:20; 11:12-13). There is one exception: "Men of Judah, judge between me and my vineyard" (5:3).
- The name "Zion" serves as object or place of God's activity (1:8, 27; 2:3; 3:16-17; 4:3-5; 8:18; 10:12, 24, 32), nowhere as acting subject in relation to God. Where "Jerusalem" does not parallel "Zion" or "Judah," it concerns God's adversary: "Jerusalem and her idols // Samaria and her idols" (10:11).

* * *

The survey shows that the characters Israel, the remnant, and Zion, who play an active, rhetorical role as YHWH's antagonists in the frame of Isa 1 and 12, do not perform in chs. 2-11 as effective agents parallel with God's activity. Their names do not regard practical counter-agency, let alone cooperation; they stand only for objects or places of YHWH's performance. He is the one character who shows on-going consistency in pragmatic terms. The frame of Isa 1 and 12, on the contrary, has a pattern of effective actants, first against YHWH, later in consonance with him. Thus it hosts a plot with a proper narrated time. This starts in Isa 1 and arrives at a first denouement in ch. 12: the forecast of YHWH's laudation. The frame connects the dispute of YHWH with his adversaries *in illo tempore* with the praise of YHWH by those who listen to him *in tempore opportuno*. This will happen exclusively on the ground of YHWH's complex activity *in tempore inter haec*, i.e. as reported and explained in Isaiah 2-11.[24]

5. Conclusion: Isaiah 1-12—The Whole Book in Preview

The starting point of this study was the question of the unity of the book of Isaiah. A provisional answer would be that the question is unnecessary, first because the material and literary unity of the book is fixed, next because it has become a unit of the canon of the Scriptures, finally because it has been accepted and read as a unit in the *Wirkungsgeschichte*. Innumerable studies have demonstrated the book's multi-layered coherence under various aspects: text form, sort of language, literary genre, oral and written tradition, composition and redaction history, reception in the Second Temple literature, the Dead Sea Scrolls and the New Testament. The quest for the unity of the biblical book will likely live on as a quest for the harmony between the various text levels comprising that unity. In any case, research of semantics is an indispensable instrument in that perspective. The way in which words are embedded and bring meaning to the complicated construct of sentences essentially determines the connection between smaller and

---

24. The time axis of Isa 2-11 follows two trails: chs. 2-5 trace the way "from the moment beyond the days" (2:2) back to the problem of the vineyard's infertility, chs. 6-11 lead forward from pregnancy, birth and growth of the child Immanuel to the moment when the shoot from Jesse takes rule (courtesy Archibald van Wieringen).

larger textual blocks in any biblical book. Since semantics play a major role in all exegetical approaches to the book of Isaiah, the research of its unity often makes the impression of a "memory game" between methods. Which procedure yields the most extensive and refined list of words and phrases at its disposal so as to decide, by means of that instrument, on diachronical and synchronical connections in this prophetic writing?

Regarding the unity of the book of Isaiah, the present study contributes one conclusion: chs. 1–12 are enclosed by a frame, the first and the last chapter, which makes the composite concerning God's dealings with Judah and Jerusalem into a miniature of the whole book. This reveals how YHWH's government will gather all flesh, i.e. Israel and the nations, to worship before his face (ch. 66). In its first section, the compound of chs. 1–12, stories about the historical Isaiah and oracles delivered by him have been transmitted, elaborated and finally assembled in such a way that they present an image of the prophet's preaching and vicissitudes.[25] The compound's frame, chs. 1 and 12, provides a rhetorical setting which describes the course that YHWH will take, according to the prophet Isaiah, with Israel and Zion, and how these actants are to comply with that initiative. The literary holder presents the salvation-historical process as a long dispute of God with his people in several scenes by means of which he carries his project into effect ("deeds by words"). It leads from YHWH's complaint against Israel and Zion and an almost definitive break away from these (Isa 1) to a new alliance of welfare for his people and to God's fame on the whole earth (Isa 12). From this perspective, YHWH is depicted as the principal acting character, with Israel and Zion as the complying character. In the anticipated outcome of the dispute, the latter two are committed to react, i.e. to give thanks to YHWH and to proclaim his glory to all nations on earth.

The hypothesis that Isa 1 and 12 form a rhetorical frame of the composites in between which presents the whole book of Isaiah on a small scale and in preview, indispensably relies on the fact that at the end of the book, it falls to Israel and Zion to proclaim the glory of YHWH's works. That far-off perspective is the result of a process which is portrayed in the book from ch. 13 onwards. Therein, the command of 12:4–6 is carried through along gradual stages of YHWH's relationship with the people involved. A wealth of studies have shown this forming an essential part of the harvest of the Isaiah research so far. Of course, what follows is not the only feasible explanation of the book's composition but one that results from the open end of ch. 12. The connected process begins with an oracle on the downfall of Babylon (Isa 13; Assur has already been dethroned in Isa 11), and takes a next step with the opening of a highway ("the Holy Way") to Zion on which "the ransomed of YHWH shall return, and come to Zion with singing" (35:10). As for the second half of the book, two appropriate references should suffice here. First,

---

25. This foundational aspect has been noted ever since Peter R. Ackroyd, "Isaiah I–XII, Presentation of a Prophet," in *Congress Volume: Göttingen 1977*, ed. Walther Zimmerli, VTSup 39 (Leiden: Brill, 1978), 16–48.

as in 11:16–12:3, the remnant *Israel* is challenged to give thanks "with joy" (בששׂון) to YHWH for his rescue from Assur; in the same way, according to 65:13–14, 18–19, the servants of YHWH will praise him "with gladness of heart" (מטוב לב) when he has segregated them from the godless powers in Judah (v. 9). Secondly, as in 12:6, *Zion* is called "to shout aloud and sing for joy" (רנה/צהל) for the presence of "the Holy One of Israel" in her midst; in the same way, in Isa 54, "the barren one" is restored as the genuine wife of YHWH and, thereupon, urged: "Sing for joy, break forth into joyful singing, and shout aloud (צהל/רנה)…for the Holy One of Israel is your Redeemer" (54:1, 5).

If it is agreed upon that the composite of Isa 1–12, on the strength of its enclosing frame, prefigures the book of Isaiah *in miniature,* this fact forms a plea for the unity of the whole in terms of pragmatics. At its opening, heaven and earth warrant the faithfulness of YHWH's word (1:2). At its closure, when readers have accomplished the journey through Isaiah's oracles, they learn that the new heavens and the new earth will bear witness to the fulfilment of God's purpose as announced in this book: "All flesh shall come to worship before my face" (66:23). The promissory interim prospect of Isa 1–12, "Truly, YHWH has done gloriously. Let this be known in all the earth" (12:5), warrants that the end of the book is not a *fata morgana.*

Chapter 9

JACOB AS A UNIFYING MOTIF IN THE BOOK OF ISAIAH

Marvin A. Sweeney

1

Modern scholarship has identified a number of unifying motifs in the final form of the book of Isaiah, such as Jerusalem or Zion, Creation, the Exodus, Exile and Return, and others.[1] But despite its ready visibility in the book, the motif of Jacob has received relatively less attention, most likely due to the recognition that Jacob is an alternative name for Israel. Although Israel might seem like an obvious motif in the book that does not require sustained analysis, the correlation of Israel with Jacob demands attention for a number of reasons, most importantly because it points to an intertextual reading of Isaiah with the Pentateuch. Jacob is one of the major ancestors of Israel in the Pentateuch—indeed, he is the eponymous ancestor of Israel, who suffers both punishment and restoration. His punishment takes the form of exile twice from his homeland due ultimately to his highhanded treatment of his brother, Esau, and his favoritism for his sons, Joseph and Benjamin. Jacob's restoration occurs at least in relation to his exile to Aram, if not also posthumously in relation to his exile to Egypt. Likewise, Jacob's descendants suffer punishment in the Pentateuch in the form of Egyptian slavery and suffering in the wilderness, but they also achieve redemption, in the form of the revelation at Sinai and their journey to the promised land of Israel.

---

1. See Marvin A. Sweeney, "The Book of Isaiah in Recent Research," in *Recent Research on the Major Prophets*, ed. Alan J. Hauser (Sheffield: Sheffield Phoenix Press, 2008), 78–92; Jacob Stromberg, *An Introduction to the Study of Isaiah* (New York: T&T Clark, 2011), esp. 97–103.

The final form of the book of Isaiah also employs Jacob as a figure who suffers punishment, exile, and restoration throughout its various components, such as the oracles of punishment and restoration in Isa 1–39 and the oracles of restoration and references to punishment in Isa 40–66. Although the present form of the book of Isaiah is focused especially on the experience of Jerusalem and Judah as signaled in the superscription of the book in Isa 1:1 (cf. Isa 2:1), the Jacob traditions, including the narratives about Jacob in Gen 25–50 and the narratives about his descendants in Exodus–Deuteronomy, also play key roles in formulating both halves of the final, synchronic literary form of the book of Isaiah in chs. 1–33 and 34–66. The present study therefore employs intertextual perspectives to examine the figure of Jacob as a unifying motif in the final form of the book of Isaiah.[2] It notes that a number of texts in Isaiah referencing Jacob have intertextual correlations with Pentateuchal texts concerning Jacob and his descendants in Gen 25–50 and Exodus–Deuteronomy. This study therefore examines the intertextual relationships between three such textual blocks, viz., Isa 2–4; 5–12; and 40–54. It argues that the texts in which Jacob appears in these textual blocks recall elements of the Jacob narratives in the Pentateuch and thereby contribute to establishing the synchronic unity of the book of Isaiah.

2

Isaiah 2–4 is a textual block within the first major portion of Isa 1–33 which constitutes a prophetic announcement concerning the cleansing of Zion for its role as the center for YHWH's world rule.[3] Following the superscription in Isa

---

2. For discussion of intertextual methodology, see especially Patricia Tull Willey, *Remember the Former Things: The Recollection of Previous Texts in Second Isaiah*, SBLDS 161 (Atlanta, GA: Scholars Press, 1997); Benjamin D. Sommer, *A Prophet Reads Scripture: Allusion in Isaiah 40–66* (Stanford, CA: Stanford University Press, 1998); Patricia K. Tull, "Rhetorical Criticism and Intertextuality," in *To Each Its Own Meaning: An Introduction to Biblical Criticisms and their Applications*, ed. Steven L. McKenzie and Stephen R. Haynes (Louisville, KY: Westminster John Knox, 1999), 156–79; Barbara Green, *Mikhail Bakhtin and Biblical Scholarship: An Introduction*, SBL Semeia Studies 38 (Atlanta, GA: SBL, 2000); Carol A. Newsom, *The Book of Job: A Contest of Moral Imaginations* (Oxford: Oxford University Press, 2003); Marvin A. Sweeney, *Form and Intertextuality in Prophetic and Apocalyptic Literature*, FAT 45 (Tübingen: Mohr Siebeck, 2005); Carleen R. Mandolfo, *Daughter Zion Talks Back to the Prophets: A Dialogic Theology of the Book of Lamentations*, SBL Semeia Studies 58 (Atlanta, GA: SBL, 2007); Marvin A. Sweeney, *Reading Prophetic Books: Form, Intertextuality, and Reception in Prophetic and Post-Biblical Literature*, FAT 89 (Tübingen: Mohr Siebeck, 2014); Marianne Grohmann and Hyun Chul Paul Kim, eds., *Second Wave Intertextuality and the Hebrew Bible*, SBL Resources for Biblical Study 93 (Atlanta, GA: SBL, 2019).

3. Marvin A. Sweeney, *Isaiah 1–39, with an Introduction to Prophetic Literature*, FOTL 16 (Grand Rapids, MI: Eerdmans, 1996), 87–112.

2:1, it begins with an announcement concerning the role of Zion as the center for YHWH's world rule (2:2–4), followed by an address concerning the cleansing of Zion for this role (2:5–4:6). The initial vision account (vv. 2–4) presents an ideal scenario in which the nations of the world will stream to Zion to learn YHWH's Torah or "instruction," which in turn leads to the cessation of war among the nations. Such a vision states one of the major ideals of the book of Isaiah as a whole. Isaiah 2:5–4:6 then begins with an invitation to the house of Jacob (2:5) to walk in the light of YHWH and, thereby, to join the nations in their pilgrimage to Zion to learn YHWH's Torah and end all war. This invitation is followed by a lengthy explanation in 2:6–4:6 concerning what needs to happen, viz., a scenario of judgment against Jacob and the nations followed by restoration, which will make the ideal scenario possible.

Interpreters have debated the diachronic dimensions of this ideal vision and its address to the house of Jacob. Some view this as a reference to the northern kingdom of Israel, but most others view it as referring to the southern kingdom of Judah. Interpretations of the setting for this ideal vision range from the time of Isaiah ben Amoz himself in the late-eighth century BCE through the Hellenistic period in the third through first centuries BCE. My own position is that Isa 2–4 is a sixth-century BCE text that refers to the exiles of Jerusalem and Judah at the end of the Babylonian exile or the beginning of the Persian period.

But when the text is read synchronically, the house of Jacob must refer to all Israel, of which Jerusalem and Judah are the remnant according to the book of Isaiah. The date of the composition then becomes less consequential, insofar as a synchronic reading of the book presumes no specific diachronic or historical setting. Such a reading strategy then opens Isaiah up for a full intertextual reading in relation to the Pentateuch, again, regardless of the Pentateuch's own diachronic setting.

The key texts for the present concern with Jacob within Isa 2–4 are 2:2–4 and 2:5, which refer respectively to the pilgrimage of the nations to "the House of the G-d of Jacob" (v. 3) and to the invitation to the house of Jacob to join the nations (v. 5). Apart from these references, the rest of the passage in Isa 2:2–4 and the whole of Isa 2–4 make it clear that the passage is concerned with Jerusalem/Zion and Judah. The use of Jacob in these two instances would then presume the whole of Israel and Judah, insofar as Jacob was the eponymous ancestor of Israel, which includes Judah as portrayed in Gen 25–35. Within the larger context of Isaiah, particularly the first portion of the book, Jerusalem and Judah would be understood to refer to "the remnant of Israel," insofar as the northern kingdom of Israel is conquered and exiled by the Assyrian empire, leaving only Jerusalem and Judah—and presumably Benjamin and Levi—to carry on. Elsewhere in the first part of the book of Isaiah, for example, Isa 11:10–16, it is understood that Israel and Judah will one day be reunited.

Isaiah 2:2–4 clearly presupposes that the nations will go up to Mount Zion, viz., the site of the Jerusalem temple, to learn YHWH's Torah and, thereby, inaugurate an ideal future in which nations will not engage in war with each other. As a prophetic announcement, the passage thereby envisions an ideal future for

Mount Zion, that is, YHWH's temple in Jerusalem, to serve as the holy center for YHWH's sovereignty over all creation, including the nations of the world that inhabit creation. The invitation to the house of Jacob in Isa 2:5 therefore would complete the ideal scenario envisioned in Isa 2:2–4 by ensuring that Israel as well as all the nations would then be gathered together at Zion to enjoy the benefits of world peace under YHWH's sovereignty.

The ideal vision of Zion's role as the holy center of the world of creation and the nations that inhabit it, together with the invitation to the house of Jacob to join the procession of the nations to Zion, relate intertextually to the account of Jacob's vision of YHWH at Luz, later to be renamed Beth El, in Gen 28:10–22. Those verses portray Jacob spending the night at Luz where he has a vision of YHWH, atop a ladder or staircase that was characteristic of many ancient temples. YHWH promises Jacob a covenant in which he and his descendants would become a great nation that would inhabit the land of Israel. As a result of this vision, Jacob erects a *matzevah* or stone monument indicating the presence of the divine at the site and renames it Beth El, "House of El" or "House of G-d." Beth El would later become one of the primary temples of the northern kingdom of Israel. Furthermore, the invitation to the house of Jacob to join the procession of the nations to Zion would recall the wilderness narratives of the Pentateuch, insofar as the journey of Israel through the wilderness would take the nation not only to the land of Israel as stipulated in the Pentateuch, but also take them to Jerusalem and the Jerusalem temple, as portrayed in the Former Prophets, especially the David and Solomon narratives in 2 Sam 1–1 Kgs 11.

The intertextual relationship between Isa 2:2–4, 5 and Gen 28:10–22 and the wilderness narratives of the Pentateuch is not one of citations; there is no demonstrable indication that these verses in Isaiah are dependent upon Genesis text or vice versa. Rather, this intertextual relationship entails placing two texts with generally analogous content from the same canonical context into dialog with each other, irrespective of the circumstances of their respective diachronic compositions.[4] The result of the intertextual dialog between the two texts, however, is compelling. The Genesis text recounts the origins of one of the early temples of the house of Jacob, in this case, the Beth El temple, which served as the royal sanctuary of the northern kingdom of Israel. For much of the ninth and eighth centuries BCE, the northern kingdom of Israel also included Jerusalem and Judah as vassals and required them to pay tribute to Israel at the Beth El sanctuary (see Amos 7–9). Such a vision portrays an early state of Israel's relationship with YHWH from the standpoint of its eponymous ancestor, Jacob. However, the Isaiah text portrays a future vision of Israel's, a.k.a., the house of Jacob's, ideal relationship with YHWH at the Jerusalem temple. Such a vision presumes that the Jerusalem temple has been restored, that the house of Jacob has been reunited and returned to the land of Israel at Jerusalem, and that the nations of the world

---

4. See Mandolfo, *Daughter Zion*, 1–28; Marvin A. Sweeney, "Isaiah 60–62 in Intertextual Perspective," in *Subtle Citation, Allusion, and Translation in the Hebrew Bible*, ed. Ziony Zevit (Sheffield: Equinox, 2017), 131–42.

have come to recognize YHWH as the sovereign deity of creation and the nations that inhabit it. Such a vision is consistent with much of the scenario of Jacob's or Israel's anticipated return to Jerusalem from Babylonian exile as portrayed in Isa 40–54 in the second part of the book.

The intertextual relationship observed here between Gen 28:10-22 and Isa 2:2-4, 5, might then be described as one of promise and fulfillment. Jacob is promised at the Beth El temple to become a great nation in the land of Israel in Gen 28:10-22 and that promise is anticipated to be fulfilled at the Jerusalem temple, also known as Zion, in Isa 2:2-4, 5. Nevertheless, it is also clear that there are differences between the two texts in that the setting shifts from the northern sanctuary at Beth El to the southern sanctuary at Jerusalem and that the divine promise expands from granting the land of Israel to Jacob to teaching divine Torah to the nations as well as to Israel. It is noteworthy, therefore, that the invitation to the house of Jacob to go up to Zion fulfills goals articulated in the Former and Latter Prophets, such as, 2 Sam 6 and Jer 30–31, as well. Altogether, Jacob's ascent to Zion in Isa 2:2-4, 5 constitutes a major rhetorical goal of the present form of the book of Isaiah, although it still remains to be fully achieved at the conclusion of the book.

3

Isaiah 5–12 constitutes prophetic instruction concerning the significance of Assyrian judgment against Israel in that it anticipates the restoration of the Davidic empire.[5] This block of material includes a large range of texts that comprise an announcement of judgment against Israel and Judah (5:1–30) and the explanation of this passage (6:1–12:6). The explanatory section includes an account of the basis for the punishment of Israel and Judah (6:1–8:15) and an announcement concerning the fall of Assyria (8:16–12:6). Altogether, chs. 5–12 portray the punishment of Israel and Judah at the hands of the Assyrian empire, together with the projected restoration of the Davidic kingdom following the downfall of the Assyrian empire. These chapters then correlate with the portrayal of Jacob's punishment and exile for his conduct in relation to his brother, Esau, his father-in-law, Laban, and his first wife, Leah. This text also correlates to the punishment and redemption of the descendants of Jacob in the Exodus and wilderness narratives in Exodus–Deuteronomy.

When considered diachronically, Isa 5–12 originate in relation to the Syro-Ephraimitic war of 735–732 BCE, in which Israel and Aram allied together in an effort to resist the Assyrian empire and enlisted the aid of their western Asian neighbors to present a unified front. When Judah balked at joining the alliance, likely for justified fears that it would never hold together when the Assyrians attacked, Israel and Aram threatened to attack Jerusalem to replace the Davidic king, whether Jotham or Ahaz, and force Judah to join the coalition. Ahaz

---

5. Sweeney, *Isaiah 1–39*, 112–211.

apparently appealed to Assyria, which destroyed Damascus and invaded Israel, thereby saving Ahaz's life and forcing him to pay increased tribute for having done so. It appears that the text was expanded over time to portray the successive Assyrian invasions of Judah, culminating in Sennacherib's 701 BCE invasion of Judah during the reign of Hezekiah as consequences of Ahaz's actions. Indeed, the later Babylonian invasion of Judah would also have been read as part of the sequence of punishment suffered by Judah within the final form of the book of Isaiah.

Chapters 5–12 are particularly important in relation to the intertextual reading of this textual block in relation to the Jacob narratives of the Pentateuch. Whereas there are no explicit statements that proved dependence on the Jacob narratives in Isa 2–4, the texts of Isa 8:16–9:6 and 10:20–26 display indications that the Jacob narratives of the Pentateuch influenced the composition of elements in Isa 5–12.

Isaiah 8:16–9:6 appears within the announcement of the downfall of Assyria and the restoration of the Davidic empire in Isa 8:16–12:6, where it constitutes initial instruction concerning YHWH's signs to Israel and the house of David. The passage begins with the prophet's expression of frustration with Israel in Isa 5:1–8:15 concerning Israel's failure to observe divine Torah (Isa 5) and King Ahaz's alleged failure to put his trust in YHWH during the Syro-Ephraimitic War (Isa 7). Following Isaiah's exclamation to "bind up the testimony" and to "seal instruction among my teachings" in v. 16, he continues in v. 17 with the statement, "And I will wait for YHWH, who is hiding his face from the house of Jacob, and I will wait for him." The passage goes on to portray problems within Israel before it announces that "the people who walked in darkness have seen great light" (9:1), which introduces a royal oracle concerning the birth of a new and righteous Davidic king (9:2–6).

The reference to YHWH's hiding the divine face from "the house of Jacob" in this passage is particularly important because it defines Israel at large as the house of Jacob, viz., the descendants of the patriarch, Jacob. But with the following anticipation that the people will ultimately see great light in the form of the birth of a new Davidic monarch, presumably Hezekiah ben Ahaz, the Isaian oracle ensures that the imagery understands the descendants of Jacob, viz., Israel and Judah, to be rightly under the rule of a Davidic monarch based in Jerusalem.

The designation of a Davidic monarch as the rightful ruler of the house of Jacob, viz., northern Israel and southern Judah, adjusts the understanding of the priority of Jacob's sons as expressed in the birth narratives of Gen 29–31. The birth narratives present an order of Jacob's sons, in which those born to Jacob's favored wife, Rachel, are destined to play the leading roles in Israel. Thus, the first four sons, Reuben, Shimon, Levi, and Judah, are all born to Jacob's wife, Leah, who is less favored. Furthermore, Reuben, Shimon, and Levi commit various infractions against their father, leaving Judah to become the first in the line of succession to their father. Subsequent sons were born to the concubines and Leah, viz., Dan and Naphtali were born to Rachel's handmaiden, Bilhah; Gad and Asher were born to Leah's handmaiden, Zilpah, and Issachar and Zebulun were later born to Leah. Although Judah would emerge as the first in line due to his priority in the order of birth, Rachel's sons, Joseph and Benjamin, would ultimately achieve priority due to Jacob's favoritism. Joseph's sons, Manasseh and Ephraim, would ultimately become the ancestors of the two major power tribes of the northern kingdom of Israel, and Benjamin would become the ancestor of the first royal tribe of northern Israel.[6]

But insofar as northern Israel was conquered and exiled during Isaiah's lifetime and Benjamin was supplanted as the royal tribe by Judah early in Israel's history, Isaiah views the tribe of Judah and the Davidic monarchy as the legitimate royal tribe and rulers of the house of Jacob.

This point is further emphasized in Isa 10:20-26, which employs the motifs of the Exodus narratives to portray Assyrian oppression of the *šĕʾār yiśrāʾēl*, "the remnant of Israel," and the *pĕlêṭat bêt yaʿăqōb*, "the escaped of the house of Jacob," in reference to the people of Israel. The motif of the remnant of Israel figures prominently in Isa, insofar as ch. 6, a first-person account of Isaiah's vision of YHWH in the Jerusalem temple, announces that YHWH plans to destroy some ninety percent of the people of Israel in order to achieve recognition as the true G-d of creation, Israel and Judah, and the nations. The motif further appears in Isa 7:1-8:15, in which Isaiah confronts Ahaz accompanied by his son, *šĕʾār yāšûb*, "a remnant shall return," as Ahaz prepares to defend Jerusalem against the anticipated Syro-Ephraimitic siege. The presence of Isaiah's son, Shear Yashub, signifies that Ahaz may suffer significant casualties, but YHWH will defend Jerusalem as promised. When Ahaz allegedly shows a lack of faith in YHWH's promise to defend the city, Isaiah then announces judgment against Jerusalem, Judah, and the house of David, until a righteous king will arise in Isa 9:1-6 and 11:1-16, who will ultimately reunite Israel and Judah and reestablish Davidic rule over the nation and the neighboring nations that had once formed part of the Davidic kingdom.

Within this context, the references to the remnant of Israel and the escaped of the house of Jacob (10:20-26) contribute to a portrayal of YHWH's punishment of Israel at the hands of the Assyrian empire, like that of the oppression of Israel by Egypt in the Pentateuch. But the passage also appears in a context in which YHWH will act to redeem Israel or the house of Jacob at the hands of Assyria through the agency of a new and righteous Davidic monarch, who will reunite the tribes of Israel and subdue those nations that had once been subject to David. Indeed, the passage concludes with (12:1-6), which quotes the song of the sea from Exod 15 to celebrate YHWH's renewed redemption of Israel and the house of Jacob in the first part of the book of Isaiah.

Overall, the references to the remnant of Israel and the escaped of the house of Jacob in Isa 5-12 refer to the birth narratives of Jacob's sons in Gen 29-31 and the narratives of Exod 1-15 to portray YHWH's punishment and redemption of Israel. The references to the birth narratives are not explicit, but the references to

---

6. Jacob's preference for his youngest sons illustrates the Israelite premise that the younger overcomes the older. See Frederick E. Greenspahn, *When Brothers Dwell Together: The Preeminence of Younger Siblings in the Hebrew Bible* (New York: Oxford University Press, 1994).

the Exodus narratives are indeed explicit to Isa 10:20–26 and 12:1–6. But instead of portraying Moses as the agent of YHWH's redemption, chs. 5–12 envision an ideal Davidic monarch, perhaps Hezekiah or Josiah, as the agent of Israel's redemption. Further references to Jacob appear in the oracles concerning the nations (Isa 13–27). These pronouncements appear in contexts that refer to the downfall of oppressors and the defense or restoration of Israel. For example, in Isa 14:1 YHWH promises to show mercy on Jacob by bringing down the Babylonian king. Isaiah 17:4 depicts Jacob's suffering at the hands of the Syro-Ephraimitic before they turn to YHWH. Further, Isa 27:6, 9 portrays Jacob's taking root and being restored in relation to YHWH's defeat of Leviathan, representing Egypt and the Nile. Finally, Isa 29:22, 23 depicts Jacob's return to YHWH following YHWH's defense of Ariel/Jerusalem.[7]

4

Isaiah 40–54 constitutes the core of what most modern scholars correctly understand to be the work of the anonymous late sixth-century prophet known only as Deutero- or Second Isaiah.[8] Deutero-Isaiah spoke at the end of the Babylonian exile or the beginning of the Persian period, when King Cyrus of Persia became king of Babylon and decreed that exiled Jews and other exiled subject nations could return to their homelands and rebuild their sanctuaries. When read synchronically, these chapters constitute a key element of the vision of Isaiah ben Amoz concerning the realization of YHWH's plans for worldwide sovereignty at Zion in Isa 34–66. Following the prophetic instruction concerning YHWH's power to return the redeemed exiles to Zion in Isa 34–35 and the royal narratives concerning YHWH's deliverance of Jerusalem and Hezekiah in Isa 36–39, chs. 40–54 constitute a prophetic instruction that YHWH is maintaining the covenant with Israel and restoring Zion. Isaiah 55, considered diachronically to constitute the conclusion to Deutero-Isaiah's work, then introduces the final section of this book (Isa 56–66) to present prophetic exhortation to adhere to YHWH's covenant.

As a prophetic instruction that YHWH is maintaining the covenant with Israel and restoring Zion, Isa 40–54 presents five key arguments following the renewed prophetic instruction to announce the restoration of Zion, which introduces the textual block in Isa 40:11. Isaiah 40:12–31 contends that YHWH is the master of creation; Isa 41:1–42:13 contends that YHWH is the master of human events; Isa 42:14–44:23 contends that YHWH is the redeemer of Israel; Isa 44:24–48:22 contends that YHWH may use Cyrus, the King of Persia and Babylon, to restore Zion; and Isa 49:1–54:17 contends that YHWH is restoring Zion. Whereas Isa 49–54 focuses on Zion, portrayed as Jerusalem, Bat Zion, or Bat Jerusalem, the four sub-units in Isa 40:12–48:21 focus on the figure of Israel,

---

7. For detailed discussion of these texts, see Sweeney, *Isaiah 1–39*, ad loc.
8. Marvin A. Sweeney, *Isaiah 40–66*, FOTL 19 (Grand Rapids, MI: Eerdmans, 2016), 1–231.

identified throughout as Jacob, the eponymous ancestor of Israel. The image of Jacob appears to be key to the argumentative strategy of the text, which draws out parallels with the experience of Jacob, qua Israel, in the Pentateuchal narratives.

The use of Jacob in the argumentative strategy of the texts begins already in Isa 40:1–11, which introduces the textual block.[9] The text has a particular focus on Jerusalem and Zion, but it is addressed to a reading or listening audience that should be identified with the exiles of Jerusalem and Judah, who are configured as the remnant of Israel/Jacob, when read in relation to the first part of the book in chs. 1–33. The name Jacob does not appear in this passage, but it is hinted at in the portions of the text that propose a new journey through the wilderness as the exiles will return from Babylon to Jerusalem. Isaiah 40:3–5 call for the clearing in the wilderness of a road for YHWH to lead the exiles home. Such a call easily draws on the traditions of the wilderness journey by Israel as it departs from Egypt on its way to the promised land of Israel. In portraying the cooperation of creation in preparing this wilderness highway, 40:4b states, "And the rugged ground shall become straight, and the rough ground will become a valley," in which the Hebrew word, *'āqōb*, literally, "twisted, crooked," indicates the rugged ground that will become straight and flat in the first stanza of this half-verse. Insofar as *'āqōb* is the root of the Hebrew name, *ya'ăqōb*, "Jacob," the text reminds the reader of the experience of the sons of Jacob, that is, the people of Israel, as they travelled the wilderness road on their way from Egypt to the land of Israel.[10]

Isaiah 40:12–31 contends that YHWH is the master of creation.[11] After presenting arguments for such a claim in 40:12–20 and 40:21–26, the third major sub-unit of this text in 40:27–31 employs rhetorical questions to conclude its argumentation and convince its reading or listening audience that YHWH is indeed the master of creation. These arguments are addressed to Jacob and Israel in v. 27 to introduce a disputation speech intended to counter the claims of Jacob and Israel that YHWH has ignored them by allowing them to suffer defeat and exile. The disputation counters that as master of creation, YHWH is not always understood, but that Jacob/Israel must trust in YHWH, who never wearies and will accomplish what YHWH has promised. Such an argument would then counter the mistrust of YHWH allegedly displayed by King Ahaz of Judah in Isa 7, as well as the claims for Israel's alleged refusal to observe YHWH's instruction in Isa 5 and elsewhere in the first part of the book. Such an argument also calls upon the audience of this text to recall that YHWH did support Jacob in the Pentateuchal narratives, despite his faults, returning Jacob to Israel twice, first from Aram and later, albeit posthumously, from Egypt.

9. Sweeney, *Isaiah 40–66*, 41–51.

10. See Marvin A. Sweeney, "Creation as Sacred Space in the Exodus Narratives," in *Lexington Theological Quarterly* 49 (2019): 1–14, for discussion of the role played by creation in the Exodus narratives, to be republished in Marvin A. Sweeney, *Visions of the Holy: Studies in Biblical Theology and Literature*. SBL Resources for Biblical Study (Atlanta, GA: SBL Press, 2023), 297–306.

11. Sweeney, *Isaiah 40–66*, 52–63.

Isaiah 41:1–42:13 argues that YHWH is the master of human events.[12] The passage begins its argumentation that YHWH has aroused a righteous one from the east, which in the context of the prophet's argumentation in Isa 40–54 refers to King Cyrus of Persia, even though he has not yet been named. By declining to name Cyrus until 44:28 and 45:1, the text builds up a sense of mystery and suspense before it reveals its purpose. But the text also appeals to past experience and identity by naming Israel and Jacob as its addressees in 41:8; it goes on to name them as YHWH's servants whom YHWH has chosen and not rejected. It names YHWH as the G-d of Israel in Isa 41:14, 17, and 20, who will redeem them and provide them with water, thereby recalling the wilderness narratives in Exod 17:1–17 and Num 20. Once again, the argumentative strategy is to call upon the audience for counterarguments, beginning in Isa 41:21 in which YHWH self-identifies as "the King of Jacob," in this case, recalling that Israel constitutes all twelve tribes based on the sons of the ancestor, Jacob, as well as recalling also YHWH's role as creator, which figures so prominently in the exodus and wilderness narratives as well as at the beginning of Genesis.

Isaiah 42:14–44:23 argues that YHWH is the redeemer of Israel.[13] Once again, this text addresses an audience configured as Jacob and Israel from the very outset in 42:14. In this case, the argumentation begins with YHWH's assertions that YHWH was the one who punished the people for their failure to observe YHWH's requirements effectively. Indeed, YHWH demands that Jacob/Israel help to remember how "your first father sinned" in v. 26. Although one might be tempted to think of Abraham, Abraham committed little in the way of sin, but Jacob indulged himself in some trickery to win the right of the firstborn and his father's blessing from his fraternal twin brother, Esau, in Gen 27–28. Jacob also spent the rest of his life dealing with analogous sibling rivalry on the part of his two wives, Leah and Rachel. But once this point is made, the passage shifts, beginning in 44:1 with assertions that YHWH is the redeemer of Israel and Jacob as demonstrated by YHWH's past actions on Israel's/Jacob's behalf. Here, YHWH addresses Jacob/Israel as "my servant," "whom I have chosen," and reassures the audience that YHWH will see to the growth of new offspring in 44:1–5. Following assertions of YHWH's role as creator and G-d, together with polemics against idols, in 42:6–20, YHWH calls upon Jacob/Israel to remember these things and addresses Jacob/Israel once again as "my servant." Altogether, these references to Jacob/Israel recall the troubled character of Jacob throughout the Pentateuchal narratives, either as the trickster who fools his brother and his father or as his descendants, who rebel against YHWH in the wilderness, even as YHWH acts to redeem Israel by bringing the nation to the promised land of Israel.[14]

12. Sweeney, *Isaiah 40–66*, 63–81.
13. Sweeney, *Isaiah 40–66*, 81–108.
14. See John E. Anderson, *Jacob and the Divine Trickster: A Theology of Deception and YHWH's Fidelity to the Ancestral Promise in the Jacob Cycle*, Siphrut 5 (Winona Lake, IN: Eisenbrauns, 2011), who focuses on both Jacob and YHWH as trickster figures in Gen 25–35.

Isaiah 44:24–48:21 argues that YHWH will use Cyrus, king of Persia and Babylon, to redeem Israel. This is the most controversial assertion on YHWH's part, insofar as it entails that YHWH will declare a foreigner, King Cyrus, as the messiah and temple builder of Israel, thereby replacing the role formerly served by the house of David.[15] The initial statement of this passage, "Thus says YHWH, your redeemer and the one who formed you in the womb," reasserts that YHWH is Jacob's/Israel's redeemer and recalls the struggle that Esau and Jacob had even when they were still in Rebekah's womb in Gen 25:19–26. YHWH's assertions about Cyrus' role as Messiah and Temple builder appear in Isa 44:28 and 45:1, the one whom YHWH, the G-d of Israel in 45:3, will use to act on behalf of Jacob/Israel, named in 45:4. YHWH demands to know if Israel should question him as creator and maker, especially when YHWH brings the wealth of Egypt and other countries to Israel. YHWH asserts that Israel was victorious due to YHWH in 45:17, that YHWH did not speak in secret, but announced publicly to the seed of Jacob what YHWH would do, apparently a reference to the earlier things mentioned throughout the first part of the book (see also Isa 45:25). After showing that the idols of the Babylonian gods, Bel and Nebo, are a burden to those who bear them in the Akitu procession, YHWH calls upon the house of Jacob/Israel to recognize that YHWH has borne them since birth in Isa 46. And after showing Bat Babel, the Daughter of Babylon, sitting on the ground without a throne in Isa 47, YHWH calls upon the house of Jacob/Israel in Isa 48 to leave Babylon, embark upon another wilderness journey where YHWH will once again provide water, and return to their homeland.

Isaiah 49–54 argue that YHWH is restoring Zion.[16] Although the focus is on Zion or Jerusalem, the textual block begins with the third so-called servant song in 49:1–6, in which YHWH speaks about the servant who was named in his mother's womb to serve YHWH's purposes. Although many interpreters correctly think that this passage references Jeremiah, who was commissioned to serve YHWH from the womb in Jer 1:4–9, it also references Jacob/Israel and explicitly names him as YHWH's servant, Israel, in v. 3.[17] Interpreters quibble over the reference in v. 6 that the servant's role is to return Jacob/Israel to YHWH, but this statement also refers to Joseph's return of Jacob's body to the land of Israel for burial in Gen 50:1–14. But even when attention turns to Jerusalem/Bat Zion beginning in Isa 49:14, the focus is the return of YHWH, identified as the G-d of Israel in Isa 52:12 and before that as the Mighty One of Jacob in Isa 49:26, to Bat Zion, the bride of YHWH, whom YHWH had abandoned. The marriage motif is important in the prophetic literature to portray the intimate relationship between YHWH and Israel or Jerusalem.[18] But the marriage motif is also central

---

15. Sweeney, *Isaiah 40–66*, 108–57.
16. Sweeney, *Isaiah 40–66*, 157–231.
17. Tryggve N. D. Mettinger, *A Farewell to the Servant Songs: A Critical Examination of an Exegetical Axiom* (Lund: Gleerup, 1983).
18. Gerlinde Baumann, *Love and Violence: Marriage as Metaphor for the Relationship between YHWH and Israel in the Prophetic Books* (Collegeville, MN: Liturgical Press, 2003).

to the Jacob narratives. Jacob goes into exile in Paddan Aram to find a bride from the family of his mother's brother, Laban. Jacob ends up marrying two of Laban's daughters, Leah and Rachel, as well as their handmaidens, Bilhah and Zilpah, and suffers due to the sibling rivalry between his wives, much as his parents suffered from his own sibling rivalry with Esau. But whereas Jacob ultimately returned home to the land of Israel with his wives and children, YHWH has been absent from the bride, Bat Zion, who is now bereft of her children, until both YHWH and her children, the people of Israel, return to her. Interpreters often think of Sarah as the matriarch who stands behind the image of the childless Bat Zion in Isa 54, but Jacob's favored wife, Rachel, was also bereft of children for a long period of time prior to the births of Joseph and Benjamin, even to the end of her life in the case of Benjamin. It is also the case that Jer 30–31, which calls upon Israel and Judah to return to Jerusalem, portrays Rachel weeping for her children in Jer 31:15. In any case, Isa 49–54 focuses especially on Jerusalem or Bat Zion, but it draws heavily on motifs from the Jacob and Rachel narratives in portraying the return of YHWH and the children of Israel to the bride, Bat Zion.

Following Isa 40–54, chs. 55–66 present only scattered references to Jacob. Overall, this textual block assigns the eternal Davidic covenant presumably to Israel at large, without identifying the audience with any other than masculine plural address forms, in Isa 55. The text then turns to prophetic instruction concerning who constitute the restored nation in Isa 56–66 in an effort to substantiate the exhortation to join YHWH's covenant in Isa 55. References to Jacob appear in Isa 58:1, 14; 59:20; 60:16; and 65:9, but these references generally refer to those who continue to sin and those who observe YHWH's expectations without clear reference to the pentateuchal Jacob narratives.[19] There is concern with YHWH's defeat of Edom in Isa 34:6 and 63:1–6, which might suggest references to YHWH's defeat of Esau to protect the righteous in Jacob/Israel against the continued enmity of Esau/Edom.

5

Interpreters have long recognized that the book of Isaiah is focused on YHWH's relationship with Jerusalem and Judah as indicated in the superscriptions in Isa 1:1 and 2:1. But the texts examined above demonstrate that both major portions of the synchronic form of the book of Isaiah in chs. 1–33 and 34–66 relate intertextually to the pentateuchal narratives concerning Israel's eponymous ancestor, Jacob, and the descendants of Jacob that ultimately form the nation of Israel. These narratives include Gen 25–35 and to some extent Gen 37–50, which portray the lifetime of Jacob, and Exodus–Deuteronomy, which portray the exodus from Egypt and the wilderness narratives concerning Israel's journey from Egypt to the promised land of Israel. They point to the influence of the Jacob narratives in the composition of Isa 1–33, particularly in chs. 2–4 and 5–12, which respectively

---

19. For detailed study of these texts, see Sweeney, *Isaiah 40–66*, ad loc.

define the ideal rhetorical goals of the book in relation to Jacob's invitation to join the nations streaming to Zion to learn YHWH's Torah and thereby end war. They also point to the punishment of Jacob at the hands of Assyria and YHWH's projected restoration of Jacob under the rule of an ideal Davidic monarch in terms that represent tremendous influence from the exodus and wilderness narratives of the Pentateuch. The second part of the book in Isa 34–66, particularly in chs. 40–54, likewise demonstrates considerable influence from the Jacob narratives of the Pentateuch, including both the exodus and wilderness narratives in chs. 40–48 and the accounts of Jacob's marriage to Rachel in the depiction of Bat Zion, a.k.a., Jerusalem, as YHWH's bride in 49–54. As the book of Isaiah currently stands, such a pattern suggests a motif of prophecy and its fulfillment, which has long been recognized in studying the final form of the book. Consideration of the Jacob motifs, therefore, has potential for evaluating the extent to which such a concern influences the compositional history of the book.

Chapter 10

CAN JEREMIAH QUOTE DEUTERO-
OR TRITO-ISAIAH? ITS IMPACT ON THE "UNITY"
MOVEMENT IN ISAIAH STUDIES*

Georg Fischer

1. *Introduction*

The relationship between Isaiah and Jeremiah is intricate. Traditionally, most scholars distinguish between two, three, or more phases for the development of the book of Isaiah. As a consequence, they assume that Jeremiah could use texts of the First Isaiah as a source, whereas they reckon for the latter part of Isaiah (ch. 40 onwards) as having dependence on Jeremiah. Among others, Ute Wendel,[1] Benjamin D. Sommer,[2] and Patricia T. Willey[3] hold this position.

This widespread opinion has recently received critique from two sides. On the one hand, research on Isaiah can demonstrate that there are many internal connections between the various parts of the book of Isaiah, thus pointing to a much stronger coherence than supposed before. Some elements in this direction are:

---

* I thank Benedetta Rossi and Dominic S. Irudayaraj for the invitation to present this paper at the ISBL congress in Rome in July 2019. Samuel Hildebrandt and Patrizia Kössler have corrected the English of this article; I am grateful to them, too.

    1. Ute Wendel, *Jesaja und Jeremia: Worte, Motive und Einsichten Jesajas in der Verkündigung Jeremias*, BThSt 25 (Neukirchen: Neukirchener Verlag, 1995).

    2. Benjamin D. Sommer, "Allusions and Illusions: The Unity of the Book of Isaiah," in *New Visions of Isaiah*, ed. Roy F. Melugin and Marvin A. Sweeney, JSOTSup 214 (Sheffield: JSOT, 1996), 156–86.

    3. Patricia T. Willey, *Remember the Former Things: The Recollection of Previous Texts in Second Isaiah*, SBLDS 161 (Atlanta, GA: Scholars, 1997).

- the frame of the entire book with the parental role of YHWH: Isa 1:2 presents him as making children grow and educating them, and Isa 66:13 compares him to a consoling mother.[4]
- the pervading use of motifs, for example, the pair צדקה and משפט, "justice and law,"[5] the expression קדוש ישראל, "the Holy one of Israel."[6]
- the recognition that Isa 55 is not an ending, but requires an extension[7]

These and other reasons indicate that the book of Isaiah may have been shaped intentionally in this way as a composite unity. Dominic S. Irudayaraj, therefore, calls it "a readable whole."[8]

On the other hand, recent research on the intertextual links with the book of Jeremiah does not support the traditional view. Several exegetes have suggested that the book of Jeremiah picks up texts from the entire book of Isaiah, including material from its later parts. This adduces an argument from outside (of Isaiah) to the issue of the unity of Isaiah.

Geoffrey H. Parke-Taylor assumes texts of the so-called Second Isaiah as sources for the "oracles against foreign nations" in Jeremiah several times.[9] Additionally, in Part X of his book, he considers that the two phrases רגע הים ויהמו גליו in Jer 31:35c take up Isa 51:15b.

Angelika Berlejung studied the relationship of Jer 10 with the polemic against idols in Deutero-Isaiah and concluded that Jer 10:3–10 takes over elements from Isa 40–46 and reads "wie ein Kompendium der Bilderpolemik aus Dtjes, deren Kenntnis vorausgesetzt werden kann."[10] Jeremiah 10 is like a short summary of what in Isaiah receives a lot of space.

I want to continue this line of thought and first present the research of Henk Leene on our topic (see subsection 2, below), before adding some other examples

---

4. Willem A. M. Beuken, *Jesaja 1–12*, HThKAT (Freiburg: Herder, 2003), 36, perceives therein "eine Bearbeitung, die den Beginn des Jesajabuchs auf sein Ende in Kap. 65–66 abstimmt." In addition, Isa 63:16 and 64:7 address God three times as "our father."

5. The pair צדקה and משפט occurs, within one verse, 14 times in Isaiah, distributed between Isa 1:27 and 59:14.

6. It has 26 occurrences, starting with Isa 1:4 and ending with 60:14.

7. See Simone Paganini, *Der Weg zur Frau Zion, Ziel unserer Hoffnung*, SBB 49 (Stuttgart: Katholisches Bibelwerk 2002), especially 193 and 199. According to him, several motifs remain open in Isa 55, and readers expect that they are clarified in a continuation.

8. Dominic S. Irudayaraj, *Violence, Otherness and Identity in Isaiah 63:1–6: The Trampling One Coming from Edom*, LHBOTS 633 (London: Bloomsbury T&T Clark, 2017), 35.

9. Geoffrey H. Parke-Taylor, *The Formation of the Book of Jeremiah: Doublets and Recurring Phrases*, SBLMS 51 (Atlanta, GA: Scholars, 2000), see parts VII and VIII.

10. Angelika Berlejung, *Die Theologie der Bilder: Herstellung und Einweihung von Kultbildern in Mesopotamien und die alttestamentliche Bilderproblematik*, OBO 162 (Fribourg: Universitätsverlag, 1998), 391. Ulrich Berges, *Jesaja 40–48*, HThKAT (Freiburg: Herder, 2008), 335, assumes similarly for the term מעצד in Isa 44:12 that Jer 10:3 borrowed it from there.

of potential textual overlap between Jeremiah and Isaiah (see subsection 3, below). It is my hope that they can offer further arguments for considering that the whole book of Isaiah was a unity when it was used for writing Jeremiah.

2. *The Contribution of Henk Leene*

With his final book,[11] the Dutch scholar Henk Leene has left a legacy. His work collects the research of his last decades, starts with Newness in the Psalms on YHWH's kingship, the same theme in Deutero- and Trito-Isaiah, in Ezekiel and Jeremiah, and concludes with their intertextual relationships.

For Leene, several passages in Isa 1–39 may be younger than Isa 40–55, and the temporal distance between Deutero- and Trito-Isaiah is small.[12] He dates these latter sections of the book to the second half of the fifth century and assumes a similar socio-religious milieu for both.[13]

More relevant for our discussion is how Leene investigates at length the links between Isaiah Jer 30–31, the "booklet of consolation."[14] I present some of his conclusions:

> The citations do not stem alone from Isa. 40–55 but also from other parts of Isaiah, and certainly from Isa. 56–66. This indicates that the authors of Jer. 30–31 did not dispose of Isa. 40–55 as an independent work, but as a prominent part of a more comprehensive prophetic book scroll.[15]

> Without Deutero-Isaiah's חדשה as background, the promise of the ברית חדשה in Jeremiah holds something incomprehensible—a promise with the shocking sound of a *contradictio in terminis*.[16]

> How would it have been possible for later readers to combine Isaiah and Ezekiel's "theology of hope" had the mediating book of Jeremiah remained unwritten?[17]

In short: *Jeremiah read Isaiah.*[18]

---

11. Henk Leene, *Newness in Old Testament Prophecy: An Intertextual Study*, OTS 64 (Leiden: Brill, 2014). On June 10, the same year, he died.
12. See Leene, *Newness*, 74, for the relationship between First and Second Isaiah; and 132–3, for distance between the two.
13. Leene, *Newness*, 134, 139.
14. Leene, *Newness*, 287–322.
15. Leene, *Newness*, 312.
16. Leene, *Newness*, 318 (author's emphasis).
17. Leene, *Newness*, 319.
18. Leene, *Newness*, 311 (author's emphasis).

Leene's position questions the traditional dating and understanding of the relationship between Isaiah and Jeremiah.[19] The basis for his questioning is the separation of the book from the (supposed) historical figure of the prophet. Jeremiah may have proclaimed his messages around 600 BCE, yet somebody could have written the scroll attributed to him at a considerably later time. This would allow us to reverse the usual sequence "Isaiah–Jeremiah–Deutero-Isaiah–Trito-Isaiah," leaving even an option for a later setting of Isa 40–66.

Leene's study enriches the understanding of the relationships of the three Major Prophets.[20] Instead of focusing on the dates given at the beginning of the respective books, he concentrates on the texts and analyzes them according to their literary character. Thus, he can free the interpretation of these prophets from long-standing misconceptions.

3. Further Examples

Leene's research opens up new perspectives for understanding the formation of the Major Prophets. This makes it possible to see the relationship between the latter parts of Isaiah[21] and Jeremiah as unfolding in the opposite direction of what is traditionally assumed. I will deal with five possible links in the following.

3.1. Parallels between Isaiah's Servant Songs and the Portrayal of the Prophet Jeremiah

The servant songs in Isaiah are some of its most distinguished texts, portraying a suffering figure with eminent importance. There are several close coincidences of those poems with specific texts in Jeremiah. Some of them form "exclusive links," meaning that they only occur in these passages. In the following I will present the most relevant ones:[22]

---

19. Leene's study concentrates on Jer 30–31, and is therefore primarily valid for those two chapters. However, as the studies of Parke-Taylor and Berlejung have shown, this seems to be true also for other parts of Jeremiah (chs. 10 and 46–51).

20. Leene also deals extensively with the book of Ezekiel and its links to Jeremiah: *Newness*, 240–79, based on several earlier articles. Especially revealing is Henk Leene, "Blowing the Same Shofar: An Intertextual Comparison of Representations of the Prophetic Role in Jeremiah and Ezekiel," in *The Elusive Prophet: The Prophet as a Historical Person, Literary Character and Anonymous Artist: Papers Read at the Eleventh Joint Meeting of The Society for Old Testament Study and Het Oudtestamentisch Werkgezelschap in Nederland en België, held at Soesterberg 2000*, ed. Johannes C. de Moor, OTS 45 (Leiden: Brill, 2001), 175–98.

21. This applies also for the book of Ezekiel; see below a few indications in 3.5.

22. For a wider exposition of this topic, see Georg Fischer, "Jeremiah, God's Suffering Servant," in *Jeremiah Studies*, FAT 139 (Tübingen: Mohr Siebeck, 2020), 249–66.

Isa 49:1 "YHWH called me from the womb."
    Jer 1:5 "Before I formed you in the womb, I knew you."

Isa 42:6; 49:6 "I make you … a light for the nations."
    Jer 1:5 "I make you a prophet for the nations."

Isa 53:7, 8c "(he …) like a lamb led to slaughter …
    he was cut off from the land of the living"
    Jer 11:19 "I was like a tame lamb led to slaughter …
        let us extirpate him from the land of the living"

Isa 53:6 "YHWH has caused the iniquity of us all to fall on him"
    Jer 15:11 "I have imposed enemies on you"

Isa 53:8a "By oppression and judgment he was taken away"
    Jer 15:15 "Don't take me away by your forbearance"

Ulrich Berges interprets the portrayal of the servant in Isaiah as a theological climax, a kind of ultimate, late development.[23] According to him, it would be strange if the author of Jeremiah, reading Isaiah, had not also picked up the idea of YHWH's servant becoming an אשם. As a result, he sees Jeremiah as the older text and the servant in Second Isaiah as an *elaboration of the presentation* of the prophet Jeremiah.[24]

But the reverse direction is just as feasible, namely, to perceive in Jeremiah an *expansion of Isaiah's portrayal* of YHWH's servant. Indications for this are:

- the addition of אלוף, "tame," for the lamb (Jer 11:19);
- the extension of time for the calling, with בטרם, "before" instead of "from the womb" (Jer 1:5);
- the change from "objective" formulations in the third person (in Isa 49:1; 53:6) to personal statements in the first person for YHWH (yet also in Isa 42:6);
- the difference between passive voices ("he was cut off, … he was taken away") and cohortative ("let us"), imperative ("don't take") in Jer 11:19; 15:15.

The distribution of these texts in Jeremiah is also significant: Jer 1 outlines his vocation; Jer 11 and 15 are the first and second confessions. Together they shape the profile of the prophet Jeremiah at prominent positions, namely at the beginning of the book, at the start of the major block Jer 11–20, and therein again in Jer 15, after God's definitive refusal to listen to any plea from Jeremiah for the

---

23. Ulrich Berges, "Servant and Suffering in Isaiah and Jeremiah: Who Borrowed from Whom?," *OTE* 25 (2012): 247–59.

24. Similarly, Katherine Dell, "The Suffering Servant of Deutero-Isaiah: Jeremiah Revisited," in *Genesis, Isaiah and Psalms*, ed. Katherine Dell, Graham Davies, and Yee von Koh, VTSup 135 (Leiden: Brill, 2010), 119–34.

people.²⁵ This can be perceived as a deliberate technique for the characterization of Jeremiah, especially in Jer 11 and 15, which both use the servant-motif after others have attacked the prophet.

This would also account for the more radical presentation in Jeremiah. In my view, it is hard to imagine that the author of Isaiah's servant songs, knowing the similar expressions in Jeremiah, would have eased them—with the result that YHWH's servant appeared as a milder version of the prophet Jeremiah.²⁶ The literary differences shown above are better explained if we assume that, as Leene wrote, "Jeremiah read Isaiah"—meaning that the author of Jeremiah took over the respective motifs from Isaiah to present Jeremiah as a personification of YHWH's servant, and that he elaborated them to make his prophet appear as the nearly perfect example for this figure.²⁷ The biographical background of Jeremiah allows imagining in a realistic way what in Isaiah remains on the level of a literary description.

3.2. Jerusalem's New Glory?

There are some interesting parallels between Isa 60 and Jer 6. Both texts portray Zion / Jerusalem, yet in different directions. Isaiah 60 shows the new splendor of it. Two aspects are: v. 6 announces "gold and incense will be brought from Sheba," and v. 18 states that "Violence will not be heard any more in your country, (nor) oppression and ruin in your territory."

Jeremiah 6 twice stands in opposition to such declarations. In v. 20, God himself asks what use "incense coming from Sheba"²⁸ might have for him; the rhetorical question is equal to a critique of it. On the one hand, if Jer 6 predates Isa 60, it seems rather odd that Isaiah did not counter explicitly the divine statement in Jeremiah. On the other hand, if the one writing Jer 6 knows Isa 60, he effectively

---

25. See the third prohibition of intercession addressed to Jeremiah in 14:11, and God's reaction at the people's prayer in 14:19–22 with 15:1–4. For the theme of intercession in Jeremiah, see Benedetta Rossi, *L'intercessione nel tempo della fine: Studio dell'intercessione profetica nel libro di Geremia*, AnBib 204 (Rome: Gregorian & Biblical Press, 2013).

26. Berges' argument of the non-use of אשם can be answered by the very marginal role of cult in Jeremiah; not even the ark of the covenant is important anymore (Jer 3:16–17), and God states provocatively that he did not command sacrifices when he led Israel out of Egypt (Jer 6:20). Isaiah 53:9 talks also about the servant's grave close to those of evildoers, presupposing his death; Jer 44 makes the prophet "disappear" in Egypt, dying at an unknown place. There may be further connections between the third servant song in Isa 50 and Jeremiah's persecution, especially in Jer 20, for example, in the motifs of "blow/strike" (root נכה) and "shame" or "derision" (with various roots).

27. Throughout the Hebrew Bible, there is no other character would resemble YHWH's suffering servant more than the prophet Jeremiah. Being misjudged is another motif that connects them.

28. This is an exclusive link; there is no other text of the Hebrew Bible linking "incense" and "Sheba."

opposed luxury imports for the temple liturgy by questioning its usefulness and putting this critique in the mouth of the LORD.

The second contrast appears in Jer 6:7, "violence and oppression are heard in it" (חמס ושד). This critical view of Jerusalem stays in explicit opposition to Isa 60:18.[29] Both phrases fit their relative contexts well: in Isaiah the new grandeur of Zion, in Jeremiah the harsh criticism of the evils of the capital. If we see Isaiah reacting on Jeremiah, this would indicate some kind of healing for the brokenness of the city—which would make sense. So also the other direction, Jeremiah drawing on Isaiah, can illuminate the relationship between these two texts. In this case, similarly to the previous opposition, Jeremiah would counter the idealized portrayal of Jerusalem in Isaiah with a series of accusations,[30] thus showing that the reality is different and that Judah's capital is accused of the combined sins of other cities. Interpreted in this way, Jer 6 confronts the idyllic vision of Isaiah.

3.3. Is there שלום?

Jeremiah 6:14 (// 8:11) refers to a doubled proclamation of שלום, "Peace! Peace!,"[31] by prophets and priests, rejecting it by the statement "and there is no peace." This is very close to the criticism in Ezek 13:10, which Leene considers as the source for Jer 6.[32] As Ezekiel has שלום only once, he goes on to ask whether already Isa 57:19 (with repeated שלום) may be in "the author's mind."[33] In fact, the doubling of שלום occurs outside the two passages of Jeremiah only in Isa 26:3; 57:19 and 1 Chron 12:19. The first passage, Isa 26, praises God: it is Judah's grateful song for YHWH who, addressed by "you," preserves his "bewährten Sinn"[34] (tested attitude, firm orientation) "(towards?) peace, peace." 1 Chronicles is certainly later than Jeremiah, and therefore cannot be its source. Isaiah 57:19 offers the closest relationship to Jeremiah. There it is a divine proclamation, directed to those[35] who are "far and near," which includes everybody. Such a universal offer is tempered by the next two verses, 20–21, which clearly limit it by the explicit exclusion of the evildoers.

Once again, if both texts did not arise independently, there are two possibilities of their interrelationship. Isaiah 57 might pick up Jer 6, clarifying the restriction of peace / wellbeing by mentioning a specific group. Or, the other way round:

29. These two are the only texts with the combination of חמס, שד and שמע.

30. Jeremiah 6 contains a kind of summary of charges, building on indictments against Gibeah (Judg 19–20), Samaria (Amos 3), and the warnings/curses of Lev 26 and Deut 28: Georg Fischer, *Jeremia 1–25*, HThKAT (Freiburg: Herder, 2005), 285.

31. One might also paraphrase it as an announcement of sure salvation.

32. Leene, "Blowing the Same Shofar," 177–83.

33. Leene, "Blowing the Same Shofar," 185.

34. This is the translation of יצר סמוך by Willem A. M. Beuken, *Jesaja 13–27*, HThKAT (Freiburg: Herder, 2007), 361 and 370.

35. The Hebrew text uses singular, but one may understand it collectively.

Jer 6 would oppose Isaiah's general announcement of salvation in YHWH's name as he attributes the repeated שלום promise to prophets. This could be a hint for referring indirectly to Isaiah, and may also be to others. Whereas "no peace" in Isa 57:19 is only directed against one group of sinners, in Jer 6:14 it is a general statement, denouncing a widespread condition. Jeremiah 6 is thus more radical than Isa 57.

3.4. Lady Zion Adorns Herself

Isaiah 54 and Jer 4 share many common expressions and motifs. Isaiah presents the restoration of Lady Zion, while Jer 4 presents her death and destruction. Gottfried Glassner has provided a list of the parallels[36] and concludes that there is an "enges Korrespondenzverhältnis" between these texts. Some of the shared elements are Jerusalem being despised (Isa 54:6; Jer 4:30), living in tents (Isa 54:2; Jer 4:20; 10:20)[37] and receiving / applying פוך ("paint") for her beauty (Isa 54:11; Jer 4:30). For Glassner, Jer 4 is the source and Deutero-Isaiah has taken over words from this text while transforming the picture to that of a resurrected city.

It seems logical that restoration presupposes previous devastation and, therefore, the sequence Jer 4 → Isa 54 makes sense. However, we have to consider the settings as "literary"; therefore it is also possible that Isaiah focuses on the renewal of the destroyed city, and Jeremiah, at a later time, concentrates on the process that led to Jerusalem's ruin. In view of the above reversals of optimistic Isaian announcements in Jeremiah, one can read the depiction of Lady Zion adorning herself for her murderers in Jer 4:30 as irony, overturning the positive estimation of Isaiah into a revelation of the naïve attitude and desperate condition of the capital.

There might still be another connection between Isaiah and Jeremiah with the motif of Zion's beauty. The expression עטרת תפארת, "crown of adornment,"[38] is a sign of Jerusalem's new glory in Isa 62:3, whereas in Jer 13:18 this symbol of splendor "has gone down from your heads," in this case of the king and the *gebirah* of Jerusalem. Once again, the passage in Jeremiah could indicate a reversal of Isaiah's announcement.

3.5. The Aftermath of Awakening

Jeremiah 31:26 contains a riddle: "Upon this, I awoke and saw, and my sleep was pleasant to me." This follows v. 25, which talks about God's act of filling the

---

36. Gottfried Glassner, *Vision eines auf Verheißung gegründeten Jerusalem: Textanalytische Studien zu Jesaja 54*, ÖBS 11 (Klosterneuburg: Österreichisches Katholisches Bibelwerk, 1991), especially 235–8.

37. The word pair אהל and יריעה referring to Jerusalem is unique to these three texts.

38. The combination of these two words is rare. Outside the two verses dealt with here, it occurs only in Ezek 16:12; 23:42, referring to Jerusalem and, in the latter case, also to Samaria, and in Prov 4:9; 16:31, for wisdom and old age.

languishing souls (נפש עיפה ,נפש דאבה). The link between both verses, especially the transition to sleep and awakening, as well as the identity of the speaker, remains unclear.

In the Hebrew Bible, Isa 29:(7–)8[39] is the closest passage Jer 31:25–26. It also has "to wake up" (קיץ) and "soul" (נפש), both twice, "weary" (עָיֵף) and the ideas of want and sleep, expressed by words such as "hungry, thirsty, to dream," but with a completely different outcome. When Zion's enemies awake from their dreaming, they will feel "empty" (ריק), in contrast to the effect on the sleeping "I" in Jer 31, who experiences comfort (עָרֵב) after awakening. Jeremiah 31:26 is a mystery. With Isa 29:6 as a possible background, it receives light, as an opposed result to the foe's attack on Jerusalem. Isaiah 29 helps to understand Jer 31:(23–)26, as the divine act of overturning the fates of the city, its surroundings, and their populations, thus leaving behind an enjoyable impression (after a kind of "night," indicated by sleep and awakening).

Jeremiah's relationship with Ezekiel points to a parallel. The end of Jer 6, in particular vv. 28–29, is difficult to understand. It alludes to a melting process, involving bronze, iron, lead and a fire ignited by bellows. It fails, does not result in achieving pure "silver" (see v. 30: כסף נמאס) and serves as an image that it is impossible to remove the wicked from the community. Ezekiel 22:17–22 is the closest text to it. There, the procedure is described more extendedly and, therefore, is easily understandable. If one knows Ezek 22, the condensed passage in Jer 6 is elucidated and becomes comprehensible.[40] In sum, viewing Isaiah and Ezekiel as sources for Jeremiah throws light on obscure and extremely short developed motifs in the latter.

4. *In Conclusion*

We started with a rather surprising question. It confronted the traditional views that (a) the book of Isaiah is composed of various parts from different times and (b) the book of Jeremiah preceded the later chapters of the book of Isaiah. The "unity movement" has challenged the first conviction about the composition of Isaiah. My aim here was to adduce additional arguments from outside the book for considering that the scroll of Isaiah was finalised as a whole earlier than has normally been supposed, already before the book of Jeremiah.

Following the line of G. Parke-Taylor, A. Berlejung and especially H. Leene, I tried to point to some close parallels between Isa 40–66 and Jeremiah, which

---

39. It speaks about a multitude of nations attacking Zion, whose effort remains vain.

40. In a similar way, Jer 23:1–4 might be a summarized form of Ezek 34, with three stages of shepherds, and Jer 31:29–30 may summarize the message of Ezek 18:1–20. Henk Leene, Georg Braulik, William L. Holladay and others share this understanding of the relationship between Ezek 34 and Jer 31; see Georg Fischer, *Jeremia 26–52*, HThKAT (Freiburg: Herder, 2005), 169–70.

led me to surmise that Jeremiah is dependent on them. On several occasions,[41] Jeremiah shows a tendency towards the literary elaboration of a source. It often displays a more critical stance and is more radical. In my view, these are signs that the author(s)[42] of Jeremiah could have known the entire book of Isaiah and reacted to it.

To be sure: I do not suggest that the book of Isaiah developed in one short process, nor do I exclude literary growth. My aim here was to present some observations that Isaiah, as a whole and in its transmitted form, could have been a source for the book of Jeremiah and predate it. In this case, Isaiah served as an inspiration for writing Jeremiah. Both books share common ideas, especially in the scroll of consolation.[43] As Leene put it for Ezekiel and Jeremiah, Isaiah and Jeremiah—at least sometimes—"blow the same shofar," yet on several occasions with different tunes, keys and modes of interpretation.

---

41. The examples adduced here cover chs. 1, 4, 6, 11, 15, 31 in Jeremiah. Part 3.5 showed additionally that the same procedure reversing former statements may also be valid for Jeremiah's connection with First Isaiah and that, like Isaiah, the book of Ezekiel, too, might be a source for Jeremiah.

42. I do not exclude the possibility of various hands being responsible for Jeremiah. However, my preference would be for there being one author, since Jeremiah displays a very complex design on various levels and a pervading intertextual working technique throughout, from the beginning to the end.

43. See, e.g., the message of restoration in Jer 30:10–11, or the comparison with a garden full of water in Jer 31:12, as in Isa 58:11.

Chapter 11

BLINDNESS IN DISCOURSE:
COGNITIVE LINKS IN ISAIAH THROUGH THE
METAPHORS IN ISAIAH 42-43 AS TEST CASES

Boris Lazzaro

"For those who are ignorant, ignorance is as bad as blindness is for those who do not see,"[1] This is what the young Plato, according to Plutarch, said to Antimachus. This short sentence condenses not only a characteristic trait of Platonic poetics,[2] but a universal cognitive constant that associates the ability to see with knowledge and, correspondingly, the inability to see with non-knowledge.[3] Something similar also happens with the sensory organ of hearing: listening represents knowledge on a metaphorical level, while deafness describes mental dullness.[4]

As recognized by many scholars,[5] the book of Isaiah is particularly representative of this analogical process. The mentioning of seeing and hearing is a

1. Plutarch, *Lys* XVIII, 5. All translations in this paper are mine.

2. See Eleftheria A. Bernidaki-Aldous, *Blindness in a Culture of Light: Especially the Case of Oedipus at Colonus of Sophocles*, AUSCLL 8 (New York: Lang, 1990), 49–55.

3. See Zoltán Kövecses, *Metaphor in Culture: Universality and Variation* (Cambridge: Cambridge University Press, 2010). For the Hebrew Bible, see Michael Carasik, *Theologies of the Mind in Biblical Israel*, Studies in Biblical literature 85 (New York: Lang, 2006), 32–43; Yael Avrahami, *The Senses of Scripture: Sensory Perception in the Hebrew Bible*, LHBOTS 545 (New York: T&T Clark, 2012), 248–55; Nicole L. Tilford, *Sensing World, Sensing Wisdom: The Cognitive Foundation of Biblical Metaphors*, SBLAIL 31 (Atlanta, GA: SBL, 2017), 58–67.

4. For the Hebrew Bible, see Tilford, *Sensing World, Sensing Wisdom*, 74–90.

5. See the bibliographic review in Boris Lazzaro, "If the Blind Walk: The Cognitive Metaphor 'Knowing is Seeing' and Its Elaboration in Isa 42,16," in *Networks of Metaphors in the Hebrew Bible*, ed. Danilo Verde and Antje Labahn, BETL 309 (Leuven: Peeters 2020), 61–78 (61 nn. 1–2).

privileged medium to express one of the central themes of the book: the hardening of the audience. However, such images do not merely revive the paradoxical order of 6:9–10. They show deeper connections among them, ones that can be grasped only at a cognitive level of the language. In fact, following the approach of Lakoff and Johnson,[6] such images can be appropriately framed as a double general cognitive metaphor: KNOWING IS SEEING and KNOWING IS HEARING, where the metaphorizing (SEEING/HEARING) is conventionally called *source* and the metaphorized (KNOWING) is called *target*. This double metaphor occurs recursively in Isaiah with a continuous variation of linguistic modulations, on the morphological, syntactic, lexical, and stylistic levels.

In this field of research, Lakoff and Johnson's cognitive approach has two advantages: (1) it allows for the collection of disparate data in a unified, simple, and well-focused framework; (2) it intercepts the links between the various linguistic modulations of the same cognitive metaphor, strengthening cohesion and coherence of the entire book on a synchronic level. Cognitive linguistics thus constitutes both a promise and a challenge for Isaianic exegesis: a promise because it clarifies aspects of the metaphorical functioning that otherwise would remain confused or unintelligible; a challenge, due to its innovative character compared to more conventional approaches to figurative language. In the present study, not being able to analyze in this context every pertinent metaphorical expression of the corpus, I limit my investigation to the images of seeing/hearing in Isa 42–43, as a test-case. Nevertheless, in this way I suggest a path of investigation that can be extended to all the occurrences of seeing/hearing metaphors within Isaiah.

1. A Fourfold Metamorphosis

Within Isa 42–43,[7] the cognitive metaphor KNOWING IS SEEING occurs four times, in 42:7; 42:16; 42:18–19; 43:8, through the modular reproduction of the stereotype of the blind. Furthermore, in 42:18–19 and 43:8, it is associated with the complementary metaphor KNOWING IS HEARING through the combined mention of the blind and the deaf. By focusing on the concept KNOWING IS SEEING, we can observe how it undergoes a peculiar elaboration in the passage from one text to another: in 42:7 the metaphor is simply inserted into the discourse; in 42:16 it undergoes a process of complexification; in 42:18–19, the same metaphor is contradicted and dissolved, then rehabilitated in 43:8, albeit through a significant modification on the cognitive level. Therefore, in the four passages mentioned, the conceptual metaphor KNOWING IS SEEING is *placed* in the discourse, then *complicated*, *contradicted*, and finally *rehabilitated*.

---

6. I am referring especially to the pioneering book of George Lakoff and Mark Johnson, *Metaphors We Live By* (Chicago, IL: The University of Chicago Press, 1980).

7. On the internal links within Isa 42–43, see Roy F. Melugin, *The Formation of Isaiah 40–55*, BZAW 141 (Berlin: de Gruyter, 1976), 106–9; Lazzaro, "If the Blind Walk," 67.

2. Placing the Metaphor (Isa 42:7)

2.1. To Open Blind Eyes

The first mention of blindness appears in Isa 42:7a: "to open blind eyes." The metaphorical value of the sentence is homologous to the peculiar use that Deutero-Isaiah[8] makes of the adjective עוּר, "blind" (together with חרשׁ, "deaf"), as denoting a lack of knowledge (cf. 42:18–20, 23; 43:8).[9] Furthermore, the metaphorical value of the utterance is contextually required by the clearly metaphorical characterization of the servant's office, announced immediately before, in 42:6b: to be "a *light* of the nations."

As a particular case of the cognitive metaphor KNOWING IS SEEING, the opening of the eyes indicates the reacquisition of the ability to understand. The syntagmatic construction √פקח *qal* + עין validates this interpretation. When referring to people, it is an idiomatic form that designates access to a new understanding of reality (cf. Gen 3:5, 7; 21:19; 2 Kgs 6:17). The phrase, however, is enriched by the adjective עוּר, declined in feminine plural, as a qualifier of the eyes (עינים עורות, "blind eyes"). With an internal metonymic process, the metaphor focuses on the organ of sight. It is a recurring expressive modality in the Isaianic repertoire (cf. 6:10; 29:10, 18; 32:3; 35:5; 44:18), capable of giving the images a certain plasticity. However, unlike 6:10; 29:10; 32:3–4; 44:18, where the metonymic process explores, one by one, various organs of perception (eyes, ears, heart, head), in 42:7a the process focuses solely on the visual element. Therefore, while the other Isaianic passages create an overall metaphorical transfer that associates a different aspect of mental understanding with each organ of the body (THE MIND IS A BODY), 42:7a focuses solely on the visual organ, the most suitable to metaphorically represent the act of knowledge.[10]

2.2. Contextual Expansions

2.2.1. Blind and prisoners (v. 7). In the broader context of v. 7, the metaphor of blindness undergoes a peculiar semantic extension.[11] Placed in parallel with 7b

---

8. This expression is used conventionally, without implying the existence of a single exilic author. Rather, it refers to the text of Isa 40–55 and to its implied author.

9. See Lazzaro, "If the Blind Walk," 67–70.

10. The metaphor of listening, however, places the stress on the interpersonal character of knowledge. On these aspects and on the general metaphor THE MIND IS A BODY, see Eve Sweetser, *From Etymology to Pragmatics: Metaphoric and Cultural Aspects of Semantic Structure*, Cambridge Studies in Linguistics 54 (Cambridge: Cambridge University Press 1991), 23–48. See also Iraide Ibarretxe-Antuñano, "Mind-as-Body as a Cross-Linguistic Conceptual Metaphor," *Miscelánea: A Journal of English and American Studies* 25 (2002): 93–119; Zoltán Kövecses, *Metaphor: A Practical Introduction*, 2nd ed. (Oxford: Oxford University Press, 2010), 254–6.

11. On the importance of context for the interpretation of a metaphor, see Josef Stern, *Metaphor in Context* (Cambridge, MA: MIT Press, 2000). In the field of cognitive linguistics, see Kövecses, *Metaphor*, 285–304.

and 7c, the opening of the eyes is related to the release of prisoners and of those who live in darkness.¹²

⁷ᵃ To open blind eyes,	לפקח עינים עורות
⁷ᵇ to get prisoners out from the dungeon,	להוציא ממסגר אסיר
⁷ᶜ from the house of confinement those who dwell in darkness.	מבית כלא ישבי חשך

The contiguity of the utterances creates a sort of equivalence between the images,¹³ or at least emphasizes their common cognitive elements. In fact, the perception of the dark, and with it the limitation of the visual field, somehow tie together the experience of the blind with that of the prisoner (ישבי חשך). Similarly, the reopening (√פקח *qal*) of the eyes and the getting out (√יצא *hiphil*) of jail find their points of correspondence in the perception of light and in the widening of the visual field. However, how are we to understand the equivalence between the images? In the sense that the blind are literally prisoners, now unaccustomed to the use of sight?¹⁴ Or, on the contrary, that imprisonment, like blindness, is a metaphor for something else, essentially a state of inner oppression? According to the metaphorical value already recognized in v. 7a, the second hypothesis appears more plausible. This conclusion is confirmed by the figurative meaning that the mention of imprisonment exhibits a little further, in v. 22,¹⁵ as well as in 49:9. In this way, mental dullness, of which blindness is a metaphor, and the suffered experience of exile, of which imprisonment is a metaphor, end up intertwining: the suffering of the deportees is coextensive with their inability to understand.

2.2.2. *Covenant of the people, light of the nations (v. 6b).* The syntactic connection between v. 6b and v. 7 further elucidates the hermeneutics of the metaphor. Isaiah 42:7 provides, in fact, the purpose of the divine commission formulated in v. 6b:

---

12. Daniel L. Smith-Christopher, "Reassessing the Historical and Sociological Impact of the Babylonian Exile (597/587–539 BCE)," in *Exile: Old Testament, Jewish, and Christian Conceptions*, ed. James M. Scott, JSJSup 56 (Leiden: Brill, 1997), 30, suggests that the correlation between blindness and captivity echoes a traditional motif in the Babylonian literature, assimilated by the exiles as a metaphorical code for their traumatic condition.

13. See Roman Jakobson, "Closing Statements: Linguistics and Poetics," in *Style in Language*, ed. Thomas A. Sebeock (Cambridge, MA: MIT Press, 1964), 358.

14. See Evode Beaucamp, "'Chant nouveau du retour' (Is 42, 10–17). Un monstre de l'exégèse moderne," *RSR* 56 (1982): 145–58 (153).

15. See Borghild Baldauf, "Jes 42,18–25. Gottes tauber und blinder Knecht," in *Ein Gott, eine Offenbarung: Beiträge zur biblischen Exegese, Theologie und Spiritualität. Festschrift für Notker Füglister OSB zum 60. Geburtstag*, ed. Friedrich V. Reiterer (Würzburg: Echter, 1991), 13–36 (32–3); Jan L. Koole, *Isaiah III*, HCOT (Kampen: Kok Pharos, 1997), I, 275; Ulrich Berges, *Jesaja 40–48*, HThKAT (Freiburg: Herder, 2008), 265.

⁶ᵇ I, the LORD, [...] have established you as covenant of the people, light of the nations, ⁷ to open blind eyes, to let prisoners out of the dungeon and from the house of confinement those who live in darkness.

On the linguistic level, the assignment is expressed by a metonymy (ברית עם, "covenant of the people") and by a metaphor (אור גוים, "light of the nations"), linked by asyndeton in a particularly dense and substantially condensed formulation.

The metonymy ברית עם is of the EFFECT-FOR-CAUSE type.[16] As such, it directly points to the result that the servant's action will help to produce: the renewed alliance between YHWH and the people, with all the benefits involved. This ennobles the mandate of the envoy, significantly including the person of the servant in the plan of salvation, and from the very beginning envisaging the positive outcome of his mission. Moreover, the salvific function supposed by the phrase ברית עם is clearly stated in the literal revival of 49:8. Here the servant is placed as a "covenant of the people," in order to revive the fortunes of the country, to reoccupy the land, declaring the end of exile, and leading the people towards freedom (vv. 8–11).

The second linguistic modulation of the task commissioned to the servant is given by the metaphor אור גוים. Conventionally, the concept LIGHT translates a vast range of situations and emotions, offering a positive evaluation: life, health, freedom, joy, truth, justice, and so on.[17] This is also evident in the Hebrew Bible repertoire.[18] In the Isaianic corpus, we can observe, for example, the use of the lexeme אור in correlation to the joy of salvation (Isa 9:1), or to law (51:4), or to moral righteousness (58:8, 10).[19]

---

16. See Kövecses, *Metaphor*, 182. For a summary of the debate around the interpretation of this syntagm, see Johann J. Stamm, "*Berit 'am* bei Deuterojesaja," in *Probleme biblischer Theologie. Gerhard von Rad zum 70. Geburstag*, ed. Hans W. Wolff (Munich: Kaiser, 1971), 510–24. See also Aarre Lauha, "'Der Bund des Volkes.' Ein Aspekt der deuterojesajanischen Missionstheologie," in *Beiträge zur Alttestamentlichen Theologie. Festschrift für Walther Zimmerli zum 70. Geburtstag*, ed. Herbert Donner, Robert Hanhart, and Rudolf Smend (Göttingen: Vandenhoeck & Ruprecht, 1977), 258–9; Willem A. M. Beuken, *Jesaja IIa*, POuT (Nijkerk: G. F. Callenbach, 1979), 124–6; Koole, *Isaiah III*, I, 230–1; Berges, *Jesaja 40-48*, 236–7.

17. See Kövecses, *Metaphor in Culture*, 36–8. On light as a metaphor for truth in Western philosophy, see Hans Blumenberg, "Licht als Metapher der Wahrheit: Im Vorfeld der philosophischen Begriffsbildung," *Studium generale* 10 (1957): 432–47.

18. See Sverre Aalen, "אור," *TDOT* 1: 160–3; Avrahami, *The Senses of Scripture*, 255–8, 265–6, 276.

19. On the metaphor of light in the book of Isaiah, see Gabriela I. Vlková, *Cambiare la luce in tenebre e le tenebre in luce: Uno studio tematico dell'alternarsi tra la luce e le tenebre nel libro di Isaia*, Tesi Gregoriana. Serie Teologia 107 (Rome: Editrice Pontificia Università Gregoriana, 2004).

In 42:6 the phrase אוֹר גּוֹיִם has a double metaphorical meaning, designating both salvation and knowledge.[20] The relevance of the metaphor to the domain of salvation is proven by various elements: (1) the connection by asyndeton with the immediately preceding metonymy בְּרִית עָם postulates the intimate link between the meanings of the two syntagms; (2) as noted in v. 7, the liberating intentionality of the divine office is made explicit; (3) in the revival of the construct אוֹר גּוֹיִם in 49:6, the saving purpose is clearly stated. The *nomen rectum* גּוֹיִם here has a mostly adjectival function,[21] expressing the range of the servant's mission, which goes beyond the physical borders of Israel.

All the same, the relevance of the metaphor of light to the conceptual domain of knowledge is supported by the syntactic connection between the phrase אוֹר גּוֹיִם and the final sentence לִפְקֹחַ עֵינַיִם עִוְרוֹת: as light, the servant will free the people from inner blindness. Moreover, light intervenes as a significant element in the metaphorical transfer from SEEING to KNOWING, conventionally expressing the radiating power of education or truth or law (cf. Isa 51:4; Pss 19:9; 43:3; 119:130; Prov 6:23; Qoh 2:13). This interpretation is confirmed by the broader context of Isa 42:1–9:[22] on the one hand, the servant's preaching includes teaching (v. 4), and on the other, YHWH expresses the intent to communicate (√נגד *hiphil* and √שׁמע *hiphil*, v. 9) his project. From this point of view, the *nomen rectum* גּוֹיִם gives the metaphor a spatial dimension, expanding the radiating force of the prophetic message and magnifying its scope: the nations themselves will learn the law from the lips of the servant (v. 1), the islands will yearn to hear about his teaching (v. 4). This is consistent with the witness function that Deutero-Isaiah accredits to foreign peoples (cf. 43:9; 52:10, 15).[23]

---

20. Hitzig had already guessed it. See Ferdinand Hitzig, *Der Prophet Jesaja* (Heidelberg: C. F. Winter, 1833), 494.

21. See *IBHS* § 9.5.3. On the double function (adjective and dative) of this noun, see n. 23, below.

22. Although the composition of vv. 1–9 is generally acknowledged to be editorial in nature, there are several indications of the synchronic unity of the pericope. See Koole, *Isaiah III*, I, 210–14.

23. Relative to the cognitive domain of knowing, the *nomen rectum* גּוֹיִם joins the adjectival function with that of a dative (see Joüon §129h and *IBHS* §9.5.2e): the light of divine revelation is *for* foreign nations, who are going to see the prodigious liberation of Israel. This cumulation of grammatical values is permitted by the semantic density of the poetic form אוֹר גּוֹיִם. This value of the *nomen rectum* does not, however, concern the cognitive domain of salvation: the nations will not necessarily be beneficiaries of salvation (see Isa 40:15, 17; 41:2; 45:1; 49:22). They will, if anything, recognize the divine intervention in favour of Israel. Note how the distinction between the two cognitive domains offers an enlightening contribution to the long-standing exegetical question regarding the presumed salvific universalism of 42:6b.

The double ascription of the metaphor אור גוים to the cognitive domains of salvation and knowledge originates from the intrinsic nature of the prophetic announcement: an unprecedented message of salvation and consolation, addressed to a people who have stopped believing in the power of YHWH (40:27). To these people God reveals himself as the only LORD (אני יהוה, 42:6, 8), announcing absolute novelties (חדשות אני מגיד, v. 9), through the mouth of the prophet.

The divine implication in this dynamic, at the same time revelatory and salvific, is highlighted by a final textual clue: the two phrases that define the mission of the servant are not introduced by the verb *to be* (as in the sentence: "you will be covenant of the people, light of the nations"), but from the verb נתן, ("I *have established* you as…"). Placed at the opening of a metaphorical sentence, this kind of verb achieves a peculiar effect, underlining the procedural nature of the metaphorical transfer and enhancing the function of the agent who carries out the transfer.[24] In this case, it is YHWH himself who is the creator of the metaphor and, with it, of salvation.

3. *Complicating the metaphor (Isaiah 42:16)*

[16a] I will make the blind walk on a way unknown to them,	והולכתי עורים בדרך לא ידעו
on paths unknown to them I will cause them to tread.	בנתיבות לא־ידעו אדריכם
[16b] I will change darkness into light before them,	אשים מחשך לפניהם לאור
and crooked places into plains.	ומעקשים למישור
[16c] These things I did for them	אלה הדברים עשיתם
nor did I abandon them.	ולא עזבתים

At v. 16, intertwining with the WAY motif, the basic metaphor KNOWING IS SEEING undergoes a process of complexification.[25] This intertwining is recognizable just at the syntactic level. In the table below it can be seen how, in v. 16a, the intertwining goes through a slavish alternation of the cognitive domains of WAY and SEEING-KNOWING.

אדריכם		לא ידעו	בנתיבות	לא ידעו	בדרך	עורים	והולכתי
SEEING-KNOWING	WAY	SEEING-KNOWING	WAY	SEEING-KNOWING	WAY	SEEING-KNOWING	WAY

At v. 16b, the synthetic parallelism between *darkness–light* and *tortuous places–plain* suggests the complementarity between the two cognitive dimensions: the prodigious change invests the atmosphere and the earth and, with them, the twofold sphere of vision and journey. The intertwining generates a strongly enigmatic statement that poses many questions: why should YHWH make the blind

24. See Christine Brooke-Rose, *A Grammar of Metaphor* (London: Secker & Warburg, 1958), 132–45.

25. In this paragraph I summarize the results of my study "If the Blind Walk," 61–77.

walk in the desert? Why not rather let the people or the redeemed walk, according to a more conventional biblical image? In its semantic impertinence, the adjective עורים imposes a figurative reading of the same dimension of the way.²⁶ The road becomes a metaphor for a different kind of path, which these anonymous wayfarers will have to take. So, if blind people are a metaphor for the exiles initiated by YHWH towards redemption, their path designates access to a new form of knowledge. Therefore, the "way" by which the blind will be led is constituted above all by the recognition of the saving plan of YHWH. In other words, it is a way of knowledge.²⁷

Ultimately, the complexification of the metaphor KNOWING IS SEEING exhibited in v. 16 has an important rhetorical function: creating a particularly vivid picture, it amplifies the paradoxical value of the people's obtuseness, of their obstinacy not to believe in the salvation offered by YHWH. Around the blind, in fact, many landscape elements change in a prodigious way: darkness gives way to light, the bumpy road becomes flat. What does not change is their physical condition, their ability to perceive the reality in front of their eyes. While facilitating the journey of the exiles towards redemption, YHWH stops before their freedom, without being able to fully heal their obstinate heart.

4. Dissolving the Metaphor (Isaiah 42:18–19)

4.1. Metaphor and Contradiction (v. 18)

At v. 18 the divine speaker begins with a paradoxical apostrophe:

¹⁸ᵃ O deaf, hear!	החרשים שמעו
¹⁸ᵇ O blind ones, fix your gaze to see!	והעורים הביטו לראות

The paradox arises because of the immediate textual adjacency between the vocatives החרשים/העורים and the imperatives הביטו לראות / שמעו related to them. Thus, two contradictory statements arise.²⁸ The paradoxical nature of the two injunctions is accentuated by the grammatical use of the imperative. Unlike 29:18, where the future forms of √שמע qal and √ראה qal agree with חרשים and עורים to delineate a splendid promise ("On that day the deaf *will hear* the words of the book and, coming out of the dark shadow, the eyes of the blind *will see*"), here, in 42:18, the same verbs command the recipients to do what is irreconcilable with their condition of deafness/blindness. In other words, the imperatives

---

26. See Lazzaro, "If the Blind Walk," 66–7.

27. The interweaving of the WAY motif with the metaphor KNOWING IS SEEING gives rise to two new metaphors: FREEDOM IS A JOURNEY and KNOWING IS WALKING TOWARDS/ENTERING. See Lazzaro, "If the Blind Walk," 73.

28. The hagiographer would not have achieved the same rhetorical effect if he had indicated his recipients in a literal way, as, for example, he does in Isa 46:3 ("Hear me, house of Jacob, and all the rest of the house of Israel") or in 48:1; 49:1; 51:7.

focus on the contradiction between two concepts (DEAFNESS/HEARING, BLIND-NESS/SEEING) that cannot coexist, because they are mutually exclusive on the cognitive and semantic level. Here the hagiographer exploits a peculiar linguistic figure, known to classical logic as *contradictio in adjecto*. It consists precisely in the immediate juxtaposition, within the same sentence, of two contradictory statements.[29]

However, in the two injunctions of v. 18, the choice of placing the vocative before the imperative signals the importance of the double metaphorical statement "deaf/blind" for the hermeneutics of the sentence.[30] Through the syntactic construction, the speaker therefore emphasizes the metaphorical signification of the two vocatives, and then contradicts it through the contiguous verbal forms "hear/fix your gaze to see." In doing so, the poet stigmatizes the logical contradiction inherent in the metaphor, somehow assimilating the metaphor to the lie.[31] After all, everyone knows that the deaf and the blind are not physically so, otherwise it could not be understood why handicapped people would be forced to do what they cannot do. Nonetheless, if the reader had any doubts, a little further on, v. 20 settles the question ("You have seen many things, but you do not pay attention to them; ears are open, but [he] does not listen").[32] In conclusion, by associating metaphor and *contradictio in adjecto*, the poet destroys the conditions of validity of the metaphor itself, making it a false and strongly ironic assertion. With this double artifice, he disqualifies the audience with considerable sarcasm, indirectly denouncing their inability to understand. While, in fact, the metaphor of the deaf/blind conveys the idea of mental dullness, the *contradictio in adjecto* prompts it, creating an unsustainable discourse on a logical level.

4.2. *The Reverse Path of the Metaphor (v. 19)*

4.2.1. *Rhetorical figures of repetition.* Having started in v. 18, the work of dissolution of the metaphor continues in v. 19. The speaker returns to the terms *deaf/blind* just enunciated to clarify their metaphorical extent. To this end, he resorts to three rhetorical figures of repetition (anadiplosis, anaphora, climax), giving his speech an insistent tone, as if to always stress upon the same concept, progressively deepening it.

---

29. See Harald Weinrich, *Metafora e menzogna: la serenità dell'arte*, Saggi 162 (Bologna: Il Mulino, 1976), 70–5, 100–1, 105, 114.

30. From the analysis of Michael Rosenbaum, *Word-Order Variation in Isaiah 40–55: A Functional Perspective*, SSN 36 (Assen: Van Gorcum, 1997), 117–18, it appears that in Isa 40–55 the vocative normally follows the verb (82% of cases). Therefore, the choice of putting the vocative before the verb, although not anomalous, is in favour of an intentional focus on the contradiction of the utterance.

31. See Weinrich, *Metafora e menzogna*, 162–7.

32. For the role of the broader context of Isa 42:18–25 for the hermeneutics of the metaphor, see Lazzaro, "If the Blind Walk," 69–70.

¹⁹ᵃ Who is blind but my servant	מי עור כי אם־עבדי
¹⁹ᵇ and deaf like the messenger I send?	וחרש כמלאכי אשלח
¹⁹ᶜ Who is blind as he who is perfect	מי עור כמשלם
¹⁹ᵈ and blind as the servant of the LORD?	ועור כעבד יהוה

Anadiplosis consists in the recovery, from v. 18, of the adjectives עור and חרש, although in reverse order (v. 19a-b). The poet therefore returns to the two concepts to reveal their referents.

The anaphora develops anadiplosis,[33] articulating itself in the alternation of the initial terms מי + adjective ("who [is] blind," v. 19a-c) and ו + adjective ("and deaf," v. 19b; "and blind," v. 19d). Anaphoric is also the repetition of the adjective עור in three stichoi out of a total of four (see v. 19a, c, d). This breaks the balance of the *blind/deaf* parallelism that would be expected to be duplicated in v. 19c-d as in v. 19a-b. In this way, the author emphasizes the visual element, the most suitable for expressing the event of knowledge.[34] The emphasis seems intentional, since what is at stake is not so much listening or obedience, but rather the intrinsic ability to understand the divine plan. Moreover, the emphasis is in line with the focus of the visual element already exhibited in vv. 7, 16 and remarked by v. 18 with the lengthening of the final phrase "fix your gaze to see" compared to the parallel "hear."

The third figure of repetition involved is climax. It intervenes in the designation of the referent, through the following honorific titles placed at the end of each stichos: "my servant" (v. 19a), "my messenger, whom I send" (v. 19b), "he who is perfect" (v. 19c), "the servant of YHWH" (v. 19d). In their succession, the epithets signal the progressive separation between the speaker and the referent. While, in fact, in the first two titles the possessive *my* underscores the relationship of mutual belonging between God and the servant, the third title ironically designates an intrinsic quality of the referent. Finally, the fourth epithet creates an inclusion with the first ("my servant"/"the servant of YHWH"), but with a conspicuous change of point of view, as if the speaker were now referring to a third person.

The intertwining of these three figures of repetition plays in favour of the disqualification of the audience, in continuity with the tone of v. 18.

4.2.2. *Inverse comparison and logic of the paradox.* While in the metaphors of vv. 7, 16, 18 the *target* is not expressly stated and can only be deduced on the basis of some contextual clues, in v. 19 it is clearly displayed. The disclosure of the identity of the accused is indeed the only argument of v. 19.

To this end, the author resorts to a rhetorical question. With it, he asks for nothing. He simply invites his interlocutor "to discard all possible answers discordant from the assertion implicit in the question."[35] The four rhetorical questions are syntactically presented as inverse comparisons, tracing back from

---

33. See Bice Mortara Garavelli, *Manuale di retorica*, 10th ed. (Milan: Bompiani, 2006), 199.

34. See §2.1 above.

35. Mortara Garavelli, *Manuale di retorica*, 133.

the *source* to the *target*. If, in fact, the usual form of the metaphor is *x is [as] y*, where *x* is the *target* and *y* is the *source*, here the syntactic construction appears inverted, giving rise to the formula *y is x*. As if, instead of the classic expression *Achilles is a lion*, one were to say: *Who can be a lion but Achilles?* As can be seen from the latter example, the interweaving of rhetorical interrogative and inverse comparison underlines the exclusivity of the comparison (only Achilles can be a lion),[36] and unusually increases the role of the *target* within the metaphorical device. The speaker points the finger at the referent, inviting the audience to detect which characteristics make him imputable as blind and deaf. To this end, in a continuous *variatio*, he uses the four epithets mentioned above to designate the referent, each time capturing different aspects of him: he is YHWH's servant, his envoy, the perfect one. The honorary character of these epithets clashes with the unmeritorious predicate *blind/deaf*, highlighting the gap between the ideal condition and the objective condition of the accused. The four honorary titles inject an additional paradoxical value into the metaphorical statements of v. 19. Let us see, case by case, how the logic of paradox moves in them.

The servant's blindness results in absurd assertion (v. 19a, d). In Isa 40–55, the noun עבד + 1 sing. suffix is used mostly as an appellative of the people, to reassure them of the salvation wrought by YHWH (41:8, 9; 44:1, 2, 21; 45:4). The connection of the appellative with the cognitive domain of SEEING-KNOWING is made explicit in 43:10, where the servant is chosen to *acknowledge* (√ידע), believe and *understand* (√בין) that YHWH is the only God. The connection is also implied in 49:3, where the servant becomes the place of the manifestation of divine glory (√פאר). The same connection is well recognizable in 42:1, a close antecedent of 42:19a and therefore particularly relevant for the hermeneutics of the passage in a perspective of text-linguistics. In the context of 42:1–9, in fact, the servant is given the task of not extinguishing the smoking lamp (v. 3), becoming himself a light to open blind eyes (vv. 6–7). The contradiction is obvious: how can light be blind? How can a blind man heal other blind people? The paradox is aggravated in v. 19d, with the use of the construct עבד יהוה, *hapax* of Deutero-Isaiah, a title that the Hebrew Bible reserves for the great leaders of Israel (Moses, Joshua, David). The paradox finds a remote solution only in 52:13–53:12: the servant, obscured by immense suffering, will finally see the light (53:11). His rehabilitation will astonish the nations, who will become spectators of an unprecedented event (52:13–15).

The deafness of the messenger (v. 19b) is a contradiction in terms: what message can an envoy who has lost the faculty of hearing possibly convey? The epithet מלאכי (with the addition of the pleonastic אשלח, as if to reiterate the concept) seems therefore intentionally selected, among all the possible designations of the referent, to create a paradoxical utterance.

---

36. In the MT, the exclusivity of the comparison is highlighted by the use of the emphatic-restrictive particle כי אם in the first stichos (v. 19a), replaced, then, in 19b, c, d by the triple use of the comparative כ. On restrictive particles, see *IBHS* §39, 3, 5d.

More intriguing is the case of v. 19c, because of the linguistic obscurity that affects the unusual formulation משלם. The appellation has been variously understood by exegetes: as a proper name (*Meshullam*), or as a *pual* participle of שלם with the meaning "the one who has experienced retribution" in a negative sense ("punished") or in a positive sense ("rehabilitated"), or with the meaning "the one who is in a covenant of peace" or, more simply, "the one who is complete, perfect." It is difficult to determine the meaning of the term unequivocally.[37] However, given the deliberately ironic and paradoxical tone of vv. 18–19 and the many ambiguities that permeate the entire section 18–25,[38] it is plausible to categorize משלם as a peculiar case of semantic ambiguity. All the same, among all the possible names of Israel, the author selects an anomalous one, attracting the attention of his listeners. At first glance, they might think it is the name of a person. Soon, however, they will be forced to grasp the meaning in order to disambiguate the metaphor, otherwise they will fall into non-sense. The reader, both ancient and modern, will have no choice but to assume a series of abductions. The meaning "the one who has experienced retribution" is undoubtedly admissible, because it is supported by the use of שלם *pual* in Jer 18:20; Prov 11:31; 13:13. Isaiah 42:19c, however, does not clarify whether it is to be understood *in bonam partem* ("he who has been rehabilitated") or *in malam partem* ("he who has been punished"). This structural ambivalence increases the irony of the metaphorical statement. Above all, it is not clear how the one who has been rehabilitated can still be affected by blindness. A similar fate hangs over the valence of "he who is in covenant of peace," supported by the contextual link with 42:6, where the servant is constituted "covenant of the people." Here too, it is hard to understand how the promoter of such a promising covenant could be reduced to blindness, even more because of the commission to open the eyes of the blind (v. 7). The meaning "he who is complete, perfect" even gives rise to a *contradictio in adjecto*: he who should be perfectly healthy is really not since he lacks sight.[39]

As we can see, however one tries to unravel the enigma of משלם, one always comes across ambiguous expressions, with varying degrees of contradiction and irony.

---

37. For *HALOT* IV, 1535, the meaning of משלם remains fundamentally uncertain. See also Roger N. Whybray, *Isaiah 40–66*, NCBC (Grand Rapids, MI: Eerdmans, 1981), 80; Claus Westermann, *Das Buch Jesaja: Kapitel 40–66*, ATD 19, 5th ed. (Göttingen: Vandenhoeck & Ruprecht, 1986), 91. On the controversial history of the interpretation of this name, see Baldauf, "Jes 42,18–25," 15–7; Koole, *Isaiah III*, I, 269; Joseph Blenkinsopp, *Isaiah 40–55: A New Translation with Introduction and Commentary*, AB 19A (New York: Doubleday, 2002), 218–19; Berges, *Jesaja 40–48*, 262.

38. See Baldauf, "Jes 42,18–25"; John Goldingay, "Isaiah 42.18–25," *JSOT* 67 (1995): 43–65.

39. In the translation, I opted for the meaning "perfect," to highlight the potential ambiguity and irony conveyed by the epithet. So does Redak; see Avroham Y. Rosenberg, *Isaiah II: Translation of Text, Rashi and Commentary*, Miqra'ot Gedolot (New York: Judaica Press, 1982), 343.

Examination of the four epithets shows that in v. 19 the contradiction is used in a systematically detracting manner. This time, however, it is not inherent in the *source* ("blind/deaf") as in v. 18, but in the *target* ("my servant," "my messenger whom I send," "he who is perfect," "the servant of YHWH"). Thus, by first questioning the *source* and then the *target*, the poet diminishes the cognitive value of the metaphor as a whole. The trouble is that the speaker in v. 19 is still YHWH. He who, in v. 7, created the metaphor of blindness, is also capable of dissolving it. YHWH exercises the same creative and sovereign power over language as he does over the cosmos.

5. *Target Replacement (Isa 43:8)*

5.1. *Contradiction and Irony*

The logical and rhetorical device of *contradictio in adjecto* also contaminates the mention of the *blind/deaf* in Isa 43:8.

8a Bring out the blind people,	הוציא עם־עור
8b who have eyes,	ועינים יש
8c and the deaf men,	וחרשים
8d who have ears.	ואזנים למו

As in 42:18, this is an introductory apostrophe, which sets the tone for the rest of the discourse.[40] However, the contradiction is less strident than in 42:18, because it does not concern the immediate exercise of the faculties of sight and hearing, but the possession of the organs deputed to the same exercise. On the surface, therefore, the contradiction is less aggressive—after all, everyone knows that the blind do not necessarily lack eyes (as happened to Zedekiah, cf. 2 Kgs 25:7), nor the deaf necessarily lack ears. If anything, the problem lies in the functioning of the sensory organs, but the author does not mention this aspect. The double statement "who have eyes"/"who have ears" is therefore redundant and, at the same time, ironic, because it provides obvious but incomplete information[41] (it is not said whether the eyes and ears work, cf. Pss 115:5–6; 135:16–17). The irony has an impact on the cognitive scope of the metaphor. Once again, it points out the metaphorical process as such, laying it bare: that Israel is blind and deaf is only a manner of speaking! This is also underlined by the hyperbole, which attributes blindness to the entire population (עם־עור, Isa 43:8a). In this way, the cognitive significance of the metaphor is diminished. So, the hypothesis that perhaps those eyes and ears might even work gains credence. In the final analysis, the peculiar conjunction of metaphorical process, *contradictio in adjecto* and irony, gives the apostrophe a tone of reproach towards its addressees.

---

40. One does not therefore understand the attempt of Georg Fohrer, *Das Buch Jesaja. III: Kapitel 40–66*, ZBK (Zurich: Zwingli-Verlag, 1967), 62, to expunge the verse as a gloss.

41. See Mortara Garavelli, *Manuale di retorica*, 167.

5.2. Metaphorical Value of the Verb יצא

The verb יצא hiphil (הוציא, "Bring out") opens the apostrophe of Isa 43:8. In the forensic scenario of vv. 8–9, the verb indicates the summoning of witnesses to trial. Nevertheless, the order to bring out the blind and the deaf raises many questions: what role can blind and deaf people play in a trial? The locution is also anomalous because, in Deutero-Isaianic lexicon, the summoning of witnesses to trial is usually conveyed by another verb, √נגש hiphil (41:21, 22; 45:21). Moreover, the placement of the metaphorical terms עור/ חרשים in immediate dependence on הוציא, raises the question whether the verb itself has metaphorical value: what kind of escape could be predicated on people who are only metaphorically blind and deaf?

Indeed, in the Deutero-Isaianic vocabulary, √יצא hiphil can denote the event of liberation from exile (48:20; 52:11[2×], 12; 55:12), as well as release from a metaphorical prison, the image of a state of inner dereliction (42:7; 49:9). The comparison with 42:7 and 49:9 is especially significant because of the common correlation of the verb יצא with the semantics of non-vision (לפקח עינים עורות, ישבי חשך, 42:7; אשר בחשך, 49:9). In 43:8 the correlation is even closer, since the author does not combine the two semantic fields by means of a parallel structure, but coordinates them directly into a single utterance, making the adjective עור the attribute of the object: "Bring out the *blind* people." The result is a paradoxical and enigmatic injunction, which, precisely because of its intrinsic anomaly, emphasizes the metaphorical value of the terms √יצא, עור, חרשים. Therefore, if blind and deaf are a metaphor for the dullness of the recipients' minds, their coming out can only indicate the abandonment of a state of dereliction that prevents them from seeing and welcoming YHWH's salvation (DERELICTION IS A PRISON). On the contrary, the contamination between the semantics of seeing and that of captivity makes it possible to reread the very mental obtuseness of the exiles as a sort of prison in which they constrain themselves. This cognitive dimension of the metaphor is supported by the context of 43:8–13, where the people are promised the acquisition of a new intelligence (√ידע and √בין, v. 10) in order to understand the identity and salvific role of YHWH (vv. 10–13).

Therefore, the author seems to deliberately select the verb יצא hiphil as an ambiguous term, which, on the one hand, is consistent with the forensic scenario of the pericope,[42] yet which, on the other, activates the cognitive metaphor DERELICTION IS A PRISON. In doing so, however, the author triggers a sort of short-circuit, since the metaphor of seeing/hearing and that of imprisonment are not entirely congruent. Unlike in 42:7, where release from prison and recovery

---

42. Some technical terms insist on this scenario: עד + suffix (vv. 9, 10, 12) designates the witness in favour; √נגד hiphil (vv. 9, 12) indicates the deposition in the courtroom; the formula אמת (v. 9) is the declaratory statement that concludes the investigation; √צדק (v. 9) expresses the acquittal of the accused. On these aspects, see Pietro Bovati, *Ristabilire la giustizia: Procedure, vocabolario, orientamenti*, AnBib 110, 2nd ed. (Rome: Pontificio Istituto Biblico, 2005), 231, 243, 276–7; Koole, *Isaiah III*, I, 307.

from blindness go hand in hand, in 43:8 the release of the blind and deaf is not accompanied by the cessation of their state of physical minority. In other words, out of metaphor, 43:8 affirms the liberation from a condition of dereliction linked to a certain mental obtuseness, and at the same time declares that this obtuseness nevertheless remains. Such a semantic-cognitive incongruity generates the expectation that Israel's inner blindness/deafness is destined to be extinguished. It is not clear, however, how this can happen.

5.3. Target Reinstating

In §§ 5.1 and 5.2, we noted the peculiar manipulative process to which the concept KNOWING IS SEEING/HEARING is subjected in 43:8. In this way, the cognitive extent of the metaphor is demeaned, and with it, the recipients of the apostrophe are ridiculed in their ability to understand. Their rehabilitation on the plan of knowledge takes place in another way, through the scenic instrumentarium of public judgement (משפט).[43]

Once transposed to the courtroom, the blind and deaf—who are so only "in a manner of speaking," as denounced by the *contradictio in adjecto*—assume the role of witnesses, a function consistent with the new setting. On a cognitive-linguistic level, the trial scenario thus imposes the emergence of new concepts, more relevant to it. Such is the concept WITNESSING, which replaces KNOWING as the *target* of the metaphor WITNESSING IS SEEING/HEARING,[44] focusing on a particular dimension of knowledge. In fact, compared to the general concept KNOWING IS SEEING/HEARING, the new metaphor stresses the witnessing subjects and the passive character of their knowledge.[45] Despite themselves, they see what they do not want to see, and hear what they do not want to hear. All this, absurdly enough, takes place during a public trial, in the presence of an international audience. It is clear, therefore, that the new setting serves only as a pretext to trigger a completely unexpected cognitive process. This can be seen from the extreme nonchalance with which the author uses the literary genre of משפט. Several anomalies actually do not fit the usual plot of a trial: neither of the two parties testifies in the courtroom; the dispute between YHWH and the foreign gods passes decisively into the background; no conclusive verdict is formulated; Israel, as we have said, is instituted in a testimonial function during the trial; still in the inquiry phase, YHWH intervenes authoritatively, in order to convince the people of his own identity, uniqueness and salvation, assuming the role of the plaintiff seeking recognition, rather than that of the judge.

---

43. See Horacio Simian-Yofre, *Sofferenza dell'uomo e silenzio di Dio: Nell'Antico Testamento e nella letteratura del Vicino Oriente Antico*, Studia Biblica 2 (Rome: Città Nuova 2005), 170–1, n. 129.

44. For a more in-depth examination of this metaphor in Hebrew Bible, see Avrahami, *The Senses of Scripture*, 225–48.

45. See Ibarretxe-Antuñano, "Mind-as-Body," 100.

The amplification of God's locutionary intervention also belongs to the ironic manipulation of the literary genre. The ample space that the author reserves for it (vv. 10–13), together with its oracular qualification (נאם־יהוה, v. 10), signal it as rhetorically determinant in the unfolding of the facts. The divine discourse has a performative value, since with it YHWH establishes his witnesses and provides the arguments to be said (YHWH is the only God, his word is truthful and worthy of faith, in him alone there is salvation). With his act of speaking, YHWH therefore creates the subjects and the object of the testimony, he establishes who must speak on his behalf and what they must report, giving full consistency to the metaphor WITNESSING IS SEEING/HEARING. The rehabilitation of the target-subjects passes through the divine word.

6. Conclusion

This study reopens an important page of Isaianic exegesis, concerning the role of the recurring images of seeing and hearing in the book of Isaiah. There is, however, a connection between them, scattered throughout the corpus, which cannot be grasped if we remain on the surface of the text. It only appears if one places oneself at a deeper level of language, on the cognitive plane. In this perspective, such images can be identified as cognitive metaphors in which the event of knowing is represented through more concrete forms of seeing and hearing.

This essay has shown the peculiar role played by the double metaphor KNOWING IS SEEING/KNOWING IS HEARING within Isa 42–43, taken as a test-case for the whole corpus. Analyzing the movement of this double metaphor, through Lakoff and Johnson's approach, has contributed in two ways to the exegesis of the text: it has surprisingly illuminated its coherence and enriched its overall hermeneutics. The metaphor, in fact, is *created* by YHWH (42:7), *complicated* (v. 16), *dissolved* (vv. 18–19), and finally *reactivated* (43:8), albeit in a modified version (WITNESSING IS SEEING/HEARING) by him. In a sense, in chs. 42–43 the metaphor KNOWING IS SEEING/KNOWING IS HEARING is born as an enormous hope, then gets complexified, dies and rises again. In its course, it plastically shows the paradox of a people insensitive to the offer of divine salvation. At the same time, it shows YHWH's obstinacy in wanting to save the people despite their obstinacy in not believing.

SECTION THREE

WORLD IN FRONT OF THE TEXT

Chapter 12

"DESOLATE" DEPICTIONS IN ISAIAH:
APPROACHING THE UNITY QUESTION, ANEW!*

Dominic S. Irudayaraj

1. *Introduction*

"Space is vast, as are the possibilities," quips Steven Schweitzer.[1] The pun in his words perceptively reflects a growing scholarly interest in space. Propelled especially by the materialistic philosophical insights of H. Lefebvre[2] and E. Soja's views on critical geography,[3] the "Spatial turn" has found echoes in literary critical arena. The growing number of spatial readings of biblical texts is an attestation to the value of this new-found approach.[4] The present work takes its cue from this trend

---

* The present study is the fruit of my semester-long (Spring 2019) Jesuit Research Fellowship at the Department of Theological Studies of Bellarmine College of Liberal Arts in Loyola Marymount University, Los Angeles, CA. I am grateful to Professors Allan F. Deck, †John C. Endres, Robbin Crabtree, Douglas Christie, and Daniel Smith-Christopher for their generous gestures that made the Fellowship both possible and fruitful.

1. Steven J. Schweitzer, "Exploring the Utopian Space of Chronicles: Some Spatial Anomalies," in *Constructions of Space I: Theory, Geography, and Narrative*, ed. Jon L. Berquist and Claudia V. Camp, LHBOTS 481 (New York: T&T Clark International, 2007), 144.

2. Henri Lefebvre, *The Production of Space*, trans. D. Nicholson Smith (Oxford: Blackwell, 1991).

3. Edward W. Soja, *Thirdspace: Journeys to Los Angeles and Other Real-and-Imagined Places* (Malden, MA: Blackwell, 1996).

4. See, e.g., Berquist and Camp, eds., *Constructions of Space I*; Jon L. Berquist and Claudia V. Camp, eds., *Constructions of Space II: The Biblical City and Other Imagined Spaces*, LHBOTS 490 (London: T&T Clark International, 2008); Jorunn Økland, J. Cornelis de Vos, and Karen J. Wenell, eds., *Constructions of Space III: Biblical Spatiality and the Sacred*, LHBOTS 540 (London: Bloomsbury T&T Clark, 2016); Mark K. George, ed.,

to prioritize space, albeit with a difference. Whereas a good number of spatial readings tend to focus on prominent themes such as Zion, Jerusalem, or city,[5] this chapter chooses to circumambulate what should otherwise be forgettable places, namely, "desolate" spaces.[6] These spaces sound a dissonant note especially in the otherwise appealing book of Isaiah. My aim, therefore, is threefold: (1) to retrace this dissonant theme, (2) to propose a spatial appropriation of the same and (3) to situate the present task within the larger, evolving interest in reading Isaiah as a composite yet unified whole.

2. Retracing "Desolate" Theme via Šmm^{cog}

Terms that depict destruction and desolation abound in Isaiah. In more than 100 occurrences of the desolate descriptions, שמם cognates (hereafter, *šmm*^{cog}) form the largest number.[7] They are not only attested across the book of Isaiah but also present themselves in a considerable variety of forms.[8] Further, though they are predicated primarily on places, there are some instances where *persons* are described with *šmm* traits, which is pertinent for this work.

The proposed circumambulation of *šmm*^{cog} in Isaiah aims to catalogue the constellation of phraseological and thematic patterning in order to highlight the "common strands that stand out and coalesce,"[9] which create "a tapestry of

---

Constructions of Space IV: Further Developments in Examining Ancient Israel's Social Space, LHBOTS 569 (London: Bloomsbury T&T Clark, 2013); Gert T. M. Prinsloo and Christl M. Maier, eds., *Constructions of Space V: Place, Space and Identity in the Ancient Mediterranean World*, LHBOTS 576 (London: Bloomsbury T&T Clark, 2013).

5. For a Zion-focused reading, see Christl M. Maier, "Daughter Zion as a Gendered Space in the Book of Isaiah," in Berquist and Camp, eds., *Constructions of Space II*, 102–18. For a Jerusalem-centered reading, see Jon L. Berquist, "Spaces of Jerusalem," in Berquist and Camp, eds., *Constructions of Space II*, 40–52. On spatial appraisals of city, see Michael P. O'Connor, "The Biblical Notion of the City," in Berquist and Camp, eds., *Constructions of Space II*, 18–39. Elsewhere I have availed a similar spatial sensibility to retrace "mountain(s)" in Micah. See Dominic S. Irudayaraj, "Mountains in Micah and Coherence: A 'SynDiaTopic' Suggestion," *JBL* 140 (2021): 703–22, https://doi.org/10.15699/jbl.1404.2021.4.

6. For a helpful survey of key theorists on place and space, see Phil Hubbard and Rob Kitchin, eds., *Key Thinkers on Space and Place*, 2nd ed. (Los Angeles: SAGE, 2011).

7. The cognates occur 21 times (cf. Figure 12.1, below). For an elaborate listing, see John D. W. Watts, *Isaiah 1–33*, rev. ed., WBC 24 (Nashville, TN: Thomas Nelson, 2005), 78–80. The present work augments Watts' list with that of Meyer. See Adlingenswil Meyer, "Šāmam," in *Theological Dictionary of the Old Testament*, ed. G. Johannes Botterweck, Helmer Ringgren, and Heinz-Josef Fabry (Grand Rapids, MI: Eerdmans, 2006).

8. Substantive forms dominate (17 out of 21, of which 12 are nominals and 5 are participles) while the verbal entries make up a total of 4 (*qal* pf [1×]; *niphal* pf [1×]; *hithpolel* [2×]). See Meyer, "Šāmam," 239.

9. I borrow this phrase from Hayes. See Katherine M. Hayes, *The Earth Mourns: Prophetic Metaphor and Oral Aesthetic*, SBLAcBib 8 (Brill, 2002), 235–6.

interwoven threads."¹⁰ In other words, it is an attempt to probe whether the textual descriptions of desolate chaos may have some promises for a coherent and meaningful reading of Isaiah.

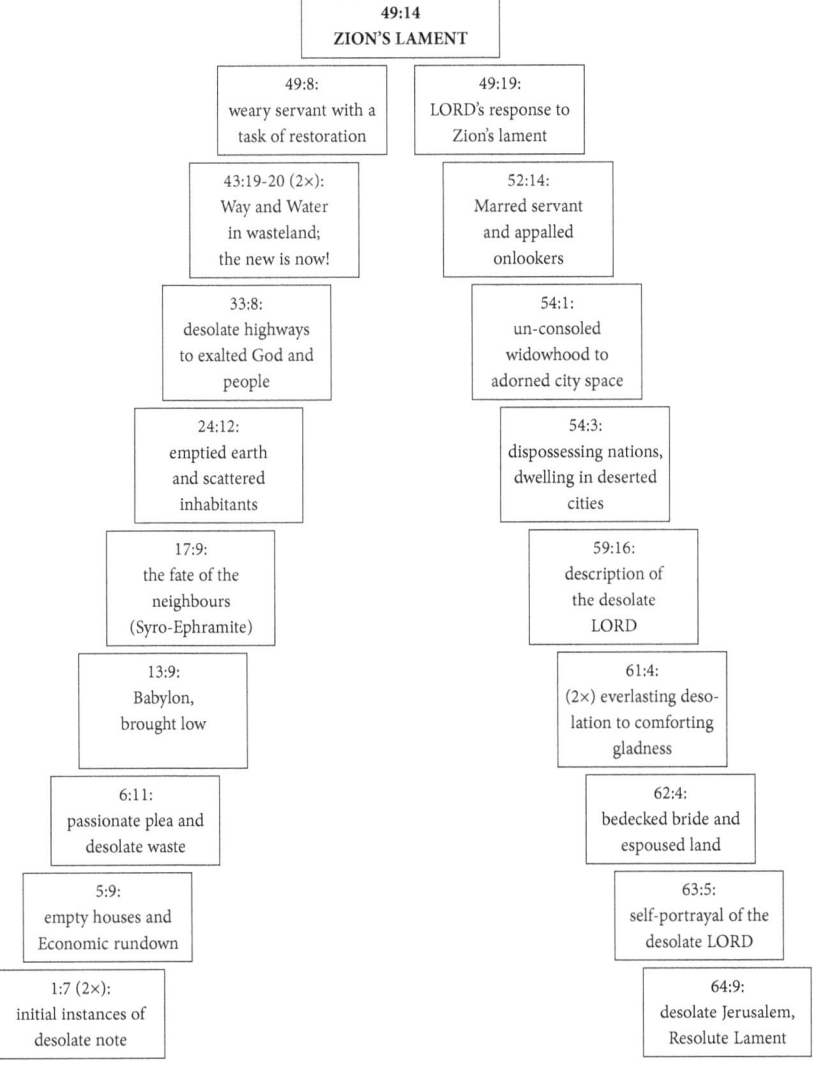

Figure 12.1 A Schema comprising the *šmm* cognates in Isaiah

---

10. The parlance is borrowed from Stulac. See Daniel J. Stulac, *History and Hope: The Agrarian Wisdom of Isaiah 28–35*, Siphrut 24 (University Park, PA: Eisenbrauns, 2018), 166.

Even a cursory sweep of *šmm*^{cog} appears to narrate its own story (cf. Figure 12.1).[11] It commences with the current state (or the coming punishment) of desolation in chs. 1, 5, 6, 13, 17, and 24. Then the tone shifts to promises of restoration in Isa 33 and 43. Restoration also features among the tasks of the servant in ch. 49. Repeated words of assurance portray the LORD's resolve to usher in the reversals in chs. 49, 52, 54, 61, and 62, including the divine warrior's involvement in these acts of reversal (59||63).[12] These initial remarks merely capture the general contours of the story around *šmm*^{cog}. All the same, even as the songs of spectacular reversal of fortunes are sung with an arresting array of images, protesting voices that intervene in these texts add a diverse tone to that chorus. Two of them, which constitute twin duets, are of interest here: (1) Zion's outcry in Isa 49 and (2) the lamenting community's passionate plea in Isa 64.[13] We begin with Zion's outburst, which transpires at the center of the schema.

3. *Theological Duet*

Isaiah 49 is noted for alternating presentations of the servant and Zion. Hyun Kim suggests that these two constitute a theological duet.[14]

Weary Servant, with a Task of Restoration: Chapter 49 begins with a discourse by the servant (vv. 1–7). Then, the LORD declares how he formed the servant and set him as a covenant (לברית) for the people in order to restore the land and allot the desolate heritages (נחלות שממות, cf. v. 8).[15] Initially though, the servant thought that he had toiled in vain. But his ensuing words of confidence reverses

---

11. For a further discussion on the details of the figure, see below (cf. section 5, Asking the Unity Question).

12. On how these parallel panes form a triptych with the intervening chapters, see Matthew J. Lynch, "Zion's Warrior and the Nations: Isaiah 59:15b–63:6 in Isaiah's Zion Traditions," *CBQ* 70 (2008): 244–63. Cf. Dominic S. Irudayaraj, *Violence, Otherness and Identity in Isaiah 63:1–6: The Trampling One Coming from Edom*, LHBOTS 633 (London: Bloomsbury T&T Clark, 2017), 71, 95.

13. Other such voices include (1) the anxious query of the "we" group (Isa 33), (2) the servant's exasperation, at least initially (Isa 49), and (3) the divine warrior's desperation (Isa 59||63).

14. The same pattern characterizes the surrounding chapters as well. See Hyun Chul Paul Kim, *Reading Isaiah: A Literary and Theological Commentary*, Reading the Old Testament (Macon, GA: Smyth & Helwys, 2016), 233–4. Sawyer, on his part, observes: "Both characters [Servant and Daughter of Zion] are introduced afresh in ch. 40. But the story of the one is completed in 40–55, while the other is developed mainly in 49–66. So, there is an overlap in 49–55. There above all the two stories intersect." John F. A. Sawyer, "Daughter of Zion and Servant of the Lord in Isaiah: A Comparison," *JSOT* 44 (1989): 99.

15. All the same, "The heritages of Israel that Deutero-Isaiah assigns to the Servant to apportion are described as 'devastated,' without further specification (Isa 49:8)." See Meyer, "Šāmam," 240.

the tone: (1) from weariness to confidence, (2) the reversal in the servant's prospects and (3) the transformation in the people and place, the text is replete with an optimistic tone. It is at this point that we hear another voice. And the voice sounds anything but optimistic.

Zion's Lament and the LORD's Reassuring Response: Zion cries out in 49:14, "The LORD has forsaken (עזב) me and my Lord has forgotten (שכח) me."[16] The contrast here is marked, which the contrastive *waw* (ותאמר) aptly captures. To this, the LORD's response comes immediately, assuring her of never being forgotten. To reiterate the same, the intimate image of a mother's mindfulness of the child in her womb (49:1–7) is adduced and even exceeded.

Nonetheless, Zion's short yet passionate outburst keeps ringing in the ears of the readers. As this is the only direct discourse of Zion in the book of Isaiah, it may pay to hear her cry closely. She exclaims: "The LORD has forsaken me; my Lord (אדני) has forgotten me" (49:14). In this poetic parallel, the subject is initially the LORD who is then addressed as *my* Lord, thus drawing the divine to her personal space only to reiterate the LORD's double disregard (forsake and forget[17]) of Zion. Hearing her cry through spatial findings can help highlight some additional details.

Spatial Reading of Zion's Outburst: Spatial theorists distinguish between First, Second, and Thirdspaces. While the first points to concrete entities, the second speaks of imagined spaces. The lived locus of the Thirdspace is an admixture of the first two and more.[18] As Ajer, through Soja observes, feelings and passionate outbursts are properly third spatial manifestations, which function as modes of struggle with a view towards emancipation.[19] In terms of this spatial model, Zion's

---

16. Meyer notes that the *hiphil* form of *šmm* occurs a total of 16 times in the Hebrew Bible and of which 10 times the subject is Yahweh. Thus, Yahweh appears to be the desolation-causing agent, par excellence. All the same, the *hiphil* form is not attested in the book of Isaiah. Meyer, "Šāmam," 242. Hrobon, however, notes, "Yhwh has afflicted Zion with 'devastation and destruction, famine, and sword' (51:19)," connecting it with Zion's desperate situation. See Bohdan Hrobon, *Ethical Dimension of Cult in the Book of Isaiah*, BZAW 418 (Berlin: de Gruyter, 2010), 66. Unless stated otherwise, biblical translations are from NRSV.

17. עזב ("forsake") occurs nine times in the desolate contexts (out of 23 times): 1:4; 6:12; 17:2, 9(2×); 49:14; 54:6, 7; 62:4. Here, Goldingay notes that abandonment is the first word out of Zion's mouth. See John Goldingay, *A Critical and Exegetical Commentary on Isaiah 56–66*, ICC (London: Bloomsbury T&T Clark, 2014), 334. Of the ten occurrences of שכח in Isaiah, six of them appear near *šmm*^{cog} instances.

18. "The third term applies to the lived reality, when the concrete spaces of the first and the ideological systems of the second are put into practice." Schweitzer, "Exploring the Utopian Space of Chronicles," 145. Here, Schweitzer draws from Lefebvre and Soja. Cf. Lefebvre, *The Production of Space*, 33; Soja, *Thirdspace*, 10, 67.

19. "Third space is found in the lived space of 'everyday life' which is a place filled with meaning, emotion, and struggle." Peter C. Ajer, *The Death of Jesus and the Politics of*

outburst initially sounds as a Thirdspace expression. It should ideally be geared towards her emancipation. At first glance, the assurance from the LORD and the attendant spectacular reversal in her fortunes seem to suggest exactly that, but for some complicating details.

Soon after Zion's outburst, the voice of the LORD arises to assure her. In fact, the LORD's speech dominates the entire discourse. If Zion laments of being forsaken and forgotten, the LORD's response addresses only the latter part. Also, whereas Zion uses the word "forget" (שׁכח) once, the LORD employs it three times and even adds an endearing image of a child in its mother's womb. To all these, Zion's response is nothing but silence. As we read on, even Zion's agency appears to be undermined because her future words (cf. "you will ask yourself," v. 21) will be supplied by the LORD. Yet, Zion continues to remain silent. Her direct discourse is never heard again in the book of Isaiah. Even the twice-uttered, double wakeup call to Jerusalem/Zion[20] (51:17; 52:1) elicits hardly any response from her. Zion's silence, when situated within the context of the promised spectacular reversals in her fortunes, is deafening. To borrow Higgins' parlance, Zion's troubling silence is akin to "degenerative speech."[21]

In short, although the Thirdspatial outburst in 49:14 appears to underscore Zion's struggle towards emancipation, the dominant voice of the LORD in the ensuing verses complicates it. And Zion's silence throughout the discourse leaves the exchange in Isa 49 anything but resolved. If this open-ended interaction characterizes the theological duet at the center of the $šmm^{cog}$ schema, there is one other duet that transpires at the bookends of the schema, to which we turn now.

Place in the Gospel of John (Eugene, OR: Pickwick, 2016), 65. Cf. Soja, *Thirdspace*, 40 n. 18. Similarly, Schweitzer observes, "Thirdspace has the potential, especially as presented by Soja, of recombining the first two perceptions of space and thus producing an opportunity for 'struggle, liberation, emancipation'" (cf. Soja, *Thirdspace*, 68). Schweitzer, "Exploring the Utopian Space of Chronicles: Some Spatial Anomalies," 145. All the same, Schweitzer (145–47) adds a corrective note via Lefebvre regarding the possibility of Secondspace being liberative and Thirdspace being hegemonic.

20. On how the motif of Zion is contested, complex, and profoundly theological in prophetic literature, including the book of Isaiah, see Frederik Poulsen, *Representing Zion: Judgement and Salvation in the Old Testament*, Copenhagen International Seminar (New York: Routledge, 2015).

21. Higgins adduces a compelling illustration from 2 Sam 13: the case of Tamar. "This process [of degenerative speech] begins with Tamar's heightened emotion, related through the formal stylization of parallelistic speech. Her utterance devolves into prose, becomes unintelligible and then inarticulate, and ends in silence. Through this degeneration, the biblical author conveys her physical brutalization, emotional breakdown, and narrative loss of agency. Tamar's ultimate silence echoes her interior and exterior desolation." Ryan S. Higgins, "He would not hear her voice: From Skilled Speech to Silence in 2 Samuel 13:1-22," *Journal of Feminist Studies in Religion* 36, no. 2 (2020): 25.

4. A Dialogical Duet

When the details of the first and the final entries of $šmm^{cog}$ are juxtaposed, noticeable parallels emerge.

	1:1–9	63:7–64:11
Covenantal overtones	my people (1:3)	my people (63:8), your people (64:9),
People's actions	rebelled against the LORD (1:2); sinful nation (1:4)	sinned, transgressed (64:5),
Your cities	masculine plural suffix (1:7)	masculine singular suffix (64:10)

Table 12.1 Parallel Features in Isa 1:1–19 and 63:7–64:11 (cf. Table 12.2)

The Initial Instance of the Desolate Note (1:7): The first mentioning of $šmm^{cog}$ occurs in the initial accusation against the covenant people ("my people," עַמִּי, v. 3) who are presented as a sinful nation (גּוֹי חֹטֵא). The same accusation employs some familial terms: evil offspring (זֶרַע מְרֵעִים) and corrupt children (בָּנִים מַשְׁחִיתִים, cf. vv. 2, 4). The ramifications are detailed in the desolate depiction of the landscape.[22]

Your country, a desolate; your cities,[23] burned with fire;[24]   ארצכם שממה עריכם שרפות אש
your land before your eyes, strangers devour it[25]   אדמתכם לנגדכם זרים אכלים אתה
and a desolate,[26] as overthrown by strangers.[27]   ושממה כמהפכת זרים

---

22. As regards the shift from the body metaphor to a realistic description of a land devastated by war, see J. J. M. Roberts, *First Isaiah: A Commentary*, Hermeneia—A Critical and Historical Commentary on the Bible (Minneapolis, MN: Fortress, 2015), 22.

23. As Mills observes, cities are the usual places of refuge. Especially in times of war, people can run inside the walled city. But a burned city indicates the very lack of such a refuge site. See Mary E. Mills, *Urban Imagination in Biblical Prophecy*, LHBOTS 560 (Bloomsbury T&T Clark, 2012), 171.

24. Comparing this to covenantal curses, Wildberger notes, "word for word, what has happened corresponds exactly to what had been included in the threats of … unfaithfulness." Hans Wildberger, *Isaiah 1-12: A Commentary*, trans. Thomas H. Trapp (Minneapolis, MN: Fortress, 1991), 27–8. However, see H. G. M. Williamson, *Isaiah 1-5: A Critical and Exegetical Commentary*, ICC (London: T & T Clark International, 2006), 65.

25. "Your land, your country, your cities" (with masculine plural suffix) occurs only once in the entire book of Isaiah.

26. 1QIsa[a] however has ושממו עליה ("and they will be appalled over it"). Roberts reads it with Isa 52:14 (also cf. Lev 26:32; Jer 2:12) as an idiom. See Roberts, *First Isaiah*, 15 n. l.

27. Since all other occurrences of מהפכת are associated with Sodom (Deut 29:22; Isa 13:19; Jer 49:18; 50:40; Amos 4:11), this text "suggests that the destruction of Sodom is archetypal of $š^emāmâ$." Meyer, "Šāmam," 244.

In short, Isa 1 outlines the people's sin and rebellion, which leads to the punishing prospects of both the land and the people.

Desolate Cities, Resolute Lament (64:9): The final entry of *šmm*^{cog} appears as part of the community lament in 63:7–64:11.

Your holy cities[28] have become a wilderness,	ערי קדשך היו מדבר
Zion has become a wilderness,	ציון מדבר היתה
Jerusalem a desolation.	ירושלם שממה

The initial lines of lament include (i) a historical survey of the LORD's loving dealing (cf. 63:7), (ii) the people's rebellion, and thus (iii) God becoming their enemy. As such, it seems to outline a thematic flow that is similar to Isa 1. For example, the "we" group of the lament acknowledges its sins[29] (cf. 64:5, 8) and notes how God handed them over to their iniquities. It is at this point that the parallel with ch. 1 ends. The "we" group swiftly shifts the focus from "sin-leading-to-punishment" logic in order to appeal to God as their father. Other shifts in their speech effectively capture the persuasiveness of their plea:

The expression "your cities" occurs only twice in the book of Isaiah—once each, in these enveloping instances of *šmm*^{cog} (1:7; 64:11). While the second person masculine plural suffix in 1:7 associates the desolate places with the people, the second person masculine singular suffix in 64:9 presents them as God's own cities. Similarly, the description of the temple as the LORD's holy place and sanctuary (63:18) later turns into the lamenting group's holy and glorious house (64:10). Together, these shifts speak of an overlap in the spaces of God and of the people.

The first instance of *šmm*^{cog} also depicts a symbiotic relationship between the people and their land: the people's violation paves the way for the land's desolation, thus indicating how the prospects of the people and their place are inextricably intertwined.

Combining the previous two observations—namely, shared space of God and of people; a symbiotic relation between people and their land—it can be surmised that, in the context of "desolate" depictions, the prospects of God, people, and land are shown to be intimately interlinked. As such, the Isaian prophetic vision holds people, place, and God symbiotically related, suggesting that their prospects are

---

28. "The expression 'holy cities,' which comes only here, underlines [that] … it is not Jerusalem's devastation alone that matters. The whole land is the 'holy land' (Zech 2:12)." See Goldingay, *A Critical and Exegetical Commentary on Isaiah 56–66*, 421.

29. 64:4b MT appears to read "It is because you have been angry that we have sinned," which seems to be a radical reversal of the typical logic. So, Childs notes that the "outrageous formation…serves only to identify the frustration of the confessing community." Brevard S. Childs, *Isaiah: A Commentary*, OTL (Louisville, KY: Westminster John Knox, 2001), 525.

mutually interconnected.[30] As such, Goldingay's translation of *hithpael* as "I am devastated" (63:5) is perceptive and persuasive.

Situating the final three verses of the lament in this shared space, the following can be observed by turning once again to the spatial triad:

- The description of the house as burned with fire (64:10a) appears to align with the Firstspace.
- The conceptions of the space as dear to the "we" group and also as the place where their ancestors worshipped outlines a Secondspace—a conceived space where the people, and their ancestors share the same worship space (64:10).[31]
- Thirdspace: From the same shared space, the "we" group voices its passionate plea (a Thirdspatial act) to the LORD: "Can you hold back, LORD, after all this? Can you remain silent, and afflict us so severely?" (64:12). In other words, faced with desolation and destruction—much of which was occasioned by one's own God—the lamenting group finds value in holding on to the same divine, or more properly, dares to goad their own God to a swift and saving intervention![32]

In sum, if the first duet in which Zion's outburst and then silence leaves the interaction open-ended, the second duet with its vision of shared space points to some promising prospects for a meaningful reading of the desolate depictions.

With these musings on the twin duets, we now turn to one remaining task of this chapter: asking the unity question, anew!

---

30. Goldingay, *A Critical and Exegetical Commentary on Isaiah 56–66*, 370. The comments of Joachimsen, which draw from memory studies, are also apt: "In this identity formation, the people and the deity stand in a mutually dependent relationship: the people shall remember and not forget who they are; they belong to God—and no other—and he [sic] cannot be without them." Kristin Joachimsen, "Remembering and Forgetting in Isaiah 43, 44, and 46," in *New Perspectives on Old Testament Prophecy and History: Essays in Honour of Hans M. Barstad*, ed. Rannfrid I. Thelle, Terje Stordalen, and Mervyn E. J. Richardson, VTSup 168 (Leiden: Brill, 2015), 55.

31. On the "inseparability of being and place," Boase avers, "The mirroring of language can be read as an implicit recognition of the permeable boundaries between people, place, and land." Elizabeth Boase, "Desolate Land / Desolate People in Jeremiah and Lamentations," in *Ecological Aspects of War: Engagements with Biblical Texts*, ed. Anne Elvey, Keith Dyer, and Deborah Guess, T&T Clark Biblical Studies (London: Bloomsbury T&T Clark, 2017), 97–115 (99).

32. As Mills notes, when faced with an insurmountable enemy, whose arrival is occasioned by the deity himself, that latter is celebrated even as it hurts; for, otherwise, when limited to human-to-human contest level, it shall not leave space for hope. See Mills, *Urban Imagination in Biblical Prophecy*, 178.

5. Asking the Unity Question

To this end, it bears to view the *šmm*^{cog} instances together in order to highlight a few thematic flows and some general patterns (cf. Figure 12.1).

As Isaiah scholarship frequently notes, the opening chapter functions as a meaningful introduction to the entire book of Isaiah.[33] The same seems to be the case with *šmm*^{cog}: already in its first instance *šmm*^{cog}, the readers are introduced to the general contours of the desolate theme: the forsaking act of the covenantal people paves the way for the punishment, in which places in perilous state form an unmistakable part.[34] Yet, something remains, which is attributed to the act of the LORD of hosts.[35]. Thus, sweeping scope of punishing judgement shares space with some positive note of remnant.[36]

Isaiah scholarship also notes that Isa 1 and 65–66 share similarities and thus function as bookends.[37] In light of this observation, an attempt to juxtapose the opening and closing occurrences of *šmm*^{cog} (Isa 1 and 63–64) helps highlight some lexical and thematic parallels which attest to yet another set of bookends that is centered on *šmm*^{cog}.

---

33. For such observations by G. Fohrer, O. Kaiser, W. J. Dumbrell, and M. A. Sweeney, see Paul D. Wegner, *An Examination of Kingship and Messianic Expectation in Isaiah 1–35* (New York: Edwin Mellen, 1992), 17 n. 20. See Roy F. Melugin, "Figurative Speech and the Reading of Isaiah 1 as Scripture," in *New Visions of Isaiah*, ed. Roy F. Melugin and Marvin A. Sweeney (Sheffield: Sheffield Academic, 1997), 295. See also Walter Brueggemann, *Isaiah 1–39*, Westminster Bible Companion (Louisville, KY: Westminster John Knox, 1998), 10–11.

34. As Hrobon notes, "the condition of the land is understood as the consequence of sin." See Hrobon, *Ethical Dimension of Cult in the Book of Isaiah*, 64.

35. It attests to some semblances of a positive note amid the dystopic descriptions. "The land is described as שממה, depopulated but not physically destroyed or without economic capacity. That is, not only the 'booth' remained but also the 'vineyard' and the 'cucumber field.'" Ehud Ben Zvi, "Isaiah 1:4–9, Isaiah, and the Events of 701 BCE in Judah," *SJOT* 5 (1991): 104. Leslie Hoppe reads a positive note already in the analogy of parent–children: "That the prophet identifies God as the parent betrayed and Israel as God's guilty children implies that judgement will not be God's last word to Israel." Leslie J. Hoppe, *Isaiah*, The New Collegeville Bible Commentary. Old Testament 13 (Collegeville, MN: Liturgical Press, 2012), 12.

36. On the theme of remnant in Isaiah, see Watts, *Isaiah 1–33*, 126–7.

37. Wegner builds on the proposals of L. J. Liebreich and R. Lack. See Wegner, *An Examination of Kingship and Messianic Expectation in Isaiah 1–35*, 19 nn. 29–30. See Edgar W. Conrad, *Reading Isaiah* (Eugene, OR: Wipf & Stock, 2002), 87–8. See also Watts, *Isaiah 1–33*, lxxv.

	1:1-9	63:7-64:11
שממה	feminine singular noun (v. 7)	feminine singular noun (64:10)
Cities	masculine plural noun and masculine plural suffix (v. 7)	masculine plural noun and masculine singular suffix (64:10)
Zion	left but vulnerable (v. 9)	Wilderness (64:10)
People's description (covenantal overtones)	sons (v. 2), my people (v. 3)	my people (63:8), your people (63:14), your holy people (63:18), your people (64:9), our father (63:16 [2×]; 64:8)
The LORD's acts	reared children, brought them up (v. 2) leaves a small remnant (v. 9)	lifted, carried them (63:9), fought against (v. 10), delivered them into their iniquity (64:7)
People's description and actions	rebelled against the LORD (v. 2); sinful nation, people laden with iniquity, offspring who do evil, children who deal corruptly (v. 4)	sinned, transgressed (64:5), iniquity-laden (63:6)
Quizzing	"why do you...?" (1:5; by the LORD)	why do you make us wander...? (63:17; from the "we" group)
Adversaries	strangers devour the [people's] land (v. 7)	our adversaries trampled your [God's] place (63:18)

Table 12.2 Parallel Features in Isa 1:1-9 and 63:7-64:11 (cf. Table 12.1)

Willem Beuken observes that across this prophetic book Isa 33 functions as a mirror text (*Spiegeltext*)[38] as it looks both backward to the previous chapters and forward to the ensuing ones. The theme of *šmm*^{cog} appears to share some semblances of this mirroring too. In mapping the details of a decimating prospect of punishment, Isa 33 points to the earlier instances of desolate depictions; and in outlining the reversal of fortunes, the text anticipates the ensuing themes of restoration.[39]

A general tone of scattering (with exilic allusions) marks the left column of the schema—especially, up to ch. 24—while repeated promises of gathering (in the context of restoration) fill the right column.

There is also a noticeable shift in the use of the divine epithets. The title "the LORD of hosts," for example, appears a notable number of nine times in the

---

38. Beuken observes that Isaiah 33 is "a 'mirror text' that reflects the themes of the book of Isaiah as a whole, looking backward to First Isaiah as well as [forward] to Second and Third Isaiah." Willem A. M. Beuken, "Jesaja 33 als Spiegeltext im Jesajabuch," *ETL* 67 (1991): 5–35, as cited in Hayes, *The Earth Mourns*, 164. Similarly, Kim observes that Isa 33 functions as a bridge pericope. It concludes the six woe-oracles (*hôy* in chs. 28–32) and also transitions to chs. 34–35; 36–39. See Kim, *Reading Isaiah*, 154.

39. This chapter also marks the beginning of a distinction among the people: the sinners will fear while the law-abiding ones will be raised, secured, and plentifully supplied!

$šmm^{cog}$-contexts of Isa 1–24. However, the title appears only one other time in the latter part (54:5) where it is used for a familial image: as the name of Zion's husband.

As regards the scope of desolation, the left column attests to a noticeable increase:

- cities, country, and land (Isa 1)
- house of the wealthy, also the noble, and "my people" (Isa 5)
- land, cities, houses, and the people (Isa 6)
- land as well as a cosmic scope (Isa 13)
- desolation in relation to Damascus and Ephraim (Isa 17)
- cosmic scope (Isa 24)
- desolation in the highways (Isa 33)[40]

An increasing specificity appears to attend the desolate terms in the restoration side of it:

- a general description of "heritages" (Isa 49:8)
- Zion's own "desolate places" (Isa 49:19)
- Zion (the personified woman) herself as "the desolate" (Isa 54:1)
- her progeny's possession of "desolate places" (Isa 54:3)
- their building of "wastes" (Isa 61)
- Zion's very name as "desolate" in the context of the coming change (Isa 62)
- the current state of Jerusalem as "desolate" (Isa 64)[41]

It can therefore be surmised that the $šmm^{cog}$ occurrences seem to narrate its own story with some notable structural patterns and thematic flows.

Unified Reading: The thematic retrace thus far has been in broad terms and also unapologetically synchronic.[42] Also, with more than 100 occurrences of desolation-related terms,[43] the choice of $šmm^{cog}$ is admittedly narrow. All the same, even if such an incidental inquiry can point to some emerging patterns, it is an attestation to the enormous prospect of a coherent reading of Isaiah.[44] All the same, I must hasten to add that the thematic flows are neither strictly linear

---

40. Though there is a general increase, it is by no means a linear one. For example, between the two cosmic scopes in chs. 13 and 24, ch. 17 has a particular focus.

41. Again, exceptions to the same do occur in the reaction of the servant's onlookers (Isa 52–53) and the Divine Warrior's twice-stated appalment (Isa 59, 63).

42. Or, more properly, a SynDiaTopic reading. For details on the meaning and relevance of this neologism, see Irudayaraj, "Mountains in Micah and Coherence."

43. Cf. section 2, "Retracing $šmm^{cog}$," above.

44. For a helpful survey of growing scholarly works on the unified reading of Isaiah, see H. G. M. Williamson, "Recent Issues in the Study of Isaiah," in *Interpreting Isaiah: Issues and Approaches*, ed. David G. Firth and H. G. M. Williamson (Downers Grove, IL: Apollos, 2009), 21–39.

nor continually evolving, which reiterates the complexity of the corpus.⁴⁵ Though vexing at the first glance, this cautions me from applying any conceptual model in a mechanical manner. In short, the challenge of the book's irreducible complexity, as well as the promise of a coherent vision, stand in creative tension. As such, the scholarly reiteration that Isaiah is a complex yet unified whole can hardly be overstated.

6. A Post-Script: Desolate Places and Resolute People

Commenting on place, people, and meaning, Tumarkin avers that "places of loss and trauma are never empty or blank; they are filled with meaning and history even when covered with ruins or new buildings."⁴⁶ Further, desolate places have the tendency to leave a lingering impact on those who circumambulate them. One such experience has been the impetus to the present work. It happened in January 2016 as part of my journey through the northern district of Sri Lanka. It was here that the final phase of the decades-long civil war unfolded. As the war records recount, the marauding army marched through this part, carpet-bombing the entire area, turning the landscape into a deathscape.⁴⁷ My travel companion, Fr. S. M. Doss, a priest from Mannar diocese, had personal painful experience of this time, having lost several family members in that war and witnessing a number of others being forced to flee.

During our visit, among the massively re-laid roads and quickly rebuilt buildings, we observed a structure, one which must have once been a home but was now reduced to a bare minimum of a few walls, filled with brutal bullet marks (cf. Figure 12.2). At Fr. Doss' suggestion, we stopped and spent some time at this ruined site. It is hard enough to visit places that mark one's own people's defeat, dispersion, and death; and it is harder still to stop and speak about it. But Doss did exactly that. His tone was certainly laced with pain and yet there was also a hint of resolve, which later elicited in me an interest to inquire into the link between desolate places and people's willingness to pause and muse over them. With this experience and interest, when I (re)read the desolate depictions in Isaiah, I felt

---

45. For a helpful survey of continuity and discontinuity in Isaiah, see Lena-Sofia Tiemeyer and Hans M. Barstad, eds., *Continuity and Discontinuity: Chronological and Thematic Development in Isaiah 40–66*, FRLANT 255 (Göttingen: Vandenhoeck & Ruprecht, 2014).

46. Maria M. Tumarkin, *Traumascapes: The Power and Fate of Places Transformed by Tragedy* (Melbourne: University Press, 2005), 225, as cited in Mills, *Urban Imagination in Biblical Prophecy*, 180.

47. According to a United Nations' estimate, the 26-year long civil war saw the killing of 80,000 to 100,000 people. For an account of the systematic violation of human rights by the Sri Lankan government forces, see Francis Boyle, *The Tamil Genocide by Sri Lanka: The Global Failure to Protect Tamil Rights Under International Law* (Atlanta, GA: Clarity Press, 2010).

drawn to juxtapose the Sri Lankan experience with the prophetic portrayals of desolate places (and people) in Isaiah.[48] When I did so, the words of Mary Mills rang true to me: "a deathscape provides a cathartic experience which 'releases from the burden of a traumatic past, but also of an anxious and uncertain present, a moment of empowerment.'"[49]

And so, I quiz myself, can Doss' pause to contemplate the bullet-dotted walls and the Isaian lament over the burnt down Temple be but two of otherwise myriad spatial instances of releasing the burden of a traumatic past towards an empowering present and a hope-inspiring future?

Figure 12.2 Bullet-dotted building in northern Sri Lanka, en route to Mullivaikkal. © Photo, by the author.

---

48. It is a move that is akin to intercultural reading. As Charlene Van der Walt, "Hearing Tamar's Voice," *OTE* 25 (2012): 182–206 (182) notes, "the intercultural Bible reading space is a dynamic creative space that allows individual readers to draw on a wealth of personal contextual knowledge as a key to interpret the Bible text."

49. Mills, *Urban Imagination in Biblical Prophecy*, 179. Cf. Tumarkin, *Traumascapes*, 42–4, 53.

Chapter 13

ZION'S DESTINY AS THEOLOGICAL DISCLOSURE: MAPPING OF A METAPHOR ACROSS ISAIAH

Gina Hens-Piazza

On the heels of a generation of scholars, whose important studies have delineated the host of traditions making up the text of Isaiah, overtures continue in search of what might qualify as the unity, or unities, binding together these 66 chapters.[1] Of the many literary approaches, the investigation of themes such as family, justice, light, righteousness, sickness, and healing number among these noteworthy pursuits.[2] Many projects, with good reason, have focused upon the centrality of Zion as a prominent thread that binds together the various traditions across this prophetic scroll.[3] After all, of the 154 times that Zion is cited in the Hebrew Bible, 47 of those iterations are found across the book of Isaiah. Ulrich Berges, among others, has made a compelling case that Zion as a personage might be a unifying key occurring repeatedly throughout this text, acquiring prophetic traits, and

---

1. Numerous studies make up these overtures. See the overview essay by Roy F. Melugin, "Isaiah 40–66 in Recent Research: The Unity Movement," in *Recent Research on Major Prophets*, ed. Alan J. Hauser, Recent Research in Biblical Studies 1 (Sheffield: Sheffield Phoenix Press, 2008), 142–94, which focuses not only upon holistic studies between Second and Third Isaiah but across the whole 66 chapters. More recently, Jacob Stromberg, "Reading Isaiah Holistically," in *An Introduction to the Study of Isaiah* (New York: T&T Clark International, 2011), 77–94, spotlights more recent studies.

2. In particular, see the set of nine essays under section IV, "Themes and Literary Motifs Spanning the Book of Isaiah," in *The Oxford Handbook of Isaiah,* ed. Lena-Sofia Tiemeyer (New York: Oxford University Press, 2020), 201–376.

3. See the overview by Stromberg "Literary Approaches in Isaiah," in *An Introduction to the Study of Isaiah*, 55–76.

ultimately resembling the *'ebed* (servant) of God.⁴ According to his study, Zion is vulnerable to the attack and scorn of the enemy in the opening chapters but still remains strong in trusting YHWH. Berges notes that in Isa 40–55, Zion initially refuses to be comforted but then gradually, and only gradually, accepts divine consolation.⁵ Finally Zion begins to manifest traits of the servant, upon whom God's spirit is bestowed.⁶ The final chapters of Isaiah endow Zion with a prophetic persona and a mission, especially to the poor in the post-exilic period. His is one of many studies tracking the journey of Zion as central in this prophetic text.

Other courses for mapping the unity across Isaiah have attended to other components to make their respective case. As early as the late 1950s, L. J. Liebreich noted terms in parallels between the first and final chapter of Isaiah, suggesting the "intention and fixed determination to make the book end in the same vein in which it begins."⁷ In follow-up essays, he noted even more correspondences between Isa 1 and 65–66. Others continued this work demonstrating the relationships and developments that tie together the opening and closing chapters of Isaiah.⁸

This study builds, first, upon the work of those who have focused upon the centrality of Zion in Isaiah and, second, upon those who have perceived connections between its opening and closing chapters. However, the exegetical camera here narrows further in that it takes up the specific metaphoric representation of Zion as female in chs. 1 and 66. This approach argues that the transformation of the metaphoric depiction of Zion from the book's beginning to its conclusion may serve as a potentially unifying linchpin for a more holistic reading of this text. Further, this study concludes with two observations: how the final personification of Zion as a female in ch. 66 contributes to the literary integrity of the concluding vision of eschatology and how this concluding celebrated personification of Zion as woman actually qualifies as a cultural exponent of the kind of realm in which such an eschatology can be realized.

Without a doubt, Zion's destiny in the book of Isaiah is one of the most pervasive themes constructing these 66 chapters. What happens to Zion and Zion's own role in this outcome designate it as a major preoccupation of this book. And the

---

4. Ulrich Berges, "Personifications and Prophetic Voices of Zion in Isaiah and Beyond," in *The Elusive Prophet: The Prophet as an Historical Person, Literary Character and Anonymous Artist: Papers Read at the Eleventh Joint Meeting of The Society for Old Testament Study and Het Oudtestamentisch Werkgezelschap in Nederland en België, Held at Soesterberg 2000*, ed. Johannes C. de Moor, OTS 45 (Leiden: Brill, 2001), 54–82.

5. Berges, "Personifications and Prophetic Voices of Zion," 81.

6. Berges, "Personifications and Prophetic Voices of Zion," 82.

7. Leon J. Liebreich, "The Compilation of the Book of Isaiah," *JQR* 46 (1956): 259–77 (276).

8. See review of many of these overtures in the essay by David Carr, "Reading Isaiah from Beginning (Isaiah 1) to End (Isaiah 65–66): Multiple Modern Possibilities," in *New Visions of Isaiah*, ed. Roy F. Melugin and Marvin A. Sweeney, JSOTSup 214 (Sheffield: Sheffield Academic Press, 1996), 188–218.

range of entities to which Zion refers is vast—a fortified city, a hilltop, a collective group, an actual people, a walled urban settlement, a holy place, a mountain. Thus, the depiction of this thematic construct exists in multiple metaphoric manifestations. Most frequently, these various depictions of Zion are portrayed specifically as a female entity. In these instances, Zion is a female person endowed with human characteristics. She is a virgin daughter, a barren woman, a prostitute, a woman in labor, a spouse, a divorced wife, a grieving mother.

1. A Word about Metaphor

These personifications qualify as a subcategory of metaphor that draws upon and impacts its own context, as well as continues to affect readers in future contexts. So, a word about metaphor is in order as to its function and its power. Regarding its own context, personification of Zion as woman is selective. While it emphasizes some features, it suppresses others of the principal subject (in this case Zion) by implying statements that normally apply to the subsidiary subject (woman) and in the process creates a new meaning.[9] Yet the functioning capacity of the metaphorical statement depends not solely upon the understanding of woman *per se*, but a specific role, status, or identity assigned to the metaphoric woman—be that virgin, daughter, wife, widow, and so on. Thus, the complexity of references signified depends, first, upon the personification of Zion as woman and, second, the specification of the woman's identity or societal role. Thus, to understand the female personification and its functioning power in the text, the role and status of women in general and then of the women defined in a particular capacity in its own context must be elaborated.

Yet how metaphors affect meaning in texts is not solely dependent upon their function in the ancient context. Reception of metaphors also plays a role. Regarding the import of this female personification of Zion on readers in future contexts, not only the function but also the power of metaphor must be taken into account. Metaphors have power to craft and organize our understanding of life. According to George Lakoff and Mark Turner, once formed and learned,

> …metaphors are just there, conventionalized, a ready and powerful conceptual tool—automatic, effortless, and largely unconscious… Metaphors give us power to conceptualize and reason, so they have power over us. Anything that we rely on consciously, unconsciously, and automatically is as much part of us that it cannot be easily resisted.[10]

---

9. Max Black, *Models and Metaphors: Studies in Language and Philosophy* (Ithaca: Cornell University Press, 1962), 44–5.

10. George Lakoff and Mark Turner, *More Than Cool Reason: A Field Guide to Poetic Metaphor* (Chicago, IL: University of Chicago Press, 1989), 62–3, as cited in Deryn Guest, "Hiding Behind the Naked Women in Lamentations: A Recriminative Response," *BibInt* 7 (1999): 413–48 (431).

Hence, metaphors have the power to define what is real and even to signify what could be reality. So Lakoff and Turner conclude, "because metaphors can be used so automatically and effortlessly, we find it hard to question them, if we can even notice them."[11]

2. The Female Zion Metaphor in Chapter 1

The opening chapter of Isaiah, which begins with the accusation speech of the LORD (vv. 2–4) and concludes with divine assurance of redemption of Zion (vv. 27–31), is widely recognized as an introduction to the book as a whole. This summary framework also offers a first encounter with Zion personified. A woe oracle with a lament (vv. 4–9) portrays Daughter Zion at risk before the enemy. "Daughter Zion is left like a shelter in a vineyard, like a hut in a field of melons" (1:8). Many translated versions render *bat-siyon* as "daughter of Zion," which would suggest a female inhabitant of the city. However, the translation here views the syntax of the Hebrew construct chain as an appositional genitive.[12] Thus daughter serves as a characteristic personifying Zion and, therefore, invites the translation "Daughter Zion."

This initial personification of Zion as daughter in the opening chapter of Isaiah summons the examination of the metaphor most dominant in the early chapters of this book. Zion is referred to as Daughter Zion six times in chs. 1–39. The use of *bat* with a geographical name frequently served as a title for a goddess in the ancient Near East.[13] Likely influenced by these ancient Near Eastern divine epithets, the title Daughter Zion occurs 26 times in the Hebrew Bible.[14] But unlike these ancient Near Eastern divine epithets, Daughter Zion is never understood as a goddess in the Hebrew Bible. Thus, an understanding of the reference "Daughter Zion" proceeds from its status as metaphor.

First, the societal understanding that enshrines the cultural category "daughter" in ancient Israel summons exposition. A daughter in the ancient Israelite context receives definition and identification in conjunction with the *bêt 'āb*, or house of the father, of which she is a member. The *bêt 'āb* was the societal unit to which the daughter belonged. She was identified with and dependent upon the father for

---

11. Guest, "Hiding," 431.
12. See William F. Stinesprin, "No Daughter of Zion: A Study of the Appositional Genitive in Hebrew Grammar," *Encounter* 26 (1956): 133–41, and GKC, 128, against F. W. Dobbs-Allsopp, "Syntagma of Bat Followed by a Geographical Name in the Hebrew Bible: A Reconsideration of Its Meaning and Grammar," *CBQ* 57 (1995): 451–70.
13. Katherine Pfisterer Darr, *Isaiah's Vision and Family of God*, LCBI (Louisville, KY: Westminster John Knox Press, 1994), 126–9, and Christl M. Maier, "Jerusalem als Ehebrecherin in Ezechiel 16," in *Feministishe Hermeneutik und Erstes Testament*, ed. Hedwig Jahnow et al. (Stuttgart: Kohlhammer, 1994), 76–101 (87–8).
14. Isa 1:8; 10:32; 16:1; 37:22; 52:2; 62:11; Jer 4:31; 6:2, 23; Lam 1:6; 2:1, 4, 8, 10, 13, 18; 4:22; Mic 1:13; 4:8, 10, 13; Zech 2:10; 9:9; Zeph 3:14; Ps 9:15 and 2 Kg 19:21.

her social and economic well-being. The father was the source of protection of the daughter in her vulnerability, especially before any threats of sexual violence. At the same time, the waywardness of the daughter or the violation of a daughter's chastity would lead to a father's dishonor (Deut 22:13–21; cf. Gen 34:31). Only when a daughter came under the domain of a husband was she released from the authority of her father. Thus, the identity of "daughter" signified a female lacking jurisdiction over herself. She was dependent upon and subjugated to the decisions and enforcements, as well as the protection, of a father.

When introduced in the first chapter of Isaiah (1:8), Daughter Zion is alone with no father in sight to keep her safe. Further, the description of her coincides with this unprotected status. She is described as "a booth in a vineyard" and "as a hut in a melon patch." Here the metaphoric personification of Zion as daughter is thickened by a further metaphor, which likens this daughter to a hut or shelter in an agricultural field, a veritable metaphor within a metaphor. This hut or booth, a structure serving day laborers, is only temporary, not stable. It is easily assaulted by severe weather or trampled by those seeking to make trouble for the landowner. Certainly the opposite of a walled or protected household or fortress, its structural status stands precariously. Thus, the comparison of Daughter Zion to this shanty of a shelter magnifies a daughter's vulnerability, her unprotected position and the ease with which she can be plundered or overcome. The violence that could threaten this easily toppled hut, here personified as Daughter Zion, receives further specification by implication in the preceding verse, where twice the condition of desolation is narrated. Verse 7 pronounces that "your country lies desolate…and your land, it is desolate." The Hebrew word šĕmāmâ, which denotes both desolation and barrenness, is used elsewhere in the biblical tradition to describe not only ravaged environmental conditions but also the ravaged state of a violated woman.[15] Having been raped by her half-brother Amnon, the tradition reports that "Tamar remained a desolate (šĕmāmâ) woman in her brother Absalom's house" (2 Sam 13:20). Hence, the state of the country and land as desolate coincides with the metaphoric description of the potentially vulnerable Daughter Zion alone in a field like a hut. She is not only vulnerable to plunder but susceptible to specifically sexual assault or violence (Deut 22:23–29). This predicated violence actualizes just a few verses later but in a way that holds her responsible. In Isa 1:21 the daughter is now designated as a prostitute.

The Hebrew root (znh), the participle form appearing here, is associated with both prostitution and fornication alike. But attention to the sociocultural and literary circumstances in each instance informs the complexity of what is meant.

Prostitution shares with fornication a fundamentally female role or profile. Yet the fact remains that both activities require male participation and typically male initiation as in Gen 38. Thus the female prostitute, though an anomaly, is a tolerated specialist who evidently accommodates the conflicting desires of men

---

15. See Christl M. Maier, *Daughter Zion, Mother Zion: Gender, Space, and the Sacred in Ancient Israel* (Minneapolis, MN: Fortress, 2008), 76–7.

for exclusive control of their wives' sexuality while at the same time having access to other women.[16]

Adding to this inequity, Deut 22:23 mandates that in instances where the woman participant is engaged to be married, only she is punished. Such asymmetry characteristic of patriarchal societies reflects the unevenness and inequalities of gender roles, values, obligations, and regulations.[17]

In ch. 1, as introduction to the whole of Isaiah, Zion's identity shifts from vulnerable daughter in v. 8 to a prostitute in v. 21. And what exactly this eclipse in personification means is clarified in the immediately following verses:

> [21] Woe, Zion[18] has become the whore.
> She that was full of justice,
> righteousness lodged in her –
> but now murderers.[19]
> [22] Your silver has become dross,
> Your beer[20] has been diluted with water.
> [23] Your princes are stubborn
> and companions of thieves.
> Everyone loves a bribe
> and runs after gifts.
> They do not defend the orphan
> and the widow's cause does not come before them.

Once righteous and just, she is now "populated by murderers." The cause of her abrupt transformation from daughter to prostitute is defined by corrupt leadership that defiled her. Those who "love bribes and run after gifts," "do not defend the orphan," and to whom "the widow's cause does not come before them" (v. 23) are earmarked here as responsible.

Here a feminist analysis does not fix upon the issue of gender as having to do only with sexed bodies. Instead, it also attends to the broader discourse latent here focusing upon issues of power, which hierarchically order social identity, relationships, and the consequences therein. Forwarding a metaphoric portrait of woman as prostitute to obscure the in-charge powerful men's lack of responsibility is itself an exercise of power. As early as Gen 3:12, the biblical creation story witnesses how the first man tries to obfuscate his culpability by blaming the

---

16. Phyllis Bird, *Missing Persons and Mistaken Identities: Women and Gender in Ancient Israel*, OBT (Minneapolis, MN: Fortress, 1997), 224–5.

17. Bird, *Missing Persons and Mistaken Identities*, 224.

18. OG identifies the city as Zion.

19. The phrase is possibly a gloss but does specify what now fills the city in contrast to what once was.

20. While translations frequently render this "wine," see *HALOT*, 738, which identifies the Hebrew here as a loan word from Akkadian.

woman when God is looking for them in the garden. And the inequities that result are not the product of creation in the garden but rather are the consequences of the fall. The resulting dictum, "you (the woman) will long for your husband, but he shall rule over you" (Gen 3:16), echoes one of the many outcomes foisted upon women for the first disobedience that disrupted the created order. Such consequences for women appear to be everywhere present in the biblical stories that follow. Again and again, the biblical tradition relates not only accounts of societal inequities that subjugate women but also forwards accounts of metaphoric women, who become the front obscuring the male religious and political leadership responsible for Israel's waywardness. One need only call to mind prophetic texts such as Jer 3:6, 8, 11, 12, where Israel is referenced as "a disloyal woman." In another instance, Lam 1–2 crafts Zion as a weeping widow whose adulterous behavior is responsible for Jerusalem's destruction. And perhaps the most graphic examples of all metaphoric women blamed for iniquity, in Ezek 16 and 23, sketch Israel and Judah as whores, detailing their activity to explain these nations' destruction. Perhaps Jacob Stromberg gets is right when he notes that "given that verses 21b-26 in this first chapter of Isaiah place fault squarely on the leadership while saying nothing about Zion's own choice in the matter, the metaphor describing her transformation into a prostitute paints her more as the victim than perpetrator of the crimes."[21] Thus the transformation of Zion's identity from threatened daughter (1:8) to prostitute (1:21) may well communicate "moral defection" and the abuse of power, but not of the metaphoric woman Zion but rather of those hiding behind her.

Five times Daughter Zion appears in these first 39 chapters along with other foreign cities identified as vulnerable or endangered daughters. The persistent metaphoric characterization further testifies to the often vulnerable or precarious status associated with the social category of daughter.[22] In response to the condemnation of Moab (15:2), Daughter Dibon initiates a lament. In 23:10, an oracle addressing Tyre informs Daughter Tarshish that her ports have been taken away so that her ships have no place to land. In that same chapter, Sidon, also addressed as daughter, is described as a raped virgin who will not recover. And the final time in these opening 39 chapters that Zion is summoned as daughter, she is referred to as Virgin Daughter Zion (37:22). The text portrays her as an instrument of insult to the enemy. She is described as "despising and scorning the enemy, tossing her head behind his back" (37:22), a reference to her being used to insult King Sennacherib of Assyria. One might question why, in this instance, Daughter Zion now becomes further designated as "Virgin Daughter Zion." Preying upon women was a well-known war tactic directed against men with whom these women were affiliated as daughters or wives. Their sexual

---

21. Stromberg, "Literary Approaches," 62.
22. Irmtraud Fischer, "Isaiah: The Book of Female Metaphors," in *Feminist Biblical Interpretation: A Compendium of Critical Commentary on the Books of the Bible and Related Literature*, ed. by Luise Schottroff and Marie-Theres Wacker (Cambridge: Eerdmans, 2012), 303–13 (310).

violation in war time was a brazen act by men demonstrating their military superiority.[23] Thus, the reference to her virgin status attests to the terrors and trauma of rape to which she would have been subject had the Assyrian military been triumphant. In this instance, reference to her status as "virgin" functions as a wartime trophy, signifying Judah's resistance before enemy assault. Hence, the overarching portrait of Daughter Zion in Proto Isaiah encompasses vulnerability, abandonment, affliction, blame, and finally as a symbol of men's military prowess despite the enemy threat.

The subsequent chapters of Isaiah all but abandon the title Daughter Zion, with only one instance in chs. 40–55 where she is told to loosen the chains around her neck (52:2), and only one other citation in chs. 56–66 where she hears that perhaps her people will be returned to her (62:11). Instead, for the span of chs. 40–66, the female Zion metaphor morphs now into an adult woman. And across these chapters Woman Zion herself is often heard describing her current state. As a mother (49:20-23; 66:8-13), she also sees herself at times as childless and barren (49:20-21; 54:1). She has been subjected to the terror of witnessing her children slain in warfare (51:17-20). As a woman she describes herself as abandoned and forgotten. While she is depicted as a bride (49:18; 61:10; 62:4-5), she is also a wife (54:5) and, in some instances, claiming to be rejected by her spouse (49:14; 50:1; 54:6; 62:4). She is even served a bill of divorce by her husband (50:1) at one point. Moreover, she is also presented as widowed without anyone caring for her (54:4). The last two images are particularly problematic because her apparent spouse is Israel's God.[24]

3. *The Female Zion Metaphor in Isaiah 66*

So how does Zion's personification in the final chapters of Isaiah fare? And how might it lend literary integrity and closure to these 66 chapters that challenge and reverse the inequities and injustice represented in the variegated and often lamentable personification of Zion across this prophetic text?

Over the years scholars have observed that the contours of what is meant by the vision of "a new heavens and new earth" of Isaiah's eschatology in 65:17-18 manifest as the restoration of the condition of the garden at creation.[25] In 65:17-24, images abound of the land being fertile and productive, people not laboring in

---

23. See Harold C. Washington, "'Lest He Die in the Battle and Another Man Take Her': Violence and the Construction of Gender in the Laws of Deuteronomy 20–22," in *Gender and Law in the Hebrew Bible and the Ancient Near East*, ed. Victor H. Matthews, Bernard M. Levinson, and Tikva S. Frymer-Kensky, JSOTSup 262 (Sheffield: Sheffield Academic Press, 1998), 185–213, for an analysis of the coincidence of sexual assault of wives and daughters in warfare in Deuteronomy and in the prophetic writings.

24. Fischer, "Isaiah," 313.

25. Claus Westermann, *Isaiah 40–66: A Commentary*, OTL, trans. David M. G. Stalker (London: SCM Press, 1969), 408; Walther Zimmerli, *Man and his Hope in the Old Testament*,

vain but enjoying the work of their hands, women bearing children without labor, and enmity among animals being resolved. As the harmony of creation is restored, one witnesses here the reversal of the consequences of the fall.

In ch. 66, the reversal prompted by this new creation manifests specifically in the transformed metaphor personifying Zion. In the opening chapter she was the endangered daughter who, like a hut in an agricultural field, remained vulnerable and unprotected. Ultimately, she was assigned the identity of a prostitute who appears more victimized and blamed than actually guilty. But in ch. 66, she not only is portrayed as restored and but becomes one of the revelatory manifestations of this new creation.

Chapter 66 consists of a collection of passages introduced by prophetic rubrics.[26] Among these, vv. 7–9 fix upon Woman Zion. Here she is no longer a daughter, a virgin, a barren woman, a woman in labor, nor a bereaved mother, a widow or divorcee, as are her previous personifications throughout Isaiah. Instead, the metaphoric depiction of female Zion is unprecedented, and its manifestation is surrounded by two images of theophany:

> [6] Listen, an uproar from the city! A voice from the temple!
> The voice of the LORD, dealing retribution to his enemies!
> [7]Before she was in labor, she gave birth.
> Before pangs came upon her, she birthed a son.
> [8]Who has heard of such a thing? Whoever saw such a thing?
> Can a land come to birth in one day?
> Can a nation be born in one moment?
> Yet, as soon as Zion was in labor, she delivered her children.
> [9]Will I open the womb and not bring to birth? says the LORD.
> Will I who brings to birth, shut the womb? says your God.
> [10]Rejoice with Jerusalem, and be glad for her, all you who love her.
> Be very joyful with her, all you who now mourn over her;
> [11]that you may suck and be satisfied at her consoling breasts;
> that you may drink deeply and delight from her glorious bosom.
> [12]For thus says the LORD,
> Behold, I will extend prosperity to her like a river,
> And the wealth of the nations like an overflowing stream that you will suck.
> You will be carried on her hip and dandled on her knees.
> [13]Like a mother who comforts her child, so I will comfort you.
> You shall be comforted in Jerusalem.

---

trans. G. W. Bowen (London: SCM Press, 1971), 158; and Emmanuel Uchenna Dim, *The Eschatological Implications of Isa 65 and 66 as the Conclusion of the Book of Isaiah* (Bern: Peter Lang, 2005), 104–6.

26. See Joseph Blenkinsopp, *Isaiah 56–66: A New Translation with Introduction and Commentary*, AB 19B (New York: Doubleday, 2003), 292, who narrates a roster of scholarly proposals that range from 3 to 7 pericopes here.

First, v. 6 preceding her description announces the noise and uproar of the coming of the LORD. Following the description of Zion in vv. 7–8, the LORD speaks in vv. 9–13 and identifies divine activity as participating in that described of Woman Zion.

The characterization of Zion and her activity, which unfolds within this divine *inclusio*, is extraordinary. She is a now fertile woman who gives birth. But in keeping with the notion of a new heaven and new earth visioned in these concluding chapters, Woman Zion gives birth in a manner that eclipses the normal birthing process. She bears offspring without pain as soon as labor begins. Though birthing more than one child, the process proceeds quickly (v. 8). Also unique to these verses and congruent with the new creation theme, Zion gives birth to new peoples (v. 8). Immediately following, God oversees the birth as if a midwife (v. 9). With the rhetorical questions, whose answers affirm God's role in creation, the LORD identifies the divine's own restorative role as associated with birthing. "Will I open the womb and not bring to birth? says the LORD. Will I who brings to birth, shut the womb? Says your God" (v. 9).

Returning to the metaphor of Zion portrayed as a mother, the LORD elaborates further her personification. Now the LORD offers divine assurance that Mother Zion will nurse them with comforting breasts. Those who drink will do so deeply until they are satisfied. Further, Israel's God promises that they will drink deeply with delight from her glorious bosom (v. 11). Hence, they will be nourished by her overflowing abundance. But not only will they be nurtured by Zion, God continues her personification here, promising how those restored will be cared for. They will be carried on her hips and dandled on her knees (v. 12).

The vividness of the personification presented by the divine description of Woman Zion—her fertile body, the labor-less process of birthing, the breasts, hips, knees of Woman Zion—is noteworthy. The sexualized denigration of a woman's body, so often portraying the iniquity of the people and even personifying Zion as a prostitute in the opening chapter of Isaiah, has been overturned and now celebrates woman's body as the locus of life and delight for the newly born.

Even more striking is the interrelationship between Zion's elaborated womanhood as mother and God's subsequent recitation. Immediately following the celebrated physical personification of Woman Zion as mother, the LORD pronounces that the divine's own participation in the restoration will be like that of a mother. "As a mother comforts her child, so I will comfort you" (v. 13). Hence, the juxtaposition of the metaphoric Woman Zion as mother with the divine's identification with mothering graphs the fertile, birthing, nurturing, mothering image of Zion on the very claims of who God will be for this people.

But Zion metaphorized as mother functions not only as the image of how restoration will be experienced and as template for how God's care will be fashioned; her description also corroborates the establishment of the new heaven and new earth. With both subtle and more literal allusions, her portrait suggests the establishment of a new creation that emancipates humanity from the consequences of the fall.

First, the explicit yet uncensored description of her physical body—breasts, hips, knees—often used to signal shame or blame by the prophets, here is set forth to signal new life and comes into focus without need to obscure or to excuse. Hence, the nakedness in the Garden of Eden, which signaled the experience of guilt from the disobedience of the first parents, is reversed by this honored and elevated description of the woman's body. Second, the consequence of the fall mandated that woman would give birth with labor and pain. That Woman Zion brings forth new children painlessly signals a new creation where such consequences have been wiped away. Third, unlike the consequences from the fall, no longer will her husband, a symbol of those who subjugate women in hierarchical frameworks, lord it over her. In this new creation, Woman Zion, personified as mother, coincides with how God will be with the community. Thus, God's identification and alliance with Woman Zion challenges and nullifies the legitimacy of social stratifications that rendered women defined, controlled, and unequal.

Yet the elevated portrait of a birthing, breast-feeding mother as metaphor for Zion still warrants some qualification. For this celebrated portrait of Zion as mother ultimately still plays into the patriarchal mindset defining woman too narrowly with regard to mere biology and sexual function. That Zion as city is often metaphorized as female has little to do with the grammatical gender of ʿîr or qiryâ. Rather cities, like women in hierarchical societies, were managed, controlled, and useful in providing food and a habitable place for life. They offered shelter and nurture for their inhabitants. While they added beauty, they also could be at the mercy of anyone hostile who entered them.[27] Hence, cities were useful and could provide functions, not unlike the view of women as mothers. So, the identification of God with Zion's motherhood as one with procreative power in ch. 66 seems to challenge and redefine the status of woman even as mother in this patriarchal context. Though functioning in the capacity of mother, there is no reference here to her status as wife. No description of a spouse precedes this narration of birth and nurturing. Instead, Zion, in her capacity to bring about new children, is identified with God as co-creator bringing about a new heaven and a new earth.

Further, this alliance between God and the personification of Woman Zion once again reaches back to the creation account. When God recognized that it was not good for "the human" (hāʾādām) to be alone, the LORD determined to provide a "companion" (Hebrew = ʿēzer).[28] Across the biblical texts, and particularly in the Psalms, ʿēzer is characteristically used to describe God, the creator and savior of Israel (Exod 18:4; Deut 33:7, 26, 29; Pss 33:20; 115:9–11; 121:2; 124:8; 146:5).

---

27. Fischer, "Isaiah," 310.

28. Though so often translated as "helper"—a translation that is totally misleading because it suggests an "assistant," a "subordinate," indeed, in too many cases an "inferior." According to Phyllis Trible, *God and the Rhetoric of Sexuality,* OBT 2 (Philadelphia, PA: Fortress, 1978), 90, "The accompanying phrase, 'corresponding to it' (kenegdô), tempers this connotation of superiority to specify identity, mutuality and equality."

Hence, in the Genesis creation story, the anticipated creation of woman anticipates one like unto God, not unlike the alliance drawn here between the Woman Zion figure as mother and God's own identification with this mother metaphor.

Some may object that the immediately following verses (vv. 14–16) concluding this section undercut the metaphoric identification of God as mother. Instead, the more typical metaphor of the militant warrior deity as one who rescues the people and destroys the enemy with fire presides as the final note in these verses. Yet the juxtaposition of God's identification with the mother Zion metaphor works to recode the sovereignty of God, as defined by the divine warrior deity that immediately follows. This Zion metaphor offers an essential addendum to such a one-dimensional theology. A deity conceived solely as the force who comes in fire, executing judgment with indignation against Israel's enemies (Isa 66:14–16), is inadequate and cannot depict the divine in its fullness.[29] The lifting up of "a new presence of strategies and values already present in the people hidden in the dominated lives of women"[30] is required. Thus, the alternative to divine omnipotence manifested in a warrior god is not impotence, but a yet to be recognized power that gives life and nurtures it.[31] Elevated to kinship with God and even functioning as the metaphor of how God will be with humanity, this extraordinary portrait of Woman Zion challenges the singularity of this warrior model offered by the previously dominant theology.

4. The Woman Zion Metaphor and Isaiah's Eschatology

In the new heaven and new earth envisioned in these final chapters of Isaiah, the portrait of God eclipses one-dimensional simplification. Instead, the mother metaphor with which God identifies, alongside the warrior metaphor, works to thicken and to disclose a more complex theology. Hence in this closing chapter, the profundity of the holy one manifests not solely as a warrior power that overpowers in vv. 14–16 but also as maternal power that brings to life, nurtures, and ultimately empowers the people.

Many have noted the parallels between the opening and closing chapters of Isaiah as grounds for arguing the literary unity of this text. Also worthy of attention are the shifts from beginning to end that render differences such as the personification of Zion as woman. These changes speak of fulfillment of what is visioned and can be actualized, as well as resolution of what was problematic and is now addressed. In the opening chapter of Isaiah, personified Zion receives

---

29. L. Juliana M. Claassens, *Mourner, Mother, Midwife: Reimaging God's Delivering Presence in the Old Testament* (Louisville, KY: Westminster John Knox Press, 2012), 55.

30. Rita Nakashima Brock, "A New Thing in the Land: The Female Surrounds the Warrior," in *Power, Powerlessness, and the Divine: New Inquiries in Bible and Theology*, ed. Cynthia L. Rigby (Atlanta, GA: Scholars Press, 1997), 158.

31. Catherine Keller, "Preemption and Omnipotence: A Niebuhrian Prophecy," in *God and Power: Counter-Apocalyptic Journeys* (Minneapolis, MN: Fortress, 2005), 29–30.

description as a daughter—vulnerable, assailable, and eventually blamed and victimized. In the intervening chapters, the metaphor portrays Zion as woman—mother, wife, divorced, bereaved, abandoned. In the final chapter, she represents not only the disclosure of the new creation but as the epitome of once-broken relationships restored. Such a shift in portrait may qualify Woman Zion as one theological linchpin in the yet to be realized Isaian eschatology.

Across this prophetic text, Zion as female metaphor "progresses from a picture of abandonment and desolation to one of glorious restoration and divine presence."[32] Metaphors are not mere literary vehicles transporting meaning. They also serve to craft and define reality, in this case a new eschatological reality. Here the metaphoric woman represents more than Zion; she makes sense only if she also functions as a cultural exponent that summons a new identity and elevated value for women in this yet to be realized eschatology. In this final chapter, the personified female is no longer threatened but celebrated and surrounded by the divine. She is no longer vulnerable, victimized, or blamed but the source of life and well-being. Finally, she is no longer the representative of a controlled or subjugated class but instead allied with God. Such reversals disclose the radicality of an eschatology that perhaps eclipsed even the prophet's own grasp, the grasp of what would be required regarding women for the eventual actualization of what Isaiah visioned as "a new heavens and new earth!!"

---

32. Rebecca W. Poe Hays, "Sing Me a Parable of Zion: Isaiah's Vineyard (5:1–7) and Its Relation to the 'Daughter Zion' Tradition," *JBL* 135 (2016): 743–61 (760).

Chapter 14

BETWEEN ABSURDITY AND HOPE:
SUFFERING IN THE BOOK OF ISAIAH

Blaženka Scheuer

The Assyrian conquest of Israel in 722 BCE and the Babylonian conquest of Judah in 587 BCE caused a decisive rift in the history of the two kingdoms. Samaria and Jerusalem were destroyed and a considerable segment of the population of the two cities was forced into exile. Only a small number of the Judahite exiles returned to Jerusalem, about 60 years after their first deportation. This experience of wars, destruction, and the near-annihilation of the Israelites is the factor that, perhaps more than any other, left a profound mark on the book of Isaiah. References to suffering can be found throughout the book. Although they primarily reflect the historical circumstances of these two wars, as the texts were collected and transmitted, the theme of suffering also became a hub for theological reflection, confronting Israelite realities time and again over the more than three hundred years of the book's composition.

The present study examines the theme of suffering in Isaiah through the lens of Albert Camus' notion of the absurd.[1] In their struggle to grasp the displacement and suffering of the Israelites, the authors/editors of the book accentuate a sense of the absurd in Israelite existence. Some of the more peculiar notions about divine punishment, such as the concept of the hardening of the heart (Isa 6:10–12), the idea of the suffering servant (52:13–53:12), and the view on YHWH's culpability

---

1. Suffering in the Hebrew Bible also has been considered from the perspective of trauma studies. See the articles in Elisabeth Boase and Christopher Frechette, eds., *The Bible through the Lens of Trauma*, SBL Semeia Studies 86 (Atlanta, GA: SBL, 2016). For a critical reflection on trauma studies and the Bible, see David Janzen, "Claimed and Unclaimed Experience: Problematic Readings of Trauma in the Hebrew Bible," *BibInt* 27 (2019): 163–85.

in the Israelite predicament (63–64) might be read as reactions to the absurdity of Israelite existence in the decades of and after the Babylonian exile.

1. *Albert Camus and the Concept of the Absurd*

Albert Camus characterizes the clash arising between a human desire for significance and meaning, on one hand, and the unresponsive and arbitrary universe on the other. Camus describes it as a feeling of incongruity in life, in which a person does not find any profound reason for living:

> The absurd is born of this confrontation between the human need and the unreasonable silence of the world. This must not be forgotten. This must be clung to because the whole consequence of a life can depend on it. The irrational, the human nostalgia, and the absurd that is born of their encounter—these are the three characters in the drama that must necessarily end with all the logic of which an existence is capable.[2]

Camus develops his understanding of the absurd, and possible human responses to it, in "The Myth of Sisyphus," a philosophical essay that he wrote in 1942 amid the horrors of World War II. Camus presents three possible ways for humans to react to the absurdity of their existence: (1) suicide, (2) faith in God, and (3) rebellion. Camus then rejects the first two options because he sees them as an escape, a way out that robs humans of their dignity and freedom. Responding to the absurd—the experience of terror or great suffering—through physical suicide is an option that takes away one of "the characters of the drama," the human subject. However, Camus argues that "the body shrinks from annihilation,"[3] which is why people go on living despite horrid experiences in life. Correspondingly, responding to the absurd through faith in God represents for Camus a philosophical suicide, which preserves the body but sacrifices the mind for an irrational belief that will enslave the person.

Camus suggests, therefore, that rebellion through an embrace of the absurd is the appropriate reaction because it retains human freedom and dignity. To illustrate this, Camus takes the myth of Sisyphus as an example. In the classical story, Sisyphus is condemned to an eternity of pointless labor: he rolls a massive stone up a mountain, but the moment that he reaches the summit, the stone rolls back down to the valley again. Although Sisyphus knows that his efforts are hopeless and his work meaningless, he is determined to continue. In this awareness of the futility of his labor and in his determination to keep on, Sisyphus embraces the absurd, chooses to live with it, and in doing so, rebels against the absurd. In his rebellion, Camus argues, Sisyphus finds meaning and happiness because amidst the meaningless suffering, he has not lost his dignity.

---

2. Albert Camus, *The Myth of Sisyphus and Other Essays*, trans. Justin O'Brien (New York: First Vintage International, 2005), 28.
3. Camus, *The Myth of Sisyphus*, 8.

Camus' understanding of the absurd illuminates the Israelites' suffering depicted in the book of Isaiah. One might object to the validity of such a project given that the Israelites have faith in a God and have, thus, in Camus' words, taken away one of "the characters of the drama" of the absurd. However, just as is the case with the myth of Sisyphus, the struggle of the Israelites with the problems of evil, human suffering, divine justice, and divine silence described in Isaiah, points to a life of absurdity—despite their recognition of the divine. Faced with endless suffering and loss, the Israelites *experience* the world as absurd.[4] The absurd is born in the clash between their cries and the silence of YHWH.

2. Whose Suffering?

Given the complex history of the composition of the book of Isaiah, a word of clarification about the point of view of this study is necessary. I look at the perception of suffering in the three parts of Isaiah from the perspective of the authors/editors that gave the book its final shape. Most scholars work from a premise that the hand responsible for the final form of Trito-Isaiah is also responsible for editing the entire book, a process that was completed no later than the third century BCE.[5] Thus, Jacob Stromberg argues that the authors of the frame around Trito-Isaiah (56:1–8 and chs. 65–66) arranged and integrated received texts (56:9–59:21; 60–62; 63:1–6; and 63:7–64:12) into the final form of Trito-Isaiah, at the same time leaving their mark on the entire book.[6] In other words, the authors/editors worked with the inherited texts, engaging in a profound dialogue with the traditions found in these texts and adapting them to the realities of their own time.[7]

---

4. For this perspective, I am indebted to Matthew H. Bowker, who applied the concept of the absurd to the book of Job; see Matthew H. Bowker, "The Meaning of Absurd Protest: The Book of Job, Albert Camus, and C. Fred Alford's *After the Holocaust*," *Journal of Psycho-Social Studies* 4 (2011): 1–21.

5. Odil Hannes Steck proposes a precise dating of the final text of the book of Isaiah to 312–311 BCE, and the final redaction of the book to a 30-year span between 302/301 and 270 BCE. See Odil Hannes Steck, *Studien zu Tritojesaja*, BZAW 203 (Berlin: de Gruyter, 1991), 30–40, 192. For critique of Steck's argument, see Joseph Blenkinsopp, *Isaiah 56–66: A New Translation with Introduction and Commentary*, AB 19B (New York: Doubleday, 2003), 57–8, and Lena-Sofia Tiemeyer, "Will the Prophetic Texts from the Hellenistic Period Stand Up, Please!," in *Judah Between East and West: The Transition from Persian to Greek Rule (ca. 400–200 BCE)*, ed. Lester L. Grabbe and Oded Lipschits, LSTS 75 (London: T&T Clark, 2011), 269–72.

6. So also Marvin A. Sweeny, *Isaiah 1–4 and the Post-Exilic Understanding of the Isaianic Tradition*, BZAW 171 (Berlin: de Gruyter, 1988), 185, who writes that "the concerns of the latter part of the book dictated the final redaction of the first part."

7. So also, Jacob Stromberg, *Isaiah after Exile: The Author of Third Isaiah as Reader and Redactor of the Book*, OTM (Oxford: Oxford University Press, 2011). Similarly, also Uwe Becker, "The Book of Isaiah: Its Composition History," in *The Oxford Handbook of Isaiah*, ed. Lena-Sofia Tiemeyer (New York: Oxford University Press, 2020), 37–56.

This process, extending over centuries, resulted in a collection of texts in which history and literary complexity are profoundly intertwined with theology. As they inherited texts and traditions from Isaiah of Jerusalem, from the prophets and communities who wrote about the exile in the spirit of Isaiah, the authors/editors of the last part of the book wanted to come to terms with YHWH's role in and indifference to their suffering. These authors/editors, who had survived the calamities of the exile, perceived themselves as the remnant of Isa 1–39, as the suffering servant of 40–55, and as the righteous, trembling servant of YHWH in 56–66.[8] In their attempts to understand the suffering of the Israelites in the past, they adapted the explanations presented by previous generations, but when trying to cope with their own suffering, the authors/editors launched a protest against the absurdity of YHWH's punishment of them. This approach is evident in Isa 6, 52:13–53:12, and 63:15–64:12.

3. Proto-Isaiah and the Maddening Nature of Punishment

3.1. Suffering...by Inference

Given that the central theme of chs. 1–39 is that of divine punishment for the sins of the Israelites through the horrors of war, one might expect elaborate references to human suffering in this part of the book. However, *explicit* references to suffering are relatively few in the first part of Isaiah. Instead, the sense of immeasurable human suffering is *to be inferred* from the numerous descriptions and metaphors of divine punishment though the violence of war and natural disasters. In these descriptions, suffering can be inferred on three levels. First, and most common, is the suffering of the people, the Israelites as a group. Their suffering is induced by physical injuries, in the form of heavy beatings and extensive wounds to their collective, metaphorical body (1:5-6; 21:10), by devastation and plundering of the land by foreign armies (1:7-8; 5:26-30; 10:6), and by violence in their frantic aggression against each other (9:17). Their suffering is also inferred in those texts that speak of their deportation into exile (5:13-14; 6:12; 7:17; 10:5-7; 39:6-7).[9] In all this, they suffer physically and emotionally through hunger, grief, anxiety, horror, and death (3:25-26; 8:21-22; 9:19-21).

The second level of suffering inferred in chs. 1–39 is that of those less fortunate in Judah and Jerusalem, those who suffer at the hands of men in power. The suffering of this group is, in fact, one of the main reasons for YHWH's collective punishment of the Israelites. The weakest in society—the orphans, the widows, the poor—stand without protection (1:17) and are abused (1:21b-23; 3:14-15; 10:2). They suffer because of the misuse of the resources by the mighty (5:8) or because of a corrupted juridical system in which they find no justice (5:23; and,

---

8. As also argued by Soo J. Kim, "Eschatology in Isaiah," in *The Oxford Handbook of Isaiah*, ed. Lena-Sofia Tiemeyer (New York: Oxford University Press, 2020), 366.

9. See further Dalit Rom-Shiloni, "Exile in the Book of Isaiah," in *The Oxford Handbook of Isaiah*, ed. Lena-Sofia Tiemeyer (New York: Oxford University Press, 2020), 296-7.

in a promise of future change, 29:20–21). To this group, we must add the wives and daughters of the men in power. Although privileged and pleasure-seeking, these women suffer the shame of public humiliation, slavery, and rape because their menfolk lost their privileges or perished in wars and were no longer able to protect them (3:16–26).

Not only the Israelites suffer. YHWH's punishment of the Israelites seems to have started a chain of events upon which the world pivoted. Hence, the Babylonians also experience dread, suffering, and death through war with the Medes (Isa 13), the Philistines suffer from the hand of YHWH (14:30b–31), Moab (15; 25:10b–12) and Edom (34), too. The Egyptians suffer from erratic frenzy against each other and from natural disasters (19:2–10), the Assyrians suffer from slavery and death (31:8–9), nations suffer due to Israelite victory (14:2), and inhabitants of the whole earth suffer from injustice, exploitation, natural disasters, and wars (24:1–13, 19–20).

While there is a strong corporate sense of anguish in these references, the third level of affliction in chs. 1–39 describes the suffering of the prophet himself, caused by the horror of the looming desolation. The prophet describes himself as suffering pain, anguish, bewilderment, confusion, horror, and violent shaking when he is shown the fate of Babylon (21:3–4),[10] and he is utterly heartbroken by the fate of Zion and Jerusalem (22:4).

In a kind of a summary of these tragedies, Proto-Isaiah ends with a strong image of human suffering: the roads are empty, the strong men are broken, and human life is worth nothing (33:7–8). Deeply affected by these events, the earth is scorched and withered (33:9).[11] Such a dissolution of the human existence is maddening and is a paradigmatically absurd predicament. Knowing that the deity in whom they put their trust, whom they believed would protect them, their king, and their land, had turned against them and was the cause of this suffering accentuated the absurdity of their existence. The world no longer made sense for them.

---

10. There has been much debate about the historical background of this text. For a short overview of different solutions, see Brevard S. Childs, *Isaiah: A Commentary*, OTL (Louisville, KY: Westminster John Knox Press, 2001), 148–51. I read this text as describing the prophet's reaction to the horrors of YHWH's punishment *per se*. When YHWH's power is demonstrated in this way, it is terrifying, regardless of whom it affects, as also argued by Delbert R. Hillers, "A Convention in Hebrew Literature: The Reaction to Bad News," *ZAW* 77 (1965): 86–90.

11. Placed between Proto- and Deutero-Isaiah, Isa 33 is best read as an intertextual reinterpretation of the events spoken of in the bulk of Isa 1–55. Thus, Sweeney labels this chapter as a "literary bridge" between the major components of chs. 1–66, and Childs as an "intertextual interpretation" of the major components of chs. 1–55. Marvin A. Sweeney, *Isaiah 1–39: With an Introduction to Prophetic Literature* (Grand Rapids, MI: Eerdmans, 1996), 430, and Childs, *Isaiah*, 246. Cf. also Willem A. M. Beuken, *Isaiah Part II. Volume 2: Isaiah Chapters 28–39*, HCOT (Leuven: Peeters, 2000), 245, who sees in this chapter an "interpretative key" to the epic of YHWH's punishment and deliverance of the Israelites in 1–55.

To understand this new reality, they needed to look for meaningful patterns and to reconsider their system of beliefs. In this process, the careful literary composition of Isa 6, the account of Isaiah's commissioning, played a pivotal role.

3.2. Absurdity of a Disrupted Relationship

The position of the vision narrative of Isaiah 6 in the book of Isaiah suggests that, for the editors, the narrative was not meant to simply account for the call of Isaiah to prophetic ministry but to explain why the prophetic intercession for the people was not enough to prevent the tragedy of the Assyrian assault on Israel and Judah at the end of the eighth century BCE. Additionally, the editors of Isaiah after the Babylonian exile applied this account also to the tragedy of the Babylonian conquest of Judah and Jerusalem in 587 BCE.[12] In this chapter, human suffering is implied in the same way as above, namely, through the tragedy of military aggression, the subsequent deportation of those who survived, and the utter desolation of the land (6:11–13).

The dynamics of absurdity are recognizable in this text. The prophet declares that this tragedy *could not* have been prevented, that YHWH was set on expelling his people from their land (6:12), and that the people were deprived of their ability to do anything that could prevent the disaster (6:9–10). In fact, both the people and the prophet were caught in an absurd existence where nothing was what it should have been: (1) the prophet, whose job would normally be to warn and intercede, was assigned to confuse and mislead; (2) the people, who would normally repent, were hindered from doing so; and (3) YHWH, whose greatness was normally demonstrated through the greatness of his people, was demonstrated through their suffering and fall. This disruption in the fundamental relationship with YHWH—and of the sense of meaningful existence tied to this relationship—defines the absurdity for the Israelites in Isa 1–39.

To counteract the absurdity of this predicament, Isa 6 offers a theological analysis that introduces grounds for hope. This is demonstrated through the suggestion that this absurd state is to be limited in time. Although the destructive force of the situation seems to be absolute, the limitation in time offers hope, albeit a very slight glimpse of it. Hope is expressed, perhaps even more explicitly, in the genre of the unit in which the divine hardening is introduced. We note that the interruption in the YHWH–Israelite relationship, illustrated with the theme of hardening of the heart, is introduced, not as a straightforward oracle of judgment,

---

12. So numerous commentaries, such as Sweeney, *Isaiah 1–39*, 140–1, and Blenkinsopp, *Isaiah 1–39*, 22–4. A great amount of literature has been written on this chapter in Isaiah, and I will refer the reader here simply to commentaries that offer a useful overview of the research, such as H. G. M. Williamson, *A Critical and Exegetical Commentary on Isaiah 1–27: In Three Volumes. Volume 2. Commentary on Isaiah 6–12*, ICC (London: Bloomsbury T&T Clark, 2018), 11–88. The theme of divine hardening has an important bearing on Isa 40–66, see Torsten Uhlig, *The Theme of Hardening in the Book of Isaiah: An Analysis of Communicative Action*, FAT/II 39 (Tübingen: Mohr Siebeck, 2009).

but as a part of a vision report featuring the incomparability of YHWH. Why is this theme juxtaposed with a vision of divine majesty? In my view, the reason is that the senselessness of YHWH's actions in history can only be tolerated if the sovereignty of YHWH's power is reaffirmed at the same time. The absurd is defused with the unfathomable. In other words, the only way for the message of the divine punishment of the Israelites, and of YHWH's distancing from them, to make sense and be accepted was precisely the certainty of YHWH's divine supremacy. Only YHWH's supremacy could counteract the absurdity of the Israelite existence because a supreme deity can never be fully comprehended by humans and can always change plans for the better regarding the human beings. Therefore, the radical hopelessness of Israelite existence after the tragedies of exile could only find its remedy in the strong belief in YHWH's power.

4. *Victimized by Yahweh: Suffering in Deutero-Isaiah*

Isaiah 40–55 acknowledges the suffering of the Israelites in the past: they were victims of war, robbed, cast into dungeons, deported, and their collective metaphorical body was scorched by YHWH's anger (42:22-25; 52:3-4). Their suffering was that of utter destruction: their temple officials were desecrated, the people annihilated (43:28; 48:10), and Jerusalem left in ruins (49:19; 51:3; 54:4). The people had been put into a "furnace of affliction" (48:10) and they had perished. That the suffering of the Israelites led to them dying is suggested by the plant and tree imagery used about them in promises of salvation: the Israelites will rise again, sprouting like grass and like willow out of a dry land that has now been watered (44:3-4). The suffering and death of the exiled Israelites is perhaps most clearly argued in Isa 53.[13] Their collective body was disfigured beyond recogni-

---

13. The identity of the sufferer in this text is contested in scholarship. In my view, the exiled Israelites are the suffering servant of Isa 53, following Tryggve N. D. Mettinger, *A Farewell to the Servant Songs* (Lund: Soc Humaniorum Litterarum Lundensis, 1983). Cf. also Fredrik Hägglund, *Isaiah 53 in the Light of Homecoming after Exile*, FAT/II 31 (Tübingen: Mohr Siebeck, 2008). This view does not deny the possibility that the poem in its origins was about an individual who suffered greatly and possibly on behalf of others, but put in the context of the Babylonian exile, it is best understood as referring to the exiled Israelites. See further Ulrich Berges, "The Servant(s) in Isaiah," in *The Oxford Handbook of Isaiah*, ed. Lena-Sofia Tiemeyer (New York: Oxford University Press, 2020), 324, and Hans-Jürgen Hermisson, "The Fourth Servant Song in the Context of Second Isaiah," in *The Suffering Servant: Isaiah 53 in Jewish and Christian Sources*, ed. Bernd Janowski and Peter Stuhlmacher (Grand Rapids, MI: Eerdmans, 2004), 16–47. For a combination of collective and individual interpretation of the servant's identity in chs. 40–55, see Rainer Kessler, "Kyros und der Eved bei Deuterojesaja: Gottes Handeln in Macht und Schwäche," in *Christus und seine Geschwister: Christologie im Umfeld der Bibel in Gerechter Sprache*, ed. Marlene Crüsemann and Carsten Jochum-Bortfeld (Gütersloh: Gütersloher Verlagshaus, 2009), 150–1.

tion, they were tormented with illness and despised by others (cf. also 49:7), they died, and they received no proper burial.

References to the *present* suffering of the Israelites function as a rhetorical device that forms the basis for YHWH's proclamation of salvation. The Israelites are instructed that they need not suffer from fear and anxiety (41:10, 13, 14; 44:8; 46:12; 51:7, 12–13); from weakness, thirst, and poverty (41:17; 55:1); from blindness and deafness (42:7, 16, 18–19); or from being unwanted by YHWH (49:14). This message, however, was met with skepticism, as we shall see below.

While Isa 40–55 declares that the suffering of the Israelites has now ended, the suffering of other peoples has not. On the contrary, those who serve other deities will suffer shame (42:17; 44:11; 45:16), Babylonians will suffer defeat in war (43:14; 46:1–2; 47), and people from Egypt and Kush will suffer slavery under the redeemed Israelites (45:14). The wicked and evil will never find peace (48:22), the enemies of the Israelites will turn to self-cannibalism (49:26), and those who do not acknowledge YHWH's redemption of the Israelites will be left in torment (50:11). In these texts, it becomes increasingly clear that Isa 40–55 also includes in these groups *those among the Israelites* who do not heed YHWH's offer of redemption, a notion that will be developed in full in the last part of Isaiah. Instead, chs. 40–55 direct the message of salvation to those among the Israelites "who pursue righteousness," "who seek YHWH," "who know the right," and carry YHWH's law in their hearts (51:1, 7). Although Isa 40–55 declares the suffering of the Israelites to be over and proclaims their utter redemption if they only accept the message and act upon it, the sense of the absurdity of their existence lingers.

4.1. Reasoning Away the Absurdity of Suffering

While half a century in the Babylonian exile might have been enough time to make the Israelites ready for divine consolation (40:1), the sense of the absurdity of Israelite existence is not alleviated with such a declaration of YHWH's return. The mistrust that YHWH earned in Isa 6 lingered, and the message about YHWH's return was met with suspicion (40:27; 49:14).

Arguments to rebuff such skepticism in chs. 40–55 follow the same pattern that we have seen in Isa 6. The first argument is that the disruption was limited in time, and YHWH was angry only for a short while (54:7). The second argument builds further on the belief in the incomparability of YHWH and firm conviction of his divine supremacy; humans cannot comprehend the ways of a supreme deity (45:9–13), who has created everything (40:18–31; 51:13–16) and has fought ancient battles (51:9–10). In dialogue with Isa 6, chs. 40–55 seem to go to great lengths to explain that the incomparability of YHWH works now for good for the Israelites. Isaiah 40–55 declares time and again how YHWH's doings now are so very new (45:15), and the Israelites are encouraged to simply accept and rejoice in their recuperation (48:6–8). Because YHWH does not think like a human and because the divine ways are incomprehensible to the Israelites (55:8–9), one might just as well repent, return to YHWH, and rejoice in the renewed relationship (55:6–7). Yet, there is a threat against the sceptics: "woe to him that quarrels with his master…" (45:9). YHWH is agitated and intimidates with a renewed violence against those who question the divine ways.

It seems that these arguments were not enough for the Israelites who had survived the horrors of a life desecrated by war, loss, and forced exile. Therefore, chs. 40–55 declare that YHWH's return to them was also out of concern for the divine reputation (48:9–11). Other deities seem to have seized the opportunity to claim dominance on account of the Israelite demise, and YHWH could not allow that.

Nonetheless, the problem of devastating suffering and the absurdity of Israelite existence in the wake of the Babylonian exile remained. The poem in 52:13–53:12 represents the most profound attempt to render the suffering of the Israelites meaningful.

4.2. Absurd Suffering of the Suffering Servant

The idea that the suffering of the innocent was to bring about salvation of the guilty was not new to the Israelites. Numerous studies have demonstrated how rooted this poem is in Israelite cultic language. The victim is passive and silent (53:7), likened to a lamb or a sheep (traditional sacrificial animals), and is said to carry off the sins of the people (נשא, Isa 53:4; cf. Lev 16:22). The sacrifice is treated as אשם, a concept that "connotes guilt resulting from an offence against God by an infraction of the ritual order, or against another person or persons, constituting a violation of the social order."[14] The suffering of the Israelites under the terrors of the Babylonian exile—they were stricken (נגוע), hurt by God (מכה אלהים), afflicted (מענה), pierced (מחלל), crushed (מדכא), and attacked (הפגיע)—was thereby given a rational explanation that made sense within the Israelite system of belief. It concludes with a joyful affirmation that the suffering remnant, this servant of YHWH has not only survived but has also been glorified.

Read through the lens of absurdity, this poem seems to address the absurd implications of the Israelites' suffering, implying that what has been lost through the events summarized in Isa 6—the familiar world defined by Israelite relationship with YHWH through the cult—has now been restored. But the problem with Isa 53 is that it represents an attempt to reason away the absurdity of suffering, to rationalize the bad, to excuse or legitimize the violence done to the victim. The human victim was dehumanized (lamb) to be kept silent. But the sacrificial lamb and the goat driven out into the desert would protest loudly if they knew. The same applied to the servant, the Israelites, their senses have been muddled (6:10), they could not understand, much less protest what was being done to them.

The authors/editors of the book of Isaiah seem to protest such an attempt at justifying the violence and suffering of the Israelites. Their protest is recognizable as a silent refutation of the explanation given in Isa 53: the servant's glorification

---

14. Joseph Blenkinsopp, "The Sacrificial Life and Death of the Servant (Isaiah 52:13–53:12)," *VT* 66 (2016): 1–14 (5). In this article, Blenkinsopp argues convincingly for the analogy between the servant's mission and the language of the Israelite sacrificial cult.

spurs satisfaction only in the deity (52:13; 53:12). The we-group—usually taken to be the Israelites who did not experience forced exile—never expresses their joy over the sacrifice, only the acknowledgment of their own ignorance of what was going on (53:1–6).[15] In a similar manner, the poem remains un-responded to in the rest of the book of Isaiah.[16] We shall see that there is a pattern by which they saw themselves as the suffering servants of YHWH, but this leads them to give voice to their protest in full (chs. 63–64).

Isaiah 53 uses the language of the cult—a pattern in Israelite relationship to the divine that the Israelites were familiar with—but it does not solve the problem of the absurdity of human suffering. On the contrary, it confirms a reality in which a sovereign deity allows suffering not only for the guilty, but now also for the innocent. While Isa 6 describes a deity who demonstrates his power through punishment of the guilty Israelites, Isa 53 demonstrates YHWH's need for satisfaction through suffering of the innocent Israelites. The absurdity of human existence under such terms is thereby restated. Such an existence will be protested in full in the last part of the book.

5. Retaining Personal Integrity: Suffering in Trito-Isaiah

References to suffering in the last part of the book of Isaiah are few but more specific. Isaiah 56–66 is bracketed with a clarification of the current sufferings of the righteous Israelites, who are persecuted by their unrighteous brethren (56:1–2; 66:5).[17] These servants of YHWH, עבדים, "those who tremble at his word," החרדים (66:2, 5), seem to have been expelled from the community by the civil and religious authority of their fellow Judahites.[18]

In between these verses, the suffering of the oppressed in the society is described in detail: they are the poor, hungry, homeless (58:6–7, 9b–10); those who suffer from corrupt courts, judicial murders; those whose lives count for nothing, who are victims of violent and deadly abuse (59:1–8). The suffering of these people, just as we have seen in chs. 1–39, seems to be a result of a collapse of

---

15. Some scholars identify the "we-group" with nations. See, for instance, Rainer Albertz, *Israel in Exile: The History and Literature of the Sixth Century B.C.E.*, SBLStBibLit 3 (Atlanta, GA: SBL, 2003), 427. In my view, only those among the Israelites who recognize the suffering of the servant for the sake of all the Israelites were counted to the "we-group" of Isa 53, as also argued by Berges, "The Servant(s) in Isaiah," 324.

16. For the influence of Isa 53 on Jewish writings in pre-Christian period, see Martin Hengel with the collaboration of Daniel P. Bailey, "The Effective History of Isaiah 53 in the Pre-Christian Period," in *Suffering Servant: Isaiah 53 in Jewish and Christian Sources* (Grand Rapids, MI: Eerdmans, 2004), 75–146.

17. For analysis and discussion of these two verses, see Blenkinsopp, *Isaiah 56–66*, 148–52.

18. As argued by most commentaries. See, for example, Blenkinsopp, *Isaiah 56–66*, 299–301.

ethical standards in the community. Although it is difficult to ascertain the identity of the oppressors, it is probable that those who oppress the poor and weak in Judahite society at the time of the Persian empire are the same group that harasses and taunts the righteous, trembling ones. This assumption is based on the fact that the punishment of the group of oppressors is the same as the punishment of those who taunt the righteous servants of YHWH: they will suffer hunger, thirst, shame, anguish, and violent death (65:11–16; 66:5). We can infer that the oppressive, taunting people are those who *right now* do not go hungry, thirsty, or are oppressed and abused. In other words, the groups of wicked oppressors, those that exclude the righteous ones from society, are the rich upper class of the community of Yehud under the Persian rule.[19]

Thus, the righteous servants of YHWH, perceiving themselves as "the heirs of the salvation announced to Israel in past Isaianic tradition,"[20] suffer in two respects: they suffer discrimination, and they suffer watching the wickedness of the powerful in their own community. They seek to restore the lost relationship with YHWH through laments and confessions of sin (59:9–15), but their efforts do not pay off. Therefore, the righteous servants of YHWH voice a powerful objection against the absurdity of their situation.

5.1. *Absurd Protest of Isaiah 63–64*

The righteous of Isa 56–66 would have experienced their existence as absurd because their firm belief in the reestablished relationship with YHWH, and the principles of existence that accompany it, did not lead to the expected results. In their theological reflection, therefore, they address the two central arguments given in the previous parts of Isaiah, arguments that concern the limitation of YHWH's anger, and YHWH's divine supremacy. Initially, they restate that precisely because YHWH is a supreme deity, YHWH must control divine anger because humans cannot endure a supreme deity's fury (57:16). This principle is particularly important in a belief system where there were no other deities to turn to.[21] Therefore, the righteous express a forceful complaint against YHWH in 63:15–64:11, a lament that is, perhaps, the most powerful expression of the absurdity of Israelite existence in the book of Isaiah.

The authors/editors of chs. 56–66 object to YHWH's continuous indifference to their needs and their suffering—a predicament that, as we have seen, defines Camus' idea of the absurd. The lament articulates the totality of Israelite dependence on YHWH, expressed through family ties (father and closest kin,

---

19. As also argued by Rainer Albertz, *A History of Israelite Religion in the Old Testament Period. Volume II: From the Exile to the Maccabees*, OTL (Louisville, KY: Westminster John Knox, 1994), 493–507. See also Blenkinsopp, *Isaiah 56–66*, 223–4.

20. Stromberg, *Isaiah after Exile*, 82.

21. In a polytheistic system, a sufferer could always turn to other deities for protection. See Angelika Berlejung, "Sin and Punishment: The Ethics of Divine Justice and Retribution in Ancient Near Eastern and Old Testament Texts," *Int* 69 (2015): 275–7.

63:16; 64:8), political relationship (their sovereign, 63:19), and cultic relationship (YHWH has invoked his name over them, 63:19).[22] Still, the expectations and cries of the Israelites are met with YHWH's disinterest: Jerusalem and the cities of Judah are desolated still, YHWH's temple continues to be trampled (63:18; 64:9–10), and the hearts of the Israelites, in spite of all the promises to the contrary, are still hardened (63:17). The experience of relentless suffering pushes the authors/editors of chs. 56–66 beyond silent acceptance or pious reflections on their own responsibility. In an echo of 6:9–10, the lament asserts that the full responsibility for their suffering is with YHWH. Therefore, they end their protest with a question that was to haunt the times and generations to come: "In view of all this, will you stand aloof, O YHWH? Will you keep silent and afflict us beyond measure?" (Isa 64:11).[23]

Accentuating YHWH's silence in 64:11, the Israelites insist on presenting themselves as witnesses, not of YHWH's power, but of YHWH's indifference. After this, the Israelites do not cry for YHWH's response any more in the book of Isaiah.

6. Conclusions

In *Rethinking the Politics of Absurdity*, Matthew Bowker develops the concept of absurdity as a psychological posture or stance that has bearing on the way an individual lives in society. The absurd stance, Bowker argues, is to refuse to make violence and suffering meaningful, to refuse to give them rational explanations, because only thus can human innocent outrage over experiences of loss, terror, and suffering be preserved.[24] The book of Isaiah bears witness to Israelite outrage over loss, terror, and the suffering of the exile. However, the purpose of the book was not to present a historical record of suffering, but to provide a theological reflection on it, explaining YHWH's role in that experience. In this confrontation between the Israelite need and the unreasonable silence of YHWH, the absurd is born. Following a chronological sequence over centuries, the suffering of the Israelites is experienced, remembered, commemorated, and protested.

Initially, YHWH's punishment of the Israelites through exile and forced displacement is corroborated and explained in Isa 6. But the chapter also presents a protest: YHWH must not rage forever. The Israelites are set in a mode of anticipation. Once the redemption is declared as realized (chs. 40–55),

---

22. See further Blaženka Scheuer, "'Why Do You Let Us Wander, O Lord, from Your Ways?' (Isa 63:17): Clarification of Culpability in the Last Part of the Book of Isaiah," in *Continuity and Discontinuity: Chronological and Thematic Development in Isaiah 40–66*, ed. Lena-Sofia Tiemeyer and Hans Barstad, FRLANT 255 (Göttingen: Vandenhoeck & Ruprecht, 2014), 163–5.

23. In Blenkinsopp's translation, Blenkinsopp, *Isaiah 56–66*, 254.

24. Matthew H. Bowker, *Rethinking the Politics of Absurdity: Albert Camus, Postmodernity, and the Survival of Innocence* (New York: Routledge, 2014), 1–18.

the experienced suffering of the Israelites is sacralized (ch. 53). Again, a silent protest, demonstrated through a relative indifference to Isa 53 in the rest of the book, bears witness to a refusal to rationalize the horrors of Israelite suffering. As the suffering and loss through exile continued to be experienced by the Israelites after the Babylonian exile, and as YHWH continued to meet the Israelite longing with silence and indifference, the authors/editors of the book of Isaiah voice their final absurd protest: they accuse YHWH of causing their suffering to which he is completely indifferent.

Bowker writes: "Absurd protest, then, has a curious aim: to attend to one's loss until some semblance of what was lost has been returned, as if by refusing to comprehend the loss, one could resurrect the object, provoke it back into presence, or 'draw God down' with our desire for explanation and restitution."[25] The absurd protest of the book of Isaiah refuses simplistic explanations, not because no good explanations had been given, but because human suffering must never be tolerated, accepted, or rationalized.[26] Yet, the authors/editors of the book of Isaiah suggest that the violent destruction of meaning in Israelite existence prior to the Babylonian exile did not only signify a loss of something good—a deprivation of YHWH's presence—but signified a recovery of something valuable, an insight worth keeping: that achieving integrity and wisdom is not done through a quiet acceptance of the destructive forces challenging human lives, but through an unyielding refusal to submit to these forces. For the Israelites of this time and onward, therefore, suffering becomes their existence and exile their home.[27]

---

25. Bowker, "The Meaning of Absurd Protest," 9.

26. Bowker argues that such absurd posture "seeks to preserve conditions of rupture, brokenness, irresolution, and meaninglessness rather that to defeat or overturn them." Bowker, *Rethinking the Politics of Absurdity*, 9.

27. Paraphrasing Emil M. Cioran who, in a reflection upon the theme of human alienation, asks: "Is it possible that existence is our exile and nothingness our home?" Emil M. Cioran, *On the Heights of Despair* (Chicago: University of Chicago Press, 1992), 106.

Chapter 15

THE ISAIANIC "UNITY MOVEMENT"
FROM A PERSPECTIVE OF TRAUMA STUDIES:
WITH A SPECIAL FOCUS ON ISAIAH 1–12

Elizabeth Esterhuizen and Alphonso Groenewald

The advent of modern exegesis put an end to the traditional understanding of the unity of the book of Isaiah as the traditional "one-prophet interpretation"[1] was replaced by Berhard Duhm's (1892)[2] proposal of a "three-book interpretation."[3] The dawn of modern Isaianic exegesis, as interpreted by Duhm in his commentary, gave rise to a new literary world in which a distinction was made between the three major sections of the book of Isaiah, namely Proto-Isaiah, Deutero-Isaiah and Trito-Isaiah,[4] which formed the foundation for all subsequent Isaianic research.[5] These three separate parts were however read and interpreted separately from each other without even considering the literary structure of the book as a whole or as a unit.

    1. The "one-prophet interpretation" had indeed been the dominant mode of interpretation in ecclesiastical and theological circles for centuries. See Marvin E. Tate, "The Book of Isaiah in Recent Study," in *Forming Prophetic Literature: Essays on Isaiah and the Twelve in Honor of John D. W. Watts*, ed. James W. Watts and Paul R. House, JSOTSup 235 (Sheffield: Sheffield Academic Press, 1996), 22–56 (25–27), who gives a helpful summary of the "one-book" approach to Isaiah.
    2. Bernhard Duhm, *Das Buch Jesaia*, 5th ed. (Göttingen: Vandenhoeck & Ruprecht, 1968).
    3. See Marvin A. Sweeney, "On the Road to Duhm: Isaiah in Nineteenth-Century Critical Scholarship," in *"As Those Who Are Taught": The Interpretation of Isaiah from the LXX to the SBL*, ed. Claire M. McGinnis and Patricia K. Tull, SBL Symposium Series 27 (Atlanta, GA: SBL Press, 2006), 243–61 (243).
    4. Tate, "The Book of Isaiah," 28–43, gives an overview of the "three-book" approach.
    5. See Ulrich Berges, *The Book of Isaiah: Its Composition and Final Form*, trans. Millard C. Lind, HBM 46 (Sheffield: Sheffield Phoenix Press, 2012), 2–3.

In recent years, however, a paradigm shift of a different nature has once again taken place in Isaianic scholarship, namely scholars have started to ask the question why the book of Isaiah was presented as a unit on one scroll, and how this book can and should be read and interpreted as a literary unit.[6] According to Gentry in the last thirty years we "have witnessed a movement away from viewing this book as a patchwork of sources to considering the meaning of the entire work as a unity. This unity, however, is often perceived as only a *redactional* unity and not an *authorial-compositional* unity."[7] According to him, the work of Ulrich Berges[8] is being instrumental in reversing the old trend and he (Berges) uses the concept of a "literary cathedral"[9] in order to indicate that the book of Isaiah should be read as a literary unity.

Regarding the ascendancy of this movement, it can be noted that Tate[10] had already stated in 1996 that "[t]he one-book approach constitutes a paradigm shift in Isaiah studies," in the post-Duhmian interpretation of the book of Isaiah. In the last 30 to 40 years the "one book of Isaiah" perspective has gained momentum with an increasing number of adherents of this approach, with its focus more on the literary features unifying the book than on the critical segmentation of the book. Although some earlier contributions had paved the way for this approach, in the opinion of Schulz,[11] it was specifically the publication of Roy Melugin's dissertation on Isa 40–55[12] in 1976 which provided the necessary impetus for

---

6. Ronald E. Clements, "The Unity of the Book of Isaiah," *Int* 36 (1982): 117–29, and Rolf Rendtorff, "The Book of Isaiah: A Complex Unity: Synchronic and Diachronic Reading," in *New Visions of Isaiah*, ed. Roy F. Melugin and Marvin A. Sweeney, JSOTSup 214 (Sheffield: JSOT Press, 1996): 32–49. See also Antti Laato, *"About Zion I will not be silent": The Book of Isaiah as an Ideological Unity*, ConBOT 44 (Stockholm: Almqvist & Wiksell, 1988).

7. Peter J. Gentry, "The Literary Macrostructures of the Book of Isaiah and the Authorial Intent," in *Bind Up the Testimony: Explorations in the Genesis of the Book of Isaiah*, ed. Daniel I. Block and Richard L. Schultz (Peabody, MA: Hendrickson Publishers, 2015), 227–53 (227).

8. Gentry, "The Literary Macrostructures," 227: "Ulrich Berges' 1998 monograph, entitled *Das Buch Jesaja: Komposition und Endgestalt*, belongs to this recent trend." This monograph was translated and published with the following title: *The Book of Isaiah: Its Composition and Final Form*.

9. Ulrich Berges, *Isaiah: The Prophet and His Book* (Sheffield: Sheffield Phoenix Press, 2012), 23.

10. Tate, "The Book of Isaiah," 43.

11. Richard L. Schultz, "The Origins and the Basic Arguments of the Multi-Author View of the Composition of Isaiah: Where are We Now and How did We Get There?," in *Bind Up the Testimony: Explorations in the Genesis of the Book of Isaiah*, ed. Daniel I. Block and Richard L. Schultz (Peabody, MA: Hendrickson, 2015), 7–32 (11).

12. See Roy F. Melugin, *The Formation of Isaiah 40–55*, BZAW 141 (Berlin: de Gruyter, 1976), 177: "The reason we could not reconstruct the history of the redaction of chapters

this new direction. The latter also played an important role in the establishment of the SBL's "Formation of the Book of Isaiah Group."[13]

This new development of the last four decades has gained momentum, becoming the dominant approach in the analysis and exegesis of the book of Isaiah. Situating the present study within this development, the following section provides a summarized introduction to Trauma Theory's implications for the analysis of biblical texts, and indeed the text of Isa 1–12 from this trauma perspective and its implication for reading Isaiah as a literary unity.

1. Trauma Theory as a Reading Lens for Biblical Texts

In an innovative—one may even claim provocative—book titled *Holy Resilience: The Bible's Traumatic Origins*[14] David Carr provides an interpretation of the origins of the Old Testament[15] in which he argues that Israel's holy writings arose from a trauma context and speak to human trauma in an ancient as well as modern context.

Since the 1970s one has noticed an exponential increase in the interest biblical scholars have shown in the insights offered by different subject fields and the contribution they can make towards Theology; for example, Anthropology, Psychology, Sociology, Political Science and Economics. A number of biblical scholars have particularly been drawn towards Trauma Theory in terms of the contribution it makes towards an interpretation of different dimensions of human suffering and the ensuing trauma implications it has on the biblical population as well as the reader of the text.[16] O'Connor especially uses Trauma and Disaster Studies, as "[t]hey serve as an 'heuristic' or 'finding' device. They offer spectacles

---

40–55 is connected to the nature of the relationships between these chapters and the book as a whole."

13. See James D. Nogalski, *Introduction to the Hebrew Prophets* (Nashville, TN: Abingdon Press, 2018), 5, on the aims and goals of this new movement. as follows: "Scholars now recognize thematic and lexical *inclusios* (literary bracketing devices framing and focusing the content for readers) linking chapters 65–66 with chapters 1–2 and 11… The creation of such links suggests that the scribes working on Isaiah recognized the developing corpus as a cohesive document in its own right. These links between older and newer material represent more than just artistic decoration. They reflect a conviction that the older material had relevance in new settings."

14. David M. Carr, *Holy Resilience: The Bible's Traumatic Origins* (New Haven, CT: Yale University Press, 2014).

15. Carr also treats the New Testament from Chapters 9 to 12 onwards (pp. 156–243).

16. Christopher G. Frechette and Elizabeth Boase, "Defining 'Trauma' as a Useful Lens for Biblical Interpretation," in *Bible Through the Lens of Trauma*, ed. Elizabeth Boase and Christopher G. Frechette, Semeia Studies 86 (Atlanta, GA: SBL Press, 2016), 161–76 (12); and Daniel L. Smith-Christopher, *A Biblical Theology of Exile*, OBT (Minneapolis, MN: Fortress, 2002), have used Trauma and Refugee Studies in order to interpret the exile.

to 'find' what is hidden beneath the opaque surfaces of human suffering."[17] A hermeneutics of trauma interrelates with the above-mentioned fields of study and inspire new understandings of individual, collective and systemic dimensions of suffering and trauma.[18] The integration of trauma theory into different theological discourses has since opened different possibilities for interdisciplinary research, not only for Theology but also for the Humanities as well.[19]

Morrow's insights in trauma theory is particularly helpful as he defines trauma "as (violent) stress that is sudden, unexpected, or nonnormative, exceeds the individual's perceived ability to meet its demands, and disrupts various psychological needs."[20] The concept of "disruption" is very helpful in order to understand many biblical texts. Trauma has the ability to shatter and fragment the previously constructed sense of self; therefore, individuals and groups seeking recovery need to find new ways to control the internalized violence (trauma) due to their experiences of disintegration. If interpreted in this way, the concept of trauma indicates an experience of "severe dislocation," which causes the "constructed sense of self" to be fragmented and shattered.[21] Trauma, therefore not only disrupts the physical locality but also the mental, spiritual and emotional sphere of individuals and communities.

Morrow's concept of disruption versus recovery can be linked to Janoff-Bulman's psychological concept of "rebuilding shattered assumptions" which she coined during the early 1990s.[22] She developed this concept in order to emphasize why it is important to understand the role which these fundamental assumptions

---

17. Kathleen M. O'Connor, "Reclaiming Jeremiah's Violence," in *The Aesthetics of Violence in the Prophets*, ed. Julia M. O'Brien and Chris Franke, LHBOTS 517 (New York: T&T Clark, 2010), 37–49 (38). See also Alphonso Groenewald, "'Trauma is Suffering that Remains': The Contribution of Trauma Studies to Prophetic Studies," *Acta Theologica Supplementum* 26 (2018): 88–102 (DOI: http://dx.doi.org/10.18820/23099089/actat.Sup26.5).

18. Frechette and Boase, "Defining Trauma," 12.

19. Eric Boynton and Peter Capretto, "Introduction. The Limits of Theory in Trauma and Transcendence," in *Trauma and Transcendence: Suffering and the Limits of Theory*, ed. Eric Boynton and Peter Capretto (New York: Fordham University Press, 2018), 1–14 (1): "Within the humanities, specifically in the past decade, trauma theory has become a robust site of interdisciplinary work. Trauma resonates with scholars in and across disciplines and has become a trope with a distinctive significance."

20. William Morrow, "Deuteronomy 7 in Postcolonial Perspective: Cultural Fragmentation and Renewal," in *Interpreting Exile: Displacement and Deportation in Biblical and Modern Contexts*, ed. Brad E. Kelle, Frank R. Ames and Jacob L. Wright, SBLAIL 10 (Atlanta, GA: SBL Press, 2011), 275–93 (281).

21. Morrow, "Deuteronomy 7 in Postcolonial Perspective," 281.

22. Ronnie Janoff-Bulman, "Rebuilding Shattered Assumptions after Traumatic Life Events," in *Coping: The Psychology of What Works*, ed. C. R. Snyder (New York: Oxford University Press, 1999), 305–23 (305–6).

play in the lives of human beings; in order to comprehend their coping mechanisms they use to cope with traumatic life events.[23] Traumatic life events challenge—we can actually say "shatter"—these basic beliefs or assumptions; and these fundamental assumptions, which are guiding human beings through life, suddenly appear totally inadequate in the face of the experience of a traumatic event.[24] This post-traumatic crisis calls for a renewal of these fundamental assumptions and this process is common in the aftermath of extreme life events.[25] This process of rebuilding can be depicted with the term resilience, being an important concept used in trauma theory.[26] To be resilient indicates the remarkable capacity of trauma survivors to survive and cope with extreme tragic experiences. To be resilient indicates the painful process of re-establishing some of the prior assumptions as well as a reappraisal of events in a positive, meaning-making way.[27] Resilience as a re-building strategy often shapes new opportunities and brings about a shift of the locus.

Carr[28] highlights the fact that Ancient Israel often suffered as a result of different periods of crisis. These crises and subsequent catastrophes over many decades and centuries did not only cause individuals to suffer; indeed, whole communities suffered and their group identities were torn apart. The prolonged exposure to trauma and traumatic events over these different periods of crisis, is firmly imbedded within the generations, which highlights and heightens inter-generational trauma. It furthermore shattered—to use Janoff-Bulman's concept—their assumptions and group identities and subsequently caused them to come to a totally new understanding of themselves. In the view of Schreiter[29] one can live from resilience, or to put it differently, resilience manifests itself in an act of identity affirmation and formation; in other words, "rebuilding shattered assumptions." Texts are social creations and therefore form a part of the process to provide explanation for claimed experience(s). Therefore, text production aims to repair shattered world views in order to restore and create

---

23. Ronnie Janoff-Bulman, *Shattered Assumptions: Towards a New Psychology of Trauma* (New York: Free Press, 1992).

24. Janoff-Bulman, "Rebuilding Shattered Assumptions," 311.

25. Janoff-Bulman, "Rebuilding Shattered Assumptions," 305–6. See also Janoff-Bulman, *Shattered Assumptions*, 115–41.

26. See Carr, *Holy Resilience*.

27. Janoff-Bulman, *Shattered Assumptions*, 140, who infers as follows: "Yet the cognitive strategies used by trauma survivors attest to the possibility for some human choice even in the face of uncontrollable, unavoidable negative outcomes. These choices reside in the interpretations and reinterpretations, appraisals and reappraisals, evaluations and reevaluations made of the traumatic experience and one's pain and suffering."

28. Carr, *Holy Resilience*, 8–9.

29. Robert J. Schreiter, "Reading Biblical Texts through the Lens of Resilience," in Boase and Frechette, eds., *Bible Through the Lens of Trauma*, 193–207 (201).

a new group cohesion.[30] In the following section the focus will be on the first subsection of the book of Isaiah and to discuss three themes which contributed to this group cohesion within the Isaianic community. The question is whether a perspective from trauma studies can contribute to the understanding of the sub-section Isaiah 1–12.

2. Isaiah 1–12

If one studies Isa 1–12 as a sub-section within the book of Isaiah from a trauma perspective, one notices that this subsection moves between judgment and salvation.[31] This movement on the one hand confirms traumatic disaster and despair and on the on the other hand this movement reverberates what could be depicted as resilience and hope.[32] It commences with an accusation against Jerusalem because of its disloyalty towards God (1:2–9)[33] and concludes with a prayer of thanksgiving for its future restoration (12:1–6).[34]

The text of Isa 1–12 thus reflects the constant threat of war and chaos which was characteristic of the lives of the Judeans.[35] On the one hand, these twelve chapters contain harsh words of judgment for the city and its leaders because of their role in creating an unjust and corrupt society, and on the other hand, they contain inspiring texts in which a future for the city and its people is imagined beyond the judgment they will experience. Therefore, the reader often has the feeling that he/she is swayed back and forth between these opposite two poles, taking the reader into one direction and then back in the opposite direction. The

---

30. David Janzen, "Claimed and Unclaimed Experience: Problematic Readings of Trauma in the Hebrew Bible," *BibInt* 27 (2019): 163–85 (165).

31. Berges, *Isaiah: The Prophet and His Book*, 24, and Leslie J. Hoppe, *Isaiah*, New Collegeville Bible Commentary 13 (Collegeville, MN: Liturgical Press, 2012), 11.

32. Elizabeth Esterhuizen, *A Study of the Tension between Despair and Hope in Isaiah 7 and 8 from a Perspective of Trauma and Posttraumatic Growth* (http://hdl.handle.net/10500/22263; Pretoria: Unisa, 2016), 59.

33. Ronald E. Clements, "Isaiah 1.1–31: Israel Summoned to Repentance—The Introduction to the Isaiah Book," in *Jerusalem and the Nations: Studies in the Book of Isaiah*, ed. Ronald E. Clements, HBM 16 (Sheffield: Sheffield Phoenix Press, 2011), 213–28 (214). See also Alphonso Groenewald, "The Transformation of the City of Zion: From Decadence to Justice and Prophetic Hope (Is. 1:1–2:5)," *HTS Teologiese Studies/Theological Studies* 72/1 (2016): 1–5 (4) (a3568) (http://dx.doi.org/10.4102/hts.v72i1.3568).

34. Hoppe, *Isaiah*, 11. See also Clements, "Isaiah 1.1–31," 214, and Alphonso Groenewald, "'For Great in Your Midst is the Holy One of Israel' (Is 12:6b): Trauma and Resilience in the Isaianic Psalm," *HTS Teologiese Studies/Theological Studies* 73/4 (2017) (a4820) (https://doi.org/10.4102/hts.v73i4.4820).

35. Elizabeth Esterhuizen and Alphonso Groenewald, "Towards a Theology of Migration: A Survival Perspective from Isaiah 1–12," *Transilvania* 10 (2021): 34–41 (36), https://revistatransilvania.ro/wp-content/uploads/2021/12/Transilvania-10.2021-34-41.pdf.

text not only puts into words the harsh realities of a political and military crisis, but also visualizes a future beyond trauma and disaster, namely of a future beyond the immediate threats.[36]

To conclude this section, we have seen that Isaiah has often been described as a prophet of judgment. The announcement of YHWH's judgment to the people and their leaders fulfils a prominent role in the message of the book and should be read against the background of the broken relationship with God. On the other hand, we have seen that the book oscillates between the announcement of judgment and salvation and that this tension characterizes the book of Isaiah.[37]

Against this background, we will only focus on two themes which form an important part of this tension between judgment and salvation, or despair and hope. These two themes can also be linked to a trauma perspective within Isa 1–12 and are the following: (1) the concept of the "We-group" and (2) the concept of "that day"/"the day of the Lord." The following discussion cannot be exhaustive, but it provides an orientation regarding these two themes.

2.1. We-group

The first theme which connects to both judgment and salvation in the book of Isaiah, and therefore is relevant for a trauma reading perspective of this book, is the idea of the protection of a small righteous group who is called the "we-group."[38] The "remnants," who will remain, are first mentioned in Isa 1:9 (שריד). Chapter 1 already contains harsh criticism of Zion's wickedness and indicates what should be done in order to bring about a change in the society. The choice is between one of two options: either to repent and "the red stains of sin will turn to white" (1:18)—in other words, have either salvation or hope—or, if not, to face disaster and despair when continuing on the old pathways. Eventually it will cause a

---

36. Hoppe, *Isaiah*, 11, infers that Isaiah "was certain that Jerusalem was to undergo a severe crisis that included political impotence and military defeat. Even more devastating would be the loss of and exile from the land that God promised to ancient Israel's ancestors. But beyond this judgment on Jerusalem was the promise of a new city ruled by a good king who led a people committed to justice."

37. Frederik Poulsen, *Representing Zion: Judgement and Salvation in the Old Testament*, Copenhagen International Seminar (New York: Routledge, 2015), 31. See also Carol J. Dempsey, "Isaiah," in *The Paulist Biblical Commentary*, ed. José E. A. Chiu et al. (Mahwah, NJ: Paulist Press, 2018), 604–66 (605): "The test is the poetic vision that captures the drama of the life of a community living under peril and promise. The main character is Isaiah, whose dynamic proclamations are filled with passion as he warns, upbraids, instructs, and comforts his people either with words of woe or words of hope."

38. Hyun C. P. Kim, *Reading Isaiah: A Literary and Theological Commentary*, Reading the Old Testament (Macon, GA: Smyth & Helwys, 2016), 17–8. He also states that "whichever reconstruction theory holds true, during and after the exile, the 'we'-group evidently signified the penitent followers of the righteous prophet as the servant's disciples and Zion's offspring—whether the remainees or the returnees" (18).

cleansing process which will lead to destruction. Chapter 1 is thus very straightforward in saying that the transformation of Zion will cause a radical judgment of the disobedient and rebellious within. In spite of the pain of the disaster being brought about by the destruction, one can assume that the positive side of this disastrous process will be that it will leave behind a righteous remnant.[39]

Berges[40] emphasizes that this is very important information which the reader receives here at the beginning of the book, consequently challenging the reader already in ch. 1 to make the decision whether he or she wants to belong to the group of the "remnant" (cf. 4:3;[41] 7:22; 10:20–22; 11:11, 16); namely the one from within, with whom God will continue the history of God's people. The concept of the remnant is noticeably prominent in the book of Isaiah, not only because of the sheer number of its occurrences in the book, but also because the tension between judgment and salvation is taken up in this motif. Regard the significance of the motif as a literary feature, King[42] infers as follows:

> [W]hile the positive aspects of the remnant in Isaiah are almost universally recognized, one neglected dimension is the use of the motif as a word of judgment itself. Here it functions not as evidence of YHWH's mercy and blessing but rather as a picture of the severity of judgment. While the former may not be completely absent, the emphasis falls on the negative aspect of the motif in the latter.

The sudden appearance of a "we"(-group), within a context where a second person plural discourse dominates, discloses a situation in both the text and in life where the author(-audience) opposes the "other"-group within the community.

---

39. Hayyim Angel, "Prophecy as Potential: The Consolations of Isaiah 1–12 in Context," *JBQ* 37 (2009): 3–10 (3). See also Barry G. Webb, "Zion in Transformation: A Literary Approach to Isaiah," in *The Bible in Three Dimensions: Essays in Celebration of Forty Years of Biblical Studies in the University of Sheffield*, ed. David J. A. Clines et al., JSOTSup 87 (Sheffield: JSOT Press, 1990), 65–87 (69).

40. Berges, *Isaiah: The Prophet and His Book*, 27.

41. See Nogalski, *Introduction*, 7, who infers as follows: "The final thematic unit in Isaiah 1–4 addresses the remnants who survive Jerusalem's destruction (4:2–6). This passage presupposes that the punishment anticipated in ch. 3 has been executed… The fact that his passage addresses those in the aftermath of Jerusalem's devastation has led a number of scholars to treat the text as a later reflection upon the consequences of Jerusalem's destruction that also anticipates a time when YHWH's glory will return to Jerusalem (4:5–6)." Webb, "Zion in Transformation," 72, also comments as follows regarding ch. 4: "Here remnant terminology is introduced for the first time, making explicit wat was implicit in chs. 1 and 2."

42. Andrew M. King, "A Remnant Will Return: An Analysis of the Literary Function of the Remnant Motif in Isaiah," *JESOT* 4 (2015): 145–69 (146).

This "we" is clearly in opposition to the plural "you" and the self-understanding of the "we"-group is defined as a group of a "few survivors" (שריד כמעט). The latter group clearly is a minority group—within the larger group—with whom it shares an experience of trauma and disaster.[43] The common notion in trauma studies is usually that when trauma presents, an individual or a section of a community within the bigger framework of a population is affected and desolate. If this is the supposition, the "we" are possibly the remaining group of trauma survivors within the broader community, which may include individuals but also the collective.

In the opinion of Conrad[44] the audience here in the beginning of the book of Isaiah is a community of survivors with a clear minority status within the Judean society (cf. Isa 1:9). This community feels powerless, as is indicated by the characterization of their opponents as the corrupt and incompetent leaders of the society (e.g. Isa 1:10, 23, 26, 27). This community suffers trauma as it is threatened by murder and bloodshed (e.g. Isa 1:21, 24). According to Smith-Christopher[45] one should always consider the impacts that suffering and traumatic events have on individuals as well as groups and specifically the effect trauma has on the "constructed sense of self."[46]

Regarding this constructed sense of the self, Morgan[47] infers that "[t]he characteristics of the remnant motif in Isaiah 1–39 differ from those in Isaiah 40–66, largely due to issues regarding composition, audience and historical concerns. From the outset of the book, Daughter Zion has already suffered from war and brutality (Isa 1:7–8), and the surviving community recognizes that it is only due to Yahweh's mercy that anyone from Judah is still alive (Isa 1:9)." In the reconstruction of their self-identity the "remnants" are the hope of the future "who will play significant roles in the theological development throughout the book of Isaiah."[48]

Although only a few would remain, this motif is an important contributing factor to the literary plotline of the whole of book of Isaiah, and "[t]he initial

---

43. Edgar W. Conrad, *Reading Isaiah*, OBT (Minneapolis, MN: Fortress, 1991), 89. See also Alphonso Groenewald, "Isaiah 1:4–9 as a Post-exilic Reflection," *JSem* 20 (2011): 87–108.

44. Conrad, *Reading Isaiah*, 156–7.

45. Daniel L. Smith-Christopher, *Micah: A Commentary*, OTL (Louisville, KY: Westminster John Knox Press, 2015), 44.

46. Morrow, "Deuteronomy 7," 281.

47. David M. Morgan, "Remnant," in *Dictionary of the Old Testament Prophets: A Compendium of Contemporary Biblical Scholarship*, ed. Mark J. Boda and J. Gordon McConville (Downers Grove, IL: IVP Academic/Inter-Varsity Press, 2012), 658–64 (660).

48. Kim, *Reading Isaiah*, 33. See in this regard Nogalski, *Introduction to the Hebrew Prophets*, 6: "In short, virtually every motif appearing in the accusatory rhetoric of Isaiah 1 returns at the end of the book as part of promises for the remnant who will survive YHWH's coming judgment."

image regarding the remnant[49] motif is that of a tenth of a people who survive divine judgment, and they serve as the 'holy seed' who will repopulate the land (Isa 6:13)."[50] The historical drama of Isa 7 and 8 presents three children with significant names, and the first to appear is *Shear-jashub* (שאר ישוב "A-Remnant-Turns Back" or "A-Remnant-Will-Return"—Isa 7:3)—the prophet's son. The child is present to embody the message and functions as a sign to both King Ahaz and his father, namely that King Rezin of Aram and King Pekah of Israel will return to their countries as the "fire stumps" that are still smouldering (7:4). What is clear is that the enemies of the north will not survive and that they will be cut down. In this context the name *Shear-jashub* embodies hope and comfort. The dualism in the name implies that there is hope, but also that despair is also a breath away. Isaiah 10 offers a further development of *Shear-jashub* when it refers to Judah's continued existence and this time is not in the context of Judah's defeated enemies (Isa 7). When YHWH declares that a "remnant will return," it is a reference to the people who will survive ("remnant of Jacob") the destruction which the southern kingdom will experience (Isa 10:20–23), firstly by the hand of the Neo-Assyrian armies, and secondly by the hand of the Neo-Babylonian armies. Even though the remnant will be dispersed among the surrounding nations (Isa 11:11–12), YHWH will see to it that they will return to the land.[51]

Seen from a trauma perspective the name *Shear-jashub* reiterates the message of hope that is available for the remnants. In order to survive the trauma, there has to be hope for a new and better outcome. The hope for a new beginning is predicted by the prophet in Isa 11. A new righteous (צדק) leader shall emerge so that "there will be a highway for the remnants of His people" (Isa 11:16) to return. Although the remnants are not saved from trauma or judgment, there is the possibility of hope through resilience. Although they are threatened by the Assyrians and later the Babylonians, they will return. The importance of the message of the remnants in the beginning of the book is to emphasize the choice they all have: either they listen to the word of YHWH, as the "we-group" do, or they can carry on in their sinful ways. The warning expressed in 1:19–20 is quite straightforward: "If, then, you agree and give heed, you will eat the good things of the earth; but if you refuse and disobey, you will be devoured by the sword. For it was the Lord (YHWH) who spoke."

2.2. "That day" (ביום ההוא) / "The day of the Lord" (יום יהוה)

The next trauma marker we can refer to in the book of Isaiah is the idea of "that day" (ביום ההוא). The high number of occurrences of "in that day" in the book of Isaiah is conspicuous: of the 45 references, 18 occur in Isa 1–12 and 22 in Isa

---

49. Righteous remnants: שאר / שארית. In Isa 1–12 (singular noun): Isa 10:20, 21(2×), 22; 11:11, 16. The rest of the book: Isa 14:22; 16:14; 28:5; 37:31, 32.
50. Morgan, "Remnant," 660.
51. Morgan, "Remnant," 660.

13–27.⁵² We encounter the first reference to "that day" (ביום ההוא) already in Isa 2:11.⁵³ The references to "that day" have multiple connotations within the first section of the book of Isaiah. Firstly, it refers to the judgment of the wicked people on "that day," because they compromised YHWH's holiness. Secondly, it is a reference to the re-establishment of YHWH's divine glory in Zion, together with the remnants referred to as the "we-group." Finally, further references to "that day" is aimed at the worship in Jerusalem and at those who threaten that worship.

The book of Isaiah contains several references to the concept the "Day of Lord"; namely with the phrase יום יהוה as well as its variations.⁵⁴ Sweeney⁵⁵ observes that the phrase "day of YHWH" (יום יהוה) and its variations appear often within chs. 1–33, and are related to the formula "in that day" (ביום ההוא). In Isa 2:12 we have a reference to the "day for the Lord of Hosts" (יום ליהוה צבאות), which gives expression to the fact that YHWH's sovereignty in rule over the nations and their idols is clearly established. The picture of the "day of YHWH" (יום יהוה) calls to the reader's mind a picture of terror and panic because YHWH's judgment is directed towards everybody who does not acknowledge YHWH. Isaiah 2:20–21 explicitly refers to the nations who will leave their idols when YHWH's divine presence is evidently inescapable.⁵⁶

Hoppe⁵⁷ notes that the motif "day of YHWH" (יום יהוה) is quite common in the prophetic tradition (cf., e.g., Isa 2:12; 13:6; Jer 17:16–18; Ezek 30:3; Joel 1:15; Amos 5:18–20). This day will speak about YHWH's victory over all the enemies, but even Israel will not be saved from YHWH's judgment because of the injustices the poor are suffering. People will abandon the other deities in favour of exclusive service to YHWH. When Isaiah describes the terrors people will experience on this day, he declares three times that people will need to hide themselves among

---

52. Berges, *The Book of Isaiah*, 148.

53. Cf. Isa. 2:11, 17, 20; 3:7, 18; 4:1, 2; 5:30; 7:18, 20, 21, 23; 10:20, 27; 11:10, 11; 12:1, 4.

54. Joel D. Barker, "Day of the Lord," in *Dictionary of the Old Testament Prophets. A Compendium of Contemporary Biblical Scholarship*, ed. Mark J. Boda and J. Gordon McConville (Downers Grove, IL: IVP Academic/Inter-Varsity Press, 2012), 132–43 (137).

55. Marvin A. Sweeney, *Isaiah 1–39: With an Introduction to Prophetic Literature*, FOTL 16 (Grand Rapids, MI: Eerdmans, 1996), 43.

56. Barker, "Day of the Lord," 137. Carol J. Dempsey, "Themes and Perspectives in the Prophets: Truth, Tragedy, Trauma," in *The Old Testament and Apocrypha*, ed. Gale A. Yee et al., Fortress Commentary on the Bible (Minneapolis, MN: Fortress, 2014), 649–71 (659), infers as follows: "Many prophetic proclamations were words of judgment. Amos inaugurated the concept of the Day of the Lord, which was a time of judgment and condemnation (5:18–20) for a people guilty of many social injustices (2:4–5, 6–8; 4:1–3; 5:7–12)." See also Göran Eidevall, *Amos: A New Translation with Introduction and Commentary*, AB 24G (New Haven, CT: Yale University Press, 2017), 162–6 for a discussion of Amos 5:18–20 regarding the "Day of YHWH."

57. Hoppe, *Isaiah*, 17–18.

the caves and the rocks in order to escape the unavoidable judgment of YHWH (Isa 2:10, 19, 21).[58]

In Isa 7 we find two narrative reports (7:1–9, 10–17) which are meant to be read together. These two reports are followed by a series of four "on that day" sayings which are made regarding future attacks form Egypt and Assyria.[59] According to Esterhuizen and Groenewald[60] the subsequent section (7:18–25) consists of four shorter passages (7:18–19, 20, 21–22, 23–25) and each of these four passages commences with the introductory phrase "on that day" (ביום ההוא). These four passages expand the warnings that had been made in the preceding narrative report concerning the king of Assyria (7:17), who will be the vehicle causing the day of judgment and disaster to take place. This will be a dim event for Judah as terror will take hold of the land and its inhabitants.[61] The first two "on that day" (ביום ההוא) sayings describe what YHWH will do to the people and the land of Judah, and the last two statements specify the impact of YHWH's actions on the people who are still living in Judah, specifically the agricultural devastation of the land.[62]

In Isa 11 the prophet spells out what it would be like for the remnants to return to Judah and Jerusalem. On "that day" a righteous rod from the stem of Jesse (Isa 11:1, 10) shall come forth and "from that day on the earth shall be full of knowledge of the Lord" (11:9). The forgotten remnant will return on a highway of his people from Assyria (11:16) and a new dawn of hope will replace the trauma which had been experienced.

At the end of the first subsection we have a short hymn of thanksgiving (12:1–6) for Jerusalem's deliverance from despair, as well as praising God for the hope and salvation that is to follow. In this song of thanksgiving the prophet praises YHWH for the promise of hope after the disaster and experience of trauma. The threefold occurrence of the noun ישועה ("salvation") emphasizes a crucial point here, namely the prophet expresses the hope that "in that day" (1a) "the comprehensive salvation accomplished by YHWH will cause the trauma to come to an end."[63]

58. Hoppe, *Isaiah*, 17–18.
59. Nogalski, *Introduction*, 9.
60. Elizabeth Esterhuizen and Alphonso Groenewald, "'And it shall come to pass on that day, the Lord will whistle for the fly which is at the end of the water channels of Egypt, and for the bee which is in the land of Assyria' (Is 7:18): Traumatic Impact of the Covid-19 Virus as a Lens to Read Isaiah 7:18–25," *HTS Teologiese Studies/Theological Studies* 77.3 (2021): 1–7 (4) (a6333) (DOI: https://doi.org/10.4102/hts.v77i3.6333).
61. See also A. Joseph Everson, *The Vision of the Prophet Isaiah: Hope in a War-Weary World: A Commentary* (Eugene, OR: Wipf & Stock, 2019), 36–7; Kim, *Reading Isaiah*, 62, and Tull, *Isaiah 1–39*, 158.
62. Nogalski, *Introduction*, 9.
63. See Alphonso Groenewald, "'For great in your midst is the Holy One of Israel' (Is 12:6b): Trauma and resilience in the Isaianic Psalm," *HTS Teologiese Studies/Theological Studies* 73, no. 4 (2017), 4 (DOI: https://doi.org/10.4102/hts.v73i4.4820).

This song of thanksgiving concludes the first major subsection of the book of Isaiah and indeed functions as a meaning-making text when read against the background of trauma and disaster described in this first major subsection. This song transcends the trauma and anticipates survival and resilience, as the "we-group" hopes that God will do something notable to them. We have read of confrontation, warning and promise and this community is now invited to become part of this story of salvation, hope and resilience.[64] In other words, this is part of a process which has been described as "rebuilding shattered assumptions."

3. Conclusion

In this contribution the focus began with a brief note on the movement which has changed the face of the studies of the book of Isaiah, namely the "unity movement" with its focus on the text of Isaiah as a literary unity—without denying the possibility that the book of Isaiah took its final form over many centuries. Secondly, the focus shifted to a brief overview of trauma theory—which has been used as a reading lens in Biblical Studies in the last two to three decades—with the implication of a trauma reading for the book of Isaiah. In the last part attention was paid to two important themes, namely the concept of the "we-group" (remnant) as well as the theme of the day of YHWH and "this day." Both these themes were briefly dealt with (only within Isa 1-12) as they have major implications for a more detailed study of the book of Isaiah—read as a literary unity—from a trauma perspective.

The prophecy of Isaiah as judgment and salvation oracles also represents the notions of despair and hope as possible tension and trauma tendencies. The themes of the remnant and the day of YHWH are both embedded in intergenerational memories and historical collective trauma. The reader is drawn into the imagined looming threat, but also out of the nothingness of despair.

The theologizing reinvention of the remnant-group is part of the process of rebuilding that can be associated with the idea of "resilience." This group has remarkably established itself to survive and to cope with the current life-experiences. However, the group has not only engaged in a reappraisal of events, but has also re-established itself in a positive and meaning-making way. We have seen that their resilience, as a re-building strategy, has shaped new opportunities with a shift of the locus. The book of Isaiah—when read as a literary unit—creates the hope that YHWH would give grace to this group of remnants, and by extension to all humanity, if they would believe the salvation that what is promised to them according to the book of Isaiah.

---

64. Groenewald, "'For great in your midst," 4.

Chapter 16

UNITY AND TRANSLATION CRITICISM:
THE CASE OF THE PESHITTA TRANSLATION

Attila Bodor

Modern biblical scholars often consider the books of the Hebrew Bible to be a puzzle made up of individual pieces originating from different sources that cannot easily be put together. This is particularly true for the study of the book of Isaiah, whose pieces are often treated as separate literary units. In contrast, ancient translations considered the Hebrew text of Isaiah in its entirety. This essay illustrates this tendency using the Syriac translation, commonly called the Peshitta (P), which offers a rare insight into the early holistic reading of Isaiah. The paper presents how the P translator unifies different Isaianic passages with the motif "God as supporter/helper." The evidence shows that reader-oriented interpretation, which often characterizes the Isaianic unity movement, has much in common with the procedures of the ancient translations.

Therefore, the early translations of the Hebrew Bible, such as P, are also an important source for exploring the holistic interpretation of Isaiah. The P renderings examined in this study indicate that, in most cases, unity in the Isaianic passages is the result of the perception/interpretation of the reader/translator. Consequently, the unity movement should pay more attention to appropriately distinguishing between the unity of the original author(s)/editor(s) and its later reception.

1. *Unity and Translation*

In his 2008 essay on the unity movement, Roy F. Melugin outlines different ways in which scholars interpret the book of Isaiah as a whole.[1] While the unity

---

1. Roy F. Melugin, "Isaiah 40–66 in Recent Research: The 'Unity' Movement," in *Recent Research on the Major Prophets*, ed. Alan J. Hauser (Sheffield: Sheffield Phoenix Press, 2008), 142–94.

movement primarily incorporates synchronic and diachronic interpretations, new approaches, such as reader-response and canonical criticism, have also been discussed.[2] Melugin uses several studies to demonstrate that the holistic reading of Isaiah is a complex issue that extends beyond the Isaianic text itself.[3] Indeed, the unity of Isaiah is also affected by readers who play a constitutive role in the interpretation of the text. As reader-response criticism has argued, readers construct the book as a whole, even though the text guides the competent reader.

This method implies that ancient translations of Isaiah should be taken into consideration because the translators, as competent readers, could also constitute the unity of a book. In fact, lexical choices, translation equivalents, and harmonizations shape the holistic reading of the original. The translation can either emphasize or neglect the intertextual links within its source text as well as create new links that construe the book differently as a whole. Therefore, assessing the target text's use of the source text, especially examining the interpretative potential that results from its translation choices, represents a rich opportunity to explore the unity of Isaiah.

However, the unity movement did not pay sufficient attention to translation criticism. For instance, Carr's essay includes a brief survey about the ancient text reception of the unity of Isaiah, but he does not touch upon the ancient translations.[4] Nevertheless, translations have increasingly gained importance in recent years, and biblical scholars have shown that they are not merely secondary text-critical tools. Instead, they are literary works that both construct and interpret the message of their source texts.[5] Hence, ancient translations are "potentially a carrier of theological motivated exegesis"[6] that may also affect the unity of their source text.

The present study focuses on this issue and examines whether and how a translation constructs the unity of a text. As a case study, the P translation of Isaiah (P-Isa) is explored,[7] which is an excellent witness to the early reception of

---

2. Melugin, "Isaiah 40–66," 177–94.

3. For a reader-oriented interpretation of Isaiah, see Edgar W. Conrad, *Reading Isaiah*, OBT 27 (Minneapolis, MN: Fortress, 1991); Katheryn Pfisterer Darr, *Isaiah's Vision and the Family of God*, LCBI (Louisville, KY: Westminster John Knox, 1994), 23–34; David M. Carr, "Reading Isaiah from Beginning (Isaiah 1) to End (Isaiah 65–66): Multiple Modern Possibilities," in *New Visions of the Book of Isaiah*, ed. Roy F. Melugin and Marvin A. Sweeney, JSOTSup 214 (Sheffield: Sheffield Academic Press, 1996), 188–218.

4. Carr, "Reading Isaiah," 193–7.

5. For a brief survey of the exegetical character of the ancient translations, see Emanuel Tov, *Textual Criticism of the Hebrew Bible*, 3rd ed. (Minneapolis, MN: Fortress, 2012), 117–22.

6. Tov, *Textual Criticism*, 120.

7. For the P translation in general, see Michael P. Weitzman, *The Syriac Version of the Old Testament: An Introduction*, UCOP 56 (Cambridge: Cambridge University Press, 1999). For P-Isa, see Ludwig Warszawski, *Die Peschitta zu Jesaja (Kap. 1–39), ihr Verhältnis zum massoretischen Texte, zur Septuaginta und zum Targum* (Berlin: Druck von H. Itzkowski,

the Hebrew text of the book. As Weitzman notes, "this is the earliest translation of the whole canon into another Semitic language...and, at the very least, shows how the Hebrew text was understood at a particular (if as yet unidentified) time and place."[8] Subsequently, this essay will focus on a single unifying motif concerning God's representation in P-Isa, namely, "God as supporter/helper."

2. A Case Study: God Is Supporter and Helper[9]

That people are not self-sufficient but require help from God represents a *leitmotif* in the Old Testament. However, the explicit statement that God helps or is a helper (i.e., the verb עזר or its substantivized form referring to God) does not occur frequently in the Hebrew Bible.[10] It is the later books of the Hebrew Bible, such as Psalms and Chronicles, that emphasize this divine attribute.[11] Accordingly, in the Hebrew text of the book of Isaiah, God is the exclusive subject of the verb עזר ("to help") in the second part of the book (Deutero-Isaiah), which likely mirrors a post-exilic redaction.[12] In contrast, P-Isa emphasizes this divine feature consistently, even in cases where the Hebrew exemplar lacks this motif. Indeed, departing from the Hebrew text, it often depicts God as a supporter (*msy'n'*) of his people or one who helps (*'dr*) his people,[13] thereby creating a new motif unifying both the text and theology of Isaiah. This study will examine five divergent renderings within P-Isa that, using the same motif, connect different passages of Isaiah and provide a unified image of God.

1897); Heinrich Weisz, *Die Peschitta zu Deuterojesaia und ihr Verhältnis zu MT., LXX. u. Trg.* (Halle: n.p., 1893); Arie van der Kooij, *Die alten Textzeugen des Jesajabuches: Ein Beitrag zur Textgeschichte des Alten Testaments*, OBO 35 (Freiburg: Universitätsverlag; Göttingen: Vandenhoeck & Ruprecht, 1981), 258–98; Attila Bodor, *The Theological Profile of the Peshitta of Isaiah*, THBS 5 (Leiden: Brill, 2021).

8. Weitzman, *The Syriac Version*, 2.

9. This section represents a slightly revised version of an earlier draft of § 1.2 (Chapter 2) of my monograph on the interpretative renderings in P-Isa: cf. Bodor, *The Theological Profile*, 37–44.

10. See *HALOT*, 811: "God helps men"—Gen 49:25 (elsewhere only in the later books of the OT, and esp. in Chronicles, is God the subject). The substantivized form of the verb עזר referring to God occurs in Exod 18:4; Deut 33:7, 29; Pss 20:3; 115:9–11; 121:2; 124:8.

11. For this verb in Chronicles, see Peter Welten, *Geschichte und Geschichtsdarstellung in den Chronikbüchern*, WMANT 42 (Neukirchen-Vluyn: Neukirchener Verlag, 1973), 158.

12. There are only four Deutero-Isaian passages where God is the subject of the verb עזר ("help"): Isa 41:10–14 (3×); 44:2 (1×); 49:8 (1×), and 50:7–9 (2×). For the redactional character of Deutero-Isaiah, see, for example, H. G. M. Williamson, *The Book Called Isaiah: Deutero Isaiah's Role in Composition and Redaction* (Oxford: Clarendon Press, 1994). Williamson suggests that Isa 40–55 both included and edited a version of the earlier Isa 1–39.

13. The P rendering of Isa 25:4 (the second example in this essay) shows that P-Isa treats these two words as synonyms.

Example 1: Isaiah 8:13b

MT	P
והוא מוראכם והוא <u>מערצכם</u>	whwyw dḥltkwn whwyw <u>msy'nkwn</u>
And he [God] is your fear and he should be <u>your dread</u>.	And he [God] is your fear and he is <u>your supporter</u>.

The Hebrew מערצכם, according to the Masoretic vocalization (מַעֲרִצְכֶם), is a defectively spelled *hiphil* participle ("your dread-inspirer"). The consonantal text should probably be understood as the noun מַעֲרִצְכֶם ("your dread"), which is parallel to מוֹרַאֲכֶם ("your fear").[14] However, the P translation renders it in an entirely different way, using *msy'nkwn* ("your supporter"); nevertheless, P-Isa seems to have known the meaning of מערצכם. The verb ערץ ("to dread, tremble") occurs 15 times in the Hebrew Bible (including six times in Isaiah), and, except for Isa 8:13, its Syriac equivalents render it appropriately.[15] For instance, in the previous verse (v. 12), לא תעריצו ("do not be in dread"), a *hiphil yiqtol* form of the same verb, is rendered as *l' tzw'wn* ("do not tremble"), a verb from the root *zw'* ("to be in motion, moved, shaken").[16]

It is important to note that this is probably not an inner-Syriac corruption because the form of *msy'nkwn* does not reflect any Syriac rendering of the verb ערץ.[17] A potential alternative explanation of this divergence is that the P rendering seeks to avoid the repetition of two synonyms: מערצכם ("your dread") and מוראכם ("your fear"). This mirrors the translation technique of P-Isa, in which repeated words are often only translated once.[18] The same technique can also be observed in the Septuagint, which renders the Hebrew synonyms only once as φόβος ("fear").[19]

However, the P version does not merely circumvent using the synonyms in the same verse. The second noun is replaced by another, *msy'nkwn* ("your

---

14. *BHS* and the major commentators of Isaiah. For a survey of the textual problems of Isa 8:13, see H. G. M. Williamson, *Commentary on Isaiah 6–12*, vol. 2 of *A Critical and Exegetical Commentary on Isaiah 1–27*, ICC (London: T&T Clark, 2018), 278.

15. The occurrences of the verb ערץ: Deut 1:29; 7:21; 20:3; 31:6; Josh 1:9; Isa 2:19, 21; 8:12, 13; 29:23; 47:12; Pss 10:18; 89:8; Job 13:25; 31:34.

16. See Jessie Payne Smith, *A Compendious Syriac Dictionary* (Oxford: Clarendon Press, 1903), 113–14. Alternatively, the Hebrew ערץ ("to be terrified, in dread") is rendered as *dḥl* ("to fear"; see Deut 1:29; 7:21), *kbš* ("to tread down, tread under foot"; see Isa 2:19, 21), and *'šn* ("to gain strength, prevail"; see Isa 47:12).

17. If P-Isa 8:13 had used the verb *zw'* as in v. 12 to render מערצכם, it would have read as an active participle form (*peal*), lacking *m*.

18. See P-Isa 8:9; 17:13; 21:11; 26:6; 40:1, 12; 41:5; 42:10, 12; 44:23; 45:1; 49:7; 54:16; 57:15, 16; 59:11; 60:3. See Warszawski, *Die Peschitta zu Jesaja*, 7; Weisz, *Die Peschitta zu Deuterojesaja*, 6.

19. However, Aquila distinguishes between the two nouns. See Joseph Ziegler, ed., *Isaias*, 3rd ed., sVtg 14 (Göttingen: Vandenhoeck & Ruprecht, 1983), 152.

supporter"), which deviates from the Hebrew source text. Thus, the Syriac rendering reinterprets the sense of its Hebrew exemplar, affecting the theological representation of the deity. While the Hebrew text of Isa 8:13, in accordance with the whole section (8:11–15),[20] stresses only the fear of God, P-Isa provides a subtler image. According to the P rendering, God is "fear" but, at the same time, a "supporter." Thus, on the one hand, the P translation adjusts the negative image of God as "dread"; on the other hand, it creates a textual link between this passage and other passages in Deutero-Isaiah in which God as a "supporter" is better accentuated. Most importantly for this study, the translation connects this passage with a further four P divergent renderings (examples 2–5) that similarly present God as a supporter/helper, thus reinforcing the unity of the book.

Example 2: Isaiah 25:4a

MT	P
כי היית מעוז לדל מעוז לאביון בצר־לו	mṭl dhwyt msy'n' lmskn' w'dwr' lbyš' b'wlṣnh
For you have been a stronghold for the poor, a stronghold for the needy in his affliction.	For you have been a supporter for the poor, and a helper for the needy in his affliction.

The Hebrew מעוז was known to the Syriac translator of Isaiah. It occurs 34 times in the Hebrew Bible (including nine times in Isaiah) and means "(mountain) stronghold."[21] P-Isa usually renders it as 'wšn' (see Isa 17:9; 23:4, 14; 27:5; 30:2, 3), which is the common Syriac equivalent of מעוז.[22] Here, however, the P translation renders מעוז as msy'n' and 'dwr', which mean "supporter" and "helper," respectively.

It seems that this divergence was influenced by the translation technique used in the P of the Old Testament. When מעוז (stronghold) is a metaphor of God, P tends to render it as "helper" (see m'drn' in Jer 16:19) or "supporter" (see msy'n' in Ps 28:8). It is also possible that by using this rendering, P-Isa seeks to circumvent the identification of God as an inanimate object.[23]

---

20. For a detailed overview of the Hebrew text of Isa 8:11–15, see Williamson, *Isaiah 6–12*, 271–300.

21. Cf. *HALOT*, 610.

22. The Syriac 'wšn' also means "strength, force, power, multitude, and a stronghold." See Payne Smith, *A Compendious Syriac Dictionary*, 408.

23. A similar rendering is also found in Isa 17:10, where צור מעוזך ("the rock of your stronghold") is rendered as tqyp' m'šnnky ("your mighty defender"). The P-Isa rendering of צור ("rock") by tqyp' ("mighty") may be regarded as a consistent interpretative translation that replaces a well-known divine image of the Hebrew Bible with another one. In all cases (17:10; 26:4; 30:29; 44:8) where God is explicitly associated with the image of the rock, P-Isa renders tqyp'. See Bodor, *The Theological Profile*, 30–7. Note that the Vetus Latina also uses the helper metaphor: *fuisti enim omni civitati humili auxiliator, et tristibus propter inopiam protectio* (the text of the Vetus Latina is taken from Petrus Sabatier [ed.], *Bibliorum*

Whatever the reason for the P divergence from the Hebrew text, the new images employed by P-Isa ("helper" and "supporter") enrich the representation of the deity with a feature that is lacking in the Hebrew exemplar. Furthermore, like the first example, P-Isa 25:4 does not only reinterpret the Isaianic text but also contributes to the unity of the book. Through choosing the supporter/helper metaphor to render מָעוֹז, the P translation integrates Isa 25:4 into the whole of Isaiah.

Example 3: Isaiah 33:2a

MT	P
יהוה חננו לך קוינו היה זְרֹעָם לבקרים	mry' rḥm 'lyn mṭl d'lyk hw sbrn hwy '*dwrn* b*spr*'
YHWH, be gracious to us, we hope; be their arm in the morning.	Lord, have mercy on us, for our hope is upon you; be our help in the morning.

In this example, the Hebrew text identifies the deity with זְרֹעַ ("arm"), stressing that God protects his people. In contrast, the P version renders the plain sense of the Hebrew text, replacing זְרֹעַ with 'dwr' ("help") and shifting the 3mp suffix ("their") to a 1cp ("our") suffix.[24] In the former case (P-Isa 25:4), P-Isa avoids identifying God as an inanimate object (i.e., "stronghold"), while here, it circumvents the identification of the deity with a part of the body (i.e., "arm"), portraying God as a person who acts in times of trouble.

It should be noted that the P rendering shows some similarities with other ancient versions, avoiding the image of the "arm" to refer to God. Nonetheless, direct textual dependency on them can be excluded in this case. The Septuagint has a different rendering: τὸ σπέρμα τῶν ἀπειθούντων ("the seed of the disobedient"), reading the consonants זרע as זֶרַע ("seed") and relating the 3ms suffix to the "disobedient" in the previous verse, Isa 33:1.[25] It follows that the main concern of the Septuagint was the correction of the suffix, which does not

---

sacrorum Latinae versiones antiquae seu Vetus Italica, 3 vols. [Reims: Reginaldum Florentain, 1743–1749]). However, it is not likely that P-Isa 25:4 directly depends on the Latin text because the two texts are quite different.

24. The MT pointing (זְרֹעָם) would normally be rendered "their arm." However, that does not fit in this context (see the parallel colon: "be gracious to us"); therefore, several commentators suggest a corrected form, זְרֹעֵנוּ ("our arm"). For example, see J. J. M. Roberts, *First Isaiah: A Commentary*, Hermeneia (Minneapolis, MN: Fortress, 2015), 421–42; Dominique Barthelémy, *Isaïe, Jérémie, Lamentations*, vol. 2 of *Critique textuelle de l'Ancien Testament*, OBO 50/2 (Göttingen: Vandenhoeck & Ruprecht, 1986), 226–7. However, other exegetes are skeptical of the emendation to "our arm:" for example, see Willem A. M. Beuken, *Jesaja 28–39*, HThKAT (Freiburg: Herder, 2010), 260.

25. See Arie van der Kooij and Florian Wilk, "Erläuterungen zu Jes 1–39," in *Psalmen bis Daniel*, vol. 2 of *Septuaginta Deutsch: Erläuterungen und Kommentare zum griechischen*

fit the context, not to circumvent the arm metaphor. The Targum is closer to the P reading as it reads תוקפנא ("our strength") for זרע and, like the P version, substitutes the Hebrew metaphor with a more concrete term, although not one of helping.

Therefore, the P rendering can be regarded as an independent interpretative rendering that achieves at least two objectives. First, it makes the sense of the Hebrew text more explicit and understandable. Second, it stresses a divine characteristic that is preferred by the P rendering of Isaiah, thereby strengthening the literary unity of the book.

Example 4: Isaiah 44:24a

MT	P
כה אמר יהוה גאלך ויצרך מבטן	hkn' 'mr mry' dprqk wgblk bmrb'' w'drk
Thus, says YHWH, your redeemer and your shaper from the womb.	Thus, says the Lord who redeemed you and formed you in the womb, and helped you.

As previous studies have shown, the P of the Old Testament often makes explicit what is implicit in the Hebrew text. Therefore, in several cases, it adds some words to make the original text more comprehensible.[26] The P additions, including those in P-Isa, mainly concern grammatical issues.[27] Yet, as Weitzman notes, "there are also cases where the translator 'improves' the text in line with his theological beliefs."[28]

The insertion of w'drk ("and helped you") into Isa 44:24a, attested only in the P version, appears to be one such theologically motivated addition.[29] This divergence cannot be traced back to another *Vorlage* as it is lacking in both the Hebrew manuscripts and other ancient versions. It is also hard to explain the addition as

Alten Testament, ed. Martin Karrer and Wolfgang Kraus (Stuttgart: Deutsche Bibelgesellschaft, 2011), 2592.

26. For example, see Craig E. Morrison, *The Character of the Syriac Version of the First Book of Samuel*, MPIL 11 (Leiden: Brill, 2001), 14–17, 57–8; Gillian Greenberg, *Translation Technique in the Peshiṭta to Jeremiah*, MPIL 13 (Leiden: Brill, 2002), 32–45; Ignacio Carbajosa, *The Character of the Syriac Version of Psalms: A Study of Psalms 90–150 in the Peshitta*, MPIL 17 (Leiden: Brill, 2008), 38–42.

27. For example, seE P-Isa 1:1, 3, 4, 8, 16, 29, 30, 31; 2:3; 5:26, 27, 28, 30; 14:7, 9; 18:5; 21:14; 22:19; 25:9; 27:4, 5; 28:11, 12; 29:16; 33:2; 38:20; 41:4; 42:22; 45:18; 47:14; 48:3; 50:11; 51:1, 6, 12, 16, 18; 54:11, 12; 56:8; 61:5. Cf. Warszawski, *Die Peschitta zu Jesaja*, 6; Weisz, *Die Peschitta zu Deuterojesaja*, 5.

28. Weitzman, *The Syriac Version*, 36.

29. However, it is usually not clear whether an addition results from the translation process or was intended to change the sense of the P text. Therefore, each case should thoroughly be investigated. See also Anthony Gelston, *The Peshiṭta of the Twelve Prophets* (Oxford: Clarendon, 1987), 131–5.

a translation or scribal error. Thus, P-Isa 44:24a appears to represent an interpretative rendering that enriches the characterization of God with a new feature appreciated by the readers of P-Isa and, as noted in the introduction, by the later books of the Old Testament.

This interpretative addition also contributes significantly to the unity of the book of Isaiah in general and ch. 44 in particular. First, in resuming an already emphasized motif in the first part of the book (8:13; 25:4; 33:2), P-Isa 44:24a highlights the connection between different passages, thus making it clear that helping is a constant characteristic of the deity. Second, with the addition, P-Isa harmonizes 44:24 with 44:2,[30] which is one of the Deutero-Isaianic passages referring to God's help: *hkn' 'mr mry' d'bdk wgblk bmrb'' d'drk* ("thus, says the Lord who made you and formed you in the womb, who helped you"). Therefore, the P rendering creates an effective parallel in Isa 44 between v. 2 and 24, emphasizing the structural and theological unity of the chapter.

Example 5: Isaiah 49:26b

MT	P
וידעו כל־בשר כי אני יהוה מושיעך <u>וגאלך</u> אביר יעקב	*wnd'wn kl bsr d'n' 'n' mry' prwqky <u>wmsy'nky</u> tqyqh dy'qwb*
And all flesh shall know that I am YHWH, your savior, <u>and your redeemer</u>, the mighty one of Jacob.	And all flesh shall know that I am the Lord,[31] your savior, <u>and your supporter</u>, the mighty one of Jacob.

Here, P-Isa appears to differ from its Hebrew exemplar for stylistic reasons. As already argued (see the first example above), the P translation often avoids synonymous words. This passage contains such a case. To avoid using the synonymous מושיע ("savior") and גאל ("redeemer") together, P-Isa 49:26b renders the second word as *msy'n'* ("supporter").

However, given the other occurrences of this divine attribute and its importance within P-Isa, the function of this divergent appears to be more than merely stylistic. Earlier, in Isa 49:8, salvation is similarly connected with the help of God: "and in the day of the salvation (ובים ישועה/*wbywm' dpwrqn'*) I helped you (עזרתיך/*'drtk*)." In this context, P-Isa 49:26 may be considered as an echo of salvation with God's help in 49:8, both verses emphasizing the relationship between the salvific act and God's help. However, the final phrase of Isa 49:26, אני יהוה מושיעך וגאלך אביר יעקב ("I am YHWH, your savior, and your redeemer, the mighty one

---

30. For the phenomenon of harmonization, see Emanuel Tov, "The Nature and Background of Harmonizations in Biblical Manuscripts," *JSOT* 31 (1985): 3–29.

31. Manuscript 7a1 omits *mry'* ("Lord"). However, following other ancient P manuscripts, it is included in the Leiden edition: see Sebastian P. Brock, ed., *Isaiah*, part. 3, fasc. 1 of *The Old Testament in Syriac According to the Peshiṭta Version* (Leiden: Brill, 1987; 2nd impression, 1993), 91.

of Jacob"), also occurs in Isa 60:16, in which P-Isa renders גאלך as *mpṣynky* ("your deliverer/redeemer"). As a result, while P-Isa 49:26 creates unity in its immediate context by connecting God's might with His help and support (thereby, reflecting the theology of 49:8), this rendering simultaneously weakens the parallel between 49:26 and 60:16 in the Hebrew source text.[32] This example thus shows the reinterpretative power of the P translation, which also affects the unity of the book of Isaiah. The divergent rendering of P eliminates important parallels in the original Hebrew but, at the same time, unifies passages that were not associated in the source text.

3. Conclusion

This essay illustrates how the P translation constructs the unity of the book of Isaiah using five divergent renderings. The examples given do not provide a comprehensive treatment of the unity constructed in P-Isa; however, based on these P renderings, conclusions can be drawn that may represent a good starting point for further, more detailed investigations into the unity created by both the P version and other ancient translations of Isaiah.

(1) P-Isa considered and rendered the book of Isaiah as a whole. The use of the same image of God, i.e., as a "supporter/helper" in different parts of the book, indicates that the book of Isaiah was received by the P translation as one single corpus.[33]

(2) P-Isa emphasizes the unity of the book of Isaiah by its lexical choices. As argued above, P-Isa harmonizes different passages of the book by the repetitive use of *msyʻn* ("supporter") and *ʻdwr* ("helper" and its derivates) as divine attributes. Using these terms in the first part of the book (chs. 1–39) is of great value as there is no correspondence to these terms in the source text of this section. The images used throughout the P translation highlight both the structural and theological coherence of the book of Isaiah. In the Hebrew version of Isaiah, God

---

32. It is noteworthy that P-Isa 49:26 in manuscript 6h3, like P-Isa 60:16, renders גאלך as *mpṣynky*, highlighting the parallelism obscured by the textus receptus of the Syriac translation. However, it is hard to decide which was the original P rendering. For the possible scenarios and their probability, see Bodor, *The Theological Profile*, 43–4.

33. Note that no caesuras are introduced by the P translator between Proto- (1–39), Deutero- (40–55), or Trito-Isaiah (56–66). The only caesura is found in P-Isa 35:2b-3 ("an admonition and an encouragement of the weak: the Savior is coming and redeems them"), which is an addition marking the midpoint of the translation. However, it is entirely or partly omitted in several manuscripts (e.g., see manuscripts 6h3, 9a1*fam*, 9l5, 11l4), suggesting that this addition goes back to a later copyist and not the translator. See Sebastian P. Brock, "Text Divisions in the Syriac Translations of Isaiah," in *Biblical Hebrew, Biblical Texts: Essays in Memory of Michael P. Weitzman*, ed. Ada Rapoport-Albert and Gillian Greenberg, JSOTSup 333 (Sheffield: Sheffield Academic Press, 2001), 214; Bodor, *The Theological Profile*, 143–4.

helps only in Deutero-Isaiah, whereas God in the P translation is a supporter and helper throughout the entire book. Thus, this divine feature creates unity, not only in the composition of the book but also in its theology.

(3) The unity of P-Isa differs from the unity of its Hebrew exemplar. This essay focuses on a motif that, because it is missing from the first part of the book (chs. 1–39), does not build upon the unity of the Hebrew text of Isaiah but somewhat undermines it. In contrast, in the P translation, God is a "supporter/helper" that represents a motif unifying and harmonizing the book of Isaiah. It is also worth noting that P-Isa does not underscore, at least explicitly, the motives that unify different passages and parts of the Hebrew exemplar of Isaiah.[34] This suggests that unity in P-Isa and, consequently, unity in the majority of ancient translations, should be considered on its own, independent from the original Hebrew text. Indeed, the unity in a translation is influenced by factors different from those influencing the unity of the *Vorlage*.

(4) The examples presented above highlight that a distinction must be made between the possible reason(s) for the P divergences and their impact on unity. The P-Isa divergences from the Hebrew exemplar may be explained in different ways. In Isa 8:13 and 49:26, P-Isa appears to avoid the repetition of two synonyms ("fear" and "dread"; "savior" and "redeemer"); in Isa 25:4 and 33:2, P-Isa circumvents the divine metaphors referring to an inanimate object ("stronghold") and an anthropomorphic image ("arm"); and P-Isa 44:24 originates from harmonization with its near context (44:2). However, the potential reasons for the P divergences do not explain why P-Isa chooses the same divine attribute to replace well-known Hebrew terms in the source text.[35] Indeed, we cannot discern the intention of the P translator at a distance of almost 2,000 years. Most likely, the idea that God helps his people was a topic of common interest across the P readership.[36] In any case, whatever the reason for the P divergences presented above, their impact on P-Isa is clear: they build up the unity of the book of Isaiah, providing a consistent view of God throughout the whole book.

---

34. For instance, Isa 35 is considered a redactional bridge between First and Second Isaiah (see Odil Hannes Steck, *Bereitete Heimkehr: Jesaja 35 als redaktionelle Brücke zwischen dem Ersten und dem Zweiten Jesaja*, SBS 121 [Stuttgart: Katholisches Bibelwerk, 1985]). Nonetheless, P-Isa does not present itself as a "bridge" text.

35. It should be noted that the reason for the "supporter/helper" renderings cannot be ascribed to the difficulty of the Hebrew source text. The Hebrew equivalents of *msy'n'* ("supporter") and *'dr* ("to help") are well attested by the Hebrew Bible and appropriately translated by the P translation of the Old Testament, including Isaiah. Furthermore, considering the other versions (1QIsa^a, Septuagint, and Targum), the possibility of another Hebrew *Vorlage* or the influence of another translation on these P readings is also unlikely.

36. For the possible reasons of the focus on this topic, see Bodor, *The Theological Profile*, 44–6.

BIBLIOGRAPHY

Aalen, Sverre. "אוֹר." *TDOT* 1: 147–67.
Abernethy, Andrew T. *The Book of Isaiah and God's Kingdom: A Thematic-Theological Approach*. NSBT 40. Downers Grove, IL: IVP Academic, 2016.
Abernethy, Andrew T. *Discovering Isaiah: Content, Interpretation, Reception*. Grand Rapids, MI: Eerdmans, 2021.
Abernethy, Andrew T. *Eating in Isaiah: Approaching the Role of Food and Drink in Isaiah's Structure and Message*. BIS 131. Leiden: Brill, 2014.
Abernethy, Andrew T. "The Ruined Vineyard Motif in Isaiah 1–39: Insights from Cognitive Linguistics." *Bib* 99 (2018): 334–50.
Abernethy, Andrew T. "Wisdom in Isaiah." Pages 334–51 in *The Oxford Handbook of Isaiah*. Edited by Lena-Sofia Tiemeyer. Oxford: Oxford University Press, 2020.
Achenbach, Reinhard. "*Lex Sacra* and Sabbath in the Pentateuch." *ZAR* 22 (2016): 101–9.
Ackroyd, Peter R. "Isaiah I–XII, Presentation of a Prophet." Pages 16–48 in *Congress Volume: Göttingen 1977*. Edited by Walther Zimmerli. VTSup 39. Leiden: Brill 1978.
Ackroyd, Peter R. *Studies in the Religious Tradition of the Old Testament*. London: SCM, 1987.
Ajer, Peter C. *The Death of Jesus and the Politics of Place in the Gospel of John*. Eugene, OR: Pickwick, 2016.
Albertz, Rainer. "Das Deutrojesaja-Buch als Fortschreibung der Jesaja-Prophetie." Pages 241–56 in *Die hebräische Bibel und ihre zweifache Nachgeschichte: Festschrift für Rolf Rendtorff zum 65. Geburtstag*. Edited by Erhard Blum, G. Christian Macholz, and Ekkehard Stegemann. Neukirchen-Vluyn: Neukirchener Verlag, 1990.
Albertz, Rainer. *A History of Israelite Religion in the Old Testament Period. Volume II: From the Exile to the Maccabees*. OTL. Louisville, KY: Westminster John Knox, 1994.
Albertz, Rainer. *Israel in Exile: The History and Literature of the Sixth Century B.C.E.* SBLStBibLit 3. Atlanta, GA: SBL, 2003.
Alexander, Joseph Addison. *Commentary on the Prophecies of Isaiah*. 7th ed. Grand Rapids, MI: Zondervan, 1976.
Amzallag, Gérard Nissim. "The Paradoxical Source of Hope in Isaiah 12." *RB* 123 (2016) 357–77.
Anderson, John E. *Jacob and the Divine Trickster: A Theology of Deception and YHWH's Fidelity to the Ancestral Promise in the Jacob Cycle*. Siphrut 5. Winona Lake, IN: Eisenbrauns, 2011.
Angel, Hayyim. "Prophecy as Potential: The Consolations of Isaiah 1–12 in Context." *JBQ* 37 (2009): 3–10.
Aster, Shawn Zelig. *Reflections of Empire in Isaiah 1–39: Response to Assyrian Ideology*. SBLANEM 19. Atlanta, GA: SBL Press, 2017.
Avrahami, Yael. *The Senses of Scripture: Sensory Perception in the Hebrew Bible*. LHBOTS 545. New York: T&T Clark, 2012.

Bailey, Daniel P. "The Effective History of Isaiah 53 in the Pre-Christian Period." Pages 75–146 in *The Suffering Servant: Isaiah 53 in Jewish and Christian Sources.* Edited by Bernd Janowski and Peter Stuhlmacher. Grand Rapids, MI: Eerdmans, 2004.

Baldauf, Borghild. "Jes 42,18-25. Gottes tauber und blinder Knecht." Pages 13–36 in *Ein Gott, eine Offenbarung: Beiträge zur biblischen Exegese, Theologie und Spiritualität. Festschrift für Notker Füglister OSB zum 60. Geburtstag.* Edited by Friedrich V. Reiterer. Würzburg: Echter, 1991.

Baltzer, Klaus. *Deutero-Isaiah: A Commentary on Isaiah 40–55.* Translated by Margaret Kohl. Hermeneia. Minneapolis, MN: Fortress, 2001.

Barker, Joel D. "Day of the Lord." Pages 132–43 in *Dictionary of the Old Testament Prophets: A Compendium of Contemporary Biblical Scholarship.* Edited by Mark J. Boda and J. Gordon McConville. Downers Grove, IL: IVP Academic/Inter-Varsity Press, 2012.

Barstad, Hans. "Isaiah 56–66 in Relation to Isaiah 40–55: Why a New Reading is Necessary." Pages 41–62 in *Continuity and Discontinuity: Chronological and Thematic Development in Isaiah 40–66.* Edited by Lena-Sofia Tiemeyer and Hans Barstad. FRLANT 255. Göttingen: Vandenhoeck & Ruprecht, 2014.

Barthel, Jörg. *Prophetenwort und Geschichte: Die Jesajaüberlieferung in Jes 6–8 und 28–31.* FAT 19. Tübingen: Mohr Siebeck, 1997.

Barthelémy, Dominique. *Isaïe, Jérémie, Lamentations.* Vol. 2 of *Critique textuelle de l'Ancien Testament.* OBO 50/2. Göttingen: Vandenhoeck & Ruprecht, 1986.

Basello, Gian Pietro. "Il Cilindro di Ciro tradotto dal testo babilonese." *RSB* 25 (2013): 249–59.

Baumann, Gerlinde. *Love and Violence: Marriage as Metaphor for the Relationship Between YHWH and Israel in the Prophetic Books.* Collegeville, MN: Liturgical Press, 2003.

Bautch, Richard. *Development in Genre between Post-Exilic Penitential Prayers and the Psalms of Communal Lament.* SBLAcBib 7. Atlanta, GA: SBL, 2003.

Beaucamp, Evode. "'Chant nouveau du retour' (Is 42, 10-17). Un monstre de l'exégèse moderne." *RSR* 56 (1982): 145–58.

Becker, Joachim. *Isaias, der Prophet und sein Buch.* SBS 30. Stuttgart: Katholisches Bibelwerk, 1968.

Becker, Uwe. "The Book of Isaiah: Its Composition History." Pages 37–56 in *The Oxford Handbook of Isaiah.* Edited by Lena-Sofia Tiemeyer. New York: Oxford University Press, 2020.

Becker, Uwe. "Gibt es ein hellenistisches Jesajabuch?" Pages 83–96 in *Prophecy and Hellenism.* Edited by Hannes Bezzel and Stefan Pfeiffer. FAT/II 129. Tübingen: Mohr Siebeck 2021.

Becker, Uwe. *Jesaja: von der Botschaft zum Buch.* FRLANT 178. Göttingen: Vandenhoeck & Ruprecht, 1997.

Becker, Uwe. "Sozialkritik in Jes 1–39 und im Amos-Buch." Pages 33–53 in *Isaiah and the Twelve: Parallels, Similarities and Differences.* Edited by Richard J. Bautch, Joachim Eck, and Burkhard M. Zapff. BZAW 527. Berlin: de Gruyter, 2020.

Becker, Uwe. "Tendenzen der Jesajaforschung 1998–2007." *TRu* 74 (2009): 96–128.

Beentjes, Panc C. "Discovering a New Path of Intertextuality: Inverted Quotations and Their Dynamics." Pages 31–50 in *Literary Structure and Rhetorical Strategies in the Hebrew Bible.* Edited by L. J. De Regt, J. de Waard, and J. P. Fokkelman. Assen: Van Gorcum, 1996.

Ben Zvi, Ehud. "Isaiah 1:4-9, Isaiah, and the Events of 701 BCE in Judah." *SJOT* 5 (1991): 95–111.

Ben Zvi, Ehud. "Observations on Prophetic Characters, Prophetic Texts, Priests of Old, Persian Period Priests and Literati." Pages 19–30 in *The Priests in the Prophets: The Portrayal of Priests, Prophets and Other Religious Specialists in the Latter Prophets*. Edited by Lester L. Grabbe and Alice Ogden Bellis. JSOTSup 408. London: Bloomsbury T&T Clark, 2004.

Ben Zvi, Ehud. "Urban Center of Jerusalem and the Development of the Literature of the Hebrew Bible." Pages 194–209 in *Urbanism in Antiquity: From Mesopotamia to Crete*. Edited by Walter E. Aufrecht, Neil A. Mirau, and Steven W. Gauley. JSOTSup 244. Sheffield: Sheffield Academic Press, 1997.

Berges, Ulrich. *The Book of Isaiah: Its Composition and Final Form*. Translated by Millard C. Lind. HBM 46. Sheffield: Sheffield Phoenix Press, 2012.

Berges, Ulrich. "Isaiah: Structure, Themes, and Contested Issues." Pages 153–70 in *The Oxford Handbook of the Prophets*. Edited by Carolyn J. Sharp. New York: Oxford University Press, 2016.

Berges, Ulrich. *Isaiah: The Prophet and His Book*. Sheffield: Sheffield Phoenix, 2012.

Berges, Ulrich. "Isaiah 55–66 and the Psalms: Shared Viewpoints, Literary Similarities and Neighboring Authors." *JBL* 141 (2022): 277–99.

Berges, Ulrich. *Jesaja 40–48*, HThKAT. Freiburg: Herder, 2008.

Berges, Ulrich. *Jesaja 55–66*. HThKAT. Freiburg: Herder, 2022.

Berges, Ulrich. "Personifications and Prophetic Voices of Zion in Isaiah and Beyond." Pages 54–82 in *The Elusive Prophet: The Prophet as an Historical Person, Literary Character and Anonymous Artist. Papers Read at the Eleventh Joint Meeting of The Society for Old Testament Study and Het Oudtestamentisch Werkgezelschap in Nederland en België, held at Soesterberg 2000*. Edited by Johannes C. de Moor. OTS 45. Leiden: Brill, 2001.

Berges, Ulrich. "Servant and Suffering in Isaiah and Jeremiah: Who Borrowed from Whom?" *OTE* 25 (2012): 247–59.

Berges, Ulrich. "The Servant(s) in Isaiah." Pages 318–33 in *The Oxford Handbook of Isaiah*. Edited by Lena-Sofia Tiemeyer. New York: Oxford University Press, 2020.

Berges, Ulrich. "'Sing to the LORD a New Song': The Tradents of the Book of Isaiah and the Psalter." Pages 213–37 in *The History of Isaiah: The Formation of the Book and Its Presentation of the Past*. Edited by Jacob Stromberg and J. Todd Hibbard. FAT 150. Tübingen: Mohr Siebeck, 2021.

Berges, Ulrich. "Trito-Isaiah and the Reforms of Ezra/Nehemiah: Consent or Conflict?" *Bib* 98 (2017): 173–90.

Berges, Ulrich. "Where Starts Trito-Isaiah?" Pages 63–76 in *Continuity and Discontinuity: Chronological and Thematic Development in Isaiah 40–66*. Edited by Lena-Sofia Tiemeyer and Hans Barstad. FRLANT 255. Göttingen: Vandenhoeck & Ruprecht, 2014.

Berges, Ulrich. "Zion and the Kingship of YHWH in Isaiah 40–55." Pages 95–119 in *'Enlarge the Site of Your Tent': The City as Unifying Theme in Isaiah*. Edited by Archibald L. H. M. van Wieringen and Annemarieke van der Woude. OTS 58. Leiden: Brill 2011.

Berges, Ulrich. "Die Zionstheologie des Buches Jesaja." *EstBib* 58 (2000): 167–98.

Berges, Ulrich, and Willem A. M. Beuken. *Das Buch Jesaja: Eine Einführung*. UTB 4647. Göttingen: Vandenhoek & Rupprecht, 2016.

Berlejung, Angelika. "Sin and Punishment: The Ethics of Divine Justice and Retribution in Ancient Near Eastern and Old Testament Texts." *Int* 69 (2015): 272–87.

Berlejung, Angelika. *Die Theologie der Bilder: Herstellung und Einweihung von Kultbildern in Mesopotamien und die alttestamentliche Bilderproblematik*. OBO 162. Fribourg: Universitätsverlag, 1998.

Berman, Joshua A. *Narrative Analogy in the Hebrew Bible: Battle Stories and Their Equivalent Non-Battle Narratives.* VTSup 103. Leiden: Brill, 2004.
Bernidaki-Aldous, Eleftheria A. *Blindness in a Culture of Light: Especially the Case of Oedipus at Colonus of Sophocles.* AUSCLL 8. New York: Lang, 1990.
Berquist, Jon L. "Spaces of Jerusalem." Pages 40–52 in *Constructions of Space II: The Biblical City and Other Imagined Spaces.* Edited by Jon L. Berquist and Claudia V. Camp. LHBOTS 490. London: Bloomsbury T&T Clark, 2008.
Berquist, Jon L., and Claudia V. Camp, eds. *Constructions of Space I: Theory, Geography, and Narrative.* LHBOTS 481. London: T&T Clark International, 2007.
Berquist, Jon L., and Claudia V. Camp, eds. *Constructions of Space II: The Biblical City and Other Imagined Spaces.* LHBOTS 490. London: T&T Clark International, 2008.
Beuken, Willem A. M. "Common and Different Phrases for Babylon's Fall and Its Aftermath in Isaiah 13–14 and Jeremiah 50–51." Pages 53–73 in *Concerning the Nations: Essays on the Oracles against the Nations in Isaiah, Jeremiah and Ezekiel.* Edited by Andrew Mein, Else K. Holt, and Hyun Chul Paul Kim. LHBOTS 612. London: Bloomsbury T&T Clark, 2014.
Beuken, Willem A. M. *Jesaja Deel IIA.* POuT. Nijkerk: G. F. Callenbach, 1979.
Beuken, Willem A. M. *Jesaja: Deel IIIB.* POuT. Nijkerk: G. F. Callenbach, 1989.
Beuken, Willem A. M. *Jesaja 1–12.* HThKAT. Freiburg: Herder, 2003.
Beuken, Willem A. M. *Jesaja 13–27.* HThKAT. Freiburg: Herder, 2007.
Beuken, Willem A. M. *Jesaja 28–39.* HThKAT. Freiburg: Herder, 2010.
Beuken, Willem A. M. "Jesaja 33 Als Spiegeltext Im Jesajabuch." *ETL* 67 (1991): 5–35.
Beuken, Willem A. M. "The Prophet Leads the Readers into Praise: Isaiah 25:1–10 in Connection with Isaiah 24:14–23 Seen against the Background of Isaiah 12." Pages 121–56 in *Studies in Isaiah 24–27: The Isaiah Workshop – De Jesaja Werkplaats.* Edited by H. Jan Bosman and Harm van Grol. OTS 43. Leiden: Brill, 2000.
Beuken, Willem A. M. "A Song of Gratitude and a Song of Malicious Delight: Is Their Consonance Unseemly? The Coherence of Isaiah Chs. 13–14 with Chs. 11–12 and Chs. 1–2." Pages 96–114 in *Das Manna fällt auch heute noch: Beiträge zur Geschichte und Theologie des Alten, Ersten Testaments: Festschrift für Erich Zenger.* Edited by Frank-Lohtar Hossfeld and Ludger Schwienhorst-Schönberger. HBS 44. Freiburg: Herder, 2004.
Beuken, Willem A. M. "The Unity of the Book of Isaiah: Another Attempt at Bridging the Gorge between Its Two Main Parts." Pages 50–62 in *Reading from Right to Left: Essays on the Hebrew Bible in Honour of David J. A. Clines.* Edited by J. Cheryl Exum and H. G. M. Williamson. JSOTSup 373. London: Sheffield Academic, 2003.
Beuken, Willem A. M. "Women and the Spirit, the Ox and the Ass: The First Binders of the Booklet Isaiah 28–32." *ETL* 74 (1998): 5–26.
Bird, Phyllis. *Missing Persons and Mistaken Identities: Women and Gender in Ancient Israel.* OBT. Minneapolis, MN: Fortress, 1997.
Black, Max. *Models and Metaphors: Studies in Language and Philosophy.* Ithaca, NY: Cornell University Press, 1962.
Blenkinsopp, Joseph. *Isaiah 1–39: A New Translation with Introduction and Commentary.* AB 19. New York: Doubleday, 2000.
Blenkinsopp, Joseph. *Isaiah 40–55: A New Translation with Introduction and Commentary.* AB 19A. New York: Doubleday, 2002.
Blenkinsopp, Joseph. *Isaiah 56–66: A New Translation with Introduction and Commentary.* AB 19B. New York: Doubleday, 2003.

Blenkinsopp, Joseph. "The Sacrificial Life and Death of the Servant (Isaiah 52:13–53:12)." *VT* 66 (2016): 1–14.

Bloch, Yigal. "Judean Identity during the Exile: Concluding Deals on a Sabbath in Babylonia and Egypt under the Neo-Babylonian and the Achaemenid Empires." Pages 43–69 in *A Question of Identity: Social, Political, and Historical Aspects of Identity Dynamics in Jewish and Other Contexts*. Edited by Dikla Rivkin Katz et al. Berlin: de Gruyter Oldenbourg, 2019.

Bloch, Yigal. "Was the Sabbath Observed in Āl-Yāḫūdu in the Early Decades of the Babylonian Exile? Reply to Oded Tammuz, 'The Sabbath as the Seventh Day of the Week and a Day of Rest: Since When?', ZAW 131 (2019) 287–294." *ZAW* 132 (2020): 117–20.

Blumenberg, Hans. "Licht als Metapher der Wahrheit: im Vorfeld der philosophischen Begriffsbildung. " *Studium generale* 10 (1957): 432–47.

Boase, Elizabeth. "Desolate Land / Desolate People in Jeremiah and Lamentations." Pages 97–115 in *Ecological Aspects of War: Engagements with Biblical Texts*. Edited by Anne Elvey, Keith Dyer, and Deborah Guess. T&T Clark Biblical Studies. London: Bloomsbury T&T Clark, 2017.

Bodor, Attila. *The Theological Profile of the Peshitta of Isaiah*. THBS 5. Leiden: Brill, 2021.

Bovati, Pietro. *Ristabilire la giustizia: Procedure, vocabolario, orientamenti*. AnBib 110. 2nd ed. Rome: Pontificio Istituto Biblico, 2005.

Bowker, Matthew H. "The Meaning of Absurd Protest: The Book of Job, Albert Camus, and C. Fred Alford's *After the Holocaust*." *Journal of Psycho-Social Studies* 4 (2011): 1–21.

Bowker, Matthew H. *Rethinking the Politics of Absurdity: Albert Camus, Postmodernity, and the Survival of Innocence*. New York: Routledge, 2014.

Boyle, Francis. *The Tamil Genocide by Sri Lanka: The Global Failure to Protect Tamil Rights Under International Law*. Atlanta, GA: Clarity Press, 2010.

Boynton, Eric, and Peter Capretto. "Introduction: The Limits of Theory in Trauma and Transcendence." Pages 1–14 in *Trauma and Transcendence: Suffering and the Limits of Theory*. Edited by Eric Boynton and Peter Capretto. New York: Fordham University Press, 2018.

Brett, Mark G. "Postcolonial Interpretation Unequal Terms: A Postcolonial Approach to Isaiah 61." Pages 243–56 in *Biblical Interpretation and Method: Essays in Honour of John Barton*. Edited by Katharine J. Dell and Paul M. Joyce. Oxford: Oxford University Press, 2013.

Brett, Mark G. "Postcolonial Readings of Isaiah." Pages 621–36 in *The Oxford Handbook of Isaiah*. Edited by Lena-Sofia Tiemeyer. New York: Oxford University Press, 2020.

Brinkman, J. A. "Elamite Military Aid to Merodach-Baladan." *JNES* 24 (1965): 161–6.

Brinkman, J. A. "Merodach-Baladan II." Pages 6–53 in *Studies presented to A. Leo Oppenheim: June 7, 1964*. Edited by R. D. Biggs and J. A. Brinkman. Chicago, IL: University of Chicago Press, 1964.

Brock, Rita Nakashima. "A New Thing in the Land: The Female Surrounds the Warrior." Pages 137–59 in *Power, Powerlessness, and the Divine: New Inquiries in Bible and Theology*. Edited by Cynthia L. Rigby. Atlanta, GA: Scholars Press, 1997.

Brock, Sebastian P., ed. *Isaiah*. Part. 3, fasc. 1 of *The Old Testament in Syriac According to the Peshiṭta Version*. Leiden: Brill, 1987; 2nd impression, 1993.

Brock, Sebastian P. "Text Divisions in the Syriac Translations of Isaiah." Pages 200–221 in *Biblical Hebrew, Biblical Texts: Essays in Memory of Michael P. Weitzman*. Edited by Ada Rapoport-Albert and Gillian Greenberg. JSOTSup 333. Sheffield: Sheffield Academic Press, 2001.

Brooke-Rose, Christine. *A Grammar of Metaphor*. London: Secker & Warburg, 1958.
Brueggemann, Walter. *Isaiah 1–39*. 1st ed. Westminster Bible Companion. Louisville, KY: Westminster John Knox, 1998.
Camus, Albert. *The Myth of Sisyphus and Other Essays*. Translated by Justin O'Brien. New York: First Vintage International, 2005.
Carasik, Michael. *Theologies of the Mind in Biblical Israel*. Studies in Biblical Literature 85. New York: Lang, 2006.
Carbajosa, Ignacio. *The Character of the Syriac Version of Psalms: A Study of Psalms 90–150 in the Peshitta*. MPIL 17. Leiden: Brill, 2008.
Carr, David M. *Holy Resilience: The Bible's Traumatic Origins*. New Haven, CT: Yale University Press, 2014.
Carr, David M. "Reaching for Unity in Isaiah." *JSOT* 57 (1993): 61–80.
Carr, David M. "Reading Isaiah from Beginning (Isaiah 1) to End (Isaiah 65–66): Multiple Modern Possibilities." Pages 188–218 in *New Visions of the Book of Isaiah*. Edited by Marvin A. Sweeney and Roy F. Melugin. JSOTSup 214. Sheffield: Sheffield Academic Press, 1996.
Carr, David M. *Writing on the Tablet of the Heart: Origins of Scripture and Literature*. Oxford: Oxford University Press, 2009.
Carroll, Robert P. "Blindsight and the Vision Thing: Blindness and Insight in the Book of Isaiah." Pages 79–93 in *Writing and Reading the Scroll of Isaiah: Studies of an Interpretive Tradition*. vol. 1. Edited by Craig C. Broyles and Craig A. Evans. VTSup 70/1. Leiden: Brill, 1997.
Chan, Michael J. "Cyrus, Yhwh's Bird of Prey (Isa. 46.11): Echoes of an Ancient Near Eastern Metaphor." *JSOT* 35 (2010): 113–27
Childs, Brevard S. *Introduction to the Old Testament as Scripture*. London: SCM, 1979.
Childs, Brevard S. *Isaiah: A Commentary*. OTL. Louisville, KY: Westminster John Knox, 2001.
Cioran, Emil M. *On the Heights of Despair*. Chicago: University of Chicago Press, 1992.
Claassens, L. Juliana M. *Mourner, Mother Midwife: Reimaging God's Delivering Presence in the Old Testament*. Louisville, KY: Westminster John Knox, 2012.
Clements, Ronald E. "שאר." *ThWAT* 7: 931–50.
Clements, Ronald E. "'Arise, Shine; For Your Light Has Come': A Basic Theme of the Isaianic Tradition." Pages 441–54 in *Writing and Reading the Scroll of Isaiah: Studies of an Interpretive Tradition*. Volume 2. Edited by Craig C. Broyles and Craig A. Evans. VTSup 70/2. Leiden: Brill, 1997.
Clements, Ronald E. "Beyond Tradition-History: Deutero-Isaianic Development of First Isaiah's Themes." *JSOT* 31 (1985): 95–113.
Clements, Ronald E. "Isaiah 1.1-31: Israel Summoned to Repentance – The Introduction to the Isaiah Book." Pages 213–28 in *Jerusalem and the Nations: Studies in the Book of Isaiah*. Edited by Ronald E. Clements. HBM 16. Sheffield: Sheffield Phoenix, 2011.
Clements, Ronald E. *Jerusalem and the Nations: Studies in the Book of Isaiah*. HBM 16. Sheffield: Sheffield Phoenix, 2011.
Clements, Ronald E. "A Light to the Nations: A Central Theme of the Book of Isaiah." Pages 57–69 in *Forming Prophetic Literature: Essays on Isaiah and the Twelve in Honor of John D. W. Watts*. Edited by James W. Watts and Paul R. House. JSOTSup 235. Sheffield: Sheffield Academic, 1996.
Clements, Ronald E. "The Unity of the Book of Isaiah." *Int* 36 (1982): 117–29.
Conrad, Edgar W. *Reading Isaiah*. OBT 27. Minneapolis, MN: Fortress, 1991.

Couey, Blake. *Reading the Poetry of First Isaiah: The Most Perfect Model of the Prophetic Poetry*. Oxford: Oxford University Press, 2015.
Dahood, Mitchell. "Hebrew – Ugaritic Lexicography V." *Bib* 48 (1967): 421–38.
Darr, Katherine Pfisterer. *Isaiah's Vision and Family of God*. LCBI. Louisville, KY: Westminster John Knox, 1994.
Davage, David. *How Isaiah Became an Author*. Minneapolis, MN: Fortress, 2022.
Davies, Graham I. *A Critical and Exegetical Commentary on Exodus 1–18*. II. *Exodus 11–18*. ICC. London: Bloomsbury T&T Clark, 2020.
Delitzsch, Franz. *Commentar über das Buch Jesaja*. 4th ed. BCAT III/1. Leipzig: Dörffling & Franke, 1889.
Dell, Katherine. "The Suffering Servant of Deutero-Isaiah: Jeremiah Revisited." Pages 119–34 in *Genesis, Isaiah and Psalms*. Edited by Katherine Dell, Graham Davies, and Yee von Koh. VTSup 135. Leiden: Brill, 2010.
Dempsey, Carol J. "Isaiah." Pages 604–66 in *The Paulist Biblical Commentary*. Edited by José E. A. Chiu et al. Mahwah, NJ: Paulist, 2018.
Dempsey, Carol J. *Isaiah: God's Poet of Light*. St. Louis, MO: Chalice, 2009.
Dempsey, Carol J. "Themes and Perspectives in the Prophets: Truth, Tragedy, Trauma." Pages 649–71 in *The Old Testament and Apocrypha*. Edited by Gale A. Yee et al. Fortress Commentary on the Bible. Minneapolis, MN: Fortress, 2014.
Dicou, Bert. "Literary Function and Literary History of Isaiah 34." *BN* 58 (1991): 30–45.
Díez Herrera, Pablo. "Clermont-Ganneau 152. El sábado en Elefantina ¿Una observancia laxa?" *EstBib* 77 (2019): 315–44.
Dille, Sarah J. *Mixing Metaphors: God as Mother and Father in Deutero-Isaiah*. JSOTSup 398. London: T&T Clark, 2004.
Dim, Emmanuel Uchenna. *The Eschatological Implications of Isa 65 and 66 as the Conclusion of the Book of Isaiah*. Bern: Peter Lang, 2005.
Dobbs-Allsopp, F. W. "Syntagma of Bat Followed by a Geographical Name in the Hebrew Bible: A Reconsideration of Its Meaning and Grammar." *CBQ* 57 (1995): 451–70.
Döderlein, Johann Christoph. *Esaias ex recensione textus hebraei ad fidem codd. quorundam mss et versionum antiquarum latine vertit notasque varii argumenti*. 3rd ed. Norimbergae et Altdorfi: George Peter Monath, 1789.
Doering, Luz. *Schabbat: Sabbathalacha und -praxis im antiken Judentum und Urchristentum*. TSAJ 78. Tübingen: Mohr Siebeck, 1999.
Dubovský, Peter. "Assyrian Downfall through Isaiah's Eyes (2 Kings 15–23): The Historiography of Representation." *Bib* 89 (2008): 1–16.
Dubovský, Peter. *Hezekiah and the Assyrian Spies: Reconstruction of the Neo-Assyrian Intelligence Services and Its Significance for 2 Kings 18–19*. BiblicaOri 49. Rome: Pontificio Istituto Biblico, 2006.
Dubovský, Peter. "Inverting Assyrian Propaganda in Isaiah's Historiography: Writing the Hezekiah-Sennacherib Conflict in the Light of the Ashurbanipal-Teumman War." Pages 365–406 in *The History of Isaiah: The Formation of the Book and Its Presentation of the Past*. Edited by Jacob Stromberg and J. Todd Hibbard. FAT 150. Tübingen: Mohr Siebeck, 2021.
Dubovský, Peter. "Sennacherib's Invasion of the Levant through the Eyes of Assyrian Intelligence Services." Pages 249–91 in *Sennacherib at the Gates of Jerusalem: Story, History and Historiography*. Edited by Isaac Kalimi and Seth Richardson. CHANE 71. Leiden: Brill, 2014.
Dubovský, Peter. "Tiglath-pileser III's Campaigns in 734–732 B.C.: Historical Background of Isa 7, 2 Kgs 15–16 and 2 Chr 27–28." *Bib* 87 (2006): 153–70.

Dubovský, Peter. "Usual and Unusual Concluding Formulas in 2 Kings 13-14: A Reconstruction of the Old Greek and Its Implication for the Literary History." *Bib* 101 (2020): 321-39.

Duhm, Bernhard. *Das Buch Jesaia*. 5th ed. Göttingen: Vandenhoeck & Ruprecht, 1968.

Eaton, John H. "The Origin of the Book of Isaiah." *VT* 9 (1959): 138-57.

Eck, Joachim. *Jesaja 1 - Eine Exegese der Eröffnung des Jesaja-Buches: Die Präsentation Jesajas und JHWHs, Israels und der Tochter Zion*. BZAW 473. Berlin: de Gruyter, 2015.

Edenburg, Cynthia. "Intertextuality, Literary Competence and the Question of Readership: Some Preliminary Observations." *JSOT* 35 (2010): 131-48.

Eichhorn, Johann Gottfried. *Einleitung in das Alte Testament*. 5 vols. Leipzig: Weidmann, 1780-1783.

Eidevall, Göran. *Amos: A New Translation with Introduction and Commentary*. AB 24G. New Haven, CT: Yale University Press, 2017.

Elayi, Josette. *Sargon II, King of Assyria*. SBL Archaeology and Biblical Studies 22. Atlanta, GA: SBL, 2017.

Esterhuizen, Elizabeth. *A Study of the Tension between Despair and Hope in Isaiah 7 and 8 from a Perspective of Trauma and Posttraumatic Growth* (URL: http://hdl.handle.net/10500/22263; Pretoria: Unisa, 2016).

Esterhuizen Elizabeth, and Alphonso Groenewald. "Towards a Theology of Migration: A Survival Perspective from Isaiah 1-12." *Transilvania* 10 (2021): 34-41.

Esterhuizen, Elizabeth, and Alphonso Groenewald. "'And it shall come to pass on that day, the Lord will whistle for the fly which is at the end of the water channels of Egypt, and for the bee which is in the land of Assyria' (Is 7:18): Traumatic Impact of the Covid-19 Virus as a Lens to Read Isaiah 7:18-25." *HTS Teologiese Studies/Theological Studies* 77.3 (2021): 1-7 (4) (a6333).

Evans, Craig A. *To See and Not Perceive: Isaiah 6.9-10 in Early Jewish and Christian Interpretation*. JSOTSup 64. Sheffield: JSOT, 1989.

Everson, A. Joseph. *The Vision of the Prophet Isaiah: Hope in a War-Weary World: A Commentary*. Eugene, OR: Wipf & Stock, 2019.

Ewald, Georg Heinrich August. *Commentary on the Prophets of the Old Testament*. 5 vols. Translated by J. Frederick Smith. London: Williams & Norgate, 1875-81.

Feuerstein, Rüdiger. "Weshalb gibt es Deuterojesaja?" Pages 93-134 in *Ich bewirke das Heil und erschaffe das Unheil (Jes 45,7). Studien zur Botschaft der Propheten, Festschrift für L. Ruppert*. Edited by Friedrich Dietrich and Bernd Willmes. FzB 88. Würzburg: Echter, 1998.

Fischer, Georg. *Jeremia 1-25*. HThKAT. Freiburg: Herder, 2005.

Fischer, Georg. *Jeremia 26-52*. HThKAT. Freiburg: Herder, 2005.

Fischer, Georg. "Jeremiah, God's Suffering Servant." Pages 249-66 in *Jeremiah Studies*. FAT 139. Tübingen: Mohr Siebeck, 2020.

Fischer, Irmtraud. "Isaiah: The Book of Female Metaphors." Pages 303-18 in *Feminist Biblical Interpretation: A Compendium of Critical Commentary on the Books of the Bible and Related Literature*. Edited by Luise Schottroff and Marie-Theres Wacker. Grand Rapids, MI: Eerdmans, 2012.

Fishbane, Michael. *Biblical Interpretation in Ancient Israel*. Oxford: Clarendon, 1985.

Fohrer, Georg. *Das Buch Jesaja*. III: *Kapitel 40-66*. ZBK. Zurich: Zwingli-Verlag, 1967.

Frahm, Eckart. "Samaria, Hamath, and Assyria's Conquests in the Levant in the Late 720s BCE: The Testimony of Sargon II's Inscriptions." Pages 55-86 in *The Last Days of the Kingdom of Israel*. Edited by Shuichi Hasegawa et al. BZAW 511. Berlin: de Gruyter, 2018.

Franke, Chris A. *Isaiah 46, 47, and 48: A New Literary-Critical Reading*. Winona Lake, IN: Eisenbrauns, 1994.

Frechette, Christopher G., and Elizabeth Boase. "Defining 'Trauma' as a Useful Lens for Biblical Interpretation." Pages 161–76 in *Bible Through the Lens of Trauma*. Edited by Elizabeth Boase and Christopher G. Frechette. SBL Semeia Studies 86. Atlanta, GA: SBL Press, 2016.

Freedman, David Noel. "Headings in the Books of the Eighth-Century Prophets." In *Divine Commitment and Human Obligation: Selected Writings of David Noel Freedman*. Edited by John R. Huddlestun. Grand Rapids, MI: Eerdmans, 1997.

Fried, Lisbeth S. "Cyrus the Messiah? The Historical Background to Isaiah 45:1." *HTR* 95 (2002): 373–93.

Fuchs, Andreas. *Die Annalen des Jahres 711 v. Chr. nach Prismenfragmenten aus Ninive und Assur*. SAAS 8. Helsinki: The Neo-Assyrian Text Corpus Project, 1998.

Gärtner, Judith. "The Kabod of YHWH: A Key Isaianic Theme from the Assyrian Empire to the Eschaton." Pages 431–46 in *The History of Isaiah: The Formation of the Book and Its Presentation of the Past*. Edited by Jacob Stromberg and J. Todd Hibbard. FAT 150. Göttingen: Mohr Siebeck, 2021.

Gärtner, Judith. "'Keep Justice!' (Isaiah 56.1): Thoughts Regarding the Concept and Redaction History of a Universal Understanding of Ṣedaqa." Pages 86–100 in *Ṣedaqa and Torah in Post Exilic Discourse*. Edited by Susanne Gillmayr-Bucher and Maria Häusl. LHBOTS 640. London: Bloomsbury T&T Clark, 2017.

Garzón Moreno, Miguel Angel. *La alegría en Isaías: la alegría como unidad y estructura del libro a partir de su epílogo (Is 65–66)*. Estella: Verbo Divino, 2011.

Gelston, Anthony. *The Peshitta of the Twelve Prophets*. Oxford: Clarendon, 1987.

Gentry, Peter J. "The Literary Macrostructures of the Book of Isaiah and the Authorial Intent." Pages 276–53 in *Bind Up the Testimony: Explorations in the Genesis of the Book of Isaiah*. Edited by Daniel I. Block and Richard L. Schultz. Peabody, MA: Hendrickson, 2015.

George, Mark K., ed. *Constructions of Space IV: Further Developments in Examining Ancient Israel's Social Space*. LHBOTS 569. London: Bloomsbury T&T Clark, 2013.

Glaßner, Gottfried. *Vision eines auf Verheißung gegründeten Jerusalem: Textanalytische Studien zu Jesaja 54*. ÖBS 11. Klosterneuburg: Österreichisches Katholisches Bibelwerk, 1991.

Goldingay, John. *A Critical and Exegetical Commentary on Isaiah 56–66*. ICC. London: Bloomsbury T&T Clark, 2014.

Goldingay, John. "Isaiah 42.18-25." *JSOT* 67 (1995): 43–65.

Goldingay, John. *The Theology of the Book of Isaiah*. Downers Grove, IL: IVP Academic, 2014.

Gray, John. *I & II Kings: A Commentary*. OTL. Philadelphia, PA: Westminster, 1976.

Gray, Mark. *Rhetoric and Social Justice in Isaiah*. LHBOTS 432. London: T&T Clark, 2006.

Green, Barbara. *Mikhail Bakhtin and Biblical Scholarship: An Introduction*. SBL Semeia Studies 38. Atlanta, GA: SBL, 2000.

Greenberg, Gillian. *Translation Technique in the Peshitta to Jeremiah*. MPIL 13. Leiden: Brill, 2002.

Greenspahn, Frederick E. *When Brothers Dwell Together: The Preeminence of Younger Siblings in the Hebrew Bible*. New York: Oxford University Press, 1994.

Groenewald, Alphonso. "'For Great in Your Midst is the Holy One of Israel' (Is 12:6b): Trauma and Resilience in the Isaianic Psalm." *HTS Teologiese Studies/Theological Studies* 73/4 (2017) (a4820). https://doi.org/10.4102/hts.v73i4.4820.

Groenewald, Alphonso. "Isaiah 1:4-9 as a Post-exilic Reflection." *JSem* 20 (2011): 87–108.
Groenewald, Alphonso. "The Transformation of the City of Zion: From Decadence to Justice and Prophetic Hope (Is. 1:1–2:5)." *HTS Teologiese Studies/Theological Studies* 72/1 (2016): 1–5 (4) (a3568). http://dx.doi.org/10.4102/hts.v72i1.3568.
Groenewald, Alphonso. "'Trauma is Suffering that Remains': The Contribution of Trauma Studies to Prophetic Studies." *Acta Theologica Supplementum* 26 (2018): 88–102. http://dx.doi.org/10.18820/23099089/actat.Sup26.5.
Grosser, Emmylou J. "What Symmetry Can Do that Parallelism Can't: Line Perception and Poetic Effects in the Song of Deborah (Judges 5:2-31)." *VT* 71 (2021): 175–204.
Grosser, Emmylou J. *Unparalleled Poetry: A Cognitive Approach to the Free-Rhythm Verse of the Hebrew Bible*. Oxford: Oxford University Press, 2023.
Guest, Deryn. "Hiding Behind the Naked Women in Lamentations: A Recriminative Response." *BibInt* 7 (1999): 413–48.
Hägglund, Fredrik. *Isaiah 53 in the Light of Homecoming after Exile*. FAT/II 31. Tübingen: Mohr Siebeck, 2008.
Hartenstein, Friedhelm. *Das Archiv des verborgenen Gottes: Studien zur Unheilsprophetie Jesajas und zur Zionstheologie der Psalmen in assyrischer Zeit*. BThSt 71. Neukirchener-Vluyn: Neukirchener Verlag, 2011.
Hartenstein, Friedhelm. "Der Sabbat als Zeichen und heilige Zeit. Zur Theologie des Ruhetages im Alten Testament." Pages 83–102 in *Das Fest: Jenseits des Alltags*. Edited by Martin Ebner. JBTh 18. Neukirchen-Vluyn: Neukirchener Verlag, 2004.
Hay, Andrew R. "An Exegetical Reflection on Isaiah 1.18." *BiTr* 20 (2016): 288–91.
Hayes, Katherine M. *The Earth Mourns: Prophetic Metaphor and Oral Aesthetic*. SBLAcBib 8. Atlanta, GA: SBL, 2002.
Hays, Christopher B. "The Book of Isaiah in Contemporary Research." *RC* 5 (2011): 549–66.
Hays, Rebecca W. Poe. "Sing Me a Parable of Zion: Isaiah's Vineyard (5:1-7) and Its Relation to the 'Daughter Zion' Tradition." *JBL* 135 (2016): 743–61.
Hermisson, Hans-Jürgen. "The Fourth Servant Song in the Context of Second Isaiah." Pages 16–47 in *The Suffering Servant: Isaiah 53 in Jewish and Christian Sources*. Edited by Bernd Janowski and Peter Stuhlmacher. Grand Rapids, MI: Eerdmans, 2004.
Hibbard, J. Todd. *Intertextuality in Isaiah 24–27: The Reuse and Evocation of Earlier Texts and Traditions*. FAT/II 16. Tübingen: Mohr Siebeck, 2006.
Higgins, Ryan. "He would not hear her voice: From Skilled Speech to Silence in 2 Samuel 13:1-22." *Journal of Feminist Studies in Religion* 36, no. 2 (2020): 25–42.
Hillers, Delbert R. "A Convention in Hebrew Literature: The Reaction to Bad News." *ZAW* 77 (1965): 86–90.
Hitzig, Ferdinand. *Der Prophet Jesaja*. Heidelberg: C. F. Winter, 1833.
Höffken, Peter. *Jesaja: Der Stand der theologischen Diskussion*. Darmstadt: Wissenschaftliche Buchgesellschaft, 2004.
Holmstedt, Robert D. "Hebrew Poetry and the Appositive Style: Parallelism, *Requiescat in pace*." *VT* 69 (2019): 617–48.
Honggeng, Guo. "The Assyrian Intelligence Activities during the Assyrian Empire." *JAAS* 18 (2004): 59–71.
Hopf, Matthias. "Die Psalmen als 'verbale Bühnen'. Ein experimenteller Blick auf die dramatisch-performativen Strukturen der Psalmen." *BZ* 65 (2021): 1–27.
Hoppe, Leslie J. *Isaiah*. New Collegeville Bible Commentary 13. Collegeville, MN: Liturgical Press, 2012.
Houtmann, Cornelis. *Exodus: Volume 3. Chapters 20–40*. HCOT. Leuven: Peeters, 1999.

Hrobon, Bohdan. *Ethical Dimension of Cult in the Book of Isaiah*. BZAW 418. Berlin: de Gruyter, 2010.

Hubbard, Phil, and Rob Kitchin, eds. *Key Thinkers on Space and Place*. 2nd ed. Los Angeles, CA: SAGE, 2011.

Ibarretxe-Antuñano, Iraide. "Mind-as-Body as a Cross-Linguistic Conceptual Metaphor." *Miscelánea. A Journal of English and American Studies* 25 (2002): 93–119.

Irudayaraj, Dominic S. "Mountains in Micah and Coherence: A 'SynDiaTopic' Suggestion." *JBL* 140 (2021): 703–22.

Irudayaraj, Dominic S. *Violence, Otherness and Identity in Isaiah 63:1–6: The Trampling One Coming from Edom*. LHBOTS 633. London: Bloomsbury T&T Clark, 2017.

Jakobson, Roman. "Closing Statements: Linguistics and Poetics." Pages 350–77 in *Style in Language*. Edited by Thomas A. Sebeock, Cambridge, MA: MIT, 1964.

Janoff-Bulman, Ronnie. "Rebuilding Shattered Assumptions after Traumatic Life Events." Pages 305–23 in *Coping: The Psychology of What Works*. Edited by C. R. Snyder. Oxford: Oxford University Press, 1999.

Janoff-Bulman, Ronnie. *Shattered Assumptions: Towards a New Psychology of Trauma*. New York: Free Press, 1992.

Janzen, David. "Claimed and Unclaimed Experience: Problematic Readings of Trauma in the Hebrew Bible." *BibInt* 27 (2019): 163–85.

Joachimsen, Kristin. "Remembering and Forgetting in Isaiah 43, 44, and 46." Pages 42–56 in *New Perspectives on Old Testament Prophecy and History: Essays in Honour of Hans M. Barstad*. Edited by Rannfrid I. Thelle, Terje Stordalen, and Mervyn E. J. Richardson. VTSup 168. Leiden: Brill, 2015.

Jones, Douglas R. "The Traditio of the Oracles of Isaiah of Jerusalem," *ZAW* 67 (1955): 226–46.

Kedar-Kopfstein, Benjamin. "שריד." *ThWAT* 7:879–82.

Kellenberger, Edgar. "Heil und Verstockung: Zu Jes 6,9f. bei Jesaja und im Neuen Testament." *TZ* 48 (1992): 268–75.

Keller, Catherine. "Preemption and Omnipotence: A Niebuhrian Prophecy." Pages 17–34 in *God and Power: Counter-Apocalyptic Journeys*. Minneapolis, MN: Fortress, 2005.

Kessler, Rainer. "Kyros und der Eved bei Deuterojesaja: Gottes Handeln in Macht und Schwäche." Pages 141–58 in *Christus und seine Geschwister: Christologie im Umfeld der Bibel in Gerechter Sprache*. Edited by Marlene Crüsemann and Carsten Jochum-Bortfeld. Gütersloh: Gütersloher Verlagshaus, 2009.

Kessler, Rainer. *Der Weg zum Leben: Ethik des Alten Testaments*. Gütersloh: Gütersloher Verlagshaus, 2017.

Kim, Brittany. *"Lengthen Your Tent-cords": The Metaphorical World of Israel's Household in the Book of Isaiah*. Siphrut: 23. University Park, PA: Eisenbrauns, 2018.

Kim, Hyun Chul Paul. "City, Earth, and Empire in Isaiah 24–27." Pages 25–48 in *Formation and Intertextuality in Isaiah 24–27*. Edited by J. Todd Hibbard and Hyun Chul Paul Kim. SBLAIL 17. Atlanta, GA: SBL, 2013.

Kim, Hyun Chul Paul. "Little Highs, Little Lows: Tracing Key Themes in Isaiah." Pages 141–66 in *The Book of Isaiah: Enduring Questions Answered Anew: Essays Honoring Joseph Blenkinsopp and His Contribution to the Study of Isaiah*. Edited by Richard J. Bautch and J. Todd Hibbard. Grand Rapids, MI: Eerdmans, 2014.

Kim, Hyun Chul Paul. *Reading Isaiah: A Literary and Theological Commentary*. Reading the Old Testament. Macon, GA: Smyth & Helwys, 2016.

Kim, Hyun Chul Paul. "The Spider-Poet: Signs and Symbols in Isaiah 41." Pages 159–79 in *The Desert Will Bloom: Poetic Visions in Isaiah*. Edited by A. Joseph Everson and Hyun Chul Paul Kim. SBLAIL 4. Atlanta, GA: SBL, 2009.

Kim, Soo J. "Eschatology in Isaiah." Pages 352–74 in *The Oxford Handbook of Isaiah*. Edited by Lena-Sofia Tiemeyer. New York: Oxford University Press, 2020.

King, Andrew M. "A Remnant Will Return: An Analysis of the Literary Function of the Remnant Motif in Isaiah." *JESOT* 4 (2015): 145–69.

Kooij, Arie van der. *Die alten Textzeugen des Jesajabuches: Ein Beitrag zur Textgeschichte des Alten Testaments*. OBO 35. Freiburg: Universitätsverlag; Göttingen: Vandenhoeck & Ruprecht, 1981.

Kooij, Arie van der, and Florian Wilk. "Erläuterungen zu Jes 1–39." Pages 2505–607 in *Psalmen bis Daniel*. Vol. 2 of *Septuaginta Deutsch: Erläuterungen und Kommentare zum griechischen Alten Testament*. Edited by Martin Karrer and Wolfgang Kraus. Stuttgart: Deutsche Bibelgesellschaft, 2011.

Koole, Jan Leunis. *Isaiah. Part III: Volume 3. Isaiah 56–66*. HCOT. Leuven: Peeters, 2001.

Kövecses, Zoltán. *Metaphor: A Practical Introduction*. 2nd ed. Oxford: Oxford University Press, 2010.

Kövecses, Zoltán. *Metaphor in Culture: Universality and Variation*. Cambridge: Cambridge University Press, 2010.

Kratz, Reinhard Gregor. "Die Redaktion der Prophetenbücher." Pages 9–27 in *Rezeption und Auslegung im Alten Testament und in seinem Umfeld: ein Symposion aus Anlass des 60. Geburtstags von Odil Hannes Steck*. Edited by Reinhard Gregor Kratz and Thomas Krüger. OBO 153. Freiburg/Schweiz: Universitätsverlag, 1997.

Kratz, Reinhard G. "Rewriting Isaiah: The Case of Isaiah 28–31." Pages 245–66 in *Prophecy and Prophets in Ancient Israel: Proceedings of the Oxford Old Testament Seminar*. Edited by John Day. LHBOTS 531. New York: T&T Clark, 2010.

Kronholm, Tryggve. "יתר." *ThWAT* 3:1079–90

Kustár, Zoltán. *"Durch seine Wunden sind wir geheilt": eine Untersuchung zur Metaphorik von Israels Krankheit und Heilung im Jesajabuch*. BWANT 154. Stuttgart: Kohlhammer, 2002.

Laato, Antti. *"About Zion I will not be silent": The Book of Isaiah as an Ideological Unity*. ConBOT 44. Stockholm: Almqvist & Wiksell, 1998.

Laato, Antti. *Message and Composition of the Book of Isaiah: An Interpretation in the Light of Jewish Reception History*. DCLS 46. Berlin: de Gruyter, 2022.

Lack, Rémi. *La symbolique du livre d'Isaïe*. AnBib 59. Rome: Pontifical Biblical Institute, 1973.

Lakoff, George, and Mark Johnson. *Metaphors We Live By*. Chicago, IL: The University of Chicago Press, 1980.

Lakoff, George, and Mark Turner. *More Than Cool Reason: A Field Guide to Poetic Metaphor*. Chicago, IL: University of Chicago Press, 1989.

Landy, Francis. "Ancestral Voices and Disavowal: Poetic Innovation and Intertextuality in the Eighth-Century Prophets." Pages 73–90 in *Second Wave Intertextuality and the Hebrew Bible*. Edited by Marianne Grohmann and Hyun Chul Paul Kim. SBL Resources for Biblical Study 93. Atlanta, GA: SBL, 2019.

Landy, Francis. "The Poetic Vision of Isaiah." Pages 393–408 in *The Oxford Handbook of Isaiah*. Edited by Lena-Sofia Tiemeyer. New York: Oxford University Press, 2020.

Lapsley, Jacqueline E. "'Look! The Children and I Are as Signs and Portents in Israel': Children in Isaiah." Pages 82–102 in *The Child in the Bible*. Edited by Marcia J. Bunge. Grand Rapids, MI: Eerdmans, 2008.

Lau, Wolfgang. *Schriftgelehrte Prophetie in Jes 56–66: Eine Untersuchung zu den literarischen Bezügen in den letzten elf Kapiteln des Jesajabuches.* BZAW 225. Berlin: de Gruyter, 1994.

Lauha, Aarre. "'Der Bund des Volkes'. Ein Aspekt der deuterojesajanischen Missionstheologie." Pages 257–61 in *Beiträge zur Alttestamentlichen Theologie. Festschrift für Walther Zimmerli zum 70. Geburtstag.* Edited by Herbert Donner, Robert Hanhart, and Rudolf Smend. Göttingen: Vandenhoeck & Ruprecht, 1977.

Lazzaro, Boris. "If the Blind Walk: The Cognitive Metaphor 'Knowing is Seeing' and Its Elaboration in Isa 42,16." Pages 61–78 in *Networks of Metaphors in the Hebrew Bible.* Edited by Danilo Verde and Antje Labahn. BETL 309. Leuven: Peeters, 2020.

Leclerc, Thomas L. *Yahweh is Exalted in Justice: Solidarity and Conflict in Isaiah.* Minneapolis, MN: Fortress, 2001.

Leene, Henk. "Blowing the Same Shofar: An Intertextual Comparison of Representations of the Prophetic Role in Jeremiah and Ezekiel." Pages 175–98 in *The Elusive Prophet: The Prophet as a Historical Person, Literary Character and Anonymous Artist: Papers Read at the Eleventh Joint Meeting of The Society for Old Testament Study and Het Oudtestamentisch Werkgezelschap in Nederland en België, held at Soesterberg 2000.* Edited by Johannes C. de Moor. OTS 45. Leiden: Brill, 2001.

Leene, Henk. *Newness in Old Testament Prophecy: An Intertextual Study.* OTS 64. Leiden: Brill, 2014.

Lefebvre, Henri. *The Production of Space.* Translated by D. Nicholson Smith. Oxford: Blackwell, 1991.

Lemaire, André. "Judean Identity in Elephantine: Everyday Life according to the Ostraca." Pages 365–73 in *Judah and the Judeans in the Achaemenid Period: Negotiating Identity in an International Context.* Edited by Oded Lipschits, Gary N. Knoppers, and Manfred Oeming. Winona Lake, IN: Eisenbrauns, 2011.

Liebreich, Leon J. "The Compilation of the Book of Isaiah." *JQR* 46 (1956): 259–74.

Liebreich, Leon J. "The Compilation of the Book of Isaiah." *JQR* 47 (1956): 114–38.

Lim, Bo H. *The 'Way of the Lord' in the Book of Isaiah.* LHBOTS 522. London: T&T Clark, 2010.

Lowth, Robert. *Isaiah: A New Translation, with a Preliminary Dissertation, and Notes, Critical, Philological, and Explanatory.* London: J. Nichols, for J. Dodsley and T. Cadell, 1778.

Lozachmeur, Hélène. *La Collection Clermont-Ganneau: Ostraca, épigraphes sur Jarre étiquettes de bois.* Vol. 1. Mémoires de L'académie des Inscriptions et Belles-Lettres 35. Paris: De Boccard, 2006.

Lund, Øystein. *Way Metaphors and Way Topics in Isaiah 40–55.* FAT/II 28. Tübingen: Mohr Siebeck, 2007.

Lynch, Matthew J. "Zion's Warrior and the Nations: Isaiah 59:15b–63:6 in Isaiah's Zion Traditions." *CBQ* 70 (2008): 244–63.

Ma, Wonsuk. *Until the Spirit Comes: The Spirit of God in the Book of Isaiah.* JSOTSup 271. Sheffield: Sheffield Academic, 1999.

Machinist, Peter. "Assyria and its Image in the First Isaiah." *JAOS* 103 (1983): 719–37.

Maier, Christl M. "Daughter Zion as a Gendered Space in the Book of Isaiah." Pages 102–18 in *Constructions of Space II: The Biblical City and Other Imagined Spaces.* Edited by Jon L. Berquist and Claudia V. Camp. LHBOTS 490. London: Bloomsbury T&T Clark, 2008.

Maier, Christl M. *Daughter Zion, Mother Zion: Gender and the Sacred in Ancient Israel.* Minneapolis, MN: Fortress, 2008.

Maier, Christl M. "Jerusalem als Ehebrecherin in Ezechiel 16." Pages 76–101 in *Feministische Hermeneutik und Erstes Testament*. Edited by Hedwig Jahnow et al. Stuttgart: Kohlhammer, 1994.

Maier, Michael P. *Völkerwallfahrt im Jesajabuch*. BZAW 474. Berlin: de Gruyter, 2016.

Mandolfo, Carleen R. *Daughter Zion Talks Back to the Prophets: A Dialogic Theology of the Book of Lamentations*. SBL Semeia Studies 58. Atlanta, GA: SBL, 2007.

Markl, Dominik. "The Babylonian Exile as the Birth Trauma of Monotheism." *Bib* 101 (2020): 1–25.

Markl, Doninik, and Georg Fischer. *Das Buch Exodus*. NSK.AT 2. Stuttgart: Katholisches Bibelwerk, 2009.

Marlow, Hilary. "Reading from the Ground Up: Nature in the Book of Isaiah." Pages 123–35 in *The Oxford Handbook of the Bible and Ecology*. Edited by Hilary Marlow and Mark Harris. New York: Oxford University Press, 2022.

Mastnjak, Nathan. "The Book of Isaiah and the Anthological Genre." *Hebrew Studies* 61 (2020): 49–72.

Mathews, Claire R. *Defending Zion: Edom's Desolation and Jacob's Restoration (Isaiah 34–35) in Context*. BZAW 236. Berlin: de Gruyter, 1995.

Melugin, Roy F. "Figurative Speech and the Reading of Isaiah 1 as Scripture." Pages 282–305 in *New Visions of Isaiah*. Edited by Roy F. Melugin and Marvin A. Sweeney. JSOTSup 214. Sheffield: Sheffield Academic, 1997.

Melugin, Roy F. *The Formation of Isaiah 40–55*. BZAW 141. Berlin: de Gruyter, 1976.

Melugin, Roy F. "Isaiah 40–66 in Recent Research: The 'Unity' Movement." Pages 142–94 in *Recent Research on the Major Prophets*. Edited by Alan J. Hauser. Recent Research in Biblical Studies 1. Sheffield: Sheffield Phoenix, 2008.

Mettinger, Tryggve N. D. *A Farewell to the Servant Songs: A Critical Examination of an Exegetical Axiom*. Lund: Gleerup, 1983.

Mills, Mary E. *Urban Imagination in Biblical Prophecy*. LHBOTS 560. New York: Bloomsbury T&T Clark, 2012.

Mills, Mary. "Wasteland and Pastoral Idyll as Images of the Biblical City." Pages 105–22 in *The City in the Hebrew Bible: Critical, Literary and Exegetical Approaches*. Edited by James K. Aitken and Hilary F. Marlow. LHBOTS 672. London: T&T Clark, 2018.

Miscall, Peter D. *Isaiah*. Readings: A New Biblical Commentary. Sheffield: Sheffield Academic, 1993.

Miscall, Peter D. *Isaiah 34–35: A Nightmare/A Dream*. JSOTSup 281. Sheffield: Sheffield Academic, 1999.

Montgomery, James A. *A Critical and Exegetical Commentary on the Books of Kings*. ICC. Edinburgh: T&T Clark, 1951.

Morgan, David M. "Remnant." Pages 658–64 in *Dictionary of the Old Testament Prophets: A Compendium of Contemporary Biblical Scholarship*. Edited by Mark J. Boda and J. Gordon McConville. Downers Grove, IL: IVP Academic/Inter-Varsity, 2012.

Morrison, Craig E. *The Character of the Syriac Version of the First Book of Samuel*. MPIL 11. Leiden: Brill, 2001.

Morrow, William. "Deuteronomy 7 in Postcolonial Perspective: Cultural Fragmentation and Renewal." Pages 275–93 in *Interpreting Exile: Displacement and Deportation in Biblical and Modern Contexts*. Edited by Brad E. Kelle, Frank R. Ames, and Jacob L. Wright. SBLAIL 10. Atlanta, GA: SBL, 2011.

Mortara Garavelli, Bice. *Manuale di retorica*. 10th ed. Milan: Bompiani, 2006.

Moughtin-Mumby, Sharon. "Feminist/Womanist Readings in Isaiah." Pages 601–20 in *The Oxford Handbook of Isaiah*. Edited by Lena-Sofia Tiemeyer. New York: Oxford University Press, 2020.

Muilenburg, James. "The Book of Isaiah: Chapters 40–66." Pages 381–733 in *IB* 5. Nashville, TN: Abingdon, 1956.

Muilenburg, James. "Form Criticism and Beyond." *JBL* 88 (1969): 1–18.

Newsom, Carol A. *The Book of Job: A Contest of Moral Imaginations*. Oxford: Oxford University Press, 2003.

Nielsen, Kirsten. *There is Hope for a Tree: The Tree as Metaphor in Isaiah*. JSOTSup 65. Sheffield: JSOT, 1989.

Nihan, Christoph. "Ethnicity and Identity in Isaiah 56–66." Pages 67–104 in *Judah and the Judeans in the Achaemenid Period: Negotiating Identity in an International Context*. Edited by Oded Lipschits, Gary N. Knoppers, and Manfred Oeming. Winona Lake, IN: Eisenbrauns, 2011.

Nitsche, Stefan Ark. *Jesaja 24–27: ein dramatischer Text: Die Frage nach den Genres prophetischer Literatur des Alten Testaments und die Textgraphik der großen Jesajarolle aus Qumran*. BWANT 166. Stuttgart: Kohlhammer, 2006.

Nogalski, James D. *Introduction to the Hebrew Prophets*. Nashville, TN: Abingdon, 2018.

Nogalski, James D. "The Role of Lady Zion in the Concluding Section of Zephaniah and Isaiah 40–66." Pages 55–73 in *Isaiah and the Twelve: Parallels, Similarities and Differences*. Edited by Richard J. Bautch, Joachim Eck, and Burkard M. Zapff. BZAW 527. Berlin: de Gruyter 2020.

Nurmela, Risto. *The Mouth of the Lord Has Spoken: Inner-Biblical Allusion in Second and Third Isaiah*. Lanham, MD: University Press of America, 2006.

O'Connell, Robert H. *Concentricity and Continuity: The Literary Structure of Isaiah*. JSOTSup 188. Sheffield: Sheffield Academic, 1994.

O'Connor, Kathleen M. "Reclaiming Jeremiah's Violence." Pages 37–49 in *The Aesthetics of Violence in the Prophets*. Edited by Julia M. O'Brien and Chris Franke. LHBOTS 517. New York: T&T Clark, 2010.

O'Connor, Michael P. "The Biblical Notion of the City." Pages 18–39 in *Constructions of Space II: The Biblical City and Other Imagined Spaces*. Edited by Jon L. Berquist and Claudia V. Camp. LHBOTS 490. London: Bloomsbury T&T Clark, 2008.

Økland, Jorunn, J., Cornelis de Vos, and Karen J. Wenell, eds. *Constructions of Space III: Biblical Spatiality and the Sacred*. LHBOTS 540. London: Bloomsbury T&T Clark, 2016.

Ortlund, Eric. "Reversed (Chrono-)Logical Sequence in Isaiah 1–39: Some Implications for Theories of Redaction." *JSOT* 35 (2010): 209–24.

Paganini, Simone. *Der Weg zur Frau Zion, Ziel unserer Hoffnung*. SBB 49. Stuttgart: Katholisches Bibelwerk 2002.

Parke-Taylor, Geoffrey H. *The Formation of the Book of Jeremiah: Doublets and Recurring Phrases*. SBLMS 51. Atlanta, GA: Scholars Press, 2000.

Parry, Donald W., and Elisha Qimron, eds. *The Great Isaiah Scroll (1Q Isa^a): A New Edition*. STDJ 32. Leiden: Brill, 1999.

Pettigiani, Ombretta. "Il motivo della vergogna come conclusione di Is 11." Pages 81–92 in *La profezia tra l'uno e l'altro Testamento: Studi in onore del prof. Pietro Bovati in occasione del suo settantacinquesimo compleanno*. Edited by Guido Benzi, Donatella Scaiola, and Marco Bonarini. AnBib Studia 4. Rome: Gregorian and Biblical Press, 2015.

Pfister, Manfred. *Das Drama. Theorie und Analyse*. 11th ed. UTB 580. Munich: W. Fink, 2001.

Polaski, Donald C. *Authorizing an End: The Isaiah Apocalypse and Intertextuality*. BIS 50. Leiden: Brill, 2003.

Porten, Bezalel. *Archives from Elephantine: The Life of an Ancient Jewish Military Colony*. Berkeley, CA: University of California Press, 1968.

Porten, Bezalel. "The Religion of the Jews of Elephantine." *JNES* 28 (1969): 116–21.

Porten, Bezalel, and Ada Yardeni, eds. *Textbook of Aramaic Documents from Ancient Egypt: Volume IV: Ostraca & Assorted Inscriptions*. Winona Lake, IN: Eisenbrauns, 1999.

Potts, Daniel T. *The Archaeology of Elam: Formation and Transformation of an Ancient Iranian State*. Cambridge: Cambridge University Press, 1999.

Poulsen, Frederik. *The Black Hole in Isaiah: A Study of Exile as a Literary Theme*. FAT 125. Tübingen: Mohr Siebeck, 2019.

Poulsen, Frederik. *Representing Zion: Judgement and Salvation in the Old Testament*. Copenhagen International Seminar. New York: Routledge, 2015.

Powell, Marvin A. "Merodach-Baladan at Dur-Jakin: A Note on the Defense of Babylonian Cities." *JCS* 34 (1982): 59–61.

Prinsloo, Gert T. M., and Christl M. Maier, eds. *Constructions of Space V: Place, Space and Identity in the Ancient Mediterranean World*. LHBOTS 576. Bloomsbury T&T Clark, 2013.

Rad, Gerhard von. *Old Testament Theology: Volume 2: The Theology of Israel's Prophetic Traditions*. Translated by David M. G. Stalker. London: Oliver & Boyd, 1965.

Rendtorff, Rolf. "The Book of Isaiah: A Complex Unity: Synchronic and Diachronic Reading." Pages 32–49 in *New Visions of Isaiah*. Edited by Roy F. Melugin and Marvin A. Sweeney. JSOTSup 214. Sheffield: JSOT, 1996.

Rendtorff, Rolf. "The Composition of the Book of Isaiah." Pages 146–69 in *Canon and Theology: Overtures to an Old Testament Theology*. Translated by Margaret Kohl. Edinburgh: T&T Clark, 1994.

Rendtorff, Rolf. "Jesaja 6 im Rahmen der Komposition des Jesajabuches." Pages 73–82 in *The Book of Isaiah: Le Livre d'Isaïe. Les oracles et leurs relectures. Utilité et complexité de l'ouvrage*. Edited by Jacques Vermeylen. BETL 81. Leuven: University Press, 1989.

Roberts, J. J. M. *First Isaiah: A Commentary*. Hermeneia. Minneapolis, MN: Fortress, 2015.

Roberts, J. J. M. "Isaiah in Old Testament Theology." *Int* 36 (1982): 130–43.

Rom-Shiloni, Dalit. "Exile in the Book of Isaiah." Pages 293–317 in *The Oxford Handbook of Isaiah*. Edited by Lena-Sofia Tiemeyer. New York: Oxford University Press, 2020.

Rosenbaum, Michael. *Word-Order Variation in Isaiah 40–55: A Functional Perspective*. SSN 36. Assen: Van Gorcum, 1997.

Rosenberg, Avroham Y. *Isaiah II: Translation of Text, Rashi and Commentary*. Miqra'ot Gedolot. New York: Judaica, 1982.

Rossi, Benedetta. *L'intercessione nel tempo della fine: Studio dell'intercessione profetica nel libro di Geremia*. AnBib 204. Rome: Gregorian & Biblical Press, 2013.

Ruszkowski, Leszek. "Der Sabbat bei Tritojesaja." Pages 61–74 in *Prophetie und Psalmen: Festschrift für Klaus Seybold zum 65. Geburtstag*. Edited by Beat Huwyler, Hans Peter Mathys, and Beat Weber. AOAT 280. Münster: Ugarit Verlag, 2001.

Samely, Alexander. "How Coherence Works: Reading, Re-Reading and Inner-Biblical Exegesis." *HBAI* 9 (2020): 130–82.

Sawyer, John F. A. "Daughter of Zion and Servant of the Lord in Isaiah: A Comparison." *JSOT* 44 (1989): 89–107.

Schaper, Joachim. "Rereading the Law: Inner-Biblical Exegesis of Divine Oracles in Ezekiel 44 and Isaiah 56." Pages 125–44 in *Recht und Ethik im Alten Testament: Beiträge des Symposiums "Das Alte Testament und die Kultur der Moderne" anlässlich des 100. Geburtstags Gerhard von Rads (1901-1971), Heidelberg, 18.-21. Oktober 2001.* Edited by Bernard M. Levinson and Eckart Otto. Altes Testament und Moderne 13. Münster: LIT, 2004.

Scheuer, Blaženka. "'Why Do You Let Us Wander, O Lord, from Your Ways?' (Isa 63:17): Clarification of Culpability in the Last Part of the Book of Isaiah." Pages 159–73 in *Continuity and Discontinuity: Chronological and Thematic Development in Isaiah 40-66.* Edited by Lena-Sofia Tiemeyer and Hans Barstad. FRLANT 255. Göttingen: Vandenhoeck & Ruprecht, 2014.

Schipper, Jeremy. *Disability and Isaiah's Suffering Servant.* Oxford: Oxford University Press, 2011.

Schmid, Konrad. "Innerbiblische Schriftauslegung. Aspekte der Forschungsgeschichte." Pages 1–22 in *Schriftauslegung in der Schrift: Festschrift für O. H. Steck.* Edited by Konrad Schmid, Reinhard G. Kratz, and Thomas Krüge. BZAW 300. Berlin: de Gruyter, 2000.

Schmid, Konrad. *The Old Testament: A Literary History.* Translated by Linda M. Malony. Minneapolis, MN: Fortress, 2012.

Schmid, Konrad. *Schriftgelehrte Traditionsliteratur. Fallstudien zur innerbiblischen Schriftauslegung im Alten Testament.* FAT 77. Tübingen: Mohr Siebeck, 2011.

Schniedewind, William M. *The Finger of the Scribe: How Scribes Learned to Write the Bible.* New York: Oxford University Press, 2019.

Schreiter, Robert J. "Reading Biblical Texts through the Lens of Resilience." Pages 193–207 in *Bible Through the Lens of Trauma.* Edited by Elizabeth Boase and Christopher G. Frechette. SBL Semeia Studies 86. Atlanta, GA: SBL, 2016.

Schüle, Andreas. "'Build Up, Pass Through.' Isa 57:14–62:12 as the Core Composition of Third Isaiah." Pages 83–112 in *The Book of Isaiah: Enduring Questions Answered Anew: Festschrift für Joseph Blenkinsopp.* Edited by Richard Bautch and J. Todd Hibbard. Grand Rapids, MI: Eerdmans, 2014.

Schüle, Andreas. "Third Isaiah. What's so Greek about It?" Pages 97–110 in *Prophecy and Hellenism.* Edited by Hannes Bezzel and Stefan Pfeiffer. FAT/II 129. Tübingen: Mohr Siebeck 2021.

Schuele, Andreas. "Who is the True Israel? Community, Identity, and Religious Commitment in Third Isaiah (Isaiah 56–66)." *Int* 73 (2019): 174–84.

Schultz, Richard L. "The Origins and the Basic Arguments of the Multi-Author View of the Composition of Isaiah: Where are We Now and How did We get There?" Pages 7–32 in *Bind Up the Testimony: Explorations in the Genesis of the Book of Isaiah.* Edited by Daniel I. Block and Richard L. Schultz. Peabody, MA: Hendrickson, 2015.

Schultz, Richard L. *Search for Quotation: Verbal Parallels in the Prophets.* JSOTSup 180. Sheffield: Sheffield Academic, 1999.

Schwartz, Ethan. "Mirrors of Moses in Isaiah 1–12." Pages 269–96 in *The History of Isaiah: The Formation of the Book and Its Presentation of the Past.* Edited by Jacob Stromberg and J. Todd Hibbard. FAT 150. Tübingen: Mohr Siebeck, 2021.

Schweitzer, Steven J. "Exploring the Utopian Space of Chronicles: Some Spatial Anomalies." Pages 141–56 in *Constructions of Space I: Theory, Geography, and Narrative.* Edited by Jon L. Berquist and Claudia V. Camp. LHBOTS 481. New York: T&T Clark International, 2007.

Scialabba, Daniela. *Creation and Salvation: Models of Relationship Between the God of Israel and the Nations in the Book of Jonah, in Psalm 33 (MT and LXX) and in the Novel "Joseph and Aseneth"*. FAT/II 106. Tübingen: Mohr Siebeck, 2019.

Seiler, D. Georg Friedrich. *Das größre biblisch Erbauungsbuch: Des alten Testamentes siebenter Theil: Die Propheten Jesaias und Jeremias*. Erlangen: zu finden in der Bibelanstalt, 1792.

Seitz, Christopher R. "The Book of Isaiah 40–66: Introduction, Commentary, and Reflections." Pages 309–552 in NIB 6. Nashville, TN: Abingdon, 2001.

Seitz, Christopher R. "The Divine Council: Temporal Transition and New Prophecy in the Book of Isaiah." *JBL* 109 (1990): 229–47.

Seitz, Christopher R. *Isaiah 1–39*. Interpretation. Louisville, KY: John Knox, 1993.

Seitz, Christopher R. "Isaiah 1–66: Making Sense of the Whole." Pages 105–26 in *Reading and Preaching the Book of Isaiah*. Edited by Christopher R. Seitz. Philadelphia, PA: Fortress, 1988.

Seufert, Matthew. "Reading Isaiah 40:1–11 in Light of Isaiah 36–37." *JETS* 58 (2015): 269–81.

Shalom, M. Paul. *Isaiah 40–66: Translation and Commentary*. ECC. Grand Rapids, MI: Eerdmans, 2012.

Simian-Yofre, Horacio. *Sofferenza dell'uomo e silenzio di Dio: Nell'Antico Testamento e nella letteratura del Vicino Oriente Antico*. Studia Biblica 2. Rome: Città Nuova, 2005.

Smith-Christopher, Daniel L. *A Biblical Theology of Exile*. OBT. Minneapolis, MN: Fortress, 2002.

Smith-Christopher, Daniel L. *Micah: A Commentary*. OTL. Louisville, KY: Westminster John Knox, 2015.

Smith-Christopher, Daniel L. "Reassessing the Historical and Sociological Impact of the Babylonian Exile (597/587–539 BCE)." Pages 7–36 in *Exile: Old Testament, Jewish, and Christian Conceptions*. Edited by James M. Scott. JSJSup 56. Leiden: Brill, 1997.

Smith, Paul A. *Rhetoric and Redaction in Trito-Isaiah: The Structure, Growth and Authorship of Isaiah 56–66*. VTSup 62. Leiden: Brill, 1995.

Soja, Edward W. *Thirdspace: Journeys to Los Angeles and Other Real-and-Imagined Places*. Malden, MA: Blackwell, 1996.

Sommer, Benjamin D. "Allusions and Illusions: The Unity of the Book of Isaiah." Pages 156–86 in *New Visions of Isaiah*. Edited by Roy F. Melugin and Marvin A. Sweeney. JSOTSup 214. Sheffield: JSOT, 1996.

Sommer, Benjamin D. *A Prophet Reads Scripture: Allusion in Isaiah 40–66*. Stanford: Stanford University Press, 1998.

Spans, Andrea. *Die Stadtfrau Zion im Zentrum der Welt. Exegese und Theologie von Jes 60–62*. BBB 175. Göttingen: Vandenhoek & Rupprecht, 2015.

Stamm, Johann J. "Berit 'am bei Deuterojesaja." Pages 510–24 in *Probleme biblischer Theologie. Gerhard von Rad zum 70. Geburtstag*. Edited by Hans W. Wolff. Munich: Kaiser, 1971.

Steck, Odil Hannes. *Bereitete Heimkehr: Jesaja 35 als redaktionelle Brücke zwischen dem Ersten und dem Zweiten Jesaja*. SBS 121. Stuttgart: Katholisches Bibelwerk, 1985.

Steck, Odil Hannes. *Gottesknecht und Zion: Gesammelte Aufsätze zu Deuterojesaja*. FAT 4. Tübingen: Mohr Siebeck, 1992.

Steck, Odil Hannes. *Die Prophetenbücher und ihr theologisches Zeugnis: Wege der Nachfrage und Fährten zur Antwort*. Tübingen: Mohr Siebeck, 1996.

Steck, Odil Hannes. *Studien Zu Tritojesaja*. BZAW 203. Berlin: de Gruyter, 1991.

Stern, Josef. *Metaphor in Context*. Cambridge, MA: MIT, 2000.

Stromberg, Jacob. "The Book of Isaiah: Its Final Structure." Pages 19–36 in *The Oxford Handbook of Isaiah*. Edited by Lena-Sofia Tiemeyer. New York: Oxford University Press, 2020.

Stromberg, Jacob. "A Covenantal Community and a New Creation after the Flood: The Wise in Daniel 11–12 and the Servants of the Lord in Isaiah." Pages 65–118 in *Isaiah's Servants in Early Judaism and Christianity*. Edited by Michael A. Lyons and Jacob Stromberg. WUNT/II 554. Göttingen: Mohr Siebeck, 2021.

Stromberg, Jacob. "Figural History in the Book of Isaiah: The Prospective Significance of Hezekiah's Deliverance from Assyria and Death." Pages 81–102 in *Imperial Visions: The Prophet and the Book of Isaiah in an Age of Empires*. Edited by Reinhard Gregor Kratz and Joachim Schaper. FRLANT 227. Vandenhoeck & Ruprecht, 2020.

Stromberg, Jacob. "Hezekiah and the Oracles Against the Nations in Isaiah." Pages 297–340 in *The History of Isaiah: The Formation of the Book and Its Presentation of the Past*. Edited by Jacob Stromberg and J. Todd Hibbard. FAT 150. Tübingen: Mohr Siebeck, 2021.

Stromberg, Jacob. *An Introduction to the Study of Isaiah*. New York: T&T Clark International, 2011.

Stromberg, Jacob. *Isaiah After Exile: The Author of Third Isaiah as Reader and Redactor of the Book*. OTM. Oxford: Oxford University Press, 2011.

Stromberg, Jacob. "Reading Isaiah Holistically." Pages 77–94 in *An Introduction to the Study of Isaiah*. New York: T&T Clark International, 2011.

Stromberg, Jacob, and J. Todd Hibbard, eds. *The History of Isaiah: The Formation of the Book and Its Presentation of the Past*. FAT 150. Tübingen: Mohr Siebeck, 2021.

Stulac, Daniel John. *History and Hope: The Agrarian Wisdom of Isaiah 28–35*. Siphrut 24. University Park, PA: Eisenbrauns, 2018.

Sweeney, Marvin A. "The Book of Isaiah as Prophetic Torah." Pages 50–67 in *New Visions of Isaiah*. Edited by Roy F. Melugin and Marvin A. Sweeney. JSOTSup 214. Sheffield: Sheffield Academic, 1996.

Sweeney, Marvin A. "The Book of Isaiah in Recent Research." Pages 78–92 in *Recent Research on the Major Prophets*. Edited by Alan J. Hauser. Sheffield: Sheffield Phoenix, 2008.

Sweeney, Marvin A. "Creation as Sacred Space in the Exodus Narratives." *Lexington Theological Quarterly* 49 (2019): 1–14.

Sweeney, Marvin A. *Form and Intertextuality in Prophetic and Apocalyptic Literature*. FAT 45. Tübingen: Mohr Siebeck, 2005.

Sweeney, Marvin A. *Isaiah 1–4 and the Post-Exilic Understanding of the Isaianic Tradition*. BZAW 171. Berlin: de Gruyter, 1988.

Sweeney, Marvin A. *Isaiah 1–39: With an Introduction to Prophetic Literature*. FOTL 16. Grand Rapids, MI: Eerdmans, 1996.

Sweeney, Marvin A. *Isaiah 40–66*. FOTL 19. Grand Rapids, MI: Eerdmans, 2016.

Sweeney, Marvin A. "Isaiah 60–62 in Intertextual Perspective." Pages 131–42 in *Subtle Citation, Allusion, and Translation in the Hebrew Bible*. Edited by Ziony Zevit. Sheffield: Equinox, 2017.

Sweeney, Marvin A. "On the Road to Duhm: Isaiah in Nineteenth-Century Critical Scholarship." Pages 243–61 in *"As Those Who Are Taught": The Interpretation of Isaiah from the LXX to the SBL*. Edited by Claire M. McGinnis and Patricia K. Tull. SBL Symposium Series 27. Atlanta, GA: SBL, 2006.

Sweeney, Marvin A. "Reading the Final Form of Isaiah as a Persian Period Text." Pages 527–37 in *The History of Isaiah: The Formation of the Book and its Presentation of the Past*. Edited by Jacob Stromberg and J. Todd Hibbard. FAT 150. Tübingen: Mohr Siebeck, 2021.

Sweeney, Marvin A. *Reading Prophetic Books: Form, Intertextuality, and Reception in Prophetic and Post-Biblical Literature*. FAT 89. Tübingen: Mohr Siebeck, 2014.

Sweeney, Marvin A. *Visions of the Holy: Studies in Biblical Theology and Literature*. SBL Resources for Biblical Study. Atlanta, GA: SBL, 2023.

Sweetser, Eve. *From Etymology to Pragmatics: Metaphoric and Cultural Aspects of Semantic Structure*. Cambridge Studies in Linguistics 54. Cambridge: University Press 1991.

Tate, Marvin E. "The Book of Isaiah in Recent Study." Pages 22–56 in *Forming Prophetic Literature: Essays on Isaiah and the Twelve in Honor of John D.W. Watts*. Edited by James W. Watts and Paul R. House. JSOTSup 235. Sheffield: Sheffield Academic, 1996.

Teeter, Andrew. "Biblical Symmetry and Its Modern Detractors." Pages 435–73 in *Congress Volume: Aberdeen 2019*. Edited by Grant Macaskill, Chistl M. Maier, and Joachim Schaper. VTSup 192. Leiden: Brill, 2022.

Teeter, D. Andrew, and Michael A. Lyons. "The One and the Many, the Past and the Future, and the Dynamics of Prospective Analogy." Pages 15–44 in *Isaiah's Servants in Early Judaism and Christianity*. Edited by Michael A. Lyons and Jacob Stromberg. WUNT/II 554. Tübingen: Mohr Siebeck, 2021.

Teeter, D. Andrew, and William A. Tooman. "Standards of (In)coherence in Ancient Jewish Literature." *HBAI* 9 (2020): 94–129.

Tiemeyer, Lena-Sofia. *The Comfort of Zion: The Geographical and Theological Location of Isaiah 40–55*. VTSup 139. Leiden: Brill, 2011.

Tiemeyer, Lena-Sofia, ed. *The Oxford Handbook of Isaiah*. New York: Oxford University Press, 2020.

Tiemeyer, Lena-Sofia. *Priestly Rites and Prophetic Rage: Post-Exilic Prophetic Critique of the Priesthood*. FAT II/19. Tübingen: Mohr Siebeck, 2006.

Tiemeyer, Lena-Sofia. "Will the Prophetic Texts from the Hellenistic Period Stand Up, Please." Pages 255–79 in *Judah Between East and West: The Transition from Persian to Greek Rule (ca. 400–200 BCE)*. Edited by Lester L. Grabbe and Oded Lipschits. LSTS 75. London: T&T Clark, 2011.

Tiemeyer, Lena-Sofia, and Hans Barstad, eds. *Continuity and Discontinuity: Chronological and Thematic Development in Isaiah 40–66*. FRLANT 255. Göttingen: Vandenhoeck & Ruprecht, 2014.

Tilford, Nicole L. *Sensing World, Sensing Wisdom: The Cognitive Foundation of Biblical Metaphors*. SBLAIL 31. Atlanta, GA: SBL, 2017.

Tomasino, Anthony J. "Isaiah 1–2:4 and 63–66, and the Composition of the Isaianic Corpus." *JSOT* 57 (1993): 81–98.

Tov, Emanuel. "The Nature and Background of Harmonizations in Biblical Manuscripts." *JSOT* 31 (1985): 3–29.

Tov, Emanuel. *Textual Criticism of the Hebrew Bible*. 3rd ed. Minneapolis, MN: Fortress, 2012.

Trible, Phyllis. *God and the Rhetoric of Sexuality*. OBT 2. Philadelphia, PA: Fortress, 1978.

Troxel, Ronald L. *LXX-Isaiah as Translation and Interpretation: The Strategies of the Translator of the Septuagint of Isaiah*. JSJSup 124. Leiden: Brill, 2018.

Tucker, Gene M. "Prophetic Superscriptions and the Growth of a Canon." Pages 56–70 in *Canon and Authority: Essays in Old Testament Religion and Theology*. Edited by George W. Coats and Burke O. Long. Philadelphia, PA: Fortress, 1977.

Tull, Patricia K. "Persistent Vegetative States: People as Plants and Plants as People in Isaiah." Pages 17–34 in *The Desert Will Bloom: Poetic Visions in Isaiah*. Edited by A. Joseph Everson and Hyun Chul Paul Kim. SBLAIL 4. Atlanta, GA: SBL, 2009.

Tull, Patricia K. "Rhetorical Criticism and Intertextuality." Pages 156–79 in *To Each Its Own Meaning: An Introduction to Biblical Criticisms and Their Applications*. Edited by Steven L. McKenzie and Stephen R. Haynes. Louisville, KY: Westminster John Knox, 1999.

Tumarkin, Maria M. *Traumascapes: The Power and Fate of Places Transformed by Tragedy*. Carlton: Melbourne University Press, 2005.

Uhlig, Torsten. *The Theme of Hardening in the Book of Isaiah: An Analysis of Communicative Action*. FAT/II 39. Tübingen: Mohr Siebeck, 2009.

Utzschneider, Helmut. *Gottes Vorstellung: Untersuchungen zur literarischen Ästhetik und ästhetischen Theologie des Alten Testaments*. BWANT 175. Stuttgart: Kohlhammer, 2007.

van der Toorn, Karel. *Scribal Culture and the Making of the Hebrew Bible*. Cambridge, MA: Harvard University Press, 2007.

Van der Walt, Charlene. "Hearing Tamar's Voice." *OTE* 25 (2012): 182–206.

Vargon, Shemu'el. "The Time of Hezekiah's Illness and the Visit of the Babylonian Delegation." *Maarav* 21 (2014): 37–56.

Vermeylen, Jacques. *Du Prophéte Isaïe à l'Apocalyptic: Isaïe I–XXXV, miroir d'un demi-millénaire d'expérience religieuse en Israël*. Volume 1. Paris: Gabalda, 1977.

Vlková, Gabriela I. *Cambiare la luce in tenebre e le tenebre in luce: Uno studio tematico dell'alternarsi tra la luce e le tenebre nel libro di Isaia*. Tesi Gregoriana. Serie Teologia 107. Rome: Editrice Pontificia Università Gregoriana, 2004.

Warszawski, Ludwig. *Die Peschitta zu Jesaja (Kap. 1–39), ihr Verhältnis zum massoretischen Texte, zur Septuaginta und zum Targum*. Berlin: Itzkowski, 1897.

Washington, Harold C. "'Lest He Die in the Battle and Another Man Take Her': Violence and the Construction of Gender in the Laws of Deuteronomy 20–22." Pages 185–213 in *Gender and Law in the Hebrew Bible and the Ancient Near East*. Edited by Victor H. Matthews, Bernard M Levinson, and Tikva Frymer-Kensky. JSOTSup 262. Sheffield: Sheffield Academic, 1998.

Watts, John D. W. *Isaiah 1–33*. WBC 24. Nashville, TN: Thomas Nelson, 2005.

Watts, John D. W. *Isaiah 34–66*. WBC 25. Nashville, TN: Thomas Nelson, 2005.

Weaver, Ann M. "The 'Sin of Sargon' and Esarhaddon's Reconception of Sennacherib: A Study in Divine Will, Human Politics and Royal Ideology." *Iraq* 66 (2004): 61–6.

Webb, Barry G. "Zion in Transformation: A Literary Approach to Isaiah." Pages 65–87 in *The Bible in Three Dimensions: Essays in Celebration of Forty Years of Biblical Studies in the University of Sheffield*. Edited by David J. A. Clines et al. JSOTSup 87. Sheffield: JSOT, 1990.

Wegner, Paul D. *An Examination of Kingship and Messianic Expectation in Isaiah 1–35*. New York: Edwin Mellen, 1992.

Weinrich, Harald. *Metafora e menzogna: la serenità dell'arte*. Saggi 162. Bologna: Il Mulino, 1976.

Weippert, Manfred. "Aspekte israelitischer Prophetie im Lichte verwandter Erscheinungen des Alten Orients." Pages 287–319 in *Ad bene et fideliter seminandum: Festgabe für Karlheinz Deller zum 21. Februar 1987*. Edited by Gerlinde Mauer and Ursula Magen. AOAT 220. Neukirchen-Vluyn: Neukirchener Verlag, 1988.

Weissenberg, Hanne von, Juha Pakkala, and Marko Marttila, eds. *Changes in Scripture: Rewriting and Interpreting Authoritative Traditions in the Second Temple Period*. BZAW 419. Berlin: de Gruyter, 2011.

Weißflog, Kay. *Zeichen und Sinnbilder: Die Kinder der Propheten Jesaja und Hosea*. Arbeiten zur Bibel und ihrer Geschichte 36. Leipzig, Evangelische Verlagsanstalt, 2011.

Weisz, Heinrich. *Die Peschitta zu Deuterojesaia und ihr Verhältnis zu MT., LXX. u. Trg*. Halle: n.p., 1893.

Weitzman, Michael P. *The Syriac Version of the Old Testament: An Introduction*. UCOP 56. Cambridge: Cambridge University Press, 1999.

Welten, Peter. *Geschichte und Geschichtsdarstellung in den Chronikbüchern*. WMANT 42. Neukirchen-Vluyn: Neukirchener Verlag, 1973.

Wendel, Ute. *Jesaja und Jeremia: Worte, Motive und Einsichten Jesajas in der Verkündigung Jeremias*. BThSt 25. Neukirchen: Neukirchener Verlag, 1995.

Wenkel, David H. "Wild Beasts in the Prophecy of Isaiah: The Loss of Dominion and Its Renewal through Israel as the New Humanity." *Journal of Theological Interpretation* 5 (2011): 251–64.

Westermann, Claus. *Isaiah 40–66*. OTL. Translated by David M. G. Stalker. London: SCM, 1969.

Westermann, Claus. "Sprache und Struktur der Prophetie Deuterojesajas." Pages 92–170 in *Forschung am Alten Testament: Gesammelte Studien*. Theologische Bücherei. Altes Testament 24. Munich: Kaiser, 1964.

Whedbee, J. William. *Isaiah and Wisdom*. Nashville, TN: Abingdon, 1971.

Whybray, Roger N. *Isaiah 40–66*. NCBC. Grand Rapids, MI: Eerdmans, 1981.

Wieringen, Archibald L. H. M. van. *The Implied Reader in Isaiah 6–12*. BIS 34. Leiden: Brill, 1998.

Wieringen, Archibald L. H. M. van. *The Reader-Oriented Unity of the Book Isaiah*. ACEBTSup 6. Vught: Skandalon, 2006.

Wieringen, Archibald L. H. M. van, and Annemarieke van der Woude, eds. *'Enlarge the Site of Your Tent': The City as Unifying Theme in Isaiah: The Isaiah Workshop – De Jesaja Werkplaats*. OTS 58. Leiden: Brill, 2011.

Wildberger, Hans. *Isaiah 1–12: A Commentary*. Translated by Thomas H. Trapp. Minneapolis, MN: Fortress, 1991.

Willey, Patricia Tull. *Remember the Former Things: The Recollection of Previous Texts in Second Isaiah*. SBLDS 161. Atlanta, GA: Scholars Press, 1997.

Williamson, H. G. M. *The Book Called Isaiah: Deutero-Isaiah's Role in Composition and Redaction*. Oxford: Clarendon, 1994.

Williamson, H. G. M. *A Critical and Exegetical Commentary on Isaiah 1–27: Volume 1. Commentary on Isaiah 1–5*. ICC. London: T&T Clark 2006.

Williamson, H. G. M. *A Critical and Exegetical Commentary on Isaiah 1–27: Volume 2. Commentary on Isaiah 6–12*. ICC. London: Bloomsbury T&T Clark, 2018.

Williamson, H. G. M. "Davidic Kingship in Isaiah." Pages 280–92 in *The Oxford Handbook of Isaiah*. Edited by Lena-Sofia Tiemeyer. New York: Oxford University Press, 2020.

Williamson, H. G. M. "Good News To or From Zion? A Reconsideration of Isaiah 40.9." Pages 13–22 in *Herald of Good Tidings: Essays on the Bible, Prophecy and the Hope of Israel in Honour of Antti Laato*. Edited by P. Lindqvist and L. Valve. HBM 97. Sheffield: Sheffield Phoenix, 2021.

Williamson, H. G. M. "Isaiah 12 and the Composition of the Book of Isaiah." *HBAI* 6 (2017): 101–19.

Williamson, H. G. M. "Isaiah: Prophet of Weal or Woe?" Pages 273–300 in *"Thus Speaks Ishtar of Arbela": Prophecy in Israel, Assyria, and Egypt in the Neo-Assyrian Period*. Edited by Robert P. Gordon and Hans M. Barstad. Winona Lake, IN: Eisenbrauns, 2013.

Williamson, H. G. M. "Recent Issues in the Study of Isaiah." Pages 21–39 in *Interpreting Isaiah: Issues and Approaches*. Edited by David G. Firth and H. G. M. Williamson. Downers Grove, IL: Apollos, 2009.

Williamson, H. G. M. "Scribe and Scroll: Revisiting the Great Isaiah Scroll from Qumran." Pages 329–42 in *Making a Difference: Essays on the Bible and Judaism in Honor of Tamara Cohn Eskenazi*. Edited by David J. A. Clines, Kent Harold Richards, and Jacob L. Wright. Sheffield: Sheffield Phoenix, 2012.

Williamson, H. G. M. "Synchronic and Diachronic in Isaian Perspective." Pages 211–26 in *Synchronic or Diachronic? A Debate on Method in Old Testament Exegesis*. Edited by Johannes C. de Moor. OTS 34. Leiden: Brill, 1995.

Williamson, H. G. M. *Variations on a Theme: King, Messiah and Servant in the Book of Isaiah*. Carlisle: Paternoster, 1998.

Williamson, H. G. M. "The Vindication of Redaction Criticism." Pages 26–36 in *Biblical Interpretation and Method: Essays in Honour of John Barton*. Edited by Katharine J. Dell and Paul M. Joyce. Oxford: Oxford University Press, 2013.

Willis, John T. *Images of Water in Isaiah*. Lanham, MD: Lexington Books, 2017.

Zakovitch, Yair. מקראות בארץ המראות (*Through the Looking Glass: Reflection Stories in the Bible*). Tel Aviv: Hakibbutz Hameuchad, 1995.

Zapff, Burkard M. *Schriftgelehrte Prophetie: Jes 13 und die Komposition des Jesajabuches: ein Beitrag zur Erforschung der Redaktionsgeschichte des Jesajabuches*. Würzburg: Echter, 1995.

Zimmerli, Walther. *Man and his Hope in the Old Testament*. Translated by G. W. Bowen. London: SCM, 1971.

INDEX OF REFERENCES

OLD TESTAMENT
Genesis
1:2	49
1:3	41
3:5	169
3:7	169
3:12	204
3:16	205
14:1	77
19:24	47
21:19	169
25–50	9, 145
25–35	146, 155
25:19–26	154
26:1	77
26:15	77
26:18	77
27–28	153
28:10–22	147, 148
29–31	149, 150
30:14	77
34:31	203
38	203
47:9	77
50:1–14	154

Exodus
1–15	150
3:4	121
3:13	121
4:41	105
7:3	105
7:14	100
8:11	100
8:18	100
8:28	100
9:7	100
9:34	100
10:1–2	100, 105
12:11	120
12:49	27
13:21	120
14:4	100
14:17–18	101
14:25	101
15	150
15:2	102, 136
15:22–27	137
17:1–17	153
17:2–11	137
17:6	120
18:4	209, 240
24:9–11	27
31:12–17	62, 67–71, 74, 75
31:13	68, 69
31:14	68–71
31:15	69, 71
31:16	68, 69
31:17	69

Leviticus
16:22	220
19:3	68
19:30	68
24:22	27
26	163
26:2	68
26:32	191

Numbers
16:29	78
20	153
20:2–13	137

Deuteronomy
1:29	241
5:6–21	68
5:12	68
5:14	70
7:21	241
11:8	87
16:3	120
20:3	241
22:13–21	203
22:23–29	203
22:23	204
23:2–10	70
23:2–9	59
23:2	59
28	163
29:22	191
31:6	241
32:13	99
32:15	99
33:7	209, 240
33:26	209
33:28	116
33:29	209, 240

Joshua
17:13	87

Judges
1:9	241
1:28	87
5:6	77
8:28	77
15:1	77
15:20	77
19–20	163

Ruth	
1:1	77
4:10	70

1 Samuel	
4:17	117
17:1	121
17:12	77
31:9	117

2 Samuel	
1	147
1:20	117
4:10	117
6	148
7	102
7:12–13	112
13	190
13:20	203
18:19–20	117
18:26	117
18:31	117
21:1	77
21:9	77

1 Kings	
10:21	77
11	147
15:3–5	85
15:11	85
22:47	77

2 Kings	
3:5	78, 79
6:17	169
12:2	79
14:3	85
14:7	79
15–16	81
15:16–22	80
15:19	82, 87
15:26	77
15:28–30	80
15:29	82
16	77
16:1–5	102
16:5–9	80
16:5	77, 78
16:7	82
16:10	82
17:1–6	81
17:3	82
18–20	40, 88
18:1	79
18:3–4	86
18:3	85
18:7	85
18:8	86
18:9	82
18:13	82
18:17–19:13	86
18:22	86
19	40
19:8	86
19:16	82
19:20	82
19:21	202
19:22	40
19:36	82
19:37	82
20	88
20:1	79
20:12–19	84
20:12	87
20:19	77
23:29	81
25	90
25:1	79
25:7	179
25:8	78
25:27	78, 79

1 Chronicles	
4:41	77, 78
5:6	82
5:17	77, 78
5:26	82
7:2	77, 78
10:9	117
12:19	163
13:3	77, 78

2 Chronicles	
9:20	77, 78
13:20	77, 78
25:19	100
26:5	77, 78
28:5–15	80
28:20	82
32:1	82
32:2	82
32:9	82
32:10	82
32:22	82
32:26	77, 78
32:31	84
33:10–13	81
36:22–23	91
36:22	91
36:23	91

Ezra	
1:1–4	91
1:1	91
1:7	91
3:10–12	91
4:2	83
9:1–2	124
9:2	26
9:4	26
9:6	124
9:8	124
9:11	124
9:14	124
10:3	26

Nehemiah	
9:25	98, 99
9:36	26
12	78
12:7	77, 78
12:22	77, 78
12:26	77, 78
12:46	77, 78
12:47	77, 78
13:15–22	72
13:15	72
13:20–22	72

Index of References

Esther		16:31	164	1:1–20	63
1:1	77	26:20	121	1:1–9	9, 191, 195
		27:9	99	1:1	23, 35,
Job					77–9, 92,
3:6	65	Ecclesiastes			130, 131,
7:1	113	2:13	172		135, 140,
7:6	121	3:19	78		145, 155,
13:25	241				244
25:6	62	Isaiah		1:2–31	130
31:34	241	1–66	39, 56	1:2–20	8, 75, 105
		1–55	4, 216	1:2–9	111, 131–
Psalms		1–39	2, 3, 15,		4, 230
8:5	62		23, 24,	1:2–5	130
9:15	202		29, 31, 40,	1:2–4	202
10:18	241		78, 95,	1:2–3	131, 134
19:4	42		96, 145,	1:2	50, 131,
19:9	172		159, 202,		133–5,
20:3	240		215–17,		139, 158,
28:8	242		221, 233,		191, 195
33:10–11	43		240, 246,	1:3–4	140
33:20	209		247	1:3	43, 99,
40:10	117	1–33	17, 48,		105, 131,
43:3	172		145, 152,		191, 195,
68:12	117		155, 235		244
71:22	40	1–32	50	1:4–9	202
78:41	40	1–27	37	1:4–8	134
89:8	241	1–24	196	1:4–7	131
89:18	40	1–12	10, 17,	1:4	40, 45,
89:19	40		19, 130,		99, 105,
106:3	70		141–3,		131, 134,
115:5–6	179		225, 227,		138–40,
115:9–11	209, 240		234, 237		158, 189,
119:130	172	1–11	135, 137		191, 195,
137:1	49	1–4	39, 232		244
121:2	209, 240	1–2	53, 227,	1:5–9	99
124:8	209, 240		230, 231	1:5–6	45, 99,
135:16–17	179	1	3, 8, 9, 39,		131, 215
137:3	49		52, 99,	1:5	131, 133,
146:5	209		130, 131,		195
			133–5,	1:6	99
Proverbs			139–42,	1:7–9	99, 191
4:9	164		188, 192,	1:7–8	215, 233
6:23	172		194, 196,	1:7	47, 99,
11:31	178		200, 202,		131, 134,
13:13	178		204, 232,		187, 191,
14:28	121		233		192, 195,
					203

Isaiah (cont.)		1:24–25	134	2:17	235	
1:8	23, 131, 133, 134, 138, 141, 202–5, 244	1:24	45, 131, 133, 140, 233	2:19	236, 241	
				2:20–21	235	
				2:20	235	
		1:25	139	2:21	236, 241	
		1:26–27	134	3	232	
1:9–10	47	1:26	132–4, 233	3:1	140	
1:9	44, 131–4, 139, 195, 231, 233	1:27–31	132, 133, 202	3:7	235	
				3:8	140	
		1:27	23, 42, 133, 139, 141, 158, 233	3:10–26	140	
1:10–20	111, 131–4			3:14–15	215	
1:10–17	71			3:14	24	
1:10	48, 50, 63, 99, 131–4, 233			3:16–4:6	33	
		1:28–29	133	3:16–4:1	33	
		1:28	133, 134	3:16–26	216	
1:11–15	132	1:29–31	36	3:16–17	141	
1:11	46, 48, 54	1:29–30	133	3:18	235	
1:12–20	134	1:29	244	3:25–26	215	
1:12	45, 132	1:30	44, 244	4:1–3	235	
1:13	8, 56, 63, 67, 71, 75, 132	1:31	99, 133, 244	4:1	235	
				4:2–6	27, 33, 232	
		2–11	8, 9, 130, 140, 141	4:2	140, 235	
1:16–17	132			4:3–5	138, 141	
1:16	244	2–5	141	4:3	232	
1:17	42, 63, 215	2–4	9, 145, 146, 149, 155	4:5–6	232	
1:18–20	132			5–12	9, 145, 148–51, 155	
1:18–19	134					
1:18	134, 231		2	232		
1:20	131, 133	2:1	23, 35, 130, 140, 145, 146, 155	5	45, 53, 105, 140, 149, 152, 188, 196	
1:21–31	131, 132, 134					
1:21–27	133	2:2–5	27, 140	5:1–12:6	148	
1:21–26	132, 205	2:2–4	146–8	5:1–8:15	148, 149	
1:21–24	133	2:2	130, 141	5:1–30	148	
1:21–23	132, 138, 215	2:3	27, 111, 138, 141, 146, 244	5:1–7	44, 111, 125	
1:21	24, 42, 132–4, 203–5, 233			5:3	45, 140	
		2:4–5	235	5:5–6	111	
1:22–23	133	2:5–4:6	146	5:6	44	
1:22	133	2:5	42, 146–8	5:7–12	235	
1:23–25	133	2:6–4:6	146	5:7	24, 140	
1:23	134, 204, 233	2:6–8	235	5:8–30	44	
		2:10	236	5:8	45, 215	
1:24–27	132	2:11	235	5:9	45, 105, 187	
1:24–26	132, 133, 138	2:12	235			
		2:13	44	5:11	45	

Index of References

5:13–14	215	6:7	99, 103	7:4–8	106, 107
5:18–20	104, 235	6:8–9	114	7:4	80, 110, 234
5:18	45	6:8	97, 124		
5:19	40, 104, 105, 140	6:9–13	114	7:5	80
		6:9–10	41, 45, 50, 53, 99, 124, 168, 217, 223	7:6	140
5:20–22	45			7:7–9	103
5:20	104			7:8	80
5:23	24, 215			7:9	80
5:24	40, 140	6:9	100, 105, 107	7:10–17	80, 103, 236
5:25	137				
5:26–30	104, 215	6:10–13	104, 105	7:11	110
5:26	104, 105, 244	6:10–12	212	7:13	112
		6:10	97–101, 105, 169	7:14–17	106
5:27	244			7:14–15	111
5:28	244	6:11–13	98, 103–5, 111, 217	7:14	105, 106, 110
5:30	104, 235, 244				
		6:11	45, 98, 99, 187	7:15–16	104
6–11	141			7:15	104, 105, 112
6–7	102, 105, 110, 111	6:12	104, 189, 215, 217	7:16–17	110
		6:13	26, 41, 44, 99, 104, 110–12, 123–5, 234	7:16	104
6	10, 96, 97, 99, 101–5, 107, 108, 113–16, 119, 123, 124, 129, 140, 150, 188, 196, 215, 217, 219–21, 223			7:17	81, 92, 106, 112, 118, 140, 215, 236
		6:16–17	105		
		7–14	35	7:18–9:6	96
		7–12	81	7:18–19	236
		7–9	78, 80, 92	7:18	81, 235
		7–8	81, 116	7:20	81, 92, 235, 236
		7	43, 77, 97, 102–8, 115, 149, 152, 234, 236	7:21–22	236
6:1–13	4			7:21	235
6:1–9	106, 107			7:22–23	104
6:1–5	97, 114			7:22	103, 111, 112, 232
6:1–4	102	7:1–9:6	96, 97, 109, 115, 140	7:23–25	44, 111, 236
6:1–2	98				
6:1	77–9, 92, 102, 109, 116	7:1–8:15	150	7:23	235
		7:1–9	236	8	108–10, 234
6:3	105, 116	7:1–2	103		
6:4	105, 112, 124	7:1	77–80, 92, 102, 103, 109, 140	8:1–9:6	97, 105
				8:1–4	105
6:5	97, 102, 109, 123, 124			8:1	105
		7:2–9	80	8:3	105
		7:2	112	8:4	81, 92
6:6–7	97, 114	7:3	103, 109, 234	8:5–10	105, 106
6:6	99			8:5–9	125

Isaiah (cont.)		9:16–17	108	11:1–16	150
8:5–8	105–7	9:16	137	11:1–11	140
8:6–8	106	9:17	44, 108,	11:1	44, 46, 236
8:6	80, 107		215	11:6–9	42
8:7	81, 92,	9:18	44	11:9	236
	106, 110,	9:19–21	215	11:10–16	146
	116	9:20	108, 137,	11:10	27, 46,
8:8	106, 107,		140		235, 236
	122, 140	10	43, 101,	11:11–16	135, 136,
8:9–10	105–7, 110		234		138, 140
8:9	241	10:1	45	11:11–12	136, 138,
8:10	106	10:2	215		234
8:11–15	242	10:4	137	11:11	81, 136,
8:11–13	108	10:5–19	81		139, 232,
8:12–13	108	10:5–15	45		234, 235
8:12	241	10:5–7	215	11:12–16	140
8:13	241, 242,	10:5–6	92	11:12–13	140
	245, 247	10:5	45, 81, 137	11:12	140
8:14	45, 140	10:6	215	11:13–14	136
8:16–12:6	148, 149	10:12	81, 92,	11:15–16	102, 137
8:16–9:6	149		138, 141	11:15	136, 137
8:16	41, 149	10:17	40, 44,	11:16–12:6	139
8:17	149		111, 140	11:16–12:3	143
8:18	105, 138,	10:20–26	149–51	11:16–12:2	139
	141	10:20–23	234	11:16	81, 136,
8:21–22	215	10:20–22	232		139, 140,
8:23	100	10:20	40, 140,		232, 234,
9:1–7	44		234, 235		236
9:1–6	104, 108–	10:21	234	12	8, 9, 33,
	12, 150	10:22	140, 234		36, 130,
9:1	108, 149,	10:24–26	101		135, 136,
	171	10:24	45, 81,		138–42
9:2–6	149		102, 138,	12:1–6	150, 151,
9:2	108		141		230, 236
9:3	108, 109	10:25	137	12:1–2	135–8
9:4–5	108	10:26–27	109	12:1	135–9,
9:5	42	10:26	102		235, 236
9:6	42, 108–	10:27	122, 235	12:2–3	139
	10, 112	10:32	138, 141,	12:2	102, 137,
9:7–10:24	140		202		138
9:7–9	108	10:33–34	44	12:3–5	135, 136
9:7	140	11–12	101, 102,	12:3–4	137
9:10–17	108		104, 111,	12:4–6	142
9:10	80		135, 140,	12:4–5	136, 138,
9:11	137, 140		142, 227,		139
9:13	108, 140		234, 236	12:4	138, 235
9:14	108	11:1–12:6	136	12:5	138, 143

Index of References

277

12:6	40, 138, 139, 143	15	216	24	49, 188, 195, 196	
13–39	135	15:2	205	24:1–13	216	
13–27	17, 19, 151, 235	16:1	23, 27, 202	24:4	46, 49, 50	
		16:3–5	23	24:6	62	
13–23	23	16:14	234	24:7	46	
13–14	40, 44, 123	17	188, 196	24:10	47, 49, 54	
13	49, 50, 52, 142, 188, 196, 216	17:2	189	24:12	187	
		17:4	151	24:19–20	216	
		17:7	40	24:23	23	
13:1–14:23	84, 90	17:9	187, 189, 242	25:4	240, 242, 243, 245, 247	
13:1	35, 135	17:10	242			
13:2	23	17:12	45			
13:4–5	37	17:13	241	25:6–8	32	
13:6	47–9, 52, 53, 235	18	33	25:6	27	
		18:1	45	25:7	27	
13:7	62	18:2	50	25:9	244	
13:9–13	37	18:3	23, 50	25:10–12	216	
13:9	187	18:5	244	25:10	27	
13:11	50	18:7	23, 27, 50	26	163	
13:19–22	49	19:2–10	216	26:3	163	
13:19–20	54	19:16–25	18	26:4	242	
13:19	47–9, 191	19:18–25	22, 27	26:6	241	
13:20–21	49	19:23–25	81	26:9	50	
13:20	47, 49	20:1	78, 79, 81–3, 92	26:18	50	
13:21–22	49, 53			27	53	
13:21	47	20:4–6	76	27:2–5	44	
13:22	47	20:4	81	27:4	44, 244	
14	35	20:6	81	27:5	242, 244	
14:1–2	23	21	44	27:6	50, 151	
14:1	151	21:1–10	84	27:9	151	
14:2–3	76	21:10	215	27:13	81	
14:2	216	21:11	241	28–35	17, 19, 33	
14:4	84, 92	21:14	244	28–33	44, 45, 50, 52	
14:7	244	21:3–4	216			
14:9	244	22	52	28–32	23, 195	
14:13–15	116	22:2	49	28–31	50	
14:13–14	103	22:4	216	28	34	
14:17	50	22:13	137	28:1	45	
14:21	50	22:19	244	28:5–6	23	
14:22	234	23:4	242	28:5	234	
14:24–27	43, 109	23:10	205	28:10–11	50	
14:25	76, 81	23:13	81	28:10	47, 50, 54	
14:28–32	98, 102	23:14	242	28:11	50, 244	
14:28	35, 78, 79, 92	23:17–18	23	28:12	244	
		24–27	18, 23, 37, 45, 49, 52	28:13	47, 50	
14:30–31	216			28:14	50	

Isaiah (cont.)		32:18	47, 50	34:14	47	
28:16–17	23	32:20	43	34:15	47, 52	
28:17	50	33	48, 50,	34:16–17	48, 49, 51	
28:23–29	23		188, 195,	34:16	47, 51, 55	
28:23	50		196, 216	34:17	47, 49, 50	
29	165	33:1	45	35–66	48	
29:1	45	33:2	243–5, 247	35	34, 45, 48,	
29:7–8	165	33:5	23, 24		50, 51,	
29:10	169	33:7–8	216		116, 117,	
29:11–12	23	33:8	187		247	
29:11	41	33:9	216	35:1	137	
29:13–14	50	33:13	46, 50	35:2–3	246	
29:15	45	33:15	24	35:5	169	
29:16	244	33:20–24	50	35:6	51	
29:17–24	23	33:21	50	35:7	51, 53	
29:18	169	34–66	17, 145,	35:8	51	
29:19	40		151, 155,	35:9	51	
29:20–21	216		156	35:10	137, 138,	
29:22	151	34–39	125		142	
29:23	40, 151,	34–35	18, 151,	36–39	17–19,	
	241		195		43, 44, 79,	
30:1	45	34	8, 34, 38,		88, 96, 97,	
30:2	242		44, 46,		102, 109,	
30:3	242		48–52, 55,		115, 117,	
30:6	98		216		119, 151,	
30:9–11	23	34:1	46, 48, 50		195	
30:11	40	34:2–4	48	36–38	40, 81	
30:12	40	34:2	52, 53	36–37	116–19	
30:15	40	34:3	49, 52	36:1–3	110	
30:18–26	23	34:4	46, 49	36:1–2	115	
30:18	24	34:5–15	48	36:1	79, 81, 83,	
30:24	43	34:6	46, 48,		92, 103,	
30:27–33	125		52-4, 155		109	
30:28	122	34:7	43	36:2–3	109	
30:29	242	34:8	47–9, 52,	36:2	116	
30:31	81		53	36:4–20	110	
31:1	40, 45	34:9	47, 49, 51,	36:6	110, 116	
31:8–9	216		52	36:9	112	
31:9	44	34:10–15	49	36:13–17	108	
32:1–8	23	34:10–12	51	36:13	115	
32:1	24	34:10	47, 51, 52	36:14	81	
32:3–4	169	34:11–12	54	36:17	81, 116	
32:3	169	34:11	47, 49, 50	36:18–20	82	
32:9	50	34:12	47, 49–52	36:21	81	
32:13	44	34:13–14	49, 53	36:37	81	
32:15–20	23	34:13	47, 51	37	103, 118	
32:16–17	24	34:14–15	49, 50	37:8–13	82	

37:8	82	40–55	2–4, 29,	40:18–31	219
37:9	81		32, 36, 37,	40:21–26	152
37:10–35	110		109, 119,	40:23	47, 51
37:11	82, 110		159, 169,	40:25	40
37:14	112		177, 200,	40:26	47, 51
37:16–20	119		206, 215,	40:27–31	152
37:16	119		218–20,	40:27	51, 152,
37:17	83, 116		223, 226,		173, 219
37:18	82		227, 240,	41:1–42:13	151, 153
37:21	83		246	41:1–4	90
37:22	119, 202,	40–54	9, 23, 24,	41:2	91, 172,
	205		145, 148,		244
37:23–24	103, 115		151, 153,	41:5–7	90
37:23	40		155, 156	41:5	241
37:25	119	40–52	48	41:8–16	25
37:29	116, 119	40–48	17, 19, 24,	41:8	41, 153,
37:30–32	110–12,		119, 156		177
	125	40–46	158	41:9	177
37:30	111	40	51, 52,	41:10–14	240
37:31	111, 234		114–17	41:10	219
37:32	110–12,	40:1–11	96, 113–	41:11–12	51
	234		20, 123,	41:13	219
37:34	116, 119		124, 129,	41:14	40, 153,
37:36–37	117		152		219
37:37	83	40:1–8	4	41:16	40
37:38	81, 82, 92	40:1–2	113–15,	41:17	153, 219
38:1	79, 87		120	41:20	4, 40, 153
38:20	244	40:1	219, 241	41:21–29	90
38:6	81, 82, 92	40:2	118, 124	41:21	153, 180
39	112, 118	40:3–5	113, 114,	41:22	180
39:1–8	84		116, 152	41:26–28	43
39:1–3	90	40:3–4	120	41:29	47, 51
39:1	84, 87, 92	40:3	120	42–43	9, 167,
39:2–3	87	40:4	152		168, 182
39:6–8	86	40:6–8	44, 113	42:1–9	172, 177
39:6–7	112, 215	40:6	114	42:1–7	24
39:6–4	118	40:9–11	113–15	42:1	42, 172,
39:6	112	40:9	115, 116,		177
39:7	45, 84, 90,		120	42:3–4	42
	92, 112	40:10–11	120, 124	42:3	177
39:8	77	40:11	116, 151	42:4	172
40–66	3, 15, 36,	40:12–48:21	151	42:5–9	90
	40, 41,	40:12–31	151, 152	42:6–20	153
	48, 95, 96,	40:12–20	152	42:6–7	177
	118, 135,	40:12	241	42:6	42, 161,
	145, 160,	40:15	172		170, 172,
	165, 206	40:17	47, 51, 172		173, 178

Isaiah (cont.)		44:1–5	25, 153	45:18	244		
42:7	168–70, 172, 176, 178–80, 182, 219	44:1	153, 177	45:20–25	84		
		44:2	177, 240, 245, 247	45:21	180		
				45:25	154		
		44:3–4	218	46–47	25		
42:8-17	25	44:8	219, 242	46	154		
42:8	173	44:11	219	46:1–2	219		
42:9	172, 173	44:12	158	46:3	174		
42:10	241	44:13	92, 93	46:5	90		
42:12	241	44:16	44	46:9–11	90, 119		
42:14–44:23	151, 153	44:18	169	46:9	51		
42:14	153	44:19	44	46:12	219		
42:16	168, 173, 176, 182, 219	44:21	25, 177	47–48	120		
		44:23	241	47	154, 219		
		44:24–48:22	151	47:1–3	120, 121		
42:17	219	44:24–48:21	154	47:1	84, 119		
42:18–25	175, 178	44:24–28	90	47:4	40		
42:18–20	169	44:24	244, 245, 247	47:12	241		
42:18–19	168, 174, 178, 182, 219			47:13–14	119		
		44:28–45:25	79	47:14	244		
		44:28–45:13	91	48	40, 154		
42:18	174–6, 179	44:28–45:1	90, 92, 93	48:1–22	24		
42:19	175–9	44:28	24, 91, 153, 154	48:1	174		
42:20	175			48:3	244		
42:22–25	218	45	119	48:6–8	219		
42:22	170, 244	45:1–13	91	48:9–11	220		
42:23	169	45:1–7	90	48:10	218		
42:26	153	45:1	24, 91, 153, 154, 172, 241	48:12–16	90		
43	188			48:14	84, 117, 119		
43:3	40						
43:8–13	180	45:3	154	48:16	90		
43:8–9	180	45:4–5	43	48:17	40		
43:8	168, 169, 179–82	45:4	25, 154, 177	48:20	25, 84, 117, 119, 120, 180		
43:9	172, 180	45:6	47, 51				
43:10–13	180, 182	45:7	42	48:21	119, 120		
43:10	24, 177, 180, 182	45:8	90	48:22	41, 219		
		45:9–13	219	49–54	17, 19, 151, 154–6		
43:12	180	45:9–10	45				
43:13	180	45:9	220	49	9, 40, 188, 190		
43:14	40, 76, 84, 219	45:11	40				
		45:13	90, 91	49:1–54:17	151		
43:15	40	45:14	51, 219	49:1–26	25		
43:19–20	187	45:15	219	49:1–7	188, 189		
43:28	218	45:16	219	49:1–6	24, 154		
44	245	45:17	154	49:1	161, 174		

Index of References

49:3	177	51:17–20	206	52:13–15	177
49:6	42, 161, 172	51:17	190	52:13	221
		51:18	244	52:14	187, 191
49:7	40, 219	51:19	189	52:15	172
49:8–11	171	52–53	196	53	10, 218, 220, 221, 224
49:8	171, 187, 188, 196, 240, 245, 246	52	118, 188		
		52:1–12	117, 120, 123, 124	53:1–6	221
		52:1–6	117, 120, 122	53:4	220
49:9	170, 180			53:6	161
49:14	154, 187, 189, 190, 206, 219	52:1–2	120–3	53:7	161, 220
		52:1	117, 118, 121, 124, 190	53:8	161
				53:9	162
49:16	45			53:10	22
49:18	206	52:2	122, 202, 206	53:11	177
49:19	23, 187, 196, 218	52:3–6	121–3	53:12	221
		52:3–4	122, 123, 218	54	40, 143, 155, 164, 188
49:20–23	206				
49:20–21	206	52:3	121, 123	54:1	143, 187, 196, 206
49:21	190	52:4	81, 84, 121, 123		
49:22	172			54:2	164
49:26	154, 219, 245–7	52:5–6	123	54:3	187, 196
		52:5	122, 123	54:4	206, 218
50–51	129	52:6	123, 124	54:5	25, 40, 138, 143, 196, 206
50	162	52:7–12	117, 120, 122		
50:1	206				
50:4–11	25	52:7–10	117, 120, 121, 123	54:6	164, 189, 206
50:4	25				
50:7–9	240	52:7–8	122	54:7	189, 219
50:8	25	52:7	117, 118, 120, 124	54:11	164, 244
50:11	219, 244			54:12	244
51:1	219, 244	52:8–9	138	54:13	25
51:3	23, 137, 218	52:8	120, 124	54:16	241
		52:9–10	23, 122, 123	54:17	22, 24, 25
51:4	171, 172			55–66	17, 19, 22–4, 155
51:6	244	52:9	120		
51:7	174, 219	52:10	120, 121, 124, 172	55	40, 58, 155, 158
51:9–10	219				
51:9	121	52:11–12	121–3	55:1–56:8	22
51:11	23, 137, 138	52:11	117, 120, 180	55:1–5	25
				55:1	45, 219
51:12–13	219	52:12	120, 154, 180	55:5	40
51:12	62, 244			55:6–7	219
51:13–16	219			55:8–9	219
51:15	158	52:13–53:12	25, 177, 212, 215, 220	55:12–13	58–60
51:16	23, 244				

Isaiah (cont.)		57:14–62:12	25	61:2	47, 48, 52,
55:12	58, 180	57:15	241		53
55:13	44, 58	57:16	241	61:3	23, 137
56–69	124	57:19	163, 164	61:4	187
56–66	2, 26, 32,	57:20–21	163	61:5	244
	36, 37, 56,	57:21	41	61:8	42
	92, 124,	58:1–12	63, 64, 66	61:10–11	24
	151, 159,	58:1–5	66	61:10	137, 206
	206, 215,	58:1	155	62	33, 188,
	222, 223,	58:3–7	59		196
	246	58:3	66, 67	62:1	23
56	22, 40	58:6–7	221	62:3	164
56:1–8	8, 23, 26,	58:8–9	66	62:4–5	206
	57, 59, 66,	58:8	171	62:4	187, 189,
	67, 69–71,	58:9–10	221		206
	74, 75, 214	58:10	171	62:5	137
56:1–2	56, 57, 59,	58:11	66, 166	62:6	23
	60, 62, 63,	58:12	64	62:7	23
	67, 69–71,	58:13–14	8, 64–7,	62:11	23, 202,
	74, 75, 221		71, 75		206
56:1	4, 24, 26,	58:13	64–7	63–66	22, 125
	42, 60, 63,	58:14	66, 155	63–64	10, 194,
	70, 75	59	64–6, 188,		221, 222
56:2	59–62, 66,		196	63	44, 52,
	68–71, 74	59:1–8	221		188, 196
56:3–8	56–9, 62,	59:9–15	222	63:1–6	22, 26, 52,
	68–70, 75	59:11	241		155, 214
56:3–7	58–60, 67	59:14–15	25, 158	63:3	52, 53
56:3–6	59	59:15–21	26	63:4	47, 48, 52,
56:3–5	45	59:15	51		53
56:3	44, 58, 70	59:16	187	63:5	25, 52,
56:4–6	70	59:17	25		187, 193
56:4–5	58	59:20	23, 25, 155	63:6	52, 53, 195
56:4	58, 59, 66,	60–62	22, 23, 33,	63:7–64:12	214
	68, 69		214	63:7–64:11	9, 22, 25,
56:5	58, 59, 70,	60	33, 40, 162		191, 192,
	74	60:3	241		195
56:6–7	58, 70	60:6	162	63:7	192
56:6	25, 59, 66,	60:9	40, 138	63:8	191, 195
	68, 69	60:14	23, 40, 138	63:9	195
56:7–8	58	60:16	155, 246	63:10	195
56:7	27, 59, 60,	60:17	24	63:11–12	93
	70, 71	60:18	162, 163	63:14	195
56:8	58–60, 244	60:20	42	63:15–64:12	215
56:9–59:21	22, 23, 214	61	188, 196	63:15–64:11	222
57	40, 163	61:1–3	24	63:16	158, 195,
57:3–13	26				223

Index of References

63:17	25, 195, 223	66:6	208	6:7	163
		66:7–9	207	6:14	163, 164
63:18	192, 195	66:7–8	208	6:20	162
63:19	223	66:8–13	206	6:23	202
64	196	66:8	208	6:28–29	165
64:4	42, 137, 192	66:9–13	208	6:30	165
		66:9	208	8:11	163
64:5	191, 192, 195	66:10	137	10	158, 160
		66:11	208	10:3–10	158
64:7	158, 195	66:12	208	10:3	158
64:8	192, 195, 223	66:13	158, 208	10:20	164
		66:14–16	210	11–20	161
64:9	187, 191, 192, 195	66:14	25, 41, 137	11	162, 166
		66:15–16	44	11:19	161
64:10	191–3, 195	66:16	26, 42, 52	13:18	164
64:11	192, 195, 223	66:17	26	13:26	121
		66:18–24	22	14:11	162
64:12	193	66:18–21	27	14:12	53
65–66	3, 22, 25, 27, 39, 54, 124, 125, 158, 194, 200, 214, 227	66:18	59	17:19–27	72
		66:19	41, 83	14:19–22	162
		66:20–23	27	15	162, 166
		66:22	67	15:1–4	162
		66:23–24	26, 27, 66	15:11	161
		66:23	56, 62–4, 67, 71, 143	15:15	161
65:3–7	26			16:19	242
65:7	113	66:24	41, 44	17:16–18	235
65:8–9	125			17:24–26	62
65:8	25	*Jeremiah*		17:27	62
65:9	25, 125, 143, 155	1	166	21:9	53
		1:1–2	77	23:1–4	165
65:11–16	222	1:3	154	24:6	53
65:13–14	143	1:4–9	154	24:10	53
65:13	25	1:5	161	26:18	77
65:14	25	1:6	154	30–31	155, 159, 160
65:15	25	1:10	53		
65:17–24	206	2:12	191	30:10–11	166
65:17–18	206	3:6	77, 205	30:10	41
65:18–19	137, 143	3:8	205	30:19	100
65:22	44	3:11	205	31	165, 166
66	9, 18, 142, 200, 207, 209	3:12	205	31:12	166
		3:16–17	162	31:15	155
		4	164, 166	31:23–26	165
66:1–2	45	4:20	164	31:25	164
66:2	26, 221	4:30	164	31:26	164, 165
66:3	26, 43	4:31	202	31:29–30	165
66:5	27, 63, 221, 222	6	162–6	31:35	158
		6:2	202	33:9–11	137

Jeremiah (cont.)

35:1	77
44	162
46–51	160
49:18	191
50–51	40
50:29	40
50:39–40	53
50:40	191
51:5	40
52:31	78, 79

Lamentations

1–2	205
1:6	202
2:1	202
2:4	202
2:8	202
2:10	202
2:13	202
2:18	202
4:22	202

Ezekiel

2:1	53
3:1	53
3:11	41
13:10	163
16	205
16:12	164
18:1–20	165
22	165
22:17–22	165
23	205
23:42	164
28:25	41
30:3	235
34	165
39:7	40

Daniel

1:21	91
6:29	91
8:25	121
10:1	91

Hosea

1–3	129
1:1	77

Joel

1:15	235

Amos

1:1	77
4:11	191
5:18–20	235
7–9	147

Micah

1:1	77
1:13	202
4:8	202
4:10	202
4:13	202

Nahum

2:1	117, 118

Zephaniah

1:1	77
3:14	202

Zechariah

2:10	202
2:12	192
7:1	79
9:9	202
14:5	77

1 Esdras

5:69	83

Tobit

1:2	83
1:13	83
1:15	83
1:16	83
1:18	83
1:21	83
1:22	83
2:1	83

Ecclesiasticus

48:18	83

2 Maccabees

8:19	83
15:22	83

NEW TESTAMENT

Matthew

5:14	42
11:15	41, 53, 55
13:9	41
13:43	41

Mark

4:9	41

Luke

8:8	41
14:35	41

John

9:7	107
9:16	107
9:39	107
12:37–40	107

Revelation

3:13	41

PSEUDEPIGRAPHA

2 Baruch

62:6	83
63:2	83
63:4	83

3 Maccabees

6:5	83

Ahiqar

3	83
4	83
5	83
7	83
10	83
11	83
13	83

14	83	9.252	83	*CG*	
15	83	9.259	83	152	72, 74
19	83	9.277	83	152 l. 2	73
23	83	9.284	83	186	73
27	83	9.287	83		
28	83	10.1	83	*COS*	
32	83	10.2	83	I, 134	88
47	83	10.6	83		
50	83	10.14	83	*PNAE*	
51	83	10.18	83	2/II, 706	86
53	83	10.184	83		
55	83	10.20	83	*RIMB 2*	
60	83	10.21	83	B.6.21.1:13	85
64	83	10.23	83	B.6.21.1:14	86
65	83	10.29–32	87		
70	83	11.19	83	*TAD*	
75	83	11.85	83	D 7.48	73, 74
76	83			D 7.16	72–74
78	83	*War*		D 7.35	73
		3.447	83		
QUMRAN		5.387	83	*RINAP*	
4Q416				1 47 r. 6'–13'	80
2 ii 8	65	CLASSICAL		2 1:234–255	82
		Apostolic Constitutions		2 82 vi 13'–8"	82
MISHNAH		7.37.3	83	3/1 1:20	86
Giṭṭin				3/1 1:23–24	86
57b	83	Aristotle		3/1 1:26	88
		Rhetoric		3/1 1:34–35	88
Megillah		2.24	83	3/1 1:5–7	86
11b	83			3/1 22 iii 18	85
		Clement		3/1 22 iv 32–53	89
Sanhedrin		*Stromata*		3/1 3:8–9	86
95a–b	83	1.141.1	83	3/1 4:48	86
				3/1, 10–11	86
MIDRASH		Herodotus			
Exodus Rabbah		*Histories*			
18.5	83	2.141	83		
JOSEPHUS		OTHER ANCIENT			
Antiquities		SOURCES			
9.232	83	*ABC*			
9.235	83	1 i 27–32	85		

INDEX OF AUTHORS

Aalen, S. 171
Abernethy, A. 1, 2, 4, 16, 32, 43, 44, 46
Achenbach, R. 74
Ackroyd, P. R. 113, 118, 142
Ajer, P. C. 189, 190
Albertz, R. 4, 221, 222
Alexander, J. A. 137
Amzallag, G. N. 135
Anderson, J. E. 153
Angel, H. 232
Aster, S. Z. 45, 81
Avrahami, Y. 167, 171, 181

Bailey, D. P. 221
Baldauf, B. 170, 178
Baltzer, K. 19
Barker, J. D. 235
Barstad, H. 15, 54, 56, 197
Barthel, J. 102, 105, 109
Barthelémy, D. 243
Basello, G. P. 90
Baumann, G. 154
Bautch, R. 25
Beaucamp, R. 170
Becker, J. 29
Becker, U. 13, 16, 18, 22, 42, 99, 102, 214
Beentjes, P. C. 21
Ben Zvi, E. 21, 194
Berges, U. 13, 14, 17–19, 22, 23, 25, 26, 30, 36, 48, 57, 63–6, 158, 161, 171, 200, 218, 221, 225, 226, 230, 232, 235
Berlejung, A. 158, 222
Berman, J. A. 96
Bernidaki-Aldous, E. A. 167
Berquist, J. L. 185, 186
Beuken, W. A. M. 17, 27, 39, 40, 43, 44, 48, 51, 59, 63, 77, 78, 102, 158, 163, 171, 195, 216, 243
Bird, P. 204

Black, M. 201
Blenkinsopp, J. 57, 61, 77, 91, 117, 118, 120, 178, 207, 214, 217, 220–3
Bloch, Y. 71, 73, 74
Blumenberg, H. 171
Boase, E. 193, 212, 227, 228
Bodor, A. 240, 242, 246, 247
Bovati, P. 180
Bowker, M. H. 214, 223, 224
Boyle, F. 197
Boynton, E. 228
Brett, M. G. 6, 26, 27, 41
Brinkman, J. A. 85, 86, 88, 89
Brock, R. N. 210
Brock, S. P. 245, 246
Brooke-Rose, C. 173
Brueggemann, W. 194

Camp, C. V. 185
Camus, A. 213
Capretto, P. 228
Carasik, M. 167
Carbajosa, I. 244
Carr, D. 7, 16, 21, 94, 200, 229, 239
Carr, D. M. 227
Carroll, R. P. 41
Chan, M. J. 90
Childs, B. S. 30, 91, 192, 216
Cioran, E. M. 224
Claassens, L. J. M. 210
Clements, R. E. 29, 41, 42, 95, 139, 226, 230
Conrad, E. W. 5, 31, 33, 41, 43, 194, 233, 239
Conroy, C. 13
Couey, B. 94

Dahoood, M. 64
Darr, K. P. 5, 32, 42, 202, 239

Index of Authors

Davage, D. 16
Davies, G. I. 100, 101
Delitzsch, F. 136
Dell, K. 161
Dempsey, C. J. 42, 231, 235
Dicou, B. 48
Dille, S. J. 43
Dim, E. U. 207
Döderlein, J. C. 2
Dobbs-Allsopp, F. W. 202
Doering, L. 72
Dubovský, P. 79–82, 86
Duhm, B. 2, 225

Eaton, J. H. 29
Eck, J. 130
Edenburg, C. 137
Eichhorn, J. G. 2
Eidevall, G. 235
Elayi, J. 83
Elgvin, T. 65
Esterhuizen, E. 230, 236
Evans, C. A. 41
Everson, A. J. 236
Ewald, J. H. A. 2

Feuerstein, R. 15
Fischer, G. 69, 160, 163, 165
Fischer, I. 6, 205, 206, 209
Fishbane, M. 20, 119
Fohrer, G. 179
Frahm, E. 82
Franke, C. A. 43
Frechette, C. 212, 227, 228
Freedman, D. N. 77
Fried, L. S. 91
Fuchs, A. 82

Gärtner, J. 67, 125
Garavelli, B. M. 176, 179
Gelston, A. 244
Gentry, P. J. 226
George, M. K. 185, 186
Glassner, G. 164
Goldingay, J. 17, 61, 65, 178, 188, 192, 193
Gray, M. 5
Green, B. 145
Greenberg, G. 244
Greenspahn, F. E. 150

Groenewald, A. 228, 230, 233, 236, 237
Grosser, E. J. 95
Guest, D. 201, 202

Hägglund, F. 218
Harrington, D. J. 65
Hartenstein, F. 71, 113, 120
Hay, A. R. 132
Hayes, K. M. 186, 195
Hays, C. B. 13
Hays, R. W. P. 211
Hermisson, H.-J. 218
Hibbard, J. T. 13, 39
Higgins, R. S. 190
Hillers, D. R. 216
Hitzig, F. 172
Höffken, P. 13
Holmstedt, R. D. 61
Honggeng, G. 86
Hopf, M. 130, 132
Hoppe, L. 194, 230, 231, 235, 236
Hoppe, L. J. 230
Houtmann, C. 69
Hrobon, B. 31, 189, 194
Hubbard, P. 186

Ibarretxe-Antuñano, I. 169, 181
Irudayaraj, D. 52, 158, 186, 188, 196

Jakobson, R. 170
Janoff-Bulman, R. 228, 229
Janzen, D. 212, 230
Joachimsen, K. 193
Johnson, M. 168
Jones, D. R. 29

Kedar-Kopfstein, B. 139
Kellenberger, E. 98, 99
Keller, C. 210
Kessler, R. 24, 218
Kim, B. 32, 42, 138
Kim, H. C. P. 43, 45, 51, 130, 188, 195, 231, 233, 236
Kim, S. J. 215
King, A. M. 232
Kitchin, R. 186
Kövecses, Z. 167, 169, 171
Kooij, A. van der 240, 243, 244
Koole, J. L. 57, 59–62, 65, 170–2, 180

Kratz, R. G. 15, 50
Kronholm, T. 139
Kustár, Z. 30

Laato, A. 31, 226
Lack, R. 31
Lakoff, G. 168, 201
Landy, F. 26, 54
Lau, W. 20, 21
Lauha, A. 171
Lazzaro, B. 167-9, 173-5
Leclerc, T. L. 24, 31, 42
Leene, H. 159, 160, 163
Lefebvre, H. 185, 189
Lemaire, A. 73
Liebrich, L. J. 3, 200
Lim, B. H. 44
Lowth, R. 2
Lozachmeur, H. 72-4
Lund, Ø. 44
Lynch, M. J. 188
Lyons, M. A. 96

Ma, W. 31
Machinist, P. 81
Maier, C. M. 138, 186, 202, 203
Maier, M. P. 16, 31
Mandolfo, C. R. 145, 147
Markl, D. 69, 84
Marlow, H. 6
Marttila, M. 21
Mastnjak, N. 94
Mathews, C. R. 51
Melugin, R. F. 3, 5, 13, 28, 38, 55, 168, 194, 199, 226, 238, 239
Mettinger, T. N. D. 154, 218
Meyer, A. 186, 188, 189, 191
Mills, M. E. 45, 191, 193, 197, 198
Miscall, P. D. 31
Montgomery, J. A. 87
Moreno, M. A. G. 16
Morgan, D. M. 233, 234
Morrison, C. E. 244
Morrow, W. 228, 233
Moughtin-Mumby, S. 6
Muilenburg, J. 3

Newsom, C. A. 145
Nielsen, K. 44

Nihan, C. 59
Nitsche, S. A. 130
Nogalski, J. 20, 227, 232, 233, 236
Nurmela, R. 21

O'Connell, R. H. 34
O'Connor, K. M. 228
O'Connor, M. P. 186
Økland, J. 185
Ortlund, E. 135

Paganini, S. 158
Pakkala, J. 21
Parke-Taylor, G. H. 158
Parry, D. W. 64
Paul, S. M. 2, 40
Pettigiani, O. 134
Pfister, M. 132
Polaski, D. C. 18
Porten, B. 72, 73
Potts, D. T. 85
Poulsen, F. 16, 42, 190, 231
Powell, M. A. 85
Prinsloo, G. T. M. 186

Qimron, E. 64

Rad, G. von 29
Rendtorff, R. 4, 14, 29
Roberts, J. J. M. 40, 80, 88, 94, 191, 243
Rom-Shiloni, D. 215
Rosenbaum, M. 175
Rosenberg, A. Y. 178
Rossi, B. 162
Ruszkowski, L. 68

Samely, A. 95
Sawyer, J. F. A. 188
Schaper, J. 57, 59
Scheuer, B. 223
Schipper, J. 45
Schmid, K. 20, 22
Schniedewind, W. M. 21
Schreiter, R. J. 229
Schüle, A. 22, 25, 72
Schultz, R. L. 21, 226
Schwartz, E. 100, 102
Schweitzer, S. J. 187, 189, 190
Scialabba, D. 67

Seiler, G. F. 1
Seitz, C. 4, 30, 94, 113
Seufert, M. 117
Simian-Yofre, H. 181
Smith, J. P. 241, 242
Smith, P. A. 57
Smith-Christopher, D. L. 170, 227, 233
Soja, E. W. 185, 189, 190
Sommer, B. D. 20, 39, 145, 157
Spans, A. 23
Stamm, J. J. 171
Steck, O. H. 14, 15, 30, 51, 214, 247
Stern, J. 169
Stinesprin, W. F. 202
Stromberg, J. 4, 13, 16, 30, 39, 49, 57, 58, 96, 98, 102, 104, 105, 109, 111, 119, 124, 125, 144, 199, 205, 214, 222
Strugnell, J. 65
Stulac, D. J. 33, 43, 187
Sweeney, M. A. 3, 17, 26, 27, 37, 39, 111, 123, 133, 136, 144, 145, 147, 148, 151–5, 157, 214, 216, 217, 225, 235
Sweetser, E. 169

Tate, M. E. 225
Teeter, D. A. 95, 96, 120
Tiemeyer, L.-S. 5, 13, 15, 21, 54, 120, 197, 199, 214
Tilford, N. L. 167
Tomasino, A. J. 39
Tooman, W. A. 95
Toorn, K. van der 21
Tov, E. 239, 245
Trible, P. 209
Tucker, G. M. 77, 78
Tull, P. K. 6, 145
Tumarkin, M. M. 197, 198
Turner, M. 201

Uhlig, T. 16, 41, 130, 217
Utzschneider, H. 130

Van der Walt, C. 198
Vargon, S. 87, 88

Vermeylen, J. 49
Vlková, G. I. 171
Vos, J. C. de 185

Warszawski, L. 239, 241, 244
Washington, H. C. 206
Watts, J. D. W. 34, 92, 186
Weaver, A. M. 83
Webb, B. G. 232
Wegner, P. D. 194
Weinrich, H. 175
Weippert, M. 22
Weissenberg, H. von 21
Weißflog, K. 42
Weisz, H. 240, 241
Weitzman, M. P. 239
Welten, P. 240
Wendel, U. 157
Wenell, K. J. 185
Wenkel, D. 43
Westermann, C. 3, 57, 178, 206
Whedbee, J. W. 43
Whybray, R. N. 178
Wieringen, A. L. H. M. van 16, 45, 131, 133, 135
Wildberger, H. 77, 78, 191
Wilk, F. 243, 244
Willey, P. T. 39, 145, 157
Williamson, H. G. M. 4, 16, 18, 21, 26, 30, 36, 37, 39, 42, 53, 63, 64, 77, 78, 98–100, 102, 109, 111, 113, 114, 130, 135, 191, 196, 217, 240–2
Willis, J. T. 44
Woude, A. van der 45

Yardeni, A. 72

Zapff, B. M. 49
Ziegler, J. 87, 241
Zimmerli, W. 206, 207

www.ingramcontent.com/pod-product-compliance
Lightning Source LLC
Chambersburg PA
CBHW071235230426
43668CB00011B/1452